C0-ARZ-385

The
LYLE
Price Guide to Collectibles and Memorabilia

The
LYLE

Price Guide to Collectibles and Memorabilia

compiled by Anthony Curtis

Perigee Books
are published by
The Putnam Publishing Group
200 Madison Avenue
New York, NY 10016

Copyright © 1988 by Lyle Publications
Glenmayne, Galashiels, Scotland
All rights reserved. This book, or parts thereof,
may not be reproduced in any form without permission.

Published simultaneously in Canada

Front cover button photos are from "Collectible
Pin-Back Buttons 1896–1986" published by Hake's
Americana & Collectibles, York, PA.

Library of Congress Cataloging-in-Publication Data

Curtis, Tony.
    The Lyle price guide to collectibles and memorabilia.

    "A Perigee book."
    Includes index.
    1. Antiques—Catalogs. I. Title.
NK1125.C887 1988   745.1'075   88-5986
ISBN 0-399-51445-7

Printed in the United States of America
1 2 3 4 5 6 7 8 9 10

CONTENTS

ACKNOWLEDGEMENTS

Abbots (East Anglia) Ltd., *The Hill, Wickham Market, nr. Woodbridge, Suffolk*
Abridge Auctions, *(Michael Yewman), Market Place, Abridge, Essex RM4 1UA*
Aldridge's, *130-132 Walcot Street, Bath, Avon. BA1 5BG*
Alfie's Antique Market, *13-15 Church Street, London.*
Alpha Antiques, *(J. J. Binns), High Street, Kingston, Herefordshire*
Allen & May, *18 Bridge Street, Andover.*
Anderson & Garland, *Anderson House, Market Street, Newcastle. NE1 6XA*
Gilbert Baitson, *194 Anlaby Road, Hull, Yorkshire*
Richard Baker & Thomson, *9 Hamilton Street, Birkenhead, Merseyside*
Ball & Percival, *132 Lord Street, Southport, Merseyside. PR9 0AE*
Banks & Silvers, *66 Foregate Street, Worcester.*
T. Bannister & Co., *7 Calbourne, Haywards Heath, W. Sussex*
Barbers Fine Art Auctioneers, *The Mayford Centre, Smarts Heath Road, Mayford, Woking.*
Bearnes, *Rainbow, Avenue Road, Torquay. TQ2 5TG*
R. A. Beck, *23 Basing Hill, London. NW11 8TE*
Tessa Bennett, *Bennett Book Auctions, 72 Radcliffe Terrace, Edinburgh.*
Yasha Beresiner, *Inter Col, 1a Camden Walk, Islington Green, London.*
Bermondsey Antiques Market, *Tower Bridge Road, London.*
Biddle & Webb, *Ladywood, Middleway, Birmingham. B16 0PP*
Bloomsbury Book Auctions, *3 & 4 Hardwick Street, London.*
Boardman Fine Art Auctioneers, *Station Road Corner, Haverhill, Suffolk. CB9 0EY*
Bonhams, *Montpelier Galleries, Montpelier Street, Knightsbridge, London. SW7 1HH*
Bonsor Penningtons, *82 Eden Street, Kingston, Surrey.*
Bracketts, *27-29 High Street, Tunbridge Wells, Kent. TN1 1UU*
John F. Bradshaw, *33 Shaw Crescent, Sanderstead, Surrey.*
J. R. Bridgford & Sons, *1 Heyes Lane, Alderley Edge, Cheshire.*
British Antique Exporters, *206 London Road, Burgess Hill, W. Sussex. RH15 9RX*
Brogden & Co., *38 & 39 Silver Street, Lincoln.*
Wm. H. Brown, *Westgate Hall, Grantham, Lincs. NG31 6LT*
Bruton, Knowles & Co., *Albion Chambers, 111 Eastgate Chambers, Gloucester. GL1 1PZ*
Buckell & Ballard, *49 Parsons Street, Banbury, Oxfordshire.*
Burrows & Day, *39/41 Bank Street, Ashford, Kent.*
Burtenshaw Walker, *66 High Street, Lewes, Suffolk.*
Lawrence Butler & Co., *Butler House, 86 High Street, Hythe, Kent. CT21 5AJ*
Shirley Butler, *Oddiquities, 61 Waldram Park Road, Forest Hill, London SE23*
Butterfield & Butterfield, *1244 Sutter Street, San Francisco.*
Button, Menhenitt & Mutton, *Belmont Auction Rooms, Wadebridge.*
Alan Cadwallender, *63 Green Street, Middleton, Manchester.*
Capes, Dunn & Co., *The Auction Galleries, 38 Charles Street, Manchester. M1 7DB*
Chancellors Hollingsworths, *31 High Street, Ascot, Berkshire. SL5 7HG*
H. C. Chapman & Son, *The Auction Mart, North Street, Scarborough.*
Christie's, *8 King Street, St. James's, London. SW1Y 6QT*
Christie's (International) S.A., *8 Place de la Taconmerie, 1204 Geneva.*
Christie's, *502 Park Avenue, New York, N.Y. 10022*
Christie's (Monaco) S.A.N., *Park Palace, 98000 Monte Carlo.*
Christie's (Hong Kong) Ltd., *3607 Edinburgh Tower, 15 Queen's Road, Hong Kong.*
Christie's, *Cornelis Schuystraat 57, 1071 JG, Amsterdam, Holland.*
Christie's East, *219 East 67th Street, New York, N.Y. 10021*
Christie's & Edmiston's, *164-166 Bath Street, Glasgow.*
Christie's S. Kensington Ltd., *85 Old Brompton Road, London. SW7 3LD*
Andrew C. Clark, *12 Ing Field, Oakenshaw, Bradford, BD12 7EF*
Clarke Gammon, *45 High Street, Guildford, Surrey.*
Coles, Knapp & Kennedy, *Georgian Rooms, Ross-on-Wye, Herefordshire. HR9 5HL*
D. G. Cook, *275 Locking Road, Weston-Super-Mare, Avon.*
Cooper Hirst, *Goldway House, Parkway, Chelmsford. CM20 7PR*
County Group Estate Agents, *102 High Street, Tenterden, Kent. TN30 6AU*
Crystals Auctions, *Athol Street, Douglas, Isle of Man.*
Alan Cunningham, *10 Forth Street, Edinburgh. EH1 3LD*
Dacre, Son & Hartley, *1-5 The Grove, Ilkley, Yorkshire.*
Dee & Atkinson, *The Exchange Saleroom, Driffield, N. Humberside. YO25 7LJ*
Dickinson, Davy & Markham, *Elwes Street, Brigg, S. Humberside. DN20 8LB*
D. A. Dolbey Jones, *35a Maclise Road, London W14.*
Wm. Doyle Galleries Inc., *175 East 87th Street, New York.*
Dreweatts, *Donnington Priory, Donnington, Newbury, Berkshire.*
Du Mouchelles Art Galleries, *409 E. Jefferson, Detroit, Michigan 48226.*
Hy. Duke & Son, *Fine Art Salerooms, Weymouth Avenue, Dorchester, Dorset. DT1 1DG*

9

Edwards, Bigwood & Bewlay, *The Old School, Tiddington, Stratford-on-Avon.*
Elliott & Green, *Auction Salerooms, Emsworth Road, Lymington, Hants. SO4 9ZE*
R. H. Ellis & Sons, *44-46 High Street, Worthing, West Sussex. BN11 1LL*
H. Evans & Sons, *Hull, Yorkshire.*
Farrant & Wightman, *2/3 Newport Street, Old Town, Swindon.*
Fellows & Sons, *Bedford House, 88 Hagley Road, Edgbaston, Birmingham. B16 8LU*
John D. Fleming & Co., *8 Fore Street, Dulverton, Somerset. TA22 9EX*
Fox & Sons, *5 & 7 Salisbury Street, Fordingbridge, Hants. SP6 1AD*
John Francis, *S.O.F.A.A., Chartered Surveyors, Curiosity Salerooms, King Street, Carmarthen. SA31 1BS*
Christopher Frost, *The Enchanted Aviary, 63 Hall Street, Long Melford, Suffolk.*
Kathleen Fullerton, *Singleton, Fernhill Heath, Worcester. WR3 7UA*
Garrod Turner, *50 St. Nicholas Street, Ipswich, Suffolk.*
Geering & Colyer, *22-26 High Street, Tunbridge Wells. TN1 1XA*
Michael C. German, *38B Kensington Church Street, London.*
Goss & Crested China Ltd., *N. J. Pine, 62 Murray Road, Horndean, Hants. PO8 9JL*
Andrew Grant, *59-60 Foregate Street, Worcester.*
Mrs. Ivy Grant, *Seas-Gu-Daighean, Lynden Lane, Stonegate, Nr. Waldhurst, Sussex. TN5 7EF*
Graves, Son & Pilcher, *71 Church Road, Hove, East Sussex. BN3 2GL*
Gray's Antique Market, *958 Davies Street, London.*
Gribble, Booth & Taylor, *West Street, Axminster, Devon.*
Arthur G. Griffiths & Son, *57 Foregate Street, Worcester.*
Rowland Gorringe, *15 North Street, Lewes, Sussex.*
Hall Wateridge & Owen, *Welsh Bridge, Shrewsbury.*
James Harrison, *35 West End, Hebden Bridge, W. Yorkshire.*
Giles Haywood, *The Auction House, St. John's Road, Stourbridge, W. Midlands. DY8 1EW*
Heathcote Ball & Co., *The Old Rectory, Appleby Magna, Leicestershire.*
Hobbs & Chambers, *'At the Sign of the Bell', Market Place, Cirencester, Gloucestershire. GL7 1QQ*
John Hogbin & Son, *8 Queen Street, Deal, Kent.*
Kevin Holmes, *Trench Enterprises, Three Cow Green, Bacton, Stowmarket, Suffolk.*
Honiton Galleries, *High Street, Honiton, Devon.*
Edgar Horn, *46-50 South Street, Eastbourne, Sussex. BN21 4XB*
Hilary Humphries, *15 Dullingham Road, Newmarket, Cambridgeshire.*
Jackson-Stops & Staff, *Fine Art Dept., 14 Curzon Street, London. W1Y 7FH*
Jacobs & Hunt, *Lavant Street, Petersfield, Hampshire. GU32 3EF*
Michael Johnston, *18 Barking Road, Needham Market, Ipswich. IP6 8ET*
G. A. Key, *Market Place, Aylsham, Norfolk. NR11 6EH*
Lacy Scott, *Fine Art Dept., 10 Risbygate Street, Bury St. Edmunds. Suffolk. IP33 3AA*
Lalonde Bros. & Parham, *The Auction Room, Oakfield Road, Clifton, Bristol. BS8 2BE*
Ruth Lambert, *Weston Favell, Northampton.*
N. J. Marchant Lane, *Salters Cottage, Bramshott, Liphook, Hants.*
W. H. Lane & Son, *64 Morrab Road, Penzance, Cornwall. TR18 2QT*
Langlois Ltd., *Westaway Chambers, Don Street, St. Helier, Jersey, Channel Islands.*
Lawrence Fine Art, *South Street, Crewkerne, Somerset. TA18 8AB*
James & Lister Lea, *11 Newhall Street, Birmingham.*
Min Lewis, *Antiques, St. David's Street, Presteigne, Powys.*
Locke & England, *18 Guy Street, Leamington Spa, Warwickshire. CV32 4DG*
Lots Road Chelsea Auction Galleries, *71 Lots Road, London. SW10 0RN*
Thomas Love & Son, *South St. John Street, Perth, Scotland.*
R. J. Lucibell, *7 Fontayne Avenue, Rainham, Essex*
Mallams, *24 St. Michael's Street, Oxford*
S. Marshall, *23 Lock Laxford, East Kilbride*
Brian & Vera Matthews, *8 The Vale, Oakley, Hamps. RG23 7LB*
May, Whetter & Grose, *Cornubia Hall, Par, Cornwall.*
John Milne, *9-11 North Silver Street, Aberdeen.*
Moore, Allen & Innocent, *33 Castle Street, Cirencester, Gloucestershire. GL7 1QD*
Morphets, *4-6 Albert Street, Harrogate, Yorkshire. HG1 1JL*
Morris, Marshall & Poole, *2 Short Bridge Street, Newtown, Powys.*
Alfred Mossop & Co., *Kelsick Road, Ambleside, Cumbria.*
McCartney, Morris & Barker, *Corve Street, Ludlow, Salop.*
Bridget McConnel, *Grays Antique Market, 58 Davies Street, London W1*
Peter McConnell, *37 Oakhurst Road, West Moors, Wimbourne. BH22 0DW*
Neales of Nottingham, *192 Mansfield Road, Nottingham. NG1 3HX*
D. M. Nesbit & Co., *7 Clarendon Road, Southsea, Hants. PO5 2ED*
Northampton Auction Galleries, *33-39 Sheep Street, Northampton.*
Nostalgia, *13 Harleslade, Brandy Cove, Bishopston.*
Olivers, *23-24 Market Hill, Sudbury, Suffolk. CO10 6EN*
Onslows Auctioneers, *14-16 Carroun Road, London. SW8 1JT*
Osmond, Tricks, *Regent Street Auction Rooms, Clifton, Bristol, Avon. BS8 4HG*

10

Outhwaite & Litherland, *Kingsway Galleries, Fontenoy Street, Liverpool. L3 2BE*
J. R. Parkinson, Son & Hamer, *14 Bolton Street, Bury, Lancs.*
Parsons, Welch & Cowell, *The Argyle Salerooms, Sevenoaks, Kent.*
Pattison, Partners & Scott, *Ryton.*
Pearsons, *Walcote Chambers, High Street, Winchester.*
Phillips, *7 Blenheim Street, New Bond Street, London. W1Y 0AS*
Phillips, *65 George Street, Edinburgh.*
Phillips, *The Old House, Station Road, Knowle, Solihull, W. Midlands. B93 0HT*
Phillips, *Marylebone Auction Rooms, Hayes Place, London.*
Phillips, *98 Sauchiehall Street, Glasgow.*
Phillips Inc. Brooks, *39 Park End Street, Oxford. OX1 1JD*
Phillips Auctioneers, *The Auction Rooms, 1 Old King Street, Bath, Avon. BA1 1DD*
Geoff Price, *37 Comberford Drive, Tiffany Green, Wednesday, West Midlands.*
Prudential Fine Art Auctioneers, *Millmead Auction Rooms, Guildford, Surrey.*
John H. Raby & Son, *21 St. Mary's Road, Bradford.*
Reeds Rains, *Trinity House, 114 Northenden Road, Sale, Manchester. M33 3HD*
S. Reeve, *17 Montague Road, Uxbridge, Middlesex.*
Renton & Renton. *16 Albert Street, Harrogate, Yorkshire.*
Riddetts, *Richmond Hill, Bournemouth Square, Bournemouth, Dorset. BH2 6EJ*
Russell, Baldwin & Bright, *Ryelands Road, Leominster, Herefordshire. HR6 8JG*
Sandoe, Luce Panes, *Wotton Auction Rooms, Wotton-under-Edge, Gloucestershire. GL12 7EB*
M. Philip H. Scott, *East View, Bedale, Yorkshire.*
Shoulder & Son, *43 Nottingham Street, Melton Mowbray.*
Robert W. Skinner Inc., *Bolton Gallery, Route 117, Bolton, Massachusetts.*
Mike Smith, *Fayre House, 31 Stockleys Lane, Tingewick, Bucks.*
Smith-Woolley & Perry, *43 Castle Hill Avenue, Folkestone.*
Jonathan H. Sneath, *Eastlyn, Fen Gate, Moulton Chapel, Nr. Spalding, Lincs.*
Mr. Solly, *13 Greenways, Beckenham, Kent. BR3 3NG*
Spear & Sons, *The Hill, Wickham Market, Suffolk.*
H. Spencer & Sons Ltd., *20 The Square, Retford, Notts.*
Stalker & Boos, *280 North Woodward Avenue, Birmingham, Michigan.*
David Stanley Auctions, *Stordan Grange, Osgathorpe, Leics. LE12 9SR*
Street Jewellery Society, *10 Summerhill Terrace, Newcastle-upon-Tyne.*
Stride & Son, *Southdown House, St. John's Street, Chichester, Sussex.*
G. E. Sworder & Sons, *Chequers, 19 North Street, Bishops Stortford, Herts.*
Christopher Sykes, *11 Market Place, Woburn, Milton Keynes.*
David Symonds, *High Street, Crediton, Devon.*
Taylor, Lane & Creber, *Western Auction Rooms, 38 North Hill, Plymouth. PL4 8EQ*
Laurence & Martin Taylor, *63 High Street, Honiton, Devon.*
Liz Taylor, *Main Street, Newstead, Melrose, Roxburghshire.*
Louis Taylor & Sons, *Percy Street, Hanley, Stoke-on-Trent.*
Terry Antiques, *175 Junction Road, London N19*
Theriault, *P. O. Box 151 Annapolis, Maryland 21404*
Osmond Tricks, *Regent Street Auction Rooms, Clifton, Bristol. BS8 4HG*
Turner, Rudge & Turner, *29 High Street, East Grinstead.*
Mrs. U. Twite, *Togford, Stogumber, Somerset. TA4 3TN*
V. & V.'s, *The Memorial Hall, Shiplake-on-Thames.*
M. Veissid & Co., *87 Park Avenue, Ruislip, Middlesex. HA4 7UL*
Vidler & Co., *Auction Offices, Cinque Ports St., Rye, Sussex.*
Wallis & Wallis, *West Street Auction Galleries, Lewes, Sussex. BN7 2NJ*
Tom Walsh, *Capricorn Curios, 48 St. Annes Road, Blackpool.*
Ward & Partners, *16 High Street, Hythe, Kent.*
Warner, Wm. H. Brown, *16-18 Halford Street, Leicester. LE1 1JB*
Warren & Wignall, *113 Towngate, Leyland, Lancashire.*
Thomas Watson, *27 North Street, Bishops Stortford.*
Way, Riddett & Co., *Town Hall Chambers, Lind Street, Ryde, Isle of Wight.*
Neil Wayne, *Old Chapel, Bridge Street, Belper, Derby.*
J. M. Welsh & Son, *The Old Town Hall, Great Dunmow, Essex. CM6 1AU*
Whiteheads, *111-113 Elm Grove, Southsea, Hants.*
Whitton & Laing, *32 Okehampton Street, Exeter, Devon.*
John Wilson, *50 Acre End Street, Eynsham, Oxford.*
Peter Wilson Fine Art Auctioneers, *Victoria Gallery, Market Street, Nantwich. CW5 3DG*
Richard Withington, *Hillsboro, New Hampshire 03244, U.S.A.*
Woolley & Wallis, *The Castle Auction Mart, Castle Street, Salisbury, Wiltshire. SP1 3SU*
Eldon E. Worrall & Co., *15 Seel Street, Liverpool.*
Worsfolds Auction Galleries, *40 Station Road West, Canterbury, Kent.*
Wyatt & Son with Whiteheads, *59 East Street, Chichester, Sussex.*
Yesterday's Paper, *40 South View, Holcombe Rogus, Wellington, Somerset. TA21 0PP.*

11

While every care has been taken in the compiling of information contained in this volume the publishers cannot accept any liability for loss, financial or otherwise, incurred by reliance placed on the information herein.

All prices quoted in this book are obtained from a variety of auctions in various countries during the twelve months prior to publication and are converted to dollars at the rate of exchange prevalent at the time of sale.

PRICE GUIDE TO COLLECTIBLES AND MEMORABILIA

H old on! Don't throw that away! So it's only perhaps an old train ticket or a matchbox that you're about to toss into the waste-basket but, unlikely as it sounds, it's worth something. That unregarded piece of trash could be the source of a useful sum of money or the beginning of a lifelong passion for you.

There is no limit to the sort of things that have unexpected value. True collectors do not only seek out bisque headed dolls, vintage cars, Old Master prints or Chelsea china. Not all of them go to the big New York sale rooms and bid in telephone number sums; they also dig in garbage dumps, haunt rummage sales and street markets, turn out their attics and use their eyes to appreciate the attractive quality of hitherto little regarded every day items. There is a profit to be made in such assorted things as railroad porters' badges, soup can labels, light bulbs, beer mats, bicycles or pictures of film stars, just as much as in Chinese porcelain or fine French furniture.

There is absolutely no limit to what is worth money. One man's trash is certainly another man's treasure and, strangely enough, once something starts to be collected, it acquires a new value. One train ticket crumpled up on a station platform is worth nothing. Ten train tickets, neatly arranged in order, form the basis of a collection that could in time be worth hundreds of dollars.

Another area for collecting is cigarette cards, first introduced by the firm of W. D. & H. O. Wills around 1885. Most of the 5000 or so sets produced are only worth a few dollars. Early examples produced by Taddy & Co. however, can be worth hundreds of dollars and if they are a set of 20 Clowns and Circus Artistes you are talking about $25,000 plus, depending on condition.

A set of twenty 'Clowns and Circus Artistes', by Taddy sold for over $25,000 by Phillips.

COLLECTIBLES & MEMORABILIA

WAGNER. PITTSBURG

Honus Wagner

Even more spectacular is the extremely rare baseball card of Honus Wagner, the Pittsburg player. Issued about 1910 this single card sold for $18,000 at Phillips.

Beer cans were introduced in 1935 and early examples feature a cone-shaped top. Over 25,000 different cans have been made and collectors prefer ringpull cans to be intact therefore, empty the contents of the can from the bottom. A 12oz. example of Pilsner Lager, made in 1955, is worth about $40.

One of the earliest patents for a cast iron mechanical novelty bank was taken out by J. Hall on December 21st 1869 for his Excelsior bank. Many of the hundreds of designs were of American manufacture and sell for between $200 and $1,000 depending on rarity. Occasionally however, a hitherto unknown example comes onto the market like one featuring a girl skipping which is worth a mammoth $15,000.

Few collectors however start out only with the aim of making money. For many of them, profit comes by accident. They collect because they like the look of something and want to own it; because it reminds them of a time when they were happy or of someone they love. Usually the initial impulse to collect begins in childhood and most of us can remember the thrill of

hunting out special colored marbles; filling up scrap books or baseball card albums; the enthusiastic swopping with friends; the anxious hunt for that elusive scrap or card that somehow always refused to come our way. It's the hunt that's the pleasure; the search combined with the gradual amassing of knowledge about the chosen subject. Only when someone has been well and truly bitten by the collecting bug, do they come to realize that their treasures represent a nest egg, worth far more than it cost to collect them in the first place.

For example, take the case of the middle aged academic who began buying second hand books while he was a student. Twenty years later he found, to his surprise, that he had assets worth well over $100,000 stacked away on his book shelves.

When he worked out how much the books had originally cost him, he discovered that no volume had been bought for more than $5 and most of them were picked up for less than $1. His treasures had been found on market stalls and at rummage sales simply because his limited income as a student meant that he could not afford new books. By 1988 some of the books were worth at least $1,000 each and none were valued at less than $200. His hours spent browsing in second hand bookshops paid off in a big way.

First Edition in three volumes of Dickens' 'Great Expectations' 1861. (Phillips) $19,200

14

It is easier to spot something that is worth money if you specialize in things that appeal to you. Car enthusiasts who cannot afford vintage vehicles can buy car mascots, or, like a man in Northern Ireland, jerricans for gasolene. Unlikely as it seems, he discovered that his collection of old cans was worth money and he began traveling all over the country picking up more unusual cans. Today he has the finest collection of jerricans in Ireland, most of them picked up from old garages, garden sheds or garbage dumps for next to nothing. Another car enthusiast realized that the introduction of modern gas stations spelt the end for the old glass globes that used to decorate the pumps. He bought one or two for the sake of nostalgia and the collection has grown into a car museum.

Oiliana is a comparatively new collecting field, the attraction being the functional advertising in the form of oil cans and pourers by firms such as Shell, Esso, Castrol and Pratts. Some of the early enamel signs might make over $200 but even humble oil pourers are keenly sought by collectors and can make as much as $40.

Comics are collected by enthusiasts all over the world, particularly American, reflecting the extensive distribution they have always had. Few collectibles have such a huge range of items available and such a vast range of prices from 25 cents to $15,000 for the No. 1 *Action* comic from June 1938 which launched Superman for its creators, Joe Schuster and Jerry Seigal.

The most widely collected British comics are *The Dandy, Film Fun, Eagle, Radio Fun, Knockout* and *The Beano* of which the first edition of July 30th 1938, complete with free Whoopee mask, is worth about $600.

With driving in mind cars on a smaller scale are also keenly sought after, particularly those produced by Dinky. Although most are worth only a few dollars, find one from the 30's and it could be worth over $1,000.

Probably the most sought after model to any Dinky collector, however, is number 992 Avro Vulcan. This model of the most famous of the R.A.F. V bombers was produced between 1955 and 1956 and differed from others in that it was made of aluminum. The bulk of the 500 or so produced were sold in North America for $1.40 cents each. Find one of these complete with its original box and you can expect to make $2,000 at auction.

Many people find that their acquisitions have a value over and above what other collectors will pay for each item because they are able to turn their hobby into a way of

A very rare Lalique glass amethyst tinted car mascot, 'Victoire', 14.7cm. high. (Christie's)
$17,000

making a living. There are several museums over the country that were started by an enthusiastic collector who fell in love with something unlikely. For instance, an out of work miner runs his own museum specializing in old pit lamps and miners' tokens. Because of his regret for the passing of an era, he picked up a few lamps and tokens when the mines were closing. He wanted something of the old way of life to be preserved. Today his collection is not only valuable in terms of money — some of the lamps he bought for next to nothing are worth $500 each — but it is also a rich source of historical evidence about the life of the past and parties of school children are brought from all over the country to see it. Instead of living on unemployment benefit, he is now a museum owner and his collection, picked up on pithead garbage dumps or bought for a few cents, is worth many thousands of dollars to any museum should he choose to sell it.

Another collector, a retired Colonel, shares his home with over seven hundred teddy bears, which have proved over the last year or so to be a phenomenal growth area. Not long after the world record of $10,000 was established at Sothebys for a short plush Steiff bear named Archibald, an even rarer muzzled bear was sold to the same buyer from California for nearly $15,000.

Margaret Steiff, a crippled dressmaker, is credited with making the first bear about 1900, but it wasn't until Teddy Roosevelt refused to shoot a bear on an organized hunt (it was, after all, tied to a stake by someone eager to please) that the Teddy Bear really took off in popularity.

Dolls too, have been hitting the headlines with new world records, for over $112,000 was paid for a rare William and Mary wooden doll which, unfortunately, was devoid of a hand and part of a lower leg.

World record breaking Steiff muzzled teddy bears, circa 1913, 'Archibald' on the left sold for $10,000 while the 20in. example on the right sold for $15,000.

World record breaking doll sold at Sotheby's for $112,000.

People buy old bar signs, advertising boards, paper window displays, enamel signs, railroad station nameboards just because they like the look of them — and later find that they have picked up a valuable asset. A man whose hobby was fishing became interested in old fishing tackle and is now one of the best known international dealers in the field for the sport of angling has been a rich source for the collector ever since the days of Isaac Walton. Salmon flies, spoons, floats, gaffs and even weights have their specialist following but the fishing reel is without doubt the most sought after item by collectors. Rare examples such as a 19th century gilt brass reel with ivory handle and spring and cog mechanism recently sold for $5,500.

A dentist gave up looking after patients' teeth when his collection of old dental instruments took over his life. Today he deals in the instruments and also writes books about them. A couple whose hobby was swimming and badminton began collecting postcards and advertising material about these sports. They've written books on the subject, deal in cards concerned with sporting subjects and travel all over the country giving lectures on their collection.

A pair of 16th century leather nose spectacles, 9cm. wide, discovered in the roof of a house. (Phillips) $2,480

Because of his job, a lighthouse keeper started collecting old postcards with pictures of lighthouses on them. Today he has one of the best collections in existence and his cards are valuable not only in money terms but also from a historian's point of view because they provide information about lighthouses which are no longer in use or sometimes even in existence. He found his cards through other dealers, in garage sales and odd lots in auctions. Few of them cost more than a couple of cents to buy and some were swopped with other collectors for cards he did not want himself, because as far as postcards are concerned there are collectors interested in every subject under the sun from bridges to bathing beauties; railroad stations to rude cartoons; foreign cities to farm yards. Today collectors pay prices ranging from $3 for a postcard of Cary Grant to anything up to $20 for one of the erotic French postcards of the 1920's.

A rare Hardy Bros. 2½in. Perfect brass fly reel of the 1891 pattern. (Phillips) $5,500

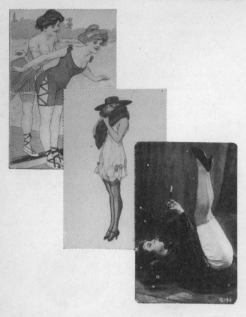

Typical saucy French postcards worth between $6 and $20.

A very rare ballooning postcard 'Lifeboat Saturday', sold by Neales of Nottingham for an amazing $2,500.

The world's first postcard was issued in Austria on October 1st 1869 and proved to be so popular that many other countries followed suit – Britain 1870, Canada 1871 and America 1873.

The first British postcards issued by the General Post Office in 1870 were designed to take the address only on one side and the message alongside the illustration on the other side. An Act of Parliament in 1902 allowed the message and address to be written on the same side leaving the other side free for a picture which greatly increased their popularity. One of the rarest examples is 'Lifeboat Saturday' which was delivered by Balloon Post from Manchester to Haslingden on September 20th 1902 and sold for the not inconsiderable sum of $2,500.

A policeman in London has shelves in his sitting room full of valuable and attractively colored Victorian poison bottles because one day, when he was chasing a suspect through rough ground, he tripped over a bottle sticking up out of a garbage dump. It was a poison bottle and because he liked the look of it, he went back to the dump and dug up several more. Then he began reading up about poison bottles and gradually his collection grew. Today some of his bottles are worth up to $1,500 each – all dug from dumps where they had been thrown away as worthless.

The scope for finding something that is worth money is immense, it covers every possible aspect of life and every interest, no matter how bizarre. Every week someone finds something new worth collecting and so another speciality is born; another market opens up for items that were disregarded before. Anything connected with golf for instance is very popular. The earliest golf balls were made of leather and filled with a concoction of boiled feathers, enough to fill a top hat. They were then hammered to a round shape and painted white. In time these were followed by the Gutta-Percha balls which were of smooth appearance and patented by Dr Paterson of St. Andrews. Early balls are extremely rare and highly collectible as can be judged by a Gourlay feathery ball in mint condition which recently sold for $8,000 at Phillips. Antique golfing items always command a premium as was witnessed by the eleven golf clubs discovered in a stick stand in the attic of Blair Castle in Scotland. The property of the Duke of Atholl these clubs, made by Jackson of Perth, sold for an amazing $100,000 at Christies.

Photograph of Sir Winston Churchill, signed, depicting him as a Lieutenant in the 4th Hussars, Cairo, September 1898. (Phillips) $3,000

One of three glass negatives taken by the Rev. Charles Lutwidge Dodgson — Lewis Carroll — in 1879. (Phillips) $16,000

Photography is another fertile area for collectors. One of the rarest cameras to come on to the market was the Thomas Sutton Panoramic Wet Plate camera made of mahogany and brass which sold for about $20,000. Just as surprising was a Kodak No. 1 from 1880 with its 57mm. F9 Periscopic Lens and Guillotine Sector Shutter which although less impressive to look at made $1,600. Don't get excited, your box Brownie which looks very similar is hardly worth anything. Attention is now focused on more recent examples as demonstrated by the $17,000 recently paid at Christies for a Leica No. 1 complete with its black enameled rangefinder and double Leica film cassette holder.

An album of 27 calotypes by D. O. Hill and R. Adamson. (Christie's) $34,000

Very rare Leica No. 1 camera complete with maker's leather case, sold for over $17,000 at Christie's.

Two 1920's silk dresses by Mariano Fortuny with Delphos pleating and stenciled belt. (Phillips) $6,000

World record auction price for pot lid 'Eastern Lady and Black Attendant', sold for over $5,000 at Phillips.

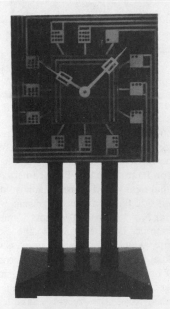

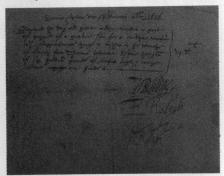

Some early signed documents can have considerable value such as this Receipt for the sale of a property signed by Sir Walter Ralegh, his wife, Elizabeth, and son Walter, which could be worth over $10,000 at auction. (Christie's)

The Sturrock Domino clock, designed by Charles Rennie Mackintosh as a wedding present to Alec Sturrock and Mary Newbery, 25cm. high. (Phillips) $84,000

An extremely rare American locomotive and tender copper weathervane, circa 1882, the locomotive reproduced in fine detail is mounted on track with two ball finials at tracks end, and attached ball counterweight, in fine original condition with verdigris surface, 17in. high, 61in. long, 8in. deep. (Robt. W. Skinner Inc.) $185,000

If there was any doubt that collecting weathervanes is a subject for serious investment it was dispelled recently when an entire auction was devoted to the sale of just one weathervane with historical connections to the patriot Paul Revere. It is rumored that weathervanes have also been disappearing mysteriously from atop some of the highest churches in New York State as a result of daring helicopter raids at dawn – a sure indication of their worth. A rare late 19th century example of a locomotive and tender weathervane, made of copper, recently sold for $185,000 – really.

Treasures can turn up anywhere – antiques shops, junk shops, garage sales or rummage sales are all good sources. Garbage dumps, however are gold mines for people with an eye for a rarity. They dig up bottles, pot lids, old clay pipes, china, decorated tiles, ironware – every piece somebody's trash from the past which is worth money today. Although milk has been sold in glass bottles since the latter part of the 19th century, they did not come into common use until after the First World War. The earliest known example "The Thatcher Milk Protector", was devised by an American, Dr Harvey P. Thatcher in 1884 and is worth about $300.

No matter how odd or unusual a find, there is always someone somewhere who yearns to own it.

Rare early light bulbs, circa 1882, worth from $340 to $600 for the Swan 'Pipless' on the left.

Light bulbs, for instance, date from about 1841 when an inventor named Starr found that a bright light could be produced by sending an electric current through a piece of carbon. One of the first successful incandescent electric lamps were made by J. W. Swan and one of his light bulbs, the 'Swan Pipless', made in 1882, is worth about $600.

The world of textiles is also a good area for the treasure hunter for a Delphos dress by the designer Mariano Fortuny could be worth over $6,000 and even

Marilyn Monroe's bra, left in a London hairdresser's, fetched the not inconsiderable sum of $1,000 at auction. Such is the magic of Monroe that the showgirl outfit she wore in the 1956 film 'Bus Stop', complete with its 20th Century Fox label, sold for nearly $30,000 at Sothebys.

Designed to keep out the cold, bedcovers were made from two thicknesses of cloth with padding sewn between. This developed into an art and before long we had the richly decorated quilts so highly prized by collectors. A rare example by Sarah Anne Wilson, consisting of thirty appliqued squares of floral and animal design, was made in 1854 and recently sold for, would you believe, $35,000.

Samplers were produced from early in the 18th century right through until after the First World War as a means of showing how adept a young girl could be at the useful art of embroidery, as well as knowing her alphabet. Most found today are 19th century and worth $200 or so but early North American examples such as one by Lydia Hart dated May 28th 1744 are extremely rare which accounts for the $37,000 it made.

An early 19th century needlework sampler, 51 x 44.5cm. (Phillips) $1,000

Tin canisters or old cookie containers used to be thrown out, disregarded by the hundreds but pretty, colored or unusual

A classic Navajo chief's blanket, woven in single strand homespun and raveled yarn, 82 x 62in. (Robt. W. Skinner Inc.) $40,000

containers can demand astonishing prices from collectors today. Collectors tend to specialize in unusually shaped containers or in ones with attractive pictures or portraits of the Royal Family, and Princess Diana and Prince Charles boxes are already being collected. Some of the most attractive are 1920's novelty containers decorated with nursery rhyme scenes or tin boxes shaped like buses, engines or books.

It seems that nothing is too everyday to be worth money — even the labels from cans of food or cleaning materials on sale in supermarkets today are being collected and show a profit for the collector within a very short period of time. Collectors of these items choose labels which are well designed, particularly attractive or which represent a significant advance in the modern way of life. Biological soap powders were a breakthrough when they first appeared and their packages were worth collecting.

It was around 1942 that the immortal cry 'Any Gum, Chum', was first heard echoing throughout Britain as the first Bubble Gum was introduced by the

American Allied Forces. The British home product didn't get under way until the early 1950's and with new issues appearing every few weeks many of these wax paper wrappers are now quite rare. Most sought after is 'Mars Attacks' issued in 1962 and quickly withdrawn because there were complaints that it frightened children — it's now worth $200.

One of a collection of twelve previously unpublished color pictures of The Beatles. (Christie's) $1,300

Fans of the Beatles in the 1960's and '70's who collected records, magazines, programs and other things relating to their idols are today sitting on a treasure trove because the big auction houses hold regular sales of pop idol memorabilia at which hundreds of dollars can be paid for an unusual record, a fan photograph, a signed concert program or even a pair of stockings with the magic name 'The Beatles' on them.

An autographed Cavern Club membership book from the early 1960's can sell for as much as $1,000 and even old copies of Beatles' sheet music sell for $3 each. Tens of thousands of printed items. are available on the Beatles who dominated not only popular music but also all youth culture for the best part of a decade. Of particular interest are those items more personally identified with the super group such as a signed concert program for 1964 which sold for $700, but for really amazing money the hand-written lyrics of 'Imagine' by John Lennon, on the reverse of an hotel bill from Majorca, sold for over $10,000. While Paul McCartney's upright piano, circa 1902, sold for $15,000. The same enthusiasm applies to Buddy Holly, Elvis Presley and the memorabilia of other more recent stars. There must be drawers and boxes full of dusty papers and magazines forgotten by one time pop fans in houses all over the country which are worth money now.

A fine Marklin clockwork tinplate Nassau-class battleship, the motor driving three propellers, the hull painted brown and two-tone gray with simulated planked deck, in its original wooden crate bearing Marklin trade label, the model 39in. long. (Christie's) $19,000

Very rare character jug, 'Churchill', designed by C. J. Noke, introduced in 1940, withdrawn by 1942, AS D6170. Wording on base: 'Winston Spencer Churchill Prime Minister of Britain 1940'. This Loving Cup was made during the Battle of Britain as a tribute to a great leader, worth over $12,000.

A Goldscheider painted terracotta group, 57cm. high. (Phillips) $3,000

These three Doulton figures, 'Wedding Morn', 'Tulips' and 'The Coming of Spring', are all worth over $1,000.

It is generally accepted that a Royal Doulton character jug inscribed 'Winston Churchill Prime Minister of Britain 1940' was withdrawn after less than a year in production because Churchill was not pleased with the likeness portrayed. As such it is an extremely rare and desirable item coveted by collectors throughout the world and is likely to fetch $12,000 plus at auction.

Even this amazing price has now been surpassed by an even rarer character jug, a pilot edition known as 'The Maori' produced in 1939, which now sells for over $12,000.

Clark Gable

Doulton produced a limited number of Toby Jugs of Chaplin in 1918. They were inscribed 'Charlie' on the base and his bowler hat formed the lid. The jugs stand 11in. high and are today very rare because less than ten are known to be in private collections, worth well over $6,000

W. C. Fields and Mae West are part of 'The Celebrity Collection', a series of six character jugs, made by Royal Doulton which were first issued as a promotional item for American Express in 1983. Groucho Marx, Jimmy Durante and Louis Armstrong were also featured but the jug of Clark Gable, designed by Stan Taylor and numbered D6709, was withdrawn in 1984 because of copyright difficulties – though not before around fifty had already been sold. As a result this rare item is now worth upwards of $5,000 while the others in the series sell for around just $100.

An extremely rare Royal Doulton character jug, 'The Maori', circa 1939, which never actually went into production. Occasionally, however, a pilot model comes onto the market and it has been reported that collectors are willing to pay around $12,000 for one.

COLLECTIBLES & MEMORABILIA

Gustav Stickley slat-sided waste-basket, circa 1907, 14in. high. (Robt. W. Skinner Inc.)

Gustav Stickley, the eldest of six brothers who died in 1942, was an American designer of furniture who signed his creations in red script. Just one of his armchairs can be worth a small fortune and even a waste-basket by him is worth over $2,000.

Rare Gustav Stickley oak 'Eastwood' chair, circa 1902, sold at Robt. W. Skinner Inc. for over $28,000.

Duck Decoys are mainly used in estuaries and ponds by hunters; are made of wood and painted in traditional colors with flat paint. Originally fashioned from mud and reeds they have now become works of art in their own right as can be judged by a pair of mid 19th century painted wooden Merganser decoys, a hen and a drake, by L. T. Holmes which sold for nearly $100,000 at Christies.

American Merganser decoy by L. T. Holmes.

Even radios have come a long way since Mr Marconi harnessed the transmission of electro-magnetic waves back in 1894 and this is the fascination for collectors. The Phillips Mains AC Super Inductance model from 1932 sells for over $200.

Anyone who wants to make a profit out of buying and selling unusual items should cast aside prejudices against 'trash' and look for the indefinable quality in something that really attracts them. They should be prepared to search out their quarry with infinite patience wherever they go and they should also take the trouble to find out as much about their subject as possible. With the growth of knowledge will come greater discrimination and the ability to spot a true rarity that is worth money. Anyone with the ability to spot an unlikely bargain knows that if they ask themselves the question "what's it worth?" the answer is very often . . . "far more than you might expect."

ANTHONY CURTIS

ADVERTISING SIGNS

There was a time when enamel advertising signs could be found pinned to every available wall surface colorfully proclaiming the purity and authenticity of every imaginable product. Indeed this was such a common practice that companies employed men whose only job was to fix these signs on site.

Now, in the 1980's, these enamel signs are among the most treasured and in some cases the most expensive examples of advertising collectibles. The most rare and desirable of these are the Victorian or Edwardian signs in mint condition. Ideally, signs should be of a size less than one meter square and feature some favorable characteristic such as a shaped edge, a figurative image or quirky period slogan, printing in full color or advertise a now obsolete product.

Reverse on glass Woolworth's sign, circa 1900, 20 x 36in. (Robt. W. Skinner Inc.) **$750**

'New England Organ Company' advertising sign, 24 x 34in. (Robt. W. Skinner Inc.) **$700**

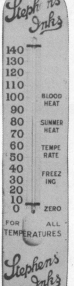

Brasso Metal Polish. (Street Jewellery) **$100**

Persil, made by Ferro Email, 1930's, 23 x 15in. (Street Jewellery) **$160**

Stephens' Inks. (Street Jewellery) **$170**

Reckitt's Blue. (Street Jewellery) **$600**

Kynoch's cartridge display board, circa 1900. **$870**

'Schlitz Brewery' tin sign, circa 1915, 24in. diam. **$435**

Large lithographed tin sign advertising Harvard Beer, circa 1910, 26¾in. wide. **$650**

Dr. Fitler's Rheumatic Syrup sign, circa 1880, 19½ x 13½in. **$2,600**

A decorative cartridge display board, arranged geometrically in stylised floral motif, 43in. square. **$5,000**

Tin advertising sign for 'Murphy Da-Cote Enamel', lithograph by H. D. Beach, Co., Ohio, circa 1925, 27 x 19in. **$650**

A 19th century roll down wall cigar advertisement, chromolithographed on canvas backed paper, 54 x 39½in. **$180**

Lithographed advertisement for Egyptienne 'Straights' cigarettes, 31in. high. **$135**

A metal Rose & Co. lithograph sign, and advertisement for 'Merchant Tailors', circa 1900, 26½in. high. **$375**

'White Rock' advertising tip tray, copy reads 'White Rock, The World's Best Table Water.' **$45**

Duke's tobacco advertising sign, America, 18½in. wide. **$260**

A metal 'El Roi-Tan' chromolithograph advertising sign, 24¼ x 20in. **$125**

'Buckeye' Farm Equipment sign, by The Winters Print & Litho Co., Springfield, Ohio', 1880-1890, 30 x 21¾in. **$480**

Tobacco advertising sign, 'Red Indian', chromolithographed on thin cardboard, circa 1900, 28 x 22in. **$450**

A shaving advertising sign, advertising 'Antiseptic Cup, Brush and Soap', circa 1910, 18¼ x 14in. **$400**

Lithograph on tin, copyrighted by Paul Jones & Co., 1903, 28½ x 22¼in. **$270**

None Such Mince Meat sign, head of an Onondaga Indian chief, circa 1890, 28 x 20in. **$2,100**

Late 19th century Elgin watch advertising sign, entitled 'My Elgin's All Right', 22 x 15in. **$190**

Bovril 'Oh Mamma Don't Forget to Order Bovril'. $800

Zebra Grate Polish. $300

Singer Sewing Machines, 11 x 7½in. (Street Jewellery) $170

Bibby's 'Cream Equivalent'. $300

Pepsi-Cola. $90

Blue Band Margarine. $80

Hudson's Soap, Easy and Safe. $100

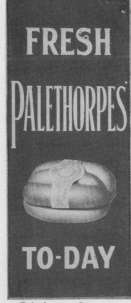

Palethorpes Sausages, Fresh Today. $120

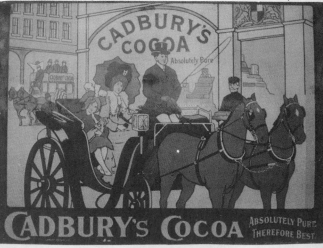

Cadbury's Cocoa, Absolutely Pure. $800

Churchman's 'Tortoiseshell' Smoking Mixture. (Street Jewellery)   **$350**

Crow Bar Tobacco.   **$200**

Fremlins Ale.   **$150**

His Master's Voice   **$250**

Elliman's Embrocation.   **$500**

Late 19th century wood advertising trade sign. (Robt. W. Skinner Inc.)
$1,800

'August Wolf Milling' advertising sign, circa 1890, 21½ x 31½in. (Robt. W. Skinner Inc.)   **$780**

Bullards' Beers. **$200**

ADVERTISING SIGNS

Karpol, Buy It Here
$150

Bird's Custard, Safeguard
Your Health.   **$250**

Burma Sauce 'The Only Sauce I Dare
Give Father'.   **$200**

Nectar Tea.
$50

Mazawattee Tea
Leaf.   **$250**

Raleigh, The All-Steel Bicycle. (Street Jewellery) **$240**

An advertising plaque bearing
Rowland's Macassar Oil, the
reverse impressed T. J. & J.
Mayer, Longport, 16 x 22cm.
(Phillips)   **$1,000**

Sunlight, Guarantee of Purity. **$900**

Komo Metal Polish. **$300**

Bird's Custard Powder.
$500

32

AERONAUTICAL

Although Wilbur Wright and his brother Orville are credited with making the first powered flight in December 1903, it was another American, Samuel Pierpont Langley, who actually invented the first aeroplane.

After achieving success with a model launched from the roof of a houseboat on the Potomac in 1896, he progressed to a full size machine and was ready to repeat the experiment early in 1903. Unfortunately, the starting mechanism failed and the aircraft plunged into the river. Professor Langley died in 1906 never having achieved his life's ambition.

The postscript to this story is, that in 1914, his former students fitted floats to Langley's 'curiosity' in an attempt to launch direct from the river- it flew like a bird.

Some of the early model planes now fetch amazing money and virtually any model made prior to 1940 is highly desirable and will do well.

Two of a set of twenty-four colored magic lantern slides depicting early ballooning and flying scenes, in original box. (Christie's) $300

A polychrome wax bust of Montgolfier, inscribed 'Discovered Aerostation, 1784', 3¾in. (Christie's) $140

A silk Stevengraph depicting a balloon and entitled 'Many happy returns of the day, made by T. Stevens of Coventry on 28th Feb. 1874', 10in. long. (Christie's) $130

Color lithograph poster published by Masileau & Co., Paris, copyright 1910, Meeting d'Heliopolis, Rougier le Gagnant sur Biplane Voisin, 17¼ x 35in. (Christie's) $200

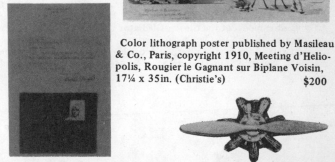

Schneider Trophy, 1931, Official Souvenir Programme, together with two others. (Christie's) $155

Annual Sporting License, U.S.A., Federation Aeronautique Internationale, together with a letter signed 1928, issued by Orville Wright. (Christie's) $330

A silver lapel badge in the form of a gnome engine with propeller, 1¾in. long. (Christie's) $80

French tinplate Paris-Tokio bi-plane, clock-work mechanism driving the wheels, circa 1935, 9in. long. $350

Geoffrey Watson — Special Shell Aviation Petrol, No. 356, published by Vincent Brooks Day & Son, 30 x 45in. (Onslows) $220

DH 60 'Gypsy Moth' G-AADP, by Stanley Orton Bradshaw, signed and dated '29, watercolor , 9 x 13¼in. (Christie's) $960

A Mettoy jet airliner, No. 2016/1, in original box with four mechanical sparking replace-ments, the box 20½in., English, circa 1935. $220

A flying scale model of the Gloster Gladiator single seater fighter Serial No. K.8032 with external details, finished in silver with R.A.F. markings, wingspan 56in. (Christie's) $580

1942 Vickers Supermarine Spitfire Mk. IX, constructor's number BR601, wingspan 36ft. 11in., length 31ft.4in. (Christie's) $111,390

An Exhibition Standard 1:30 scale model of the prototype Panavia Tornado F-2 Multi Role Combat Aircraft, wingspan 17½in. (Christie's) $5,000

A large scale model of the British airship R100-G-FAAV, 10ft. long, with tower, 4ft. (Christie's) $2,000

Studio of Roy Nockolds — Sopwith Transport Ditched in the Sea near Shipping, signed, on board — 20 x 30in. (Onslows) $450

American Flyer Manufacturing Co., Model No. 560 spring-driven monoplane, 54cm. long, span 60cm., boxed. (Phillips)
$300

A Tipp Lufthansa turbo-prop airliner, battery powered, 22½in. long with a Tipp Bi-plane, 20¼in. wide, circa 1935. $570

Studio of Roy Nockolds — Hawker Fury 1 Serial No. K2074, signed and dated 1940, watercolor, 15 x 19in. (Onslows) $400

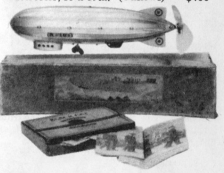

DH 60 'Gypsy Moth' G-AADS, by Stanley Orton Bradshaw, signed and dated '29, watercolor , 9¼ x 13in. (Christie's) $650

A pre-war Japanese R101 airship by GK, the aluminum body with tinplate gondolas and fins, 13in. long, together with newspaper cuttings, circa 1930. $660

A Tipp R101 tinplate Zeppelin, German, circa 1930, 25½in. long. $1,650

After Gamy — Garros Gagne le Grand Prix de l'Aero Club, hand-colored lithograph, 17¾ x 35¾in. (Onslows) $75

A color lithograph poster inscribed 'Graceful Parachute Descent', published by H. Miller Junr. & Co., 28 x 18in. (Christie's) $260

One of four silver place-setting holders depicting a Wright flyer, 1½in. high, in presentation case. (Christie's) $700

An ivory paper knife, reputed to have been salvaged from Manfred von Richthofen's aircraft, 12in long. (Christie's) $700

A blue enamel oval snuff box, the cover painted with a hot air balloon over the country-side, 2¼in. long. (Christie's) $800

A commemorative plate depicting Immelmann's Fokker III monoplane, by N. Roe, oil, signed, inscribed and dated 1981, 9in. diam. (Christie's) $250

A pair of sheepskin-lined flying trousers, type B-1. (Christie's) $150

A white metal souvenir spoon commemorating the journey of Norwegian airship 'Norge' in 1926, 5in. long. (Christie's) $80

A sheepskin-lined U.S. Army flying jacket, type B-3, size 48. (Christie's) $300

A complimentary Season Pass to the London Aero-drome, Hendon, 1914, issued to John F. Plummer, together with a collection of other related material. (Christie's) $250

An openface pocket watch, the white face inscribed 'Shock proof lever, Swiss made' and depicting a mono-plane, 2in. diam. (Christie's) $110

AMERICAN INDIANWARE

Interest in the material culture of the American Indians has led to a number of specialist sales being devoted to their crafts.

Working with tools of bone or ivory and using all available materials such as animal hides, quills, corn husks, willow and beads they produced artefacts of both great practical use and beauty. The buffalo provided the Indians with food, clothing and shelter. Hides were also painted and used in a decorative way.

Beadwork was introduced in the mid 16th century in the south, and in the north and east in the 18th and 19th century. The use of certain types and colors of beads helps the historian to determine the extent of 'white' contact with certain groups of Indians.

Plains child's quill vest with cloth lining, 10½in. wide. (Robt. W. Skinner Inc.) $950

Woodlands beaded coat with double collar, fringed edge and silk applique. (Robt. W. Skinner Inc.) $8,000

Iroquois corn husk false face society mask with fringed edge, 15in. long. (Robt. W. Skinner Inc.) $600

Early Woodlands beaded bandolier bag in blue wool flannel with red straps, 35in. long. (Robt. W. Skinner Inc.) $4,000

Kwakiuth wood ceremonial food bowl in the shape of a whale, 24¾in. long. $8,000

Haida Indian argillite pipe carved with totemic animals, 6¼in. long. $1,600

American Indian North-East Woodlands ball-headed club, 21½in. long. $23,000

A Southwestern polychrome canteen, Zia, 19th century, painted over a cream slip in black and red, 10¾in. deep. (Robt. W. Skinner Inc.) $1,200

'Sioux Maiden', by Gerda Christofferson, pastel portrait, signed and dated '57, 19 x 24in. (Robt. W. Skinner Inc.) $375

A Southwestern polychrome jar, Zia, with indented base, flaring sides and tapering rim, 12½in. diam. (Robt. W. Skinner Inc.) $1,000

Yuma polychromed female figure with traditional horsehair coiffure, inscribed 'Yuma, Arizona Indian 1931', 8in. high. (Robt. W. Skinner Inc.) $375

'Apache Mountain Spirit Dance', by Carl Nelson Gorman, signed 'Kin-Ya-Onny-Beyeh', oil on canvas, 19½ x 23½in. (Robt. W. Skinner Inc.) $900

A Hopi wood Kachina doll, 'Mahuu' (locust), with black, mustard and rose decoration over a white painted body, 15¾in. high. (Robt. W. Skinner Inc.) $1,200

Basket Maker, by Patrick Robt. Desjarlait, tempera, signed, 14 x 17in. (Robt. W. Skinner Inc.) $1,300

A Southwestern polychrome storage jar, San Ildefonso, of tall rounded form, 12½in. high. (Robt. W. Skinner Inc.) $700

Navajo Germantown serape, finely woven on a red ground, 47 x 68in. (Robt. W. Skinner Inc.) $2,300

'Long Hair Dancer', by Bruce Timeche, tempera, signed, 10 x 13in. (Robt. W. Skinner Inc.) $275

Southwestern pottery dough bowl, Cochiti, the interior painted over a cream slip in black foliate motifs, 14in. diam. (Robt. W. Skinner Inc.) $1,200

'Warrior', by Velino Shije Herrera, signed 'Ma-Pe-Wi '45', tempera on white paper, 9½ x 12½in. (Robt. W. Skinner Inc.) $700

A Southwestern basketry tray, Apache, woven in devil's claw on a dark golden field, 19in. diam. (Robt. W. Skinner Inc.) $1,400

Two Plains paint decorated parfleche containers, Crow, a shoulder bag, 12 x 13in. and a case 12 x 23½in. (Robt. W. Skinner Inc.) $500

A Southwestern polychrome basketry tray, Yavapai, woven in red and dark brown designs on a golden field, 14½in. diam. (Robt. W. Skinner Inc.) $950

Navajo Germantown weaving, woven on a red ground in black and white, 41 x 69in. (Robt. W. Skinner Inc.) $1,300

'Eagle Dancer', by Raymond Chavez, signed, 13 x 17¼in. (Robt. W. Skinner Inc.) $300

'Rattle for Germination', by Fred Kabotie, tempera, signed, 15 x 22½in. (Robt. W. Skinner Inc.) $900

Southwestern pottery jar, Zia, painted over a pinky cream slip in black and red, 12¾in. diam. (Robt. W. Skinner Inc.)
$1,000

'Untitled', by Gerda Christofferson, pastel portrait, signed and dated '57, 18½ x 24in. (Robt. W. Skinner Inc.)
$260

A Hopi polychrome pottery canteen, painted over a creamy yellow slip in dark brown linear and 'Koshare' figural decoration, 3¼in. high. (Robt. W. Skinner Inc.)
$200

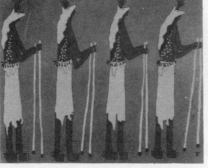

'Owl Kachina', by Peter Shelton, acrylic on paper, signed 'Hoyewva '64', 14 x 21in. (Robt. W. Skinner Inc.)
$500

'Deer Dancers', by Harry Fonseca, signed in interlocking initials, dated 1975 on back, acrylic on canvas board, 20 x 23in. (Robt. W. Skinner Inc.)
$450

Southern Plains painted buffalo fur robe, 92in. long, 67in. wide. (Robt. W. Skinner Inc.)
$500

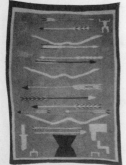

Large Navajo pictorial weaving, woven on a red field in mustard, white and navy, 61 x 88in. (Robt. W. Skinner Inc.)
$2,300

Northwest coast mask, Bella/ Bella Coola, of polychrome cedar wood, 12.5/8in. high. (Robt. W. Skinner Inc.)
$49,000

'King of the Herd', by Quincy Tahoma, tempera, signed and dated '53, 6½ x 10in. (Robt. W. Skinner Inc.)
$650

AMUSEMENT MACHINES

Now that highly sophisticated video games and complex electronically operated machines dominate the amusement arcades, attention is wistfully returning to the great mechanical devices of a bygone age.

Fast gaining in popularity with collectors, amusement machines form a fascinating collection and offer an excellent investment potential.

The promise of challenge and entertainment suggested by these evocatively named contraptions is almost irresistible. One may have one's fortune told, test one's grip, take part in a death dive and experience the delights of one pennyworth of the Gay Deceiver — all good clean fun.

'Haunted House' automaton in wooden case with glazed window, circa 1935, 70in. high. **$530**

'The Night Watchman', coin-operated automaton by The British Automatic Co. Ltd., circa 1935, 66½in. high. **$1,000**

'The Haunted House', coin-operated automaton, circa 1935, 70½in. high. **$930**

Caillie gambling machine with five coin slots, circa 1910, 25½in. high. **$330**

Gottlieb & Co. 'World Fair' pinball table with glass top, 51in. long. **$200**

'Laughing Sailor', amusement machine, coin-operated bearing Ruffler & Walker plaque, 68½in. high, circa 1935. **$1,000**

AMUSEMENT MACHINES

'The Drunkard's Dream', coin-operated automaton, 66½in. high, circa 1935. **$1,000**

Caillie Brothers grip-test amusement machine in green-painted case, circa 1910, 59in. high. **$1,000**

'The Burglar', coin-operated automaton, circa 1935, 67in. high. **$770**

'Great Race' game, coin-operated, in oak casing, 47in. wide, circa 1925. **$880**

Ahrens '22-Man Football' game, coin-operated, in oak casing, circa 1930, 43¾in. wide. **$1,000**

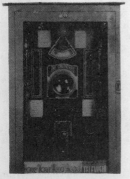

Green Ray 'Television' amusement machine, circa 1945, 75in. high. **$420**

Arhens 'Test Your Strength' amusement machine in painted wooden case, circa 1922, 79in. high. **$880**

'Zodiac' coin-operated fortune-teller, circa 1940, 24½in. high. **$245**

'Playball' Allwin with seven winning chutes, in oak case, circa 1920, 27½in. high. **$140**

Ahrens stereoscopic viewer in oak cabinet, circa 1925, 68in. high. **$1,000**

Auto Stereoscope in oak casing with coin slot, circa 1930, 22½in. high. **$330**

'Test Your Grip' amusement machine with iron grip handle, circa 1925, 50in. high. **$775**

Early Genco pinball bagatelle table with glass top, circa 1935, 39in. long. **$600**

'Pussy' Shooter, amusement machine, circa 1935, 76in. high. **$620**

American coin-operated mutoscope 'Death Dive', circa 1915, 50in. high. **$700**

White City 'Screen Stars' gambling machine in oak casing, circa 1940, 26½in. high. **$140**

AMUSEMENT MACHINES

A '**Little Wonder**' Allwin-type machine, circa 1925, 32½in. high. **$265**

A 19th century random number selector, signed Jno. Wright, Sept. 1897, 10in. wide. **$155**

Coin operated mechanical sweepstakes game, manufactured by RMC, trademark Rock-Ola, circa 1930?, 12in. high. (Robt. W. Skinner Inc.) **$700**

Coin operated mechanical football game, manufactured by The Baker Novelty Co., circa 1933, 17½in. high. (Robt. W. Skinner Inc.) **$310**

Brooklands '**Totalisator**' bandit with coin slot, circa 1939, 24in. high. **$245**

The '**French Execution**' coin-slot automaton, circa 1935, 84in. high. **$1,000**

A '**Stars of the Silver Screen**' machine, circa 1935, 27in. high. **$700**

Rare prohibition gambling machine with metal body, circa 1930, 6in. high. **$285**

An '**Aeroplane**' Allwin-type machine, circa 1940, 33in. high. **$200**

ARMOR

Although full suits of armor are a little bulky to contemplate collecting, quite apart from costing anything from a few hundred to many thousands of pounds, such articles as gauntlets, arm and shoulder defences and particularly breastplates can lead to an interesting and not too expensive collection.

Independent breastplates have been known since the 14th century, and examples of these can of course be on the dear side, but those from later centuries can be found from as little as $100 upwards.

Beware of reproductions, however, for they have been made for the last hundred years. All those I have seen come complete with a suitable hole or dent where the heart is, along with the story about how the plowman turned it up where the battle of Culloden (or suitable local shindig) took place.

  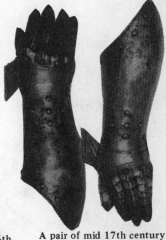

A pair of German articulated gauntlets, circa 1580, from a 'black and white' suit of armor. (Wallis & Wallis) $660

A composite suit of late 16th century cuirassier's half armor. $2,500

A pair of mid 17th century Cromwellian elbow gauntlets, fully articulated with finger scales. (Wallis & Wallis) $360

A rare 16th century Turkish cuisse (knee and thigh defence), one-piece knee now with brass rivet heads. (Wallis & Wallis) $200

Prussian Regt. of Garde du Corps officer's parade cuirass. (Christie's) $6,500

A South German or North Italian articulated gauntlet, circa 1510, 10in. long. (Wallis & Wallis) $280

45

An articulated right-hand gauntlet, circa 1600, with flared cuff. (Wallis & Wallis) $140

A 17th/18th century mail coat with short sleeves. (Christie's) $280

An etched and gilt pauldron from a Pisan armor, circa 1580. (Wallis & Wallis) $120

A Cromwellian period pikeman's breastplate and tassets, armorer's mark. (Wallis & Wallis) $1,000

A kebiki-laced kuchiba-iro-odoshi tosei-gusoku. (Christie's) $5,000

Early 17th century pikeman's breastplate together with associated simulated five lame tassets. (Christie's) $850

A breastplate probably adapted in the early 19th century. (Wallis & Wallis) $400

A pair of Indian 18th century gold damascened arm defences, bazu band, 12in. (Wallis & Wallis) $450

A 17th century breast and bullet proof backplate, turned over borders and distinct medial ridge. (Wallis & Wallis) $800

An interesting English Civil War period reinforcing breastplate. (Wallis & Wallis) $440

A pair of 17th century Indian arm guards bazu band made for a princeling, 10in. (Wallis & Wallis) $400

A 15th century Turkish breastplate, Krug, struck with the St. Irene arsenal mark. (Wallis & Wallis) $280

A cuirassier's three-quarter armor, circa 1640, the whole mounted on a plastic dummy and wooden base. $11,000

A suit of armor dated Tenmon gonen (1536). (Christie's) $4,500

A Georgian copy of a fully articulated and fluted 16th century Maximilian full suit of armor. (Wallis & Wallis) $7,150

A pair of late 19th century French cuirassier's breast and back plates, brass studs to borders. (Wallis & Wallis) $400

A Continental articulated breastplate, circa 1700, of swollen form with medial ridge. (Wallis & Wallis) $400

A 17th century Continental breastplate with twin studs for fastening and shoulder straps. (Wallis & Wallis) $300

Original letters and documents written or signed by the famous names of history in all fields, from great authors to naval and military leaders, Kings and Queens, scientists, artists and musicians, provide a fascinating field for the private collector, as well as the raw material for historical and literary research. The collector will find himself in competition with the research libraries of the world, but will also have the reward of working alongside historians with a common aim. There is a particular demand for literary letters and for royal documents, but any piece of paper or parchment bearing a famous name is likely to be of some value. The signatures of many of our popular entertainers and recent sportsmen are of little worth, but there is always the chance that they may gain interest in the future.

The value of any letter or document will depend on many factors, most importantly the identity of the writer and the scarcity of the signature. In addition, the contents and condition are significant and must always be taken into account. There are numerous facsimile reproductions, not only of important letters but of routine notes like the acknowledgements sent out by Churchill in response to messages of greetings, and forgery has long been a popular pastime. It is sensible to buy from a reputable dealer who will guarantee the authenticity of everything he sells.

Although most of the examples illustrated are indicative of the upper end of the market there is still a wealth of material from lesser personalities which can be bought at prices well within the reach of most collectors.

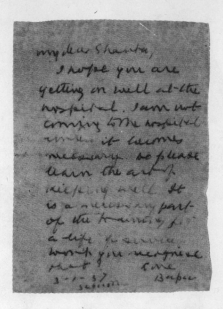

M. K. Gandhi: Fine series of sixteen Autograph letters signed ('Bapu'), 21 pages 8vo, June 1936 to December 1939. $7,000

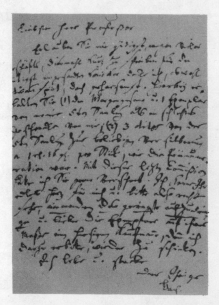

Carl Philipp Emanuel Bach, fine autograph letter signed, 1 page, octavo, Hamburg, 14 December 1785. $11,000

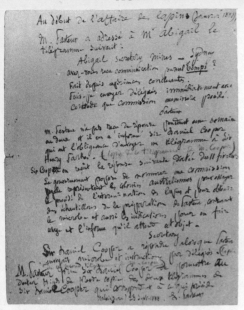

Louis Pasteur: Autograph statement signed,
1 page 4to, 23 September 1888. $1,200

Elizabeth I, important letter signed
Elizabeth R at head, to Sir Nicholas
Throckmorton, her ambassador to
Scotland, containing a major statement
about Elizabeth's policy towards the
fate of Mary Queen of Scots, July 1567.
$33,000

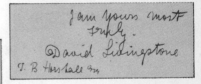

David Livingstone, autograph
letters arranging to procure beads
for next visit to Africa, 4 pages,
8vo, to J. B. Horsfall MP,
Kensington Palace Gardens,
January 1858. $880

Albert Einstein, autograph letter
signed about relevance of Lanczos'
work to Einstein's theories on
relativity, 1 page, Princeton 1949.
$2,100

Leon Trotsky, highly important autograph letter
signed, written a month before his deportation to
Mexico, 4 pages, quarto, 22 November 1936. $3,300

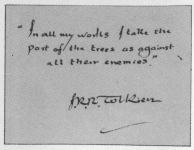

J.R.R. Tolkien, autograph statement signed 'In all my works I take the part of the trees as against all their enemies', on an oblong slip of paper. $310

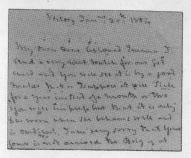

Horatio Nelson, fine autograph letter signed Nelson and Bronte to Emma Hamilton, 4 pages, quarto, sending a watch for their child and mentions that a comb is on its way to Emma etc., Victory, 20 January 1804.
$5,000

Mary Queen of Scots, remarkable autograph letter written at the age of 11 to her mother Mary of Guise announcing her intention to make her first communion, one page, folio, Meudon Easter 1554.
$10,000

Charles Edward Stuart: Autograph document, signed ('Charles P.R.'), 50 x 126mm., Paris 4 May 1747. $1,300

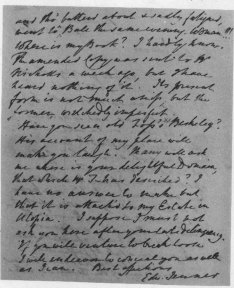

Robert Browning: Autograph receipt, signed, 1 page 16mo; Florence, 17 July 1854. $250

Edward Jenner: Autograph letter signed, 2 pages 4to, with address, 30 December 1821, (last page). $1,700

Sir Winston Spencer Churchill: Autograph letter, signed ('Winston S.C.'), 1 page 8vo, Treasury Chambers, Whitehall, 1 February 1926. $640

Franz Liszt: Autograph letter signed, 2 pages 8vo with envelope, 'Lundi' n.d. (last page). $770

W. H. Auden, autograph manuscript of his 'Ode to the George Washington Hotel' comprising 60 lines with 2 revisions signed and inscribed to the Manager and all staff, 5 pages, octavo and small quarto. $1,100

Donathien Sade, autograph letter, unsigned, to his lawyer Gaufridy, relating to the scandal caused by Sade's keeping a number of young girls at his chateaux for his pleasures, 4 pages, quarto, Provence, June 1775. $1,100

Henry VIII: Document signed, 1 page folio (oblong) on vellum, 1 May 1545. $10,000

Charles Darwin: Brief autograph letter signed, 1 page 8vo, 3 February n.y. $1,500

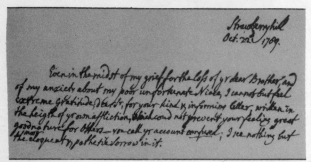

H. Walpole, fine autographed letter signed, to Captain Waldegrave, 2 pages, quarto, Strawberry Hill, 22 October 1789. $960

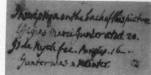

Horace Walpole: Autograph inscription, 4 lines on a small card, ca. 6½ x 3¼mm., unsigned, n.d. $70

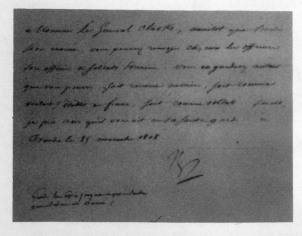

Napoleon I: Letter signed ('Np') to Clarke, ½ page 4to, 28 November 1808. $900

Charles II, letter relating to plantations in America, 1672, (Robt. W. Skinner Inc.) $2,000

AUTOMATONS

The genius of the 18th and 19th century craftsmen is perhaps best exhibited in his ability to construct the most ingenious and delicate of automatons. Developed by the Swiss Jacquet-Droz family, and later by the French, mechanical toys grew in complexity until the mid-Victorian era, by which time most occupations, from shoe cleaning to piano playing, had been interpreted with mechanical ingenuity to make delightful adult playthings.

Most depend solely on the driving power of a spring, but many inventors propelled their machines by compressed air, water, sand, mercury and steam. The best examples, worth hundreds or even thousands, are by Vaucanson, Robertson and Rechsteiner, particularly writing and drawing automatons, and talking dolls developed by Von Kempelen.

Mass production of mechanical toys reared its head about 1870 with the rising German tin plate industry and, craftsmanship inevitably suffering, they became simply playthings for children.

A thriving trade developed in importing these toys from Germany to England mainly as a result of their popularity with adults buying for young people for it is a matter of record that they held only a limited appeal for children their subject matter being considered somewhat sophisticated and their independence of movement thought to be 'off putting'.

Adults, however, continued to buy most enthusiastically and to preserve these fascinating pieces and it is thanks to them that we have so many good examples to wonder at and enjoy today.

A musical automaton of a bisque headed doll beside a dressing table, marked Simon & Halbig, S & H 6, the doll 15in. high. (Christie's) $3,000

A picture automaton, the timepiece in the church facade activates the clockwork mechanism, probably French, 35in. long.
$1,500

German bisque automaton, dolls by Armand Marseille, circa 1890, 12in. high. (Theriault's)
$1,250

AUTOMATONS

Early 20th century enamel singing bird automaton, 3¼in. high. (Robt. W. Skinner Inc.) $1,500

A Pussy Band Printed Paper automaton, circa 1910, 18in. high. $580

A German musical automaton, 'Musical Troupe' with seven bisque dolls, circa 1880, dolls 7in. high. $4,000

A singing bird automaton, the domed brass cage with hinged door, French, circa 1900, 21½in. high. $1,760

A 19th century clockwork lady knitting automaton, Germany, 21in. high. (Robt. W. Skinner Inc.) $1,800

A composition headed automaton modeled as a standing Chinese man, 30in. high, French 1880. (Christie's) $9,000

French bisque automaton by Emile Jumeau, circa 1890, 19in. high overall. (Theriault's) $4,275

French bisque automaton, probably Farkas, circa 1920, 12in. high. (Theriault's) $1,000

French musical automaton of a girl seated, smelling flowers, by Leopold Lambert, circa 1880, 19¾in. high. $3,300

AUTOMATONS

An automaton handcart with two Armand Marseille bisque headed dolls, 19½in. long, German, circa 1910. $1,760

Late 19th century German Boy on Swing automaton, 44in. high. $1,210

German automaton with bisque dolls, circa 1890, 26in. wide, with ten mechanical actions. $10,000

French-type bisque automaton, 18in. high, circa 1890. (Theriault's) $2,000

A singing bird automaton with clock, Swiss, probably by Jacquet Droz, circa 1785, 20in. high. (Christie's) $44,000

French bisque automaton by Leopold Lambert, circa 1900, 20in. high. (Theriault's) $3,000

French musical automaton of a piano player, circa 1915. $2,200

A bisque headed automaton, the German head impressed 5/0, probably French, circa 1900, 18in. high. $925

Late 19th century French landscape automaton on ebonised base, 22in. high. $880

AUTOMATONS

19th century wooden and papier-mache automaton, 36in. high. (Theriault's) $1,400

A sailor's hornpipe automaton, English, circa 1880, 14 x 16in. $1,500

A musical automaton of a dancing couple by Vichy, French, circa 1860, 13½in. high. $2,600

An advertising display automaton on oak base, circa 1930, 25in. wide. $1,750

A mid 19th century German portable barrel organ automaton, 52cm. wide. (Phillips) $9,000

A German 19th century automaton of an organ grinder with miniature dancers, on a garden stage. (Phillips) $3,750

A musical automaton of a conjuror, probably by L. Lambert, French, circa 1880, 16in. high. $2,800

A 19th century European singing bird automaton, 22in. high. (Robt. W. Skinner Inc.) $2,250

A 19th century bisque-headed Magicienne automaton. (Phillips) $11,000

AUTOMOBILIA

It all started in Britain around the 1890's. In those days cars were bought by the wealthy and driven by chauffeurs. Then 'sporty types' adopted the new hobby of motoring and, becoming owner-drivers, created a demand and a market for new and improved 'extras'.

Of the wide range of accessories including, radiator caps, oil cans, hub caps, steering wheels, mascots, speedometers, fascia panels and other related gadgets, the massive head-lamps once fixed to fast cars such as Lagondas and Alvis are most enthusiastically collected.

Evidence of the increasing nostalgia for the early days before road tax, insurance or speed limits, is clearly demonstrated by the hordes of visitors and traders attending autojumbles, specialized sales and special events.

Collectibles range from postcards, petrol coupons and tax discs selling for around one dollar to the rare and coveted sales brochures of Bugatti and Ferrari. These exotic pro-ductions sell for a considerably higher price as will collectibles associated with M.G., Bentley and Rolls-Royce. Motor racing in general and Brooklands Track in particular are also high interest areas.

Books on most aspects of motoring are collected and range from under seven dollars to over two hundred dollars for Laurence Pomeroy's magnum opus on Grand Prix cars. Magazines too are in demand with 'Autocar', 'Motor Sport' and 'Speed' the most popular examples.

A spelter smoker's compen-dium modeled as a sports roadster, 9in. long. (Christie's) $600

Souvenir of the Brooklands Automobile Racing Club, July 6th 1907. (Onslows) $200

A nickel plated Milegal 'Meter', 4¼in. diam. (Onslows) $100

Mahogany showcase made from a brass Rolls Royce Silver Ghost radiator shell with Spirit of Ecstasy mascot, 35in. high. $400

Smith's tachometer calibrated from 1000 to 2500 rpm, 6½in. diam., plaque inscribed and dated 1933. $400

A chromium plated and gilt desk timepiece modeled as an Edwardian tourer, 8½in. high. (Christie's) $900

57

AUTOMOBILIA

Bugatti Sales Brochure.
$80

Esso petrol pump globe.
(Onslows) $140

Car head lamp with 4in. diam.
reflector, 10in. high, circa 1910.
$100

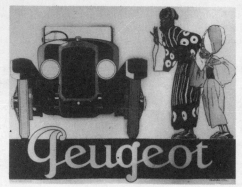

An 18kt. gold key-ring
modeled as a Rolls-Royce
radiator, 3in. overall.
(Christie's) $300

Peugeot, by Rene Vincent, lithograph
in colors, printed by Draeger, 1170 x
1540mm. (Christie's) $1,600

Le Rire, special 13 July
number, 1901 for the Paris-
Berlin automobile race,
brochure. (Christie's)
$150

A Pratts post war glass petrol
pump globe. (Onslows)
$600

A chromium plated and
enameled B.A.R.C. Brook-
lands badge, stamped 1367,
3¾in. high. (Onslows) $800

One of two photographs of
Leyland-Thomas No. 1 Babs,
signed by Parry Thomas.
(Onslows) $240

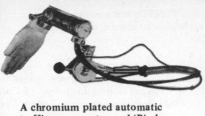

A chromium plated automatic traffic warner, stamped 'Birglow Auto Signal Pat. 375944, Pat. 376564, Reg. design 767816', 42in. long. (Christie's) $320

A motoring picnic hamper, four settings, marked Coracle, 22½in. long. (Christie's) $1,400

Early 20th century Bleriot brass head lamp, 12in. high. $90

Harrods Ltd. Automobiles, Petrol Steam Electric Cars, Motorcycles Accessories of All Descriptions, catalog with prices and text, circa 1903. (Onslows) $260

Two of twenty-one R.A.C.I. dashboard plaques, late 1920's early 1930's, approx. 3 x 2in. (Christie's) $1,100

De Dion Bouton poster, circa 1903. $200

A chromium plated decanter in the form of a Bugatti radiator, by Classic Stable Ltd., 6¾in. high. (Onslows) $520

An A. T. Speedometer Co. Ltd. Bentley 6½ or 8 liter speedometer, and a rev counter. (Onslows) $400

Accessory Catalog, pre 1914. $25

BADEN-POWELL ITEMS

Robert Stephenson Smyth Baden-Powell was the greatest British hero of the early years of the 20th century, long before he started his Scouting movement for which he is best remembered today.

Victorian crowds followed him everywhere because he was famous as the saviour of Mafeking which he had successfully defended in a long siege against the Boers in 1900. To mark his achievement all sorts of souvenirs bearing his image were produced ranging from clay pipes to plates, statuettes, cookie jars, cigarette cards, badges, Vesta cases and teapots.

These are all collected today as are Baden-Powell's own writings and drawings, for he was an accomplished artist, and artefacts from the early years of the Boy Scout movement which he founded in 1908.

A plaster bust of Baden Powell, 10in. high. $70

Staffordshire oval wall plate with wavy edge featuring Lieut.-Col. R. S. S. Baden Powell. $50

Staffordshire figure of Baden Powell with cannon, 22in. high. $300

Crystal glass two-handled vase, engraved with a portrait of Baden Powell, on four short feet, 11in. high, slight crack. $25

An unusual teapot featuring Baden Powell in Boer War uniform together with scouts in a camping scene. $70

Tall Staffordshire milk jug with gilt decoration and portrait of Baden Powell. $40

BADGES

There are many interesting aspects to a collection of badges. Through a study of their regimental motifs, numerals, materials and design, one may follow the changes and reforms of the system as well as the history of particular regiments.

A start can often be made on a domestic level. Most families have, at one time or another had a serving soldier in the family and for sentimental reasons soldiers tend to keep their badges.

A cap badge may be identified as such by the fastening. Usually this consists of a prong, a slide or two metal loops designed to be fastened by a split pin. A cap badge is normally larger than those designed to be worn on a uniform collar.

It is a good idea to consult an old Army List for information on who wore what and when.

A U.S.A. gilt and enameled sterling silver badge of The Joint Chiefs of Staff, by H. S. Meyer Inc., New York, (Wallis & Wallis) $70

A military style white metal Canadian cap badge of the Carbide Chemicals Co. (Wallis & Wallis) $60

A Turkish Empire official's French silver gilt pin-back shield badge. (Wallis & Wallis) $180

An officer's silver Maltese Cross pouch belt badge of The King's Royal Rifle Corps, HM Birmingham 1917. (Wallis & Wallis) $120

A Nazi Govt. Admin. official's field gray sleeve badge to the rank of Regierungsamtmann. (Wallis & Wallis) $250

An officer's 1855 (French) pattern gilt shako plate of The 63rd (Manchester) Regt. (Wallis & Wallis) $200

A late Victorian other rank's brass helmet plate of The Canadian Medical Staff Corps. (Wallis & Wallis) $130

An other rank's cap badge of The 2nd Vol. Bn. The Worcester Regt., S. Africa 1900-02 scroll below. (Wallis & Wallis) $40

An Indian brass puggaree badge worn by gun lascars of the Artillery Train. (Wallis & Wallis) $80

A Georgian officer's copper gilt shoulder belt plate of The W(?) Volunteer Infantry. (Wallis & Wallis) $150

A Panzer troop's standard bearer's sleeve badge embroidered in silver bullion and black and pink thread. (Wallis & Wallis) $170

A late Victorian white metal helmet plate of The Rajputana-Merwa Railway Vol. Rifles. (Wallis & Wallis) $300

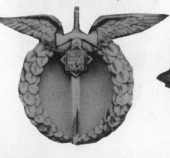

A trooper's helmet plate of The 5th Dragoon Guards. (Wallis & Wallis) $100

A silver World War II Free Czech Air Force pilot's badge, by Spink, with pricker numbering on the reverse '309', 3 lug attachment. (Wallis & Wallis) $200

A Victorian officer's gilt, silvered and enamel helmet plate of The Border Regt., first pattern, worn 1881-91. (Wallis & Wallis) $620

An officer's pre 1881 gilt and silvered Glengarry badge of The 72nd (Duke of Albany's Own) Highlanders. (Wallis & Wallis) $710

An other rank's white metal cap badge of The 4th Vol. Bn. The Queen's Regt. (Wallis & Wallis) $130

A William IV officer's gilt helmet plate of The Warwickshire Yeomanry Cavalry. (Wallis & Wallis) $200

An officer's silvered plaid brooch of The Black Watch. (Wallis & Wallis) $130

A George I King's Messenger's badge, by Francis Garthorne, circa 1720-23. (Phillips) $20,250

A Victorian hollow-cast gold plaid brooch of the Clan Mackinnon, 1.2oz. Troy. (Wallis & Wallis) $400

An other rank's white metal Glengarry of The Royal Limerick County Militia. (Wallis & Wallis) $160

A Georgian other rank's brass bearskin plate, die-stamped 1801-16 Royal Arms and motto. (Wallis & Wallis) $800

A brass cap badge of The 1st V.A. Bn. Home Guard. (Wallis & Wallis) $80

Bruce Bairnsfather was the war artist who created the famous cartoon character 'Old Bill'. The longsuffering, archetypal 'Tommy' of World War I. During and after the war, a vast range of 'Bairnsfatherware' was produced.

These wares fall into seven main categories:

Original paintings, drawings, sketches and letters by Bairnsfather.

Pottery items bearing 'Fragments from France' cartoons and models of Old Bill's head.

Bystander Products. Original 'Fragments from France' cartoons, postcards, (there are 56 available in a complete set) jig-saws and prints.

Metal Ware. Car Mascots of Old Bill, ash trays, etc.

Theater and Cinema ephemera including posters, advertising postcards, magazines and photographs of the various plays and films made about Old Bill or by Bairnsfather.

Books and Magazines about or by Bairnsfather.

Miscellaneous: Dolls, handkerchiefs, badges, glass slides.

The market is still in its infancy and these wares are currently largely overlooked and inexpensive. A boost to the market is assured, however, by publication of the first priced and illustrated catalogue to Bairnsfatherware 'In Search of the Better 'Ole' (Milestone Publications, 62 Murray Road, Horndean, Hampshire PO8 9JL). England

Once a collectors' market is established the demand for 'Old Bill' products is self generating the more the interest grows, which indicates good prospects for a healthy investment.

Grimwade bowl with transfers of 'Old Bill'. $60

A 'Temporary Gentleman' in France, by Bruce Bairnsfather. $30

Grimwade shaving mug with transfers of 'Old Bill' and Arms of Margate. $80

Carlton shrapnel Villa 'Tommies dugout somewhere in France'. $60

Grimwade mug 'Well if you know of a better 'ole go to it'. $70

Grimwade bowl 'What time do they feed the sealions Alf?' $60

Carlton 'Old Bill' British Empire Exhibition. $100

Grimwade pottery plate 'When the 'ell is it goin' to be strawberries?' $60

Carlton 'Old Bill' with colored balaclava 'Yours to a cinder Old Bill'.$150

'Old Bill' pottery head, white. $70

'Old Bill', doll in fair condition. $80

Metal car mascot of 'Old Bill' $200

As more and more people develop an awareness of the historical and artistic value of paper money the popularity of this subject as a collecting field continues to rise.

Over the years banknotes have been made from a variety of materials including the fabric of a khaki shirt sleeve (Boer War), silk, leather and even seal skin but today, many collectors focus their attention on the beauty of the engraved note.

It is not often realized that top security printing firms reckon on a twenty five year training period for the handful of portrait engravers who make it to the top of their profession. It can take six months to engrave a steel plate yet the collector can buy a piece of 'miniature art' for as little as two dollars.

The earliest notes available, at a reasonable price, are those of the Ming Dynasty dated 1368 and worth about $720 but inflation has left the new collector with a wide variety of inexpensive examples to choose from. German hyper-inflation has left notes for collectors at just one dollar each and French Revolution issues can still be picked up for as little as $6.

An interesting collection can be built around the many emergency issues hand signed by such notable figures as General Gordon, Garibaldi, Louis Kossuth and notes such as those designed by Baden-Powell (Siege of Mafeking) and Benjamin Franklin (War of Independence).

Many modern banknotes of the world have only a short life as leaders such as Idi Amin or Bokassa come and go and these will provide a fascinating historical reference.

Billets de Confiance, small card notes issued during the French Revolution. They vary in price from **$30** to **$1,000**

Theresienstadt Concentration Camp Notes, originally designed by inmates of the camp, the S.S. decided Moses was too Aryan and altered the portrait to look more like Fagin. Worth about **$15**

Ceylon 100 rupees, proof, probably unique. Little is known about Victorian issues of Ceylon. Worth **$1,500**

3000 tengas, Russian note of Bukhara 1918, worth about **$40** but much rarer than the price suggests. Many hundreds of different Russian notes exist and are often hard to identify.

National Bank of Egypt £1, 1898. One of the earliest Egyptian notes known. This 'Specimen' would fetch about $1,500, but as an issued note it catalogs at $4,900.

British North Borneo Company $1, 1922. Formerly a Crown Colony the notes are all scarce and popular. This note catalogs in the Standard Catalog of World Paper Money by Albert Pick at $800.

Union Bank of Australia £50 specimen, 1905, only 3 or 4 known to exist. Probably fetch in excess of $2,000 in auction.

Belfast £10 of 1965, they were still hand-signed at this time in Ireland. Worth about $80.

North of Scotland Bank £100, 1930, rare note, canceled, but uncanceled notes would still be valid. Worth $500.

Union Bank of Scotland £100 specimen, taken over by the Bank of Scotland. Worth $500 to a collector.

Government of India, One Thousand Rupees, 2nd June 1913, Bombay, scarce. (Christie's) $360

Proof Guernsey £1, 1867, Channel Islands notes are well collected and this rarity would fetch $800 to $1,000.

U.S.A. **Stamford Bank $5**. A 'broken bank'. Thousands once existed but 90% went bankrupt leaving colorful paper behind them. Worth **$50**.

Russia: 1819 **10 roubles** State Assignat. (Phillips) **$100**

Royal Bank of Scotland £1 dated 9th February 1750, on watermarked paper, rare. (Christie's) **$1,700**

Bank of England £5, 1869, signed by Dixon as Cashier. 'White' Fivers were first issued in 1793 and continued until Sept. 1956. A Dixon £5 catalogs at **$1,700** in the specialist 'English Paper Money Catalogue' by Vincent Duggleby.

Commerical Bank of Scotland £5, 1935. Beautiful notes make Scotland one of the most collected areas of paper money. In circulated condition it would be worth **$25** but uncirculated as much as **$130**

BAROMETERS

Torricelli, as every schoolboy knows, invented a method of producing the vacuum. In 1660, Robert Boyle adapted Torricelli's technique to the production of a weather glass. Naturally enough, it was not long before the device attracted the attentions of many a notable horologist and instrument maker. Among these was Daniel Quare, Thomas Tompion, John Patrick, Henry Jones and Charles Orme, any of whose works attracts enormous sums of money. As can be seen, however, not all barometers are equally expensive.

By midway through the 18th century, rococo scrolls were often incorporated in the design of barometer cases which, by the final quarter of the century, had evolved into the ever-popular wheel (or banjo) shape. Most have mahogany, or occasionally satinwood, frames with delicate boxwood stringing on the edges and silvered dials enclosed by convex glass. Good examples incorporate in their designs such extras as thermometers, hygrometers, spirit-levels and even clocks — each device adds a bit to the value.

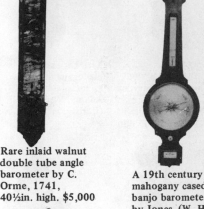

A 19th century Adie's Sympiesometer by Crichton, London, in mahogany case. (Dreweatt Watson & Barton) $1,300

A George I walnut signal barometer, the brass plate inscribed Made by John Patrick in the Old Bailey London, 36¼ x 29½in. (Christie's) $9,250

Rare inlaid walnut double tube angle barometer by C. Orme, 1741, 40½in. high. $5,000

A 19th century mahogany cased banjo barometer by Jones. (W. H. Lane & Son) $340

A Georgian inlaid mahogany wheel barometer. (Warren & Wignall) $640

An early 18th century oyster veneered stick barometer, circa 1705. (Dreweatts) $5,800

A 20th century classical Revival gilt carved barometer, Italy, 38in. long. (Robt. W. Skinner Inc.) $540

Victorian oak cased Admiral Fitzroy barometer with weather glass, the thermometer, 46in. long. (Reeds Rains) $400

BAROMETERS

A Sheraton period wheel barometer, by J. B. Roncheti. (Woolley & Wallis) $6,000

Late 18th century mahogany stick barometer, plate signed G. Adams, 39¼in. high. (Christie's) $1,700

An early 19th century mahogany wheel barometer, the 8½in. diam. dial signed Negretty & Co. (Phillips) $650

A 19th century French crossbanded mahogany wheel barometer, Paris 1740, 110cm. high. (Phillips) $1,200

A late 17th century walnut stick barometer, the engraved brass plates for Summer and Winter, 48in. high. (Christie's) $3,000

A 19th century wheel barometer, the 12in. dial inscribed Zuccani, London, 57in. high. (Parsons, Welch & Cowell) $700

A late 19th century oak American Forecast or Royal Polytechnic bulb Cistern barometer, 107cm high. (Phillips) $600

A George III mahogany stick barometer, by J. Somalvico & Son, London, 45in. high. (Christie's) $1,000

BAYONETS

The earlier bayonets were of the "plug" type; that is, they had hilts which fitted tightly into the barrel of muzzle loaders so that, having fired off his gun at the onrushing attackers, a soldier without time to reload could plug the bayonet in and convert his gun into a kind of pike. He could, too, if he was kept standing around in the rain for a long time waiting for his officers to decide to begin the battle, plug the bayonet in and keep his charge dry. Only, since the hilts were usually made of wood which swelled when wet, he sometimes couldn't get the bayonet out again in time and was left struggling while the opposing army took pot shots at him from a safe distance. Embarrassing, to say the least.

So, ever eager not to lose every possible chance of scoring a hit, the military mind came up with the idea of a bayonet with a socket handle which fitted round the outside of the gun barrel, with the blade bent out of the way of discharging bullets.

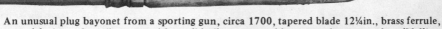

An unusual plug bayonet from a sporting gun, circa 1700, tapered blade 12¼in., brass ferrule, turned fruitwood swollen grip, with small bulbous top and brass tang button washer. (Wallis & Wallis) $120

A U.S. M. 1917 Bolo bayonet, blade 10½in., by Plumb, Phila., 1918, with wood grip, in its canvas covered scabbard, the leather tip stamped 1917. (Wallis & Wallis) $100

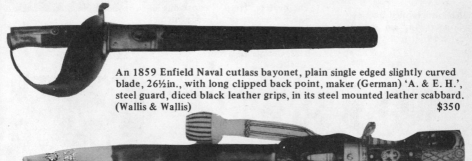

An 1859 Enfield Naval cutlass bayonet, plain single edged slightly curved blade, 26½in., with long clipped back point, maker (German) 'A. & E. H.', steel guard, diced black leather grips, in its steel mounted leather scabbard. (Wallis & Wallis) $350

A Nazi Police dress bayonet, plated blade, 12½in., by Carl Eickhorn, white metal mounts, staghorn grips with police emblem, eagle's head pommel, in its leather scabbard with white metal mounts and a dress knot. (Wallis & Wallis) $200

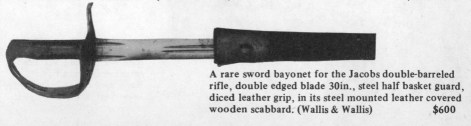

A rare sword bayonet for the Jacobs double-barreled rifle, double edged blade 30in., steel half basket guard, diced leather grip, in its steel mounted leather covered wooden scabbard. (Wallis & Wallis) $600

BEATLES

Tens of thousands of printed items are available on the fab four who dominated not only popular music but also all youth culture for the best part of a decade. For the enthusiast today the hard decision is not what to collect but rather what not to collect. The Beatles Book is the bible and a run should not be too difficult to amass; original 1960's sheet music in nice condition is harder to find than one would think; while gems such as the hand bill for Shea Stadium turn up as a happy surprise.

Of particular interest are those items more personally identified with the super group such as an autographed Cavern Club membership book for 1961 which can command as much as $1,000. Even more sought after would be a signed Royal Variety Performance program such as one recently sold by Sotheby's for well over $2,000.

But for really amazing money the hand-written lyrics of 'Imagine' by John Lennon, on the reverse of an hotel bill from Majorca dated 20/4/71, will command over $10,000.

An autographed Beatles Concert program, signed, circa 1964. $920

The Beatles, 'Help', Parlophone 33½ r.p.m., mono, 1965, signed on the cover by each of The Beatles, and inscribed 'All the Best, George Harrison'. (Christie's) $2,400

The Beatles in Shea Stadium, hand bill and concert tickets, 1966. $650

The Beatles in America, 1964. $20

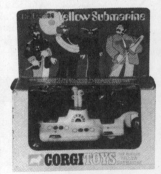

A Corgi 'Yellow Submarine' toy, the die cast scale model with two opening hatches revealing figures of The Beatles, circa 1967, 5in. long, in original box. (Christie's) $240

A pair of Beatle woven nylon stockings printed with caricatures of the Beatles, circa 1965. $560

Abbey Road, The Borough of St. Marylebone, enameled street sign, 30 x 18in. $1,280

A Beatles gold disc for the LP 'Sgt. Peppers Lonely Hearts Club Band', presented to the Beatles by EMI, dated 1967. $28,600

The Beatles at Carnegie Hall, 1964. $30

One of four polychrome Richard Avedon psychedelic posters of The Beatles, produced for the Daily Express, circa 1967, each 27½ x 19½in., together with another of the four Beatles, 15½ x 40½in. (Christie's) $560

The Beatles Book, Monthly No. 6, 1964. $8

An autographed Cavern Club membership book for 1961, containing the signatures of Pete Best, Johnny Lennon, George Harrison and Paul McCartney, 1961. $925

The Beatles in Mathew Street, a bronze by A. Curran, 1978, 32in. high. $3,080

'Help' Premier, comprising two tickets to the London premier and program leaflet, 1965. $300

John Lennon's Broadwood upright piano, with letter of authenticity. $17,600

A copy of the Marriage Certificate of John Winston Lennon and Yoko Ono Cox, contracted at the Registrar's Office, in the City and Garrison of Gibraltar, by Governor's Special Licence, on 20th March, 1969. (Christie's) $6,000

A gold Beatles disc for 'The Beatles Story', on Capitol, circa 1964. $3,740

'Long Long Long' Sheet Music, 1968. $4

A set of hand 'Reindeer' bells, with red wooden handle used by John Lennon for the recording of 'Happy Christmas (War Is Over)', 1972, 12in. long.(Christie's) $1,400

The Beatles, Peter le Vasseur, 'Illustration for the Beatles Song "In My Life" ', dated 1969, oil on board, 8½ x 8½in. (Christie's) $1,300

'Our First Four', a cardboard presentation folder containing the first four 45 r.p.m. records produced by Apple Records Ltd., 13½ x 9½in. (Christie's) $440

An autographed 'Help' premier program signed by Ringo Starr, John Lennon, Paul McCartney, Jane Asher, George Harrison and Pattie Boyd. $1,210

The Beatles LP, VJ 1092, the first LP released in the United States. $90

BEATLES

George Harrison letters to a fan, a handwritten letter encouraging the fan to buy 'From Me To You', dated 1963. $400

Seven concert programs relating to the Beatles, 1962-65. $1,280

Astrid Kirchherr, original portrait photograph of John Lennon, George Harrison and Stuart Sutcliffe, 1960. $1,320

A Beatle Bubble Gum Machine by Oak Mfg. Co. Inc., American, circa 1965. $840

A rare photograph sold with copyright and negative of the Beatles and NME Poll Winners Trophy, Wembley 1964. $1,100

A Christmas card for 1970 from Apple made from foam rubber. (Worrall's) $240

The Beatles, a signed menu for the Supper Party following the Royal World Premiere "Help!". (Christie's) $840

The Beatles 1962, copyright Harry Hammond, mounted on card. $485

An autographed Beatles concert program signed on the front by all four members of the group, Blackpool, 1964. $700

BELLEEK

One of the most distinctive forms of porcelain is Belleek, produced in Co. Fermanagh since 1863.
It is made of a parian paste with an unusual iridescent pearly glaze, which is modeled into a variety of ornamental wares; particularly pieces featuring shells, marine forms and an open basketwork design.

The firm originally traded as David McBirney and Company, and some of the original designs are still in production to this day. Earlier works are often marked "Belleek Co. Fermanagh" with the printed trademark of an Irish wolfhound and harp, while later works, after 1891, usually bear the trademark together with "Co. Fermanagh, Ireland".

A Belleek 'dolphin' candle-stick, modelled as a putto seated on a dolphin, 19.5cm. high, no. D343. (Phillips) $1,400

A pair of Belleek candlestick figures of a boy and girl basket bearer, 22cm. high. (Phillips) $7,200

A Belleek First Period figure of 'The Crouching Venus', 18¼in. high. (Christie's) $1,600

A pair of Belleek figures of 'Meditation' and 'Affection', 35cm. high, nos. D1134 and D20. (Phillips) $3,600

One of a pair of Belleek nautilus vases, naturally modeled and heightened in pink, 21cm. high. (Christie's) $2,000

A Belleek figure of a cooper standing before two barrels forming vases, 21cm. high. (Christie's) $4,000

BERLIN WOOLWORK

Berlin woolwork is a simplified system of embroidery originating in Berlin in the early 19th century and similar in concept to the modern painting by numbers kit.

The designs, usually of exotic birds and flowers or copies of famous paintings, were first printed on squared paper. The needlewoman, working in wools, then transferred these patterns to a canvas most commonly using the tent or cross stitch, and often embellished the work with beads or cut pile areas. The finished product was generally applied to footstools, chairs and firescreens but, if the proud creator was particularly pleased, the work was often mounted in a rosewood or maple frame and hung on the wall of the living room to be admired by all. A popular subject for pictures was the sailing ship and a great number of these were worked by sailors during the long sea voyages.

By the 1830's, designs were being printed directly on to the canvas itself, and as the popularity of woolwork grew in both Europe and America so did the number of patterns available; reaching 14,000 designed for the British market alone around 1840. Early examples are often more subdued in color than the later which, after the discovery of the purple analine dye became a little bit gaudy.

Berlin woolwork saw its decline in the 1870's, supposedly after criticism that it debased the art of embroidery, but I think its relative frivolity just did not gel with the more austere furniture which was beginning to dominate fashionable taste in the last quarter of the century.

Mid 19th century Berlin woolwork picture of a Turk, 29 x 25½in. (Christie's) $750

A Victorian needlework panel, possibly a stool cover, 38 x 27in. (Christie's) $1,200

A Berlin woolwork cushion with a large central medallion and sprays of flowers, 18in. square. (Christie's) $2,000

BIBLE BOXES

These chests are commonly referred to as bible boxes although they were also used for storing and transporting important documents, books and small items of value. They were of particularly sturdy construction so that they might withstand the rigors of a long journey by horse-drawn carriage.

Popular in the days when almost every family possessed a bible — sometimes the only reading material kept in a house— these boxes were constructed of oak, usually decorated with low relief carving frequently incorporating a date or initials and fitted with hinges and a strong lock. The bible, not only read for spiritual guidance, also provided a record of the family history and this valuable register of births, marriages and deaths could be kept safely under lock and key in a stout box such as this. The boxes, like the bibles, were passed on from generation to generation and remained popular in that form until around the time of William and Mary.

The earlier boxes with flat tops date from the 16th century and are usually about 61cm. wide and as much as 25.5cm. deep. Later examples often have a sloping lid which could be used as a lectern to rest a book upon whilst reading.

Writing boxes developed about the same time as bible boxes, are usually much shallower. As the style developed it became the custom to fit writing boxes with feet and later to place them on a stand until finally they became free standing pieces of furniture.

By the William and Mary period, demand had somewhat abated, possibly because every family possessing one had kept it in good order for succeeding generations.

17th century oak bible box. $250

An oak bible box showing the Stuart Coat-of-Arms, retaining the original handblocked paper. $500

An oak bible box, its front and sides carved with two rows of flutings, with a reeded edge to the top, circa 1600. $700

Commonwealth carved oak bible box, 1657, 2ft. wide. $1,000

BICYCLES

The invention of the bicycle brought a new way of life to many Victorian men and women by making it possible for even the lowest paid workers in that society to experience independence and mobility for the first time and at a very low cost.

Nowadays, pre-1900 bicycles are very much in vogue and fairly expensive. In the seventies, when demand was restricted to a small group of enthusiasts, their value showed only a moderate improvement and it is not so long ago that $1,000 seemed like a lot to pay for a bicycle. Now we see that some fine examples will fetch thousands of dollars.

One does not have to pay that type of money to start a collection however, for there are many examples from early in the 20th century which can be bought for more modest sums.

A late 19th century child's bicycle with 16in. detachable driving wheel. (Christie's) $800

Beck boneshaker or Michaudine, circa 1867-69, built at the Lister Works, Holloway, London. (Christie's S. Kensington) $1,000

A 'Pedestrian Hobby Horse' bicycle. (Phillips) $4,000

Waltham fixed-wheel bicycle, circa 1890, possibly American and assembled in Britain. (Christie's S. Kensington) $800

Tandem tricycle, frame no. 189, probably built in Coventry, circa 1888. (Christie's S. Kensington) $8,000

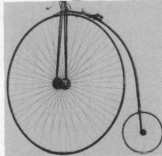

Ordinary bicycle, circa 1885, driving wheel diameter is 57in. (Christie's S. Kensington) $2,500

BONDS & SHARE CERTIFICATES

Officially known as Scripophily, this specialized area centers around the collecting of Share Certificates and Bonds issued by Companies and Governments since the 17th century.

Early certificates were printed on vellum (calf skin) which holds a particular appeal for some collectors but there are many other interesting features upon which to base a collection.

For excellence the work produced by the famous security printing firms such as Waterlow, Bradbury Wilkinson and the American Banknote Co., provide us with some beautiful pieces which are always in great demand for their visual appeal. Apart from the artistic appearance of the certificates however, one may decide to trace and record the history of one company in particular or even collect only those bonds and share certificates which have been signed by one of the many famous people connected with their issue. Obviously a collection of the signatures of important personages has a special attraction.

Of the many and diverse branches of industry represented in this field collectors favor those certificates issued by companies involved in mining, the railroads and most other forms of transport but all of these factors mentioned-historical interest, artistic merit, significant signatures, will have a bearing on the desirability and market value of a document.
It is worth noting that while shares issued in the United Kingdom are generally considered to be the property only of the person named on the document, American and Canadian shares are often made out 'To the bearer' and, if the company should still be in existence and can be traced, these could have a market value well above that of the actual document.

Le Nouveau Monde, 1851 share in this Company, for working Gold Mines in California. $30

Russian 1822 Loan, £111 Bond, handsigned by Nathan Meyer Rothschild. $150

Bald Mountain Mining Co., Colorado, share certificate dated 1880. $40

Chicago, Burlington & Quincy Railroad Co.,
share certificate dated 1892.   **$16**

Central Van Lead Mining Co. Ltd., certificate
dated 1877 in this Welsh Company.   **$40**

Confederate Bond, $500, dated 1862. **$36**

Bond for the City of Warsaw, dated 1903, 100
roubles.   **$40**

Western Australia, Lake Way Goldfield 1899
Ltd., share certificate, 1899.   **$20**

Sidi Salem Company of Egypt share certificate,
£4 share, dated 1909.   **$25**

Aylesbury Market Co., £10 share dated 1864.
$30

**North Hallenbeagle Tin & Copper Mining Co.
Ltd., 1860,** share in this popular Cornish mine.
$30

An early **Cinema** share dated 1910. **$16**

Perfect Blind-Stitch Sewing Machine Co. Ltd.,
share certificate 1903. **$12**

Bath Sanitary Steam Laundry Co. Ltd., share
certificate dated 1884. **$20**

Cape of Good Hope Diamond Mining Co. Ltd.,
bearer warrant dated 1881. **$60**

BOOKS

Book Collecting is a growing market which every year attracts new devotees among people who have previously only looked on books as 'good reads' for whiling away long journeys. Now the collecting of books is becoming one of the new 'Commodity markets' and a safe resort for money against inflation. There is fierce bidding at specialized book auctions all over the country and the days are sadly gone when a box of mixed books which might well contain a first edition could be picked up for a few cents at a local shop.

For a book enthusiast to buy wisely it is essential to learn something about the subject and then to specialize for this is a huge world indeed.

Some categories are more popular than others — medicine has a dedicated but fairly small following as has war-like subjects and books about military regiments. Books dealing with travel, topography and wild life of every kind come near the top of the popularity poll especially if they contain fine plates and illustrations.

The snobbism that sometimes shows itself in more specialized books is refreshingly absent in the world of modern firsts. Much sought after are Penguin first editions in paperback — especially the first thirty and those brought out during the war when they were printed on thin paper and their fragility made it difficult for them to survive. Rarity is a quality which makes any book collectible.

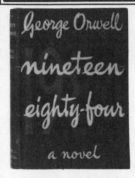

Orwell (G.): Nineteen Eighty-Four, First Edn., 1949. (Phillips) $1,000

C. Dickens: Great Expectations, 3 vols., 1st Edn., 32pp. of advertisements, original cloth gilt, 1861. (Phillips) $19,200

Fowles (J.): The Collector, First Edn., 1963. (Phillips) $180

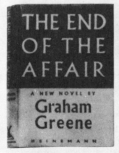

Greene (G.): The End of the Affair, First Edn., 1951. (Phillips) $70

Legge (Capt. W. V.): A History of the Birds of Ceylon, 34 hand-col. litho plates, 4to, 1880. (Phillips) $1,700

Golding (W.): Lord of the Flies, First Edn., 1954. (Phillips) $300

BOOKS

The Bible bound with Book of Common Prayer, engraved title dated 1672, printed title 1679. (Phillips) $3,200

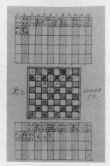

Sydenham Edwards: The new Flora Britannica, 61 hand-colored plates, quarto, 1812. (Phillips) $1,700

Koch and Kellermeistern von Allen Speison Getrenken, title printed in red and black woodcuts, Frankfurt, 1554. (Phillips) $4,160

Greco Gioachino, 1600-c.1634, Manuscript entitled 'The Royall Game of Chess', comprising 95 games executed in pen, ink and green wash. (Phillips)

$1,408

A 17th century miniature Book of Psalms with embroidered cover, England, 2 x 3¼in. (Robt. W. Skinner Inc.)

$2,000

Ferdinand Berthoud, L'Art De Conduire Et De Regler Les Pendules Et Les Montres, First Edition, Paris 1759, 12mo, modern calf. (Christie's) $760

Lopez de Sigura (R.R.): Il Givoco de gli Scacchi . . . First Italian Edn., trans. G. D. Tarsia, woodcut initials, small 4to, Venice, 1584. (Phillips) $1,120

E. Dodwell: Views in Greece, 30 hand-colored views, folio, 1821. (Phillips) $6,400

J. B. Selves, Tableau des Desordres dan l'Administration de la Justice, green morocco gilt with arms of C. A. Regnier, Paris, 1812. (Phillips)

$535

BOOKS

Ludolphus de Saxonia — Dat Boeck vanden Leuen ons Liefs heren Jhesu Cristi, folio, Zwolle, Pieter van Os, 20th Nov., 1495. (Phillips) $18,000

P. Vergilius Maro: The Pastorals, 2 vols., 3rd Edn., editor R. J. Thornton, half calf, 1821. (Phillips) $3,800

Henry J. Elwes: A monograph of the Genus Lilium, 48 hand-colored plates by W. H. Fitch, folio, 1880. (Phillips) $6,400

James Scott of Edinburgh Binding, The Holy Bible containing the Old and New Testaments, London, J. Baskett, 1741 bound with Psalms of David, Edinburgh, A. Kincaid, 1772. (Phillips) $1,800

T. S. Eliot: The Waste Land, Ltd. Edn., No. 92 of 300, Officina Bodoni, 1961. (Phillips) $1,000

Doves Press, Alfred Lord Tennyson, Seven Poems and two Translations, Limited Edition, by Cobden-Sanderson, signed and dated 1903. (Phillips) $1,200

Omar Khayyam, Rubaiyat, trans. E. Fitzgerald, 16 color plates, by W. Pogany, g.e. by Riviere, circa 1930. (Phillips) $1,000

Capt. Robert Melville Grindlay: Scenery Costume and Architecture on the Western Side of India, folio, R. Ackermann, 1826. (Phillips) $2,880

Vale Press, R. Browning, Dramatic Romances and Lyrics, Limited Edition of 210, 1899. (Phillips) $1,000

BOOKS

John Watson Stewart, The Gentleman's and Citizen's Almanack, g.e., Dublin, T. and J. W. Stewart, 1755. (Phillips) $950

Binding — Dante Alighieri: La Divini Commedia, some col., green mor, gilt with black overlay abstract design and small gold stars, g.e. by D. Etherington, 4to, Bergamo, 1934. (Phillips) $600

The History of Guy, Earl of Warwick, n.d. (Phillips) $320

Irish Binding: Book of Common Prayer, contemporary red morocco, lined case, Cambridge, John Baskerville, 1760. (Phillips) $1,434

Leybourn (William), Cursus Mathematics, Mathematical Sciences In Nine Books, London 1690. (Christie's) $2,276

Roscoe (William): Monandrian Plants of the Order Scitamineae, from Lord Derby's library with his bookplate, 112 hand-col. plates, 1828. (Phillips) $8,500

Lunardi (Vincent): An Account of the First Aerial Voyage in England, 2nd Edn., small 4to, 1784. (Phillips) $360

W. L. Buller: History of the Birds of New Zealand, 1st Edition, 35 colored plates, by J. G. Keulemans, London, 1873, 1 volume. (Prudential Fine Art) $2,200

Jeu de la Giraffe, circa 1820. (Phillips) $560

BOTTLE OPENERS

Small and useful objects like bottle openers were, and still are, considered to be the ideal material for advertising purposes.

Usually marked with the company name, a date and perhaps a few words announcing a new product they were generally inexpensive to manufacture and could be given to customers as a token of goodwill.

Some examples produced to commemorate a special event were sold as souvenirs.

Items of 'local' interest as well as novelty pieces will always attract a higher premium.

All metal rachet top bottle opener. $6

A novelty Crown cork bottle opener, the turned wooden bottle forms the handle, the opener is stamped 'An Tsin Tir Adheanta', 5¾in. long. $40

A Scandinavian Crown cap opener, circa 1860, 6in. long. $35

A Crown cork opener in cast iron and sheet metal with double sided 'Crown Opener Rd. 702661' $6

Chromium plated bottle opener and bottle top with screw fitting. $1

Key-shaped combined bottle opener and cork-screw. $10

A novelty golf ball Crown cork bottle opener, stamped 'Made in England', 3½in. long. $25

A Crown cork bottle opener and all steel pocket corkscrew, maker's name 'Made & Pat'd. in USA Vaughan Chicago', 3in. long. $45

An English silver Crown cork bottle opener of Art Deco design, date letter 'D' for 1939 and initials WW, 3½in. long. $70

An advertising pocket Crown cap bottle opener, on one side the Johnnie Walker gentleman and on reverse is 'Born 1820 Still Going Strong', 1½in. long. $90

Skyline Bottle Boy, all chrome helical corkscrew with two Crown cork openers, 5in. long. $15

A heavy pewter paperweight and bottle opener, stamped on base 'Ducky' by Kirby & Beard of Paris, circa 1930. $135

BOTTLES

Bottles most popular with collectors fall into four categories:—

1. Mineral water, beer and other beverage bottles.
2. Quack medicine and 'Cure All' bottles.
3. Glass and stone ink bottles.
4. Poison bottles.

Most collections start with a mineral water bottle, the most popular being Hiram Codd's marble-stoppered lemonade bottle, and the transfer-printed stone ginger beer bottle. Especially sought after are colored varieties of the Codd bottle. A few years ago they could be bought for under $20, but today, the dark green and amber varieties change hands at about $150 and the cobalt blues well over $200.

The patent medicine 'quack cure' category also shows an indication of some staggering increases in value. Not long ago a Warners Safe Cure Bottle, green in color could be bought for less than $30. Today you may be lucky enough to pick one up for $100.

The variety of both stone and glass ink bottles to be found is vast, ranging from a simple eight-sided variety to the most sought after of all, the cottage ink, so called because it was molded in the form of a small cottage with doors and windows. Until recently these were considered to be worth between $20 and $30. Now, because of demand, they average around $80 and certain very rare examples go to overseas collectors at around the $500 mark.

Poison bottles too are becoming a very specialized category with the cobalt blue varieties the most valued. Of particular interest would be a blue poison bottle shaped rather like a submarine or in the figural form of a skull and crossbones which are considered so rare that the price would be negotiable between buyer and seller.

Prices Patent Candle Co. cough medicine in a cobalt blue bottle. $80

An early wine bottle of dark-green metal, circa 1670, 19.5cm. high.
$900

Radam's Microbe Killer bottle, heavily embossed, 10¼in. high. $90

'Dewars' Peace whiskey flask by Royal Doulton, 7in. high.
$200

'The Adaptable Hot Water Bottle & Bed Warmer'. $30

A rare cobalt blue Hiram Codd's marble stoppered bottle. $240

Virol bone marrow
pot, 9in. tall, $24;
4½in. tall, $4.

Fishers Seaweed Extract
bottle with bulbous
neck, 5in. high. $50

Small blue glass perfume
bottle with crown stopper,
3in. high. $15

A rare mid 17th cen-
tury green glass sealed
wine bottle, 19.5cm.
high. $6,000

A late 19th century
Thatcher Milk Pro-
tector. $300

An early Bellarmine
stoneware bottle,
8¼in. high. $500

'Lynaris' Niagara
Patent amber glass
bottle, 8½in. high.
                 $150

Guinness's Extra Stout,
bottled by Globe Bottling
Co., Dunfermline. $80

Prices Patent Candle
Co. bottle of cobalt
blue, 7¼in. high. $60

A sealed and dated
green glass wine bottle
of mallet shape, dated
1738, 8¾in. high.
                 $800

Eclipse patent wasp
waist cobalt blue
bottle, 8in. high. $350

A. J. Smith & Co. pictorial
whiskey flagon, $40, non-
pictorial $20.

BOTTLES

Martin poison bottle with shaped neck, 4½in. long. $80

'Warners Safe Cure' bottle with embossed lettering. $110

A mid blue crescent shape poison bottle 'Not To Be Taken', 5in. high. $10

Glass bottle with embossed Madonna and Child, containing holy water, 5in. tall. $25

A rare ginger beer by W. A. Scott, Montrose, with swing stopper. $400

Zara Seal bottle, 10¼in. high. $25 (smaller examples 4in. high, $40.)

Sir Robert Peel stoneware reform flask, 9¼in. tall. $350

Billows Patent (small size). Aqua colored, with one flat side which has a groove near its base to retain the round glass stopper, 7½in. high. $600

Dockhead black glass flask by Wm. Jackson, 7¾in. long. $300

Stone Codd. Brown stoneware standard Codd shape and seal but both bottle and round marble stopper are made of stoneware, 8½in. high. $2,000

Aqua glass Codd's bottle, 8½in. high. $5

Amber glass Hamilton bottle, 8¾in. long, $140, aqua glass. $8

BRONZE ANIMALS

Bronze groups of animal sculpture became a popular art form in the 19th century. When Antoine-Louis Bayre exhibited his 'Tiger Devouring a Gavial' at the Salon of 1831 it caused a commotion in the French art world. The general enthusiasm led to other artists adopting animals as the subject of their work and so a group emerged to become known as — les animaliers.

For the first time, animals were depicted in art as they are in nature: docile, active, resting, feeding, dramatic in combat and always in realistic detail.

Notable artists from this period include P. J. Mene, Isadore Bonheur, Jules Moigniez and Christophe Fratin.

A bronze group of two tigers attacking an elephant, signed Seiya, Meiji period, 27cm. long. (Christie's) $540

One of a pair of bronze rabbits, signed Tsunemitsu saku, late Meiji/Taisho period, one 19cm. high, the other 21cm. long. (Christie's) $2,750

A 19th century bronze model of a seated ape, unsigned, 16cm. high. (Christie's) $3,200

Late 17th century South German bronze figure of a lion, on a squared marble base, 9½in. high. $2,300

A 19th century bronze spelter model of a camel with saddle, 10½in. high. (Christie's) $1,200

A late 19th century English bronze model of a wild cat crouching on a rocky promontory, cast from a model by J. Macallan Swan, 23.5cm. high. (Christie's) $3,400

A bronze figure of a stag, the oval base inscribed P. J. Mene, circa 1843, 8½in. high. (Anderson & Garland) $1,200

A bronze model of a rat, signed Muroe tancho saku, Meiji period, 14cm. long. (Christie's) $820

Bronze figure of a horse, by Isadore-Jules Bonheur, France, 32in. long. (Robt. W. Skinner Inc.) $8,000

Bronze figure of a pheasant, by Jules Moigniez, French, 20¾in. high. (Robt. W. Skinner Inc.) $3,000

One of a pair of large 19th century French bronze groups of a setter with a pheasant and a pointer with a hare, signed J. Moigniez, 42cm. high. (Christie's) $13,500

A 19th century gilt bronze figure of a sporting hound, 'Tom', signed Barye Fils, 8½in. high. (Peter Wilson & Co.) $360

A 19th century French bronze model of a Shetland pony carrying a dead stag, signed I. Bonheur, 22.5 x 25.5cm. (Christie's) $975

A 19th century French bronze group of a ten point stag brought down by two Scottish hounds, cast from a model by A. L. Barye, 39 x 57cm. (Christie's) $8,000

A bronze model of a stag and a fox, signed Fratin, 22½in. wide. (Christie's) $1,000

BUBBLE GUM WRAPPERS

The peak of production in Bubble Gum wrappers spans a period of twenty years dating from 1953-1973. In America however, where wrapper collecting is extremely popular, examples are available from the early thirties onwards.

It was not until around 1942 that the immortal cry 'Any gum chum?' was first heard echoing throughout Britain as they were introduced to the sticky delights of bubble gum by the American allied forces. The British home product did not really get under way until the early 1950's and the big name to emerge from this fiercely competitive field was that of the company A. & B.C.

As part of their promotional campaigns bubble gum manufacturers started to release picture card issues and with each new series a new wrapper featuring art work strongly influenced by topical events in film, television, football and pop music.

Apart from the hardy perennials like Tarzan, Superman and Popeye wrappers depicting The Beatles, Cliff Richard and The Monkees all proved to be extremely popular as did heroes of the Wild West such as The Legend of Custer. The 1957 launching of the satellite Sputnik stimulated an increase in the production of wrappers bearing a space travel theme.

With new issues appearing every few weeks all of these products had a very short 'shelf life' with the result that many of these wax paper wrappers are now quite rare.

One of the most sought after is 'Mars Attacks' issued in 1962 but quickly withdrawn because there were complaints from parents that it frightened their children — it's now worth $200.

'Legend of Custer', 1968, A. & B. C. Chewing Gum Ltd. $20

'Dollar', 1953, A. & B. C. Chewing Gum Ltd.
$10

'Civil War News', 1965, A. & B. C. Chewing Gum Ltd. $20

BUBBLE GUM WRAPPERS

'Mars Attacks', 1962, Bubble Inc. $200

'Roy Rogers', 1955, Times Confectionery Co. Ltd. $30

'Superman in the Jungle', 1968, A. & B. C. Chewing Gum Ltd. $30

'Outer Limits', 1964, Bubble Inc. $40

'Hocus Pocus', 1955, Wow Productions Ltd. $50

'My Chum' (Popeye), 1945, Klene's, Holland, imported. $50

BUCKLES

Buckles have presented an interesting fashion feature throughout the centuries. Essentially a piece of jewelry, they have been styled for daywear and to sparkle in the evening. They were worn at the belt, on a garter at the knee and on shoes. It is reported that men wore buckles as an indication of their social status and some were so large, they almost covered the whole instep.

Buckles were often included in a parure — a set of matching jewelry — and reflect the changing styles. Examples include those made of precious metals and set with gem-stones and the rather ornate Victorian style of gilt, silver filigree, beads or jet.
Emphasis was placed on the use of metal during the Art Nouveau period and it is buckles from this period that have become most popular with collectors today.

A Guild of Handicrafts Ltd. silver enamel and amethyst buckle/cloak clasp, designed by C. R. Ashbee, circa 1902, 13.75cm. wide. $13,500

Early 16th century German silver gilt buckle and belt end. $2,750

A Faberge silver gilt and enamel buckle, 1899-1903. $1,500

A fine late 18th century shoe buckle of polished steel decorated with crystal stones set in silver. $80

18th century iron buckle with fern leaf motifs, 3½in. long. $20

1930's brass butterfly belt buckle. $10

A Lalique gold, diamond, opal and enamel choker buckle, circa 1900, 7.5cm. wide. $35,000

A Russian silver gilt shaped buckle with a dagger clasp. (Christie's) $170

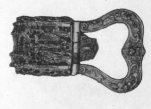

Late 15th/16th century South German silver gilt belt buckle, 4.3/8in. overall. $2,250

95

BUTTER STAMPS

Butter stamps have a lot to commend them as suitable objects for collecting. They are small, quite readily available and offer an attractive range of interesting motifs.

Most commonly made of sycamore with a turned wood handle and a hand carved design on the base, the topic of the design will help to identify the source: a swan and bullrushes suggests a riverside farm, a sheep — a hill farm, and so on.

A popular American butter stamp bears a tulip motif and other themes include birds, dates, wheatsheaves, a heart and even a little motto entreating one to 'Eat Good Butter'.

Less common examples in boxwood and those designed to commemorate a special event are of particular interest to the collector.

A 19th century American butter stamp, carved with a lamb, 3in. diam. (Robt. W. Skinner Inc.) $300

Sycamore wood butter marker, circa 1830, 5in. diam. (Christopher Sykes) $75

An American 19th century wooden handleless butter stamp with incised anchor, 3½in. diam. (Robt. W. Skinner Inc.) $80

An American 19th century wooden butter stamp carved with a running fox, 2½in. diam. (Robt. W. Skinner Inc.) $160

A 19th century American wooden butter stamp of shell design, 3½in. diam. (Robt. W. Skinner Inc.) $110

A 19th century American wooden butter stamp with incised deer, 4in. diam. (Robt. W. Skinner Inc.) $330

A 19th century American wooden butter stamp showing a bird on a branch, 3in. diam. (Robt. W. Skinner Inc.) $240

An American 19th century wooden oval butter stamp with carved eagle standing on a globe, 5½in. long. (Robt. W. Skinner Inc.) $390

A 19th century American wooden butter stamp carved with a cow, 3½in. diam. (Robt. W. Skinner Inc.) $160

CADDY SPOONS

Although it is doubtful if the luck of an English farmer will be repeated when he found a 16th century silver spoon worth thousands while rethatching his cottage roof, there are still plenty of prizes to be found in old cutlery drawers.

Most sought after are the early seal top and apostle spoons which have a cast finial joined to the flattened stem with a 'V' joint. Of more unusual form are moat spoons, for scooping the floating debris from the surface of a cup of tea, mustache spoons which have a barrier on the leading edge of the bowl and castor oil spoons designed to administer the beneficial elixir with as little hardship as possible.

The most likely prize to be found, however, are caddy spoons which generally have a large ornate bowl and very short handle, find one of these in the form of an eagle and we are talking about over $2,000.

Bright cut caddy spoon, Birmingham, 1798. (Dreweatts) $110

A Victorian caddy spoon, the bowl formed as a shell, by John Foligno, 1854. (Christie's) $1,125

A Victorian caddy spoon, the bowl formed as a shell, by C. T. & G. Fox, 1841. (Christie's) $2,000

A George IV caddy spoon, by C. Reily and G. Storer, 1828. (Christie's) $600

A Regency caddy spoon by Edward Farrell, 1816. (Christie's) $2,500

A Victorian silver gilt caddy spoon, the bowl formed as a mussel shell, by Francis Higgins, 1849. (Christie's) $1,500

A vine chased caddy spoon, by Hilliard & Thomason, Birmingham, 1852. (Dreweatts) $160

Jockey cap caddy spoon, by Thos. Willmore, Birmingham, 1798. (Dreweatts) $350

Fiddle pattern caddy spoon, Birmingham, 1814. (Drewatts) $125

A Victorian caddy spoon, the bowl formed as acanthus foliage, by John Figg, 1844. (Christie's) $2,600

A Victorian caddy spoon formed as a broom, by Charles Fox, 1863. (Christie's) $820

A William IV caddy spoon, the bowl formed as a limpet shell, 1830, maker's mark WT. (Christie's) $1,400

CAMERAS

Cameras were first produced on a commercial scale at the end of the 19th century and the Victorians quickly developed a passion for the art of photography. Their veritable mania for documentation led them to record all manner of events from the Grand Tour to the day a young man paraded proudly in his first pair of long trousers.

Today, as the race goes on to develop smaller, lighter, slimmer, fully automatic cameras, the trade in old plate cameras and all the paraphernalia of the Victorian studio, is thriving. Made with the precision of scientific instruments most of these cameras are still in usable condition but they have taken on more than a utilitarian appeal and are now treasured for their intrinsic quality.

A few years ago a good Victorian brass and wood plate camera could be bought easily for as little as $20; after all, who wanted old cameras? Then a few enthusiasts began collecting in a serious way and, suddenly, plate cameras were changing hands at ten times as much.

Even some cameras made as recently as ten years ago have acquired a commercial value to collectors — often far in excess of the guide lines worked out by manufacturers for trade-in prices on new equipment.

One of the rarest examples to come on to the market was the Sutton Panoramic Wet Plate Camera which fetched $20,000 at auction, the resulting publicity bringing two more to light which also sold for about the same figure. Although these were exceptional prices, there are many cameras, like the Powell's stereoscopic camera or the Compur Leica, which sell for well over $2,000.

Most, however, change hands for a good deal less than this, but still at prices which would send anybody up into the loft for a search.

Wet-plate camera by W. W. Rouch, London, circa 1864, 5 x 5in. $1,500

A Thornton-Pickard quarter-plate triple extension field camera. (Onslows) $340

An Alpa Reflex 35mm. s.l.r. camera, Mod. 6, No. 38996, with Kern Switar, Schneider and Alpa lenses. (Christie's) $500

Newman & Guardia Nydia folding plate camera, 3¼ x 4¼in., in original leather case, circa 1905. $340

A. C. Lawrance 'Clifford' drop-plate camera, 4 x 5in., with Goerz Doppel-Anastigmat, 150mm. lens, English, circa 1890. $330

ICA Universal Juwel 440 folding plate camera, 13 x 18cm., Germany, circa 1925. $340

Ensign Tropical special reflex camera, 3¼ x 4¼in., in teak body, circa 1930. $300

A prototype V.P. mono-rail camera in aluminum casing, with Tessar lens. (Christie's) $600

Newman & Guardia New Ideal Sibyl folding camera, 3¼ x 4¼in., circa 1925. $160

A Kodak no. 1 camera, with 57mm. f 9 periscopic lens, guillotine sector shutter, 17cm., American, circa 1880. $1,600

Postcard size Tropical stereoscopic reflex camera. (Christie's) $7,400

A Sinclair Tropical Una hand and stand camera, 3¼ x 5¼in., with Zeiss f 6.3 lens in Newman & Sinclair shutter, English, circa 1925. $1,430

Sanders & Crowhurst 'The Birdland' reflex camera, 4 x 5in., circa 1908. $320

Marion's metal miniature camera, 1¼ x 1¼in., in mahogany case, circa 1884. $2,800

A stereoscopic sliding box camera, with two simple lenses, in mahogany body on baseboard, 9in. long, English, circa 1860. $925

Prestwich Manufacturing Co. 35mm. hand-crank movie camera, circa 1915, 18 x 24mm. $480

A 2¼ x 2¼ Redding's Luzo roll-film camera in brass re-inforced mahogany casing, Patent No. 17328. (Christie's) $900

A Stirn's Waistcoat detective camera, No. 5065, in nickel-plated brass casing, taking six circular exposures on circular plate. (Christie's) $960

A rare J. Frennet stereo reflex camera, 7 x 15cm., with twin Zeiss Protarlinse 244mm. lenses, Belgian, circa 1900. $440

A four lens multiple exposure camera, probably by J. Lancaster & Sons, taking four 2 x 1½in. exposures on one quarter plate, in mahogany casing. (Christie's) $2,400

A Zeiss Contaflex 35mm. twin-lens reflex camera, No. Z 42268 with a Sonnar taking lens and a Sucher-Objectiv lens, and an exposure meter. (Christie's) $900

CANE HANDLES

Walking sticks have been with us for thousands of years — arousing in man an acquisitive instinct for just about that long.

Sticks were made from cane or a variety of woods and decorated with many materials but, it was usually the cane handle which received most attention to detail and design. The most elegant sticks have tops mounted in gold, silver or porcelain and many more versatile sticks are designed to conceal gadgets such as a snuff box, a watch or even a hidden camera.

During the second half of the 19th century glass walking sticks were made at the Nailsea glass works near Bristol. These glass sticks were hung on the wall in the belief that they had the power to ward off disease from the household.

German walking stick with slender ebonized hardwood shaft, circa 1905, 39in. long. $840

A gold mounted smoky quartz parasol handle, cane shaft, overall length 13¾in. (Christie's) $2,000

A Meissen cane handle in the shape of Joseph Frohlich lying on top of a barrel, circa 1743, 13.5cm. $9,000

Ebony blackamoor's head knop cane, with named silver collar. (Woolley & Wallis) $180

A Girl in a Swing type cane holder modeled as the head of a masked lady, circa 1765, 2.1/8in. high. (Christie's) $560

A Colonial stick, the handle carved with a lioness's head. (Woolley & Wallis) $315 £210

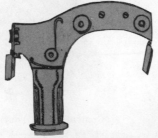

Late 19th century malacca walking cane with scrimshaw ball-grip set with a compass, 81.5cm. long. $265

Ben Akiba miniature walking stick camera, (Christie's) $6,800

Top of the handle of a captain's 'going ashore' cane. $20,000

CAR MASCOTS

These decorative symbols introduced around 1905, are usually made of cast metal though sometimes of wood or glass.

Of the wide range of designs, including those issued by car manufacturers, such as, the Rolls Royce Spirit of Ecstasy and the American company Lincoln's greyhound, the magnificent mascots designed by the French glass artists Sabino and Lalique are the most highly prized.

Many car owners had mascots made to their own designs and these offer a great variety of interesting subjects for the collector.

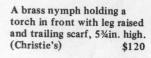

A brass bust of Minerva, stamped, 6in. high, on circular plinth.(Christie's) $280

'Cinq Chevaux', a Lalique car mascot molded in clear glass, etched France No. 1122, 11.5cm. high. (Christie's) $4,750

A brass nymph holding a torch in front with leg raised and trailing scarf, 5¾in. high. (Christie's) $120

A nickel plated speed nymph clutching a scarf, by Lejeune, stamped Reg. AEL, 6in. high. (Christie's) $300

'Grenouille', a Lalique car mascot in clear and satin finished glass molded as a seated frog, 6.3cm. high. (Christie's) $6,000

A cast silver radiator mascot by Omar Ramsden, 1935, 12.8cm., 21.5oz. (Lawrence Fine Art) $1,750

CARD CASES

In the days when polite society expected printed notice of an intended visit, the calling card played a vital role. It is said that fashionable ladies of the 19th century, anxious to impress others with their status, would display cards presented to them by those of considerable social consequence, in a large open dish placed on the drawingroom table. The most important being well to the top.

Cards were often delivered by a footman but the common practice was to carry several personal cards in a case.

Card cases are almost always of slim and rectangular shape and made from a variety of materials such as gold, silver, ivory, tortoiseshell, Tunbridgeware, mother-of-pearl, papier mache and leather. They are often beautifully decorated and sometimes marked with the original owner's monogram or inscribed to commemorate an event.

A Chinese ivory card case, carved in shaped panels with figures and buildings in garden and river scenes. (Lawrence Fine Art) $100

A Victorian shaped silver card case, by Edward Smith, Birmingham 1852, 10.1 cm. (Lawrence Fine Art) $530

An Indian card case inlaid with mosaic panels and borders of tinted ivory and metal. (Lawrence Fine Art) $25

A papier mache card case, inlaid with mother-of-pearl and gilt with a Chinese river scene. (Lawrence Fine Art) $25

A Chinese ivory card case, deeply carved with numerous figures and buildings in landscapes. (Lawrence Fine Art) $145

A mother-of-pearl card case, inlaid in a trellis pattern with an engraved bird and flowers, with paua shells. (Lawrence Fine Art) $50

CARLTON WARE

This Staffordshire earthenware and pottery was produced by Wiltshaw and Robinson at Stoke on Trent from 1890 till 1957. From 1958, the firm was re-titled Carlton Ware Ltd. They are best known for porcelain vases produced in the 1920's with bright enameling and gilded decorations, often on black backgrounds, and painted with flowers or fan motifs. The firm's usual mark is circular enclosing a swallow and topped by a crown. Some pieces are marked Carlton Ware.

Decoration is varied from Art Deco designs of lustrous trees in unusual colors, Kate Greenaway style fairies, fantastic and mythical birds and even traditional Chinese chinoiserie designs.

Standard Carlton Ware vase of pale blue ground with tube lined floral decorations on primary colors, also blue inside the vase, 165mm. high. (Goss & Crested China) $170

Pale pink shaped vase with Art Deco design, 195mm. high. (Goss & Crested China) $250

Oviform vase with dark gray ground simulating nightfall, signed by E. F. Paul, with Kate Greenaway style fairies design, 230mm. high. (Goss & Crested China) $1,100

Egyptianesque jardiniere with frieze decoration and hieroglyphics on a blue ground, 160mm. high. (Goss & Crested China) $1,900

Vibrant lustrous red 'Rouge Royale' leaf, one of a series introduced after 1930, 220mm. long. (Goss & Crested China) $20

Deep red jug with gold handle and sea-green interior, one of the famous birds series, featuring fantastic and mythical birds, 295mm. high. (Goss & Crested China) $400

CARTE DE VISITE

The earliest recorded mention of the Carte de Visite in La Lumiere, 1854, credits two Frenchmen with — 'an original idea for the use of small portraits'.

The Carte de Visite consisted of a portrait, usually full length and measuring approximately 2½ x 3½ins., mounted on a slightly larger card designed as a calling card, which often carried reference to the photographer on the reverse side. The cost might have been anything up to a shilling.

The idea was promoted by one, Disderi, who, having captured the interest of the people, then applied for a patent.

By 1862, 'cartemania' was sweeping society and Disderi is reputed to have earned as much as $100,000 annually from his studio work.

The bestselling Carte de Visite of all time was W. Downey's portrait of the Princess of Wales (1867), which achieved a sale of 300,000 copies.

Princess of Prussia. (W. & D. Downey). $20

Example of early 'tin type' photograph. $80

Mr. Herbert Gladstone, M.P. $18

Le Sultan. (Abdullah Freres). $25

Queen Victoria — Court size card. (Hughes & Mullins). $16

Miss Anderson. $18

105

CHAIRS

Over the years, as rooms have been changed and modernized, many a good chair has been relegated to the attic. It was probably thought at the time that while it was too good to be thrown away it was not worthwhile trying to sell it.

At first glance, an old rickety chair may not strike one as the perfect object for the sitting room but, once restored a transformation can take place.

The Victorian cabriole leg dining chair is probably the nicest chair to have been produced during the Victorian period, dating from about 1850 to the end of the century.

With their full balloon backs and French influenced cabriole legs these chairs achieved a degree of elegance soon to be lost as the popular taste turned towards more ponderous styles. The better made examples of this style were those produced at the beginning of their period of popularity and were usually of rosewood, walnut or mahogany, often with fine floral carving on the backs and knees and the most beautifully carved scroll feet; later chairs were often of beech or oak construction and not so well made or finely carved.

Throucout the late Victorian era, dining chairs tended to be heavy and ponderously respectable in style, drawing room chairs being somewhat lighter and bedroom chairs were often positively frivolous. The superabundance of down to earth kitchen chairs in the Windsor style is due to the fact that almost every joinery shop in the country found them easy to produce from whatever wood was to hand. They were produced from about 1830 until the end of the Victorian era and were particularly popular in working class homes and in country districts.

Remember, a pair of chairs is worth more than two singles and a set of four is worth a lot more than two pairs, and so on.

One of a pair of 19th century Chinese armchairs, inlaid with mother-of-pearl. (H. Spencer & Sons) $1,160

A Georgian period Provincial child's rocking armchair. (Woolley & Wallis) $740

An oak chair designed by W. Cave, with drop-in seat, circa 1900. $770

Gustav Stickley spindle Morris chair, circa 1907, with sling seat, 32½in. wide. (Robt. W. Skinner Inc.) $3,000

Mid 19th century walnut salon chair with molded and pierced rail, and serpentine padded seat. $1,250

Late Victorian mahogany framed armchair with turned legs and arm supports. (John Hogbin & Sons) $240

CHAIRS

One of a set of four Victorian walnut side chairs on French cabriole front supports. (Reeds Rains) $1,160

A Louis XVI beechwood fauteuil with cartouche-shaped back and seat frame carved with marguerites. (Woolley & Wallis)
                    $1,400

One of a set of six Regency ebonized dining chairs with bowed seats, four stamped SG. (Christie's) $3,675

One of a pair of Regency mahogany bergeres, with distressed upholstery in ribbed frames. (Christie's) $7,500

One of a pair of George II giltwood open armchairs, the backs and seats covered with contemporary tapestry woven in wool and silk, 41½in. high. (Christie's)
                    $145,000

A William IV mahogany armchair with scrolled shaped leather upholstered back and seat and ring-turned tapering legs. (Christie's)
                    $4,755

One of a set of six carved hardwood chairs. (F. H. Fellows & Sons)
                    $4,200

A Gustav Stickley willow armchair, circa 1907, 39in. high, 31in. wide. (Robt. W. Skinner Inc.) $500

One of a set of four Dutch marquetry inlaid dining chairs with drop-in seats. (Worsfolds) $1,800

CHAIRS

Elizabethan Revival mahogany platform rocker, by G. Hunzinger, New. York, circa 1882, 39in. high. (Robt. W. Skinner Inc.) $735

Victorian oak revolving office chair. (British Antique Exporters) $200

One of a pair of Regency mahogany hall chairs, the sabre back legs joined by ring-turned stretchers. (Christie's) $9,000

Charles II walnut, child's high chair with original adjustable footrest and retaining bar. (James & Lister Lea) $2,000

A Regency metamorphic library armchair attributed to Morgan & Saunders, the seat opening to reveal four treads. (Christie's) $7,000

One of a pair of laminated rosewood chairs, attributed to J. H. Belter, circa 1855, 38in. high. (Robt. W. Skinner Inc.) $3,700

A Regency beechwood tub armchair, the back filled with cane and with green leather squab cushion. (Christie's) $2,000

A Thonet bentwood rocking chair (paper label under seat). (Reeds Rains) $175

One of a pair of rush-backed wing armchairs. (Bonham's) $840

CHAMBER POTS

The chamber pot or 'po' – from the French pot de chambre – was usually supplied as part of a toilet set consisting of a jug, basin, soap dish and slop pail. The quality of material and design varies enormously and includes the simple transfer printed earthenware pot, the better quality and colorful Mason's ironstone pot and the elegant fine porcelain pot enameled and gilded by a factory such as Limoges. Chamber pots were also made of silver and gold.

Most collectible pots, apart from the obvious, are those bearing some kind of novel decoration like the frog illustrated or those with a portrait of Napoleon or a watching eye painted on the inside on the bottom surface. Early 19th century potters produced many pots bearing an inscription – some amusing, some crude and these too are highly collectible.

A blue and white chamber pot painted with peony and bamboo issuing from rockwork, circa 1750, 18.5cm. diam. (Christie's) $2,750

Child's white china potty. $8

Sunderland luster pottery chamber pot with an applied frog and cartoon face in the interior. (Cooper Hirst) $640

An English china chamber pot, by Brown-Westhead, Moore & Co., circa 1870, with polychrome rhododendron decoration on cream ground. $70

A pewter chamber pot, stamped with crown and other marks. (Lots Road Galleries) $160

Floral china chamber pot, 1850, (British Antique Exporters) $65

A Victorian two-handled chamber pot, 9¼in. diam. (Dickinson, Davy & Markham) $100

One of two chamber pots, circa 1750, 15.5cm. wide, 12.5cm. diam. (Christie's) $4,750

Late Victorian silver chamber pot, with a scroll handle. (Woolley & Wallis) $1,000

CHECKS & BILLS OF EXCHANGE

An offshoot of the more established practice of collecting Banknotes is that of collecting checks. These can be quite inexpensive and will provide a source of great interest and fun.

A collection will be more readily defined by the introduction of a theme perhaps focusing on a particular bank, group of banks or a local area.

As with most printed paper collectibles, the more attractive and well printed the item, the more desirable the item is to a collector. However, never forget the rarity and age factor — early items are usually more scarce and interesting, but may be less attractive.

Lloyds Bank Ltd., Tonbridge, unused check form dated 1893. **$7**

Colonial Bank, Kingston, Jamaica, unusual piece dated 1909. **$10**

Bank of New York, 1869. **$8**

Glyn, Mills, Currie & Co., now Williams & Glyn's, check dated 1892. **$2**

Royal Bank of Scotland, circa 1855, unused check form from the Campbelton Branch. **$12**

Central Bank of New Jersey, 1873. **$6**

First National Bank, Cooperstown, New York, 1895. **$4**

National Bank of the Republic, Private check for the New York and New Haven Railroad Co., dated 1865. **$8**

Barclay & Co. Ltd., Saffron Walden, 1910.
$3

Bank of Otterville, Missouri, check dated 1901.
$5

Midland Bank Ltd., overprinted on London Joint City & Midland Bank Ltd., Brigg, 1924. $3

Messrs. Gosling & Sharpe, now part of Barclays, check dated 1831. $10

The Brazil Bank, Indiana, 1873 check on this American Bank. $10

Mills, Errington, Bawtree & Co., Colchester, unused check form dated 1880. $10

Hongkong & Shanghai Banking Corporation, London, Bank Draft on the Yokohama branch, 1888. $12

Commercial Bank Corporation of India & The The East, Draft from Bombay to their correspondents in London, dated 1866. $30

Mechanics & Traders Bank of Brooklyn, privately printed 1889 check for Theodore S. Bird's Dry Dock. $10

Blackstone National Bank, Boston, U.S.A., 1875. $6

CHEESE DISHES

It is not often realized that throughout the 19th century people were well used to expecting fresh milk, butter and cheese, for cows were actually kept in the center of large towns for this purpose right up until the First World War.

Most large houses of the period actually had their own dairy set in the coolest part of the house, usually facing north, where they regularly made butter, curds and whey and cheese.

It became fashionable in the 19th century to partake of cheese after dinner and this custom saw the production of vast numbers of decorative china cheese dishes able to grace the diningroom as opposed to the rather plain functional dishes which rarely left the kitchen. Unfortunately some of the larger Stilton cheese dishes have become somewhat redundant for it would cost a king's ransom to fill one.

Staffordshire pottery cheese dish with floral decoration. $25

Stilton cheese dish and cover in the style of Wedgwood, circa 1900, 12in. high. (Lots Road Galleries) $200

Wilkinson Ltd. 'bizarre' cheese dish and cover, 1930. $130

A tall Stilton cheese dish and cover with molded basket weave design, 12in. (Dickinson, Davy & Markham) $130

Booth's blue and white wedge-shaped cheese dish. $40

Late 19th century majolica circular section cheese dish and cover, 10½in. diam. $100

Early 19th century Chamberlain's Worcester dish. $925

A George Jones majolica cheese dome and stand. (Dreweatts) $720

Late 19th century majolica cheese dish with domed cover, 10in. diam. (Robt. W. Skinner Inc.) $500

As with annuals, the prime motivation for collecting children's books is nostalgia. Some people merely wish to re-read books from their childhood while others wish to amass collections of fine first editions. This means that a 'reading copy', ie. rather worn copy of a later edition of Richard Crompton's William books can be had for $2 while a scarce first edition with dust wrapper of the same book may cost $40. Popular subjects for collecting are early chromolithographed color books, alphabets, artists such as Mabel Lucie Atwell, and also novels by Enid Blyton, W. E. Johns, Frank Richards etc. There are some artists whose work alone sells a book – Lear, Cruikshank, Tenniel, Ernest Shepherd who illustrated so many of A. A. Milne's books, Arthur Rackham, E. H. Detmold, Jessie M. King and Kay Nielsen (a man, by the way). Fairy story books by Andrew Lang were often illustrated by people like Austen Dobson, Linley Sanbourne, Kate Greenaway, T. Bowick and Randolph Caldecott.

Early children's books like Hornbooks and Chapbooks are of course immensely valuable but they do not turn up every day and when they do the prices they fetch ensure that they will be bought up by libraries or learned institutions.

Every second hand bookshop has its children's section and most collectors combine purchases from these with books bought from specialist mail order dealers.

Condition is all important and because the books were often given rough handling by their original owners those in pristine condition are very rare – and consequently very highly priced when they come up for sale.

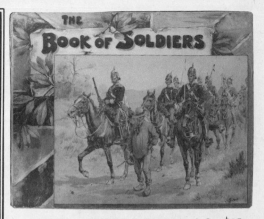

The Book of Soldiers, E. P. Dutton & Co. $25

The Big Book for Girls, 1927. $5

The House That Jack Built, George Routledge & Sons. $40

Robinson Crusoe, Nister Publications, circa 1900. **$20**

Treasure Hunt, Puzzle Book, circa 1940. **$10**

The Young Fur Traders, by R. M. Ballantyne. **$3**

Rosy Cheeks, Nister Untearable. **$25**

The Alphabet Book, 1880's. **$30**

Andersen's Fairy Tales, Anne Anderson Illustrations, 1930's. **$15**

Little Frolic, 1930's $20

Mickey Mouse Annual 1947. $20

Boys Who Became Famous, by F. J. Snell, 1924. $5

From Many Lands, America, Father Tuck Series, 1904. $30

Buck Jones Annual 1958. $10

The Arabian Nights, Hodder & Stoughton, 1949. $40

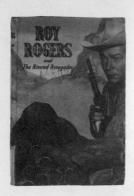

Roy Rogers, Adprint Ltd., 1952. $3

Film Fun Annual 1941. $50

Ameliaranne and the Green Umbrella, 1939 $20

The Animal ABC, Deans Diploma Series No. 28.$15

Little Wide Awake 1890. $50

Some Farm Friends, circa 1900. $20

Merry Hearts 1896. $75

CHRISTMAS CARDS

The Christmas card originated in Britain as one man's personal stationery in an issue of one hundred copies. Today over three billion cards a year sell in the U.S.A. alone. While exceptionally early and decorative cards now fetch high prices it is still possible to purchase attractive late Victorian cards for a dollar or two and bundles of 1930's art deco beauties will turn up in grandma's attic for free.

The illustrations on early cards are notably 'non-festive' by today's standards showing mainly children and animals at play, lots of flowers and lace, circus acrobats in full flight and even sad little dead robins with their feet in the air. The cards often carried the most sobering even macabre messages.

A Happy Christmas To You. $5

'A Casket of Good Wishes', 150 x 100mm., embossed, opens up to reveal verse. $15

With Loving Christmas Greetings. $15

God Bless You With A Happy Christmas. $5

A Merry Christmas. $15

May Your Christmas Be Happy. $10

CHRISTMAS CARDS

Wishing You A Joyous
Christmas. $2

A Happy Christmas. $3

The Seasons Greetings. $10

Christmas Bring You
Many Joys. $5

1843 Christmas card , designed by John Calcott
Horsley, sent by Sir Henry Cole to William
Makepeace Thackery.   (Phillips) $4,250

A Whole Catalogue Of
Xmas Joys Be Yours.
                    $15

Wish Best Wishes For A
Happy Christmas. $6

Ring Joy and Peace and Happiness.
                    $6

A Happy Christmas. $6

Jolly Xmas Crushes and
Sweet Xmas Jams. $7

Loving Christmas Greeting
and Best Wishes. $10

Here's My Pug and Little
Kitty. $8

118

CIGAR BOX LABELS

Because the label was presumed to reflect the quality of the contents of the box these labels are invariably of the highest quality. Fine art work combines with superb color printing to produce a very decorative item. No collection of packaging is complete without a few of these and they frame up to make a fine decoration to hang on the wall.

Also sought after are the cigar bands themselves for they depict an infinite variety of colorful subjects including flags, flowers, butterflies, vintage cars, famous painters and capital cities. Most of these are issued in sets of 24, 36 or 48 and mounted and framed these too will make a decorative wall hanging.

Peter Gabler, Long Hill, Conn., 'Gabler's Judge'. $7

O-Claire, The Perfect Cigar. $5

Victory. $2

Don Rey. $2

El Arte Cigar Co., 'Prima Lucia'. $5

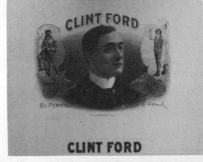

T. E. B. & Co., 'Clint Ford'. $7

CIGARETTE CARDS

Cigarette cards were the 'commercial breaks' of the 1870's until the end of the Second World War. During that time more than 5,000 sets of cards were produced ranging in subject over every possible aspect of life and interests from royalty to railway trains.

Before the arrival of the cardboard slide-action packet, cigarettes were presented in a thin paper packet with a piece of card inserted to protect the cigarettes from damage.

American manufacturers with a keen eye for the promotional main chance were the first to put a picture on the cards and around 1885 W.D. & H.O. Wills of Bristol became the first firm to issue these cigarette cards in Britain. They were an immediate success and soon eagerly collected by youngsters throughout the land.

Many of the cards were of high artistic merit and since most offer some information on the subject illustrated on the other side, a collection soon became an important source of general knowledge on an abundant range of subjects and made up a richly illustrated history of the times. Early cards show a preference for Kings and Queens and famous statesmen but later issues encompass an endless variety of topics — Sports Personalities, Air Raid Precautions, Stars of Screen and Stage, How to Swim, Do You Know and so on.

Nowadays collectors tend to be of more mature years and collections very valuable assets indeed. A complete set of Taddy's Clowns issued early this century in a series of twenty sold recently for the amazing sum of $25,000. It is important always to bear in mind that the condition of cigarette cards has a direct bearing on their value and dog eared, creased or marked sets are worth considerably less than those in pristine condition.

Gems of French Architecture, W. D. & H. O. Wills, Series of 50, 1917. $60

Fire-Fighting Appliances, John Player & Sons, Series of 50, 1930. $20

National Fitness, Spine, Waist & Arms, Ardath, Series of 50, 1938. $10

Wild Animals of the World, Adkin & Sons, Series of 50, 1923. $25

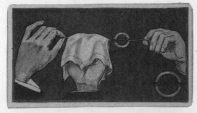

Magical Prizes, R. & J. Hill Ltd., The Mysterious Ring, Series of 50, 1938. $25

Aviation Series, W. D. & H. O. Wills, Series of 50, 1910. **$60**

How to Swim — Series of 50. 1935. **$6**

Fish & Bait — Series of 50. 1910. **$16**

Do You Know? — 4 Series of 50. 1922-33. **$10–$16** Set

Celebrated Bridges, John Player & Sons, Series of 50, 1903. **$130**

Birds & Eggs — Series of 50. 1906. **$70**

Shadowgraphs, F. & J. Smith's, Series of 25, 1915. **$130**

Airmen & Airwomen, Carreras Ltd., Series of 50, 1936. **$25**

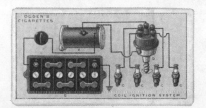

Applied Electricity — Series of 50. 1928. **$25**

Military Motors, W. D. & H. O. Wills, Series of 50, 1916. **$40**

CIGARETTE CARDS

Races of Mankind, F. & J. Smith's, Series of 40, 1900.   **$1,500**

Keep Fit, Lambert & Butler, Series of 50, 1937.   **$8**

Kings of Speed — Series of 50. 1939.   **$6**

Cope's Golfers — Series of 50. 1904.   **$550**

Stars of Screen & Stage — Series of 48. 1935.   **$10**

Time & Money — Series of 50. 1908.   **$50**

Women on War Work — Series of 50. 1916.   **$160**

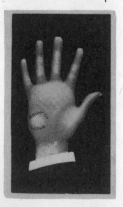

Palmistry, Carreras Ltd., Series of 50, 1933.   **$8**

Clowns & Circus Artistes — Series of 20.   **$25,000**

CIGARETTE CASES

Some indication of the widespread popularity of the smoking habit can be seen in the abundance of delightful cigarette cases on the market today. This is a popular subject for collectors, mainly because they are plentiful, attractive and, although they were designed to house only the smaller cigarettes, in use they re-create the elegance of times past.

Cigarette cases were made from gold, silver, tortoiseshell, papier mache and enamel ware. The box lid was usually a feature of the decoration and here the variety is infinite. They may be inset with precious stones, engraved, painted or inlaid with contrasting materials. The earliest examples are of formal design, demonstrating the skills of the silversmith and engraver, but after it became fashionable for women to smoke, the designs take on the bold and colorful patterns of the modernist era.

A Continental plated cigarette case enameled with a collie dog on a sky background, circa 1910. (Phillips) $300

A 1930's cigarette case, silver and two-color gold colored metal, with stripes of black lacquer, 11.75cm. wide. $700

A French enameled cigarette case by Eugene Grasset, circa 1900. $600

An Imperial two-color gold and jeweled presentation cigarette case by Bok, St. Petersburg, 1899-1908, 9.7cm. $4,500

A French silver, black lacquer and crushed eggshell cigarette case and a cigar piercer, London 1925, 11cm. wide. $485

A German .935 standard cigarette case, signed Reznicek. (Andrew Grant) $1,250

123

CIGARETTE LIGHTERS

Most of the old cigarette lighters on the market today date from around 1900, and there are still many interesting and unusual examples available at a very modest price.

This is a good area for investment. Particularly in the early experimental types and patented examples which demonstrate a skilful facility in combining ideas to good effect.

There is a combined battery operated torch and petrol lighter, an evening purse cum dance card lighter and a lighter skilfully disguised to conceal a cosmetic compact.
Some of the most interesting lighters date from the period of the first World War when they were handmade from shell cases and other sundry equipment.

Silver cased petrol cigarette lighter by Tiffany & Co., New York. $110

An Alfred Dunhill silver gilt and enamel cigarette box and lighter, London hallmarks for 1929. (Christie's)
$1,500

Polo petrol cigarette lighter, circa 1920. $8

An 18kt. gold lighter watch, with the 'Dunhill Unique' lighter mechanism, London 1926. $2,860

Late 19th century spelter table lighter. $60

A Dunhill 'Bijou' lady's 18kt. plain gold petrol lighter, Pat. 143752 Fab. Suisse, 3.2cm. high. (Christie's) $650

Sixty or seventy years ago small boys used to stand outside tobacconists asking 'Got any cigarette cards, mister?'. In the late forties youngsters went around picking up empty packets and tearing off the fronts. Cards had been discontinued during wartime and the packet front was a sort of substitute.

Things are on a firmer footing now with hundreds of serious collectors. There is also a keen following abroad, especially in Brazil, Czechoslovakia, Hungary and Great Britain.

The formation of the British Cigarette Packet Collectors' Club in 1980 coincided with the publication of the one and only book on the subject of cigarette packet design, Cigarette Pack Art by Chris Mullen, published by Hamlyn. The club was the brainchild of Mr Nat Chait, a retail tobacconist from Richmond in Surrey whose knowledge of the trade over many years is unsurpassed, while his collection of items of pre-1914 vintage is probably the finest in the country.

Collectors ages range between 9 and 69. Collections range in size from a few hundred to tens of thousands. The current world record holder, Mr Vernon Young, has in excess of 60,000. Compared with cigarette cards prices are low for the hobby is relatively new, and as a consequence the field for research is large. Cigarettes have sold in Britain since 1851. General awareness regarding their packaging did not come about for almost 100 years.

'Grand Parade', packet of twenty cigarettes, by P. J. Carroll & Co., 1953. $1

'Lucky Dream', packet of twenty cigarettes by Lucky Dream Cigarette Co., 1950. $3

'Island Queen', packet of twenty cigarettes by P. J. Carroll & Co. Ltd., circa 1935. $4

'Apple Blossom', packet of ten cigarettes by Kriegsfeld & Co., circa 1910.   **$10**

'Rose', paper packet of five cigarettes, by China Tobacco Co., circa 1900.   **$10**

'Turf', cigarette packet slide, Film Favorites, 1947.   **$1**

'New Alliance', packet of five cigarettes by David Corre & Co., circa 1902.   **$10**

'All Gay', packet of five cigarettes, by W. J. Harris, circa 1900.   **$10**

'Turkish Blend', packet of twenty cigarettes by B. Morris & Sons Ltd., 1970.   **$2**

CLARICE CLIFF

Clarice Cliff, who was apprenticed to A.J. Wilkinson Ltd., and later became art director at both the Royal Staffordshire Pottery and a subsidiary company Newport Pottery, produced vases, jars and tableware in a glazed pottery painted in combinations of vibrant yellow, orange and red, or purple, green, blue and orange. These works are distinctive not only in color content but often in shape. One of the better known examples is a teaset molded in the shape of corn on the cob and painted yellow.

Patterns to look for include Bizarre, Inspiration Bizarre, Biarritz, Crocus and Fantasque. Although most pieces are easy to identify and there are still many good examples on the market, trade tends to be between collectors and the prices high.

A superb wall plaque by Clarice Cliff painted with a scene inspired by Diaghilev's costume design for The Ballet Russe. (Christie's)
$15,000

A Clarice Cliff Bizarre oviform jug in the 'Snake Tree' pattern, 6¾in. high. (Christie's) $700

A Clarice Cliff Bizarre circular wall charger, 45.6cm. diam. (Christie's)
$755

A Clarice Cliff Fantasque baluster shaped vase, 16¼in. high. (Christie's)
$2,200

A Clarice Cliff Bizarre cubist breakfast set painted with geometric designs in red, blue, green and ocher, circa 1931. (Christie's) $1,000

A Clarice Cliff Fantasque single-handled 'Isis' vase, printed marks, 24.6cm. high. (Lawrence Fine Art)
$615

BRACKET CLOCKS

Earliest examples resembled truncated grandfather clocks, having square brass faces and plain ebony cases – though they sometimes had a little gilt enrichment. There is a glazed door at the rear, through which can be seen the finely engraved backplate, and a handle on the top enables the piece to be carried from room to room. All English bracket clocks run for at least eight days without rewinding, and nearly all early examples have a fusee movement. This, in the simplest terms, is a top-shaped brass contraption which houses the mainspring whose unwinding is controlled by means of gut, wire or something similar to a miniature bicycle chain coiled round the outside of the 'top'.

Continental clock movements – which can be recognized by the gear teeth set actually on the drum containing the mainspring – are not as sought-after as their English counterparts – whose drums are toothless.

CARRIAGE CLOCKS

Clocks intended for use while traveling – with their spring-driven movements – had been used to a small degree since the sixteenth century but they never really caught on until the French clockmakers began to produce them en masse in the 19th century.

Carriage clocks made during the early 19th century usually had quite fine cast brass cases, with thick beveled glass windows resting in grooves in the frame. The glass at the top was large; later it became much smaller and was let into a metal plate. Carrying handles are usually round on these early 19th century clocks, tapering towards the ends and, because there is often a repeat button on the top front edge, the handles usually fold backwards only.

A red walnut quarter repeating bracket clock, signed on the chapter ring Asselin, London, 19in. high. (Lawrence Fine Art) $1,750

A George II ebonized grand sonnerie bracket clock, the dial signed Thos. Hughes, London, 9¾in. high. (Christie's) $10,000

A Charles II ebonized striking bracket clock, the dial signed Hen. Jones, London, 16in. high. (Christie's) $6,000

A 19th century French ormolu carriage clock, the lever movement striking on a gong, 8½in. high. (Phillips) $1,500

Late 19th century French brass repeating alarm carriage clock, the dial signed E. Caldwell & Co., Phila., 7½in. high. (Reeds Rains) $1,560

A 19th century French gilt brass carriage clock, signed E. Dent, Paris, 944, 5½in. high. (Phillips) $3,700

LANTERN CLOCKS

The first truly domestic timepieces were called lantern clocks. Proper old lantern clocks run for thirty hours and only have an hour hand — the minute hand was not introduced until about 1690 — but this is not to say that a clock with only one hand dates necessarily from the 17th century, for the smaller, local clockmakers continued to turn out the less complicated, one-handed timepieces for a further hundred years.

Earliest examples either stood on a bracket or were equipped with an iron ring at the back. This allowed the clock to be hung on a nail driven into the wall and it was leveled and steadied by means of spikes at the base.
Many of the early lantern clocks had a weight supported on a rope.

LONGCASE CLOCKS

At first, faces were eight to nine inches square, of brass, with flowers and scrolls engraved in their centers. These increased to about ten inches square by the 1680's, when the wider cases were introduced. From the beginning of the 18th century, faces were usually twelve inches square, or larger following the introduction of the arch.
This was in widespread use by 1720 and, on early examples, was often less than a semicircle.
After 1750, an engraved brass or silvered face without a chapter ring was often used, and from 1775, a cast brass or enameled copper face was introduced.

During the last quarter of the 18th century, manufacturers turned their attentions to quantity rather than quality, making such economies as the use of white painted wood or iron faces after 1790.

Wing alarm lantern clock, circa 1700, 15½in. high. $3,000

An Italian brass and iron lantern clock, circa 1700, 35cm. high. (Christie's) $6,000

A lantern clock, the chapter ring signed T. Cranbrook, 13½in. high. $2,750

Late 17th century Swiss clock with iron dial, 40cm. high. (Christie's) $3,000

A Georgian mahogany longcase clock, by J. Hart, Yarmouth, 7ft. 6in. high. (Phillips) $4,000

A Gustav Stickley oak tall case clock, circa 1902-04, 71in. high. (Robt. W. Skinner Inc.) $10,765

MANTEL CLOCKS

As a basic rule French mantel clocks are nearly all decoration while English models are nearly all clock.

Early French makers to look for are Lepine, Janvier, Amand, Lepaute and Thuret, who started to use a great deal of elaborate scrollwork at the end of the 17th century. If you find a clock by any of these makers you have certainly found a clock. Things to look for are a verge escapement — which is loosely indicated by a horizontally turning crown wheel with sharp teeth just above the pendulum — a painted face or porcelain numerals and a winding hole placed in the face where you least expect it. Pendulums should be pear shaped bobs on brass rods.

By the 19th century, everyone decided they wanted one of these flashy French clocks to add an air of opulence to the lounge. Consequently, manufacturers began doing a spot of overtime.

The word that really matters in any description is 'ormolu' — that is, it is made of a hard metal, such as brass, which is rough cast before being chiseled and engraved by hand and, finally, coated with a thin amalgam of gold and mercury.

Cheaper 19th century mass produced clocks have a similar appearance — at first glance — but they are made of spelter. This is a soft metal which is simply cast and gilded. Clocks with decoration of this kind should sell for about a quarter of the price of the ormolu pieces. The infallible test is to scratch the underside of the clock; if the gold color comes away to reveal gray metal, it's spelter, if brass is revealed it's ormolu. Another test is to tap the case sharply with a coin. If the sound is sharp and pingy, you have hard metal; if it is a dull thud, you have soft.

An Italian ormolu and cut glass portico mantel clock with chased dial, signed Ld Lacroix a Turin, 16½in. high. (Christie's) $2,300

An ormolu mounted porphyry tripod vase clock of Athenienne form, 20in. high. (Christie's) $12,500

A Regency gilt bronze automaton mantel clock, the case in the form of a bird cage, signed Borrell, London, 1ft.7in. high. (Phillips) $10,000

A small Restoration ormolu mantel clock in Louis XV style, the enamel dial signed S. Devaulx Palais Royal 124, 11in. high.
          $1,000

An Empire carved mahogany and veneer shelf clock, by Hotchkiss & Benedict, N.Y., circa 1825, 39in. high. (Robt. W. Skinner Inc.)
          $695

A Continental gilt metal candle alarm with florally engraved plinth case, 5in. high. (Christie's)
          $1,295

A late Empire bronze ormolu and griotte marble mantel clock, 17½in. wide. (Christie's) $2,000

An Empire ormolu mantel clock, the silk-suspended countwheel striking movement with enamel dial, 19in. wide. (Christie's) $3,240

A gilt metal calendar strut clock, the backplate stamped Thos. Cole, London, 5½in. high. (Christie's) $3,675

A George III mahogany mantel timepiece, the dial signed Absolon, London; 10in. high. (Phillips) $1,000

An Art Deco green onyx mantel clock with ivory figures carved after a model by F. Preiss, 25.2cm. high. (Christie's) $3,240

A French 19th century ormolu mantel clock, on an oval rosewood plinth under a glass shade, 1ft.3in. high. (Phillips) $1,400

A Regency rosewood mantel timepiece, the dial signed Arnold & Dent, Strand, London, 10¼in. high. (Phillips) $1,300

An ornate metal elephant clock with eight-day chiming movement, outside count wheel, 21in. high. (Andrew Grant) $1,200

An Empire carved mahogany shelf clock, by Riley Whiting, Conn., circa 1825, 29½in. high. (Robt. W. Skinner Inc.) $345

A Regency ormolu mantel clock, the dial in drum-shaped case, 9½in. wide. (Christie's) $1,800

A French red marble perpetual calendar mantel clock and barometer, 18½in. high. (Lawrence Fine Art) $1,500

A French Louis XVI style black marble and ormolu mounted mantel clock, 1ft. 9in. high. (Phillips) $1,900

A Louis XVI white marble and ormolu mounted mantel clock, the dial signed Hardy A Paris, 1ft.2in. high. (Phillips) $1,700

A three-dimensional wood model picture clock showing a French Chateau, under glass dome, 21½in. high. (Andrew Grant) $2,400

A Royal Presentation ormolu mounted ebony grande sonnerie spring clock by Thos. Tompion, London, No. 278, circa 1700, 28in. high. (Christie's) $365,000

A Swiss automaton mantel clock, 9in. high.(Christie's) $3,455

An early 19th century ormolu mantel clock, 1ft.9in. high. (Phillips) $1,360

A mahogany mantel clock, by Breguet, 11¼in. high. (Phillips) $8,400

SKELETON CLOCKS

It is a widely held belief that skeleton clocks — almost all of which were made during the 19th century — were the work of apprentices, made during their final year of study and so designed that examiners could observe the working and workmanship of each part with a minimum of effort.

While this might well have been the practice from which the style originated, its popularity throughout the Victorian period necessitated the masters' involvement in their manufacture. English models are of fret-cut brass, with silvered brass chapter rings, and are usually to be found on wooden bases beneath glass domes — for they are naturally prone to dust damage.

Another variety is the French skeleton clock. This is usually much smaller, having solid front and backplates — often engraved on later examples — and enameled chapter rings.

WALL CLOCKS

Although wall clocks of a sort had been in existence for quite some time, it was not until Pitt imposed a tax on clocks, in 1797, that the impetus was given for the manufacture of large wall clocks which could be hung in public places for all to see. This is why many large wall clocks are still known today as Act of Parliament Clocks.

By the arrival of the Regency period, wall clocks had reduced in size to about eighteen inches in width, many veneered in rosewood with brass scroll inlay. The larger, Victorian, wall clocks are referred to as Vienna regulators and have a mahogany case and an elaborate pendulum. You will most probably find one driven by means of a spring, but those employing weights are better quality as a rule.

15 in. brass skeleton timepiece with strike and chain drive, under dome. (Worsfolds) **$460**

An English brass striking skeleton clock of York Minster type, on wood base with glass dome, 59cm. high. (Christie's) **$2,625**

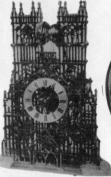

A brass three-train 'Westminster Abbey' skeleton clock, striking on gong and nest of eight bells having mercury pendulum, 24in. high. (Andrew Grant) **$8,400**

A George III mahogany wall timepiece, the 12in. silvered dial signed Jefferys, London, 1ft. 4½in. high. (Phillips) **$2,400**

A late 17th century Italian day and night clock, signed Jean Baptiste Gonnon a Milan, 20 x 23½in. (Lawrence Fine Art) **$5,000**

A Georgian mahogany wall timepiece, dial signed Field, Bath, 3ft. 7in. high. (Phillips) **$1,200**

CLOISONNE

Cloisonne is a technique of enameling developed in the 10th century. It consists of soldering fine wires on to a solid base to form a pattern of small cells which are then filled with colored enamel: the wire acting as a wall to prevent adjacent colors from running together. When fired, the wires remain visible and become an integral part of the design.

This method differs from Champleve enamel where actual depressions are cut into the metal base and then filled with enamel paste and fired as before.

Although a few older pieces are to be found, most of the examples seen today date from the 19th century when enamel was returned to popularity by Alexis Falize. He was a French silversmith who began importing and selling Chinese cloisonne articles while also adapting the technique for his own products.

Late 19th century cloisonne cabinet decorated in various colored enamels, 14.5 x 9 x 12cm. (Christie's) $1,500

A pair of 19th century cloisonne enamel and gilt bronze cockerels, 17½in. high. (Bermondsey) $3,000

A cloisonne enamel and gilt bronze mounted censer and domed cover with large lotus finial, 18th century, 53cm. high. (Christie's) $5,600

A 17th century cloisonne enamel pear-shaped vase with taotie and loose ring handles, 39cm. high. (Christie's) $1,295

A 16th century cloisonne enamel tripod circular dish decorated on a pale-blue ground with a meander of peony and hibiscus, 19.8cm. diam. (Christie's) $1,400

Late 19th century cloisonne enamel oviform vase with flaring neck, 61.5cm. high. (Christie's) $6,000

A 16th century Ming cloisonne enamel globular tripod censer, 12.8cm. diam. (Christie's)
$4,000

A small cloisonne enamel and gilt bronze circular box and cover, Qianlong five-character mark, 6.5cm. diam. (Christie's)
$325

A 16th/17th century Ming cloisonne enamel deep bowl with widely everted rim, 27.5cm. diam. (Christie's)
$3,455

A cloisonne enamel dish, the blue ground decorated with a quail, 18in. diam. (Lawrence Fine Art)
$220

Cloisonne vase decorated with dragons on a dark-blue field, converted to a reading lamp, 19in. high. (Peter Wilson)
$200

A cloisonne enamel circular box and flat cover, Qianlong, 32.7cm. diam., wood stand. (Christie's)
$4,800

Late Qing Dynasty cloisonne enamel and gilt bronze double moon-flask, formed as two circular flattened bottles conjoined, 36cm. high. (Christie's)
$2,500

One of a pair of 19th century cloisonne enamel figures of zebras.
$67,000

A cloisonne enamel and gilt bronze tripod censer and domed cover, Qianlong/Jiaqing, 39cm. high. (Christie's)
$3,500

American comics are collected by enthusiasts all over the world reflecting the extensive distribution they have always had. Few collectibles have such a huge range of items available and such a vast range of prices. Action Comics Number 1, if you could find a copy would cost you around $15,000 while at the other extreme scores of titles are readily available at only a few dollars.

It was in Action Comics launched in June 1938 that the far-famed Superman character made his debut and then only after his creators Joe Schuster and Jerry Seigal had seen their work rejected by almost every major publishing house in America.

Essential reading is the Overstreet Price Guide which lists and values all the American comics ever published in its 350 plus pages.

More Fun Comics, No. 47, September 1939. $50

Top Notch, 'Galleon's Ghost', 1935. $6

Detective Comics, No. 28, June 1939, 'Batman'. $2,000

Batman, No. 1, Spring Issue 1940, 'The Batman and Robin'. $5,000

Batman, D. C. Comics, 1977. $4

Adventure Comics, No. 72, March 1942, 'Sandman'. $600

New Adventure Comics, No. 27, June 1938. **$90**

Walt Disney's, No. 1. **$2,500**

Comics on Parade, 'Li'l Abner', No. 45. **$25**

Action Comics, No. 1, June 1938, 'Superman'. **$15,000**

Diamond Dick, Boy's Best Weekly, 1901. **$8**

All-American Comics, No. 16, July 1940, 'Green Lantern'. **$2,400**

Movie Comics, No. 1, April 1939. **$60**

All Star Comics, No. 1, Summer Issue, 1940. **$1,200**

Halt, No. 4, June 1945, Duchess Publishing. **$2**

Andy Panda, No. 85.
$40

Walt Disney's Comics,
No. 99. $55

Punch Comics, No. 16.
$25

All-American Comics, No. 1,
April 1939.   **$300**

Diamond Dick, The Boys Best
Weekly, 1900.   **$8**

Superman v. Muhammad Ali,
D. C. Comics, 1978. $5

Captain Marvel Adventures,
No. 21.   **$110**

Spook Suspense Mystery,
No. 29. $40

The Purple Claw, No. 1.
$30

Although nostalgia is the main motivation for comic collecting, an increasing number of people now appreciate comic art for its own sake and a growing amount of research is being carried out by individuals all over the country to identify and catalogue the various artists and authors.

As with any hobby, the most interesting and valuable collections are those which have been built up around a central theme, for example, the work of a particular author or artist, or stories of a particular type. One of the most widely collected artists is Dudley Watkins who drew Desperate Dan for the 'Dandy', Lord Snooty for the 'Beano' and many other comic strips and story illustrations for D. C. Thomson.

Rowland Turner who drew several issues of the 'Super Detective Library' and 'Thriller Picture Library' is another artist whose work is in great demand and any comic containing examples of his art commands a premium price.

The ill-fated boy's magazine the 'Ranger' which only lasted for forty weeks in 1965-66 contained the now legendary Trigan Empire, magnificently drawn by Don Lawrence and printed in full color. Other artists of note are Eric Parker and Frank Hampson who drew the innovative Dan Dare for the 'Eagle'.

The most popular stories tend to be those of the science fiction/fantasy type. The comic 'TV21' (1965-69) specializes in comic strips, best of Jerry Anderson's TV series 'Thunderbird', 'Fireball XL5', 'Sting Ray' and 'Super Car' and copies of this comic changes hands at up to $6 each.

To bring us up-to-date '2000 A.D.', with its science fiction comic strip, has become something of a cult and early issues, only five or six years old, may bring up to $10 each.

The Magnet, Jan. 15th 1921. $4

The Beano Comic, July 30th 1938. $600

Radio Fun, Oct. 15th 1938. $120

Knock-Out Comic and Magnet, No. 90, Nov. 1940.   **$10**

2000 A.D., No. 3, March 1977.   **$9**

The Dandy Comic, No. 340, March 1947. **$10**

The Pioneer, Feb. 10th 1934.   **$10–$30**

The Rover, 'Hawkeye', No. 745, July 1936.   **$7**

The Boy's Own Paper, Enlarged Christmas Number, Dec. 1927.   **$3**

Pluck.   **$4**

The Skipper, No. 367, September 1937.   **$8**

The Champion, 'Zoom the Racing Speed Cop', Dec. 1935.   **$6**

COPPER & BRASS

Copper and brass have been used for making an enormous range of generally functional household articles on a commercial scale for over 300 years. Originally there were many flaws on the surface but this was alleviated with improved production methods in the 18th century.

Be it candlesticks or kettles, trivets or jelly molds, a choice often has to be made as to what to collect but all will enhance the home if you don't mind the cleaning.

With early pieces it is often the patina built up over centuries which accounts for most of the value so care in cleaning is recommended.

There are many reproductions on the market, some very difficult to identify so don't hesitate to ask in antiques shops. Most dealers are willing to pass on the benefit of their experience and knowledge and all are obliged to give an accurate description.

A Benham & Froud brass kettle designed by Dr. C. Dresser, on three spiked feet, 24.5cm. high. (Christie's) $650

A Victorian brass and wood paper rack, circa 1880. (British Antique Exporters) $36

Copper milk churn with cover. (Ball & Percival) $135

A 16th century European brass alms dish, depicting Adam and Eve in the Garden of Eden, 15¾in. diam. (Robt. W. Skinner Inc.) $415

Victorian copper firescreen with inset mirror, circa 1880. (British Antique Exporters) $65

One of a pair of Anglo-Indian brass jardinieres on later stained oak bases, 41in. high. (Christie's) $4,105

A large 16th/17th century brass Nuremburg alms dish, the rim stamped with flower heads, 21in. (Dreweatts) $920

Victorian brass coal bucket 1880. (British Antique Exporters) $110

Late 19th century brass gong with hammer. (British Antique Exporters) $150

Barlow's patent brass candlestick, Birmingham, England, circa 1839, 7.3/8in. high. (Robt. W. Skinner Inc.) $695

A George III brass and steel basket grate, 34¼in. wide, 30½in. high. (Christie's) $8,500

One of a pair of 18th/19th century brass wall sconces, dated 1750, 17¾in. high. $485

Large embossed brass jardiniere on claw feet. (Ball & Percival) $560

Victorian copper kettle, circa 1850. (British Antique Exporters) $100

An early 17th century English brass warming pan, dated 1613, 12in. diam., the wood handle a later replacement. $330

A Tibetan gilt copper figure of Buddha, seated in dhyanasana, sealed, 8in. high. (Lawrence Fine Art) $355

Victorian brass jardiniere on paw feet, 1880. (British Antique Exporters) $85

An 18th century Dutch brass wine cooler on stand. (Phillips) $6,800

A circular embossed brass double ended box, 1.7/8in. diam., with bust of Duke of Wellington on one side. (Wallis & Wallis) $40

A 17th century brass candlestick engraved 'For the use of ye Company of Joyners and Carpenters', dated 1690, 9in. high. (Gorringes) $10,000

Late 19th century Art Nouveau style brass coal box. (British Antique Exporters) $125

Victorian pressed brass bellows, circa 1880. (British Antique Exporters) $50

A pair of Federal late 18th/ early 19th century bell metal andirons, 24in. high. (Christie's) $1,835

An early 20th century Arts & Crafts hammered copper umbrella stand, 25in. high. (Robt. W. Skinner Inc.) $555

An oval brass planter with gadroon embossed decoration, 13in. high. (Peter Wilson) $300

A William and Mary brass table candlestand with a pair of scroll arms, 8in. wide. $2,500

Early 19th century copper coal helmet, also a matching shovel, 17½in. high. (Peter Wilson) $600

Mid 19th century copper jelly mold with fluted column decoration, 6in. diam. (Peter Wilson) $220

Pair of mid 18th century brass table candlesticks, probably French, 7¼in. high. $770

A Robin Banks enamelled copper charger, RB monogram 1986, 39.4cm. diam. (Christie's) $300

An 18th century Spanish brass flagon, 8.5in. high. (Woolley & Wallis) $400

Benedict Art Studios hammered copper wall plaque, N.Y., circa 1907, 15in. diam. (Robt. W. Skinner Inc.) $800

Gustav Stickley hammered copper umbrella holder, circa 1905, no. 273, 27¼in. high. (Robt. W. Skinner Inc.) $700

CORKSCREWS

Most of the corkscrews, or bottle screws, we see around today, date from the middle of the 19th century. Earlier examples do exist, some going back to the 17th century, but these are extremely rare.

The earliest examples were made of steel and consisted of a simple spiral fixed to a wooden handle. It was only later that more complex designs were introduced with handles made of engraved brass, silver, steel, bone, horn and ivory. The handles were often styled in the shape of animals, birds or some more unusual novelty theme.

The Victorian penchant for new inventions ran riot during the 19th century and hundreds of different corkscrew based devices, in all shapes and sizes, were made; many of them patented. Other devices, such as a bottle dusting brush or any number of other small tools, are often incorporated into the handle. Any corkscrew combined with a gadget will be of interest to a collector and this will be reflected in the selling price.

At one time, the corkscrew was one of the essential tools of day to day living. Even miniature scent bottles were sealed with a cork and the ladies often carried small, intricately designed silver versions for this purpose. Sometimes a Victorian housekeeper would attach a small corkscrew, fitted with a hanging loop to her chatelaine, alongside all the other necessary bits and pieces. (The chatelaine being an ornamental bunch of short chains bearing keys, pencil, scissors etc., which is then attached to the belt at the waist. A similar version, in miniature, could be attached to a gentleman's watch chain and, again, a miniature corkscrew was a popular item.)

There was, at one time, a very pleasing custom for a house guest, upon writing to thank his host, to include the gift of a corkscrew, perhaps with some words of praise engraved on the handle.

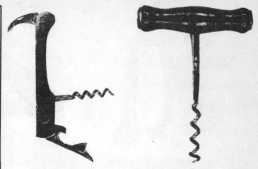

Waiter's Friend stamped 'Hebel' and Made in Germany, 4½in. long. $28

A corkscrew with turned oak crossbar, steel shank and helical worm, circa 1870, 4¼in. long. $10

Combination pocket penknife and corkscrew by John Watts of Sheffield, 3½in. long. $55

A plated champagne tap with integral pointed end above which are the holes for drawing the champagne through, tap 5in. long. $115

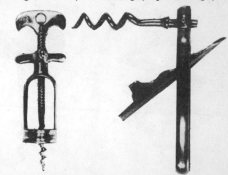

Early 20th century French polished steel corkscrew, the open barrel with perfect bladed worm with point, 6in. overall length. $115

A pocket corkscrew made of steel, stamped Universal Pat. June 27, 05 (1905), 5½in. long open. $350

A nickel plated bar corkscrew 'Original Safety', manufactured by Gaskell & Chambers, 10in. high. $250

Waiter's friend corkscrew with fluted worm and blade inscribed 'John Watts, Sheffield', 3¼in. long. $55

Pocket folding bow corkscrew in steel, circa 1880, 3in. long closed. $40

A corkscrew with dusting brush and suspension ring, the baluster turned brass stem terminating in a small Henshall type brass button, circa 1810, 6in. high. $135

Clough type of pocket corkscrew with wooden sheath printed with advertisement for Cowbroughs Nourishing Ale for Invalids, made in U.S., 4in. long. $55

A double action corkscrew of the Thomason's 1802 type with brass barrel, turned bone handle and dusting brush, 9in. long extended. $490

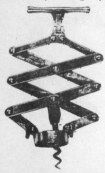

An all-steel concertina type corkscrew stamped 'Ideal Perfect' and 'Brevete & Depose', length 9¾ x 4¼in. closed. $250

A 19th century corkscrew/ Codd bottle opener with plain steel shank and turned ashwood handle, circa 1875, 4½in. long. $150

A narrow rack King's Screw corkscrew by Thos. Lund, with perfect turned rosewood crossbar complete with dusting brush inner thread, 7¼in. long closed. $1,000

COSTUME

Period costume has always held a fascination for collectors so it comes as no surprise when a garment one or two hundred years old fetches a high price.

The current trend, however, shows some astonishing prices paid for clothes from as recent a period as the 1950's.

Elegant dresses of the 20's, 30's and 40's are eagerly sought after by the fashion conscious to be worn today and, all but the rare and flimsy, are likely to be in wearable condition. From the 1900's onward fashionable women were known to change their clothes up to four times a day leaving us the legacy of a multitude of garments showing scant signs of real wear. The named labels to look for are Dior, Cheruit, Chanel, Nini Ricci and Fortuny 'Delphos'.

Clothes that once belonged to well known personalities fall into a category of their own and fetch the high prices of a specialized market.

A Dragon robe, the black gauze ground embroidered with coiling dragons. (Reeds Rains) $1,240

A boy's side fastening tunic of white pique embroidered in red cord with scrolling flowers. (Christie's) $280

Boned and laced corset in pink cotton with lace trim, French, 1880's. $90

A muslin dress with an underdress of saxe blue silk taffeta, circa 1880. (Christie's) $600

A pair of white kid gloves with deep cuffs of white satin embroidered in silver thread and sequins, mid 17th century. (Christie's) $5,200

A lady's waistcoat of white cotton quilted in white silk and embroidered in yellow and red wools, English, circa 1730. (Christie's) $5,600

Fold-over shawl with black silk center, borders woven in fine wool and silk and sewn on by hand, Paisley or Norwich, 1830's, 4ft.6in. x 4ft.8in. $260

A Japanese cotton indigo-dyed double-ikat kimono, 20th century. $110

A mid Victorian orange and purple flowered cream silk dress with boned bodice and slight train. (Dacre, Son & Hartley) $340

A suit of rust-colored wool with deep cuffs and wide skirts, circa 1760. (Christie's) $10,000

A dress of ivory satin printed in vertical bands of gray fleck design and a larger pink and gray chine design, circa 1834. (Christie's) $2,400

A fine full length evening mantle of gray facecloth, by Rouff, 13 Boulevard Hausmann, Paris, 1900. (Christie's) $220

Militia great coat with attached cape, coarse blue wool, Massa., circa 1855. (Robt. W. Skinner Inc.) $1,060

A dress of pale pink silk figured with sprays of flowers, the sleeves, bodice and hem decorated with pink satin rouleaux, circa 1815. (Christie's) $760

A jacket and skirt of maroon figured silk brocaded with white stripes sprigged in pink and blue, circa 1770. (Christie's) $5,200

A cotton dress printed with sprigs of brown leaves, with a handkerchief front, circa 1810. (Christie's) $760

A dress of ivory silk woven with satin stripes, the bodice trimmed with ivory satin and with blond lace, lined with silk, circa 1830. (Christie's) $2,800

A sleeved waistcoat of emerald green figured, voided silk, woven with sprays of flower heads, English, circa 1730. (Christie's) $1,800

A gentleman's suit of voided velvet woven with pink and black sprigs against a pale blue silk ground, French, circa 1790, together with a waistcoat, circa 1770. (Christie's) $560

A 1920's flamingo pink ostrich feather cape and fan, fan 110cm. wide, 70cm. tall. (Chelsea Auction Galleries) $360

Shawl of silk and wool with pattern woven in orange, red, yellow, green and brown on cream ground, Norwich, circa 1840's, 4ft.6in. x 4ft.9in. $240

An open robe of pale yellow silk luster, the neckline edged with 18th century Binche lace. (Christie's) $3,600

A gentleman's suit of deep blue satin, French, Lyons, circa 1770. (Christie's) $6,000

An open robe of cotton printed overall with red and blue convolvulus with red stems against a gray ground, circa 1785. (Christie's) $4,400

CRESTED CHINA

The value of crested china may be determined by three factors: theme, rarity and condition in that order. The most popular themes are: The Great War, Buildings; Animals (including birds); Transport; Memorials; Statues, Cartoon/Comedy Characters; Comic/Novelty; Sport; Alcohol and Musical Instruments. This list is by no means exhaustive but it does cover the main spheres of interest among collectors. Rarity is self-explanatory; a 'Bomb Thrower' is rarer than a 'Cenotaph' and therefore is worth more. These two factors may be summed up as 'Collectibility', for example a scarce animal would be worth far more than, say, a unique billiken because there is far more demand for the animal from theme collectors. Thus supply and demand play an important part. It should always be borne in mind that even the most attractive and rare crested cup and saucer will never be worth more than a few dollars whereas a rare military piece could command as much as $200.

Condition is the third factor which affects price. Crested china produced by other manufacturers was never as fine as that of the Goss factory. The other producers were not interested in the high standard that Goss set himself, they were only concerned with jumping on the crested china bandwagon and producing wares as quickly and as cheaply as possible for the profitable souvenir trade which was rapidly developing.

Having made the point that crested china factories were not that particular about the quality of their products it follows that many pieces were substandard even before leaving the factory. Such manufacturers' imperfections do not affect value, however, damage occurring in the period subsequent to manufacture such as cracks or chips affect value considerably.

Model of a **Tank** by Arcadian China. $30

Model of the '**Forth Bridge**' by Carlton China, 166mm. long. $75

Children Playing in the Sand, by Grafton China. $100

Donkey, by Arcadian China. $50

Model of a **Lifeboatman** by Arcadian China, 85mm. high. $20

Grenade with flames at top by Aynsley China, 88mm. high. $40

Figure of **Lady Godiva** by Arcadian China, 75mm. high. $60

'**Mary Queen of Scots Bed**', by Carlton, 90mm. long, a superbly modeled historical piece. (Goss & Crested China) $120

Grafton China, '**The Bomb Thrower**', 140mm. high. (Goss & Crested China) $220

Willow Art cartoon character couple sitting in armchair, '**Dr. Beetle and Sunny Jim**'. (Goss & Crested China) $100

The '**Biddenden Maids**', a 12th century pair of Siamese twins. (Goss & Crested China) $80

Carlton '**John Citizen**', carrying sack of 'Housing', 'Unemployment' and 'Taxes' problems. (Goss & Crested China) $140

Carlton child riding donkey, on oval base, can be found inscribed '**This beats going to school**'. (Goss & Crested China) $60

Crime and detection are endlessly fascinating, appealing to the intellect in the details of the detecting and to rather baser instincts as they inspire shock and horror. In the nineteenth century magazines detailing true crimes such as Famous Crimes and the Police gazette sold readily and continued through the Edwardian era to be replaced by the 'pulp' magazines such as 'Mystery Novels', 'Candid Detective' etc.

These magazines from the 1920's and 1930's are of two types, the purely fictional and the supposed accounts of true crimes. The fictional tales were generally illustrated with line drawings but the true crime magazines such as Famous Crime Cases were illustrated with horrifying photographs of bodies, weapons and murderers in chains. Less sensational were the many digest-sized magazines such as London Mystery and Ellery Queen's which specialised in traditional tales of detection without the shock and horror sensationalism of the 'pulps'.

In America cover art is collected particularly these magazines depicting bondage situations. There are also specialist collectors of magazines featuring Mickey Spillane and Hank Janson.

Stories or factual articles on drug abuse or drug trafficking also have their followers and magazines featuring such copy will often sell for double the normal price.

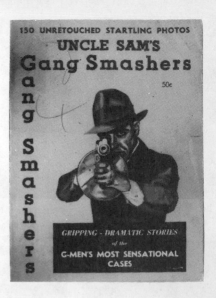

Uncle Sam's Gang Smashers, 1937. $30

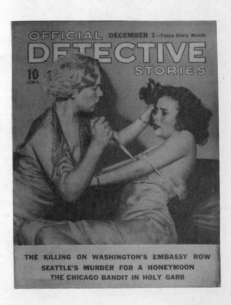

Official Detective Stories, Dec. 1936. $13

20th Century Crime Cases,
Oct. 1946. $6

Suspense, Mystery, Adven-
ture, Crime, Sept. 1958. $2

Famous Crime Cases,
Every Story True, June
1945. $6

Smashing Detective Stories
Sept. 1953. $4

Underworld, Edited by Hank
Janson, Vol. 1 No. 2. $6

Super Detective, No. 4,
1950. $6

10 True Crime Cases,
April 1949. $4

Manhunt, Detective Story
Monthly, Sept. 1953. $2

Greatest Detective Cases,
Dec. 1944. $8

Gangster Women, Larceny In Her Soul, Oct. 1946.   **$6**

Ellery Queen's Mystery Magazine, May 1953. **$2**

Startling Crime Cases, Every Story True, Sept. 1950.   **$4**

Mystery Novels Magazine, May 1935.   **$12**

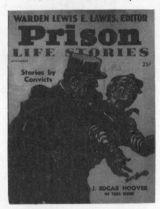

Prison Life Stories, Dec. 1935, Vol. 1 No. 3. **$25**

Candid Detective, Nov. 1938, Vol. 1 No. 1. **$30**

Gripping Detective Cases, Nov. 1946.   **$4**

London Mystery Selection, Sept. 1959.   **$2**

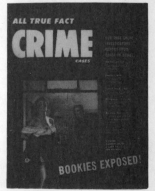

All True Fact Crime Cases Oct. 1952.   **$4**

CURTAINS

To the untrained eye, a bundle of old curtains in a corner of the attic is precisely that, and no more. If you are having a clear out, and have established that they are the wrong size for the sitting room, wouldn't fit in the back bedroom, then for goodness sake, if they look a bit speculative don't throw them out. Old textiles can be worth money.

A length of fabric designed by, for example, Morris & Co., would be quite a rare find. In 1861, William Morris, along with other well-known painters, an architect and an engineer, set up this company whose aims were, to produce decorative articles of the very finest quality, for 'the people'. His designs, taken from plant and animal forms, are extremely attractive and still very popular today.

The company provided, in today's terms, a complete house furnishing service, supplying everything that could possibly be required within a household, from a stained glass window to a set of teaspoons.

William Morris designed textile in 'peacock and dragon' pattern, circa 1878, 89 x 63in. (Robt. W. Skinner Inc.) $800

One of a set of four Jacobean crewel-work bed hangings, embroidered in colored wools, 3ft.1in. wide. (Lawrence Fine Art) $4,750

One of a pair of printed plush curtains, 1890's, 130cm. wide. $770

One of a set of three wool and silk Templeton's curtains, designed by Bruce Talbert, circa 1880, together with two pelmets. $4,750

A Morris & Co. printed cotton double-sided curtain, selvedge with printed Oxford St. mark, 1891, 181.5cm. wide. $700

One of a pair of Morris & Co. wool curtains and matching pelmet, designed by Wm. Morris, 1880's, 'Bird' pattern, 250 x 240cm. $5,500

DE MORGAN

Towards the end of the 19th century many European potters were experimenting with the old Italian and Islamic methods of painting pottery with metallic luster

William De Morgan the English ceramic designer, was one of the first to achieve success in this field and his work has a distinctive and rare quality.

Throughout his working life he teamed up with other well known artists such as William Morris, Joe Juster, Halsey Ricardo and Frederick and Charles Passenger to produce vases, tiles and dishes.

His first pottery workshop was at Chelsea, his second at Merton Abbey near London and the third, which closed down in 1907, was at Fulham. His early tiles are unmarked but subsequent marks from Merton Abbey 1882-1888, show W. De Merton Abbey, with a sketched abbey within a rectangle. Marks from the Fulham factory include, DM over a tulip and William De Morgan & Co., Sands End Pottery, Fulham.

A De Morgan luster vase, decorated by Fred Passenger, 1890's, 32.6cm. high. $1,300

A William de Morgan wall plate designed by Chas. Passenger, 47cm. diam. (Christie's) $2,500

A De Morgan luster vase, decorated by James Hersey, impressed Sand's End mark, painted initials and numbered 2227, 21.1cm. high, 1888-97. $500

A De Morgan charger, decorated by Chas. Passenger, 1890's, 41.5cm. diam. $10,000

A De Morgan vase decorated in shades of mauve, green, blue and turquoise with panels of flowers, 1890's, 15.6cm. high. $450

A De Morgan plate, decorated by F. Farini, 1890, 22.8cm. diam. $750

DECANTER LABELS

Decanter labels have always struck me as very worthwhile articles to collect, for not only are they small and reasonably plentiful, but there are also rare examples worth hundreds of dollars which add spice to the search. They are made in a variety of materials, including silver, enamel, porcelain and Sheffield plate and come in a variety of shapes including oval, shield and rectangular.

Dating from about 1730, they were used in wealthier homes to identify the contents of the opaque bottles of the period, while lesser mortals made do with stuck-on handwritten parchment labels.

Most were individually made until the Victorian period, when mass production took over, but their real demise followed the Grocers' Licences Act of 1860, which allowed wine to be sold in single bottles, provided a paper label indicated their contents.

There are, of course, numerous modern die-stamped reproduction labels to be found, but these are fairly easily distinguishable from the heavier original examples.

A more watchful eye is necessary, however, to spot old labels (usually Madeira) renamed with more saleable titles like brandy or whisky. This practice is indicated by very thin metal on the face, and sometimes old lettering may even be revealed by huffing on the surface.

The rarest labels are those made of Battersea enamel (and I mean Battersea enamel made from 1753 to 1756, not the many other forms of enamel which have attracted the name). The originals are usually quite large, about 7.5cm. across, with a wavy outline, and could be worth hundreds of dollars.

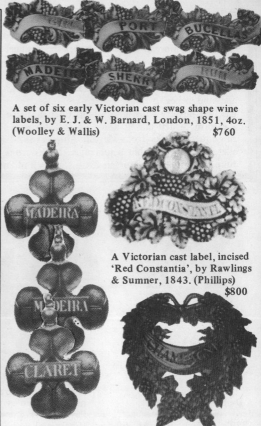

A set of six early Victorian cast swag shape wine labels, by E. J. & W. Barnard, London, 1851, 4oz. (Woolley & Wallis) $760

A Victorian cast label, incised 'Red Constantia', by Rawlings & Sumner, 1843. (Phillips) $800

A set of three George III cast four-leaf clover wine labels, probably by B. Smith, London, 1807. (Christie's) $600

One of three silver gilt wine labels for Champagne, Port and Claret, by B. Smith, 1808, 3in. high, 7oz.5dwt. (Christie's) $4,970

A Victorian stamped-out hunting horn wine label, incised 'Port', by G. Unite, Birmingham, 1857. (Phillips) $600

A George III cast scallop shield wine label, 'Sherry', by Wm. Eley, 1814. (Phillips) $580

DECANTERS

Over the years decanters have changed shape in accordance with styles and a good representative collection will include as many different shapes as possible. The best known are ships' decanters — or Rodneys, mallet shaped decanters, taper decanters perhaps in blue or green, and square decanters — shaped to fit into decanter boxes for fortification during the days of coach travel.

These boxes became less popular when the tantalus with its locking frame system was introduced in the mid 19th century. The tantalus, a case in which decanters are visible but locked up, takes its name from Tantalus, the son of Zeus who, as a punishment, was made to stand in water that ebbed when he would drink, overhung by grapes that drew back when he reached for them!

One of a pair of cut glass decanters and stoppers of club shape, circa 1820. (Christie's) $865

A Galle enameled glass bottle of flattened flask shape with stopper, 30.25cm. high. $660

A green baluster decanter with lozenge stopper, 9½in. high. (Christie's) $320

A 'Lynn' decanter of mallet shape, the body lightly molded with horizontal ribs, circa 1775, 23cm. high. (Christie's) $1,000

A Hukin & Heath 'Crow's foot' decanter, designed by Dr. C. Dresser, electroplate and glass, with registration lozenge for 1879, 24cm. high. (Christie's) $12,500

A Guild of Handicraft hammered silver and green glass decanter, the design attributed to C. R. Ashbee, with London hallmarks for 1903, 22.5cm. high. (Christie's) $2,500

DECOYS

The ancient hunter in search of food, practised decoying by imitating the sounds that animals make. Then, observing that a bird feeding or swimming on a pond represented safety to other birds, he fashioned the decoy.

The first decoys were of primitive style, fashioned from mud and reeds but now decoy making has become the art of professionals.

Decoys are mainly used on estuaries and ponds. They are made of wood and painted in traditional colors with flat paint. They are generally larger than life size; sometimes by half the natural size, sometimes twice as large, for out on the rough water, the larger decoys are spotted sooner.

Decoys of many species may be found. The gulls and crows were often placed on the banks near to where the duck decoy was tethered in order to improve the setting.

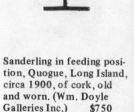

A life size carved and painted black duck, Birchler, circa 1925, full length 18in., 19in. high. (Robt. W. Skinner Inc.) $3,650

Two late 19th century painted wooden decoys, one 10in. long, the other 11½in. long. (Christie's) $440

Sanderling in feeding position, Quogue, Long Island, circa 1900, of cork, old and worn. (Wm. Doyle Galleries Inc.) $750

Black-bellied plover with applied wings from South Jersey, bill replaced. (Wm. Doyle Galleries Inc.) $700

A painted cedar hen canvasback decoy, made by L. T. Ward Bros, 1936, 15in. long. (Christie's) $5,310

Black-bellied plover in feeding position. (Wm. Doyle Galleries Inc.) $200

A painted wooden oversized Golden Eye decoy, by 'Gus' Aaron Wilson, circa 1880/1920, 20in. long.(Christie's) $2,425

Black-bellied plover by A. Elmer Crowell, E. Harwich, Mass., full sized, original paint. (Wm. Doyle Galleries Inc.) $12,000

A Canada goose decoy, by George Boyd, early 20th century, 29in. long. (Christie's) $2,425

American bittern from New England, decorative. (Wm. Doyle Galleries Inc.) $400

A pair of painted wooden American merganser decoys, a hen and drake, by L. T. Holmes, circa 1855/65. (Christie's) $93,500

Sandpiper, factory made, original paint and stick. (Wm. Doyle Galleries Inc.) $270

A painted wooden primitive brant decoy, three-piece laminated construction, 18in. long. (Christie's) $335

A painted wooden Maine flying scoter decoy, by 'Gus' Aaron Wilson, circa 1880/1920, together with two black-painted wooden duck decoys. (Christie's) $6,275

A painted wooden hollow constructed Canada goose decoy, by Chas. H. Hart, Mass., circa 1890/1915, 20½in. long. (Christie's) $4,400

DEDHAM POTTERY

With the failure of the Chelsea Keramic Art Works in 1891 a consortium of Boston businessmen reformed the company as Chelsea Pottery under the management of Hugh Robertson. After problems with the kilns however, the company moved to Dedham, Massachusetts and were again reformed under the name Dedham Pottery.

At first they produced only plates decorated with either rabbits, dolphins or elephants but later progressed to vases and general tableware under the direction of William Robertson who succeeded his father Hugh in 1908.

The factory is mainly known for its crackle glaze finish and traded successfully until ceasing production in 1943.

Early 20th century Dedham pottery plate with Fairbanks house, 8½in. diam. $3,500

Early 20th century Dedham pottery turkey trivet, 6in. diam. $660

A Dedham pottery elephant charger, Mass., circa 1929, 12in. diam. $1,500

Late 19th century Dedham pottery experimental drip vase, 6¼in. high. $800

Early 20th century Dedham pottery plate, stamped and dated 1931, 8¾in. diam. $2,500

Late 19th century Dedham pottery vase with oxblood and black glaze, 7¼in. high. $2,000

DENTAL INSTRUMENTS

The first statutory law relating to dentistry was an Act passed in 1579 which, although forbidding barbers to act as surgeons, did allow them to continue to draw teeth!
These were tough times. The traveling 'dentist' trudged around from town to town lugging a bag of very primitive implements and performing dentistry, of a sort, on patients anesthetized by gin. It was not unknown for the dentist to anesthetize himself from time to time.
Times change however, and with the development of effective and hygienic dentistry came an improved technology applied to instruments and equipment.
Everything from a simple probe to a massive cast iron, adjustable dentist's chair will be included in this fascinating category and most of the equipment collected today is precision made and of the finest quality.

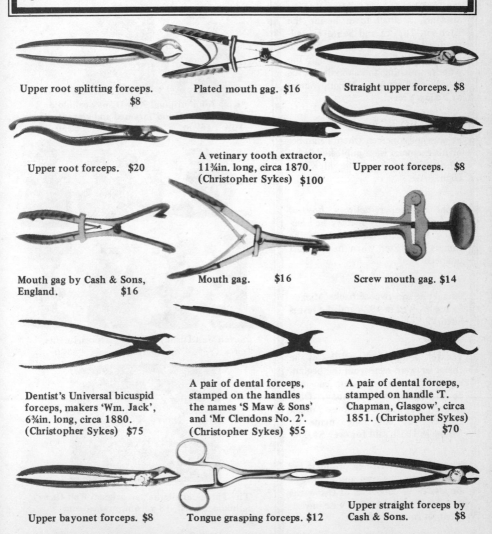

Upper root splitting forceps. $8

Plated mouth gag. $16

Straight upper forceps. $8

Upper root forceps. $20

A vetinary tooth extractor, 11¾in. long, circa 1870. (Christopher Sykes) $100

Upper root forceps. $8

Mouth gag by Cash & Sons, England. $16

Mouth gag. $16

Screw mouth gag. $14

Dentist's Universal bicuspid forceps, makers 'Wm. Jack', 6¾in. long, circa 1880. (Christopher Sykes) $75

A pair of dental forceps, stamped on the handles the names 'S Maw & Sons' and 'Mr Clendons No. 2'. (Christopher Sykes) $55

A pair of dental forceps, stamped on handle 'T. Chapman, Glasgow', circa 1851. (Christopher Sykes) $70

Upper bayonet forceps. $8

Tongue grasping forceps. $12

Upper straight forceps by Cash & Sons. $8

DISNEYANA

Few people would argue the point that the fourth son of Elias and Flora Disney, born on Sunday, December 5th 1901, at 1249 Tripp Avenue, Chicago, has made the greatest contribution to the world of fun and laughter.

His formative years were spent on the family farm at Marceline in Missouri, a small town beside the Atchison Topeka and Sante Fe railroad, where on hot summer days he would walk for miles through the woods, watching the animals, on his way to cool off in the languid waters of Yellow Creek.

Success on a small scale came when he was just nineteen when a number of his cartoons were published in his school magazine at the McKinley High.

From newspaper delivery boy to handyman at a jelly factory he eventually became a cartoonist on the Kansas City Star when he was just nineteen.

After one or two setbacks Mickey Mouse evolved in 1928 and the rest is history.

The full commercial qualities of the character were seen from the beginning and toys from this era can now be worth amazing money. Only recently a Mickey Mouse organ grinder, just 6in. long, made by Distler in 1930, sold for over $4,000.

The market for Disney products has always been universal and enthusiastic and eager collectors of Disneyana can be confident of a wise investment set for a rosy future.

Unusual tinplate and composition Minnie Mouse and pram, probably by Wells, 7½in. long, circa 1933. $2,000

'King John' original Walt Disney celluloid from 'Robin Hood', framed and glazed, 13¼ x 16½in. $250

Seven Walt Disney opaque glass ornaments, circa 1935, 4½in. to 7in. $800

'The Three Caballeros', an original Walt Disney celluloid, signed, 18 x 16in., framed and glazed. $3,000

'Jiminy Cricket', original Walt Disney celluloid, framed and glazed, 16¼ x 17½in. $650

Back and front of German tinplate Mickey Mouse mechanical bank, circa 1930, 6¾in. high. $500

Pinocchio doll, with clockwork movement within the articulated legs, circa 1942, 7½in. high. $450

The Mickey Mouse Fire Brigade, 1936. $70

Pinocchio doll by Ideal Novelty & Toy Co., 7¼in., circa 1945. $400

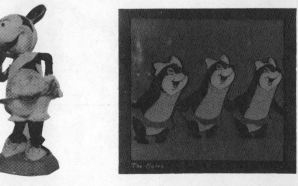

American Mickey and Minnie Mouse, plaster painted models, 9in. high, circa 1945. $200

'The Moles', a celluloid taken from 'Song of the South', framed and glazed, 12¼ x 10½in. $150

One of two original hand paintings on celluloid, from the Walt Disney film Snow White and the Seven Dwarfs, 6½ x 9½in. (Christie's) $1,300

Alarm clock, clockface depicting the Three Little Pigs, circa 1935, 6in. high. $300

Lead model Mickey and Minnie Mouse barrel organ group. (Hobbs & Chambers) $80

Mickey Mouse, stuffed toy by Dean's Rag Book Ltd., circa 1930, 6¼in. high. $350

Walt Disney's Pinocchio, 1940. $25

'Minnie Mouse', stuffed toy by Dean's Rag Book Ltd., circa 1930, 7in. high. $200

'Felix the Cat', large plush-covered toy with cloth bow tie, 28½in. high, circa 1930. $1,500

Four Disney stuffed figures, comprising a velveteen Mickey Mouse and Pluto; two corduroy 'Widgets', late 1930's-40's. (Christie's) $575

Glazed earthenware musical jug depicting the 'Three Little Pigs', circa 1935, 10in. high. $300

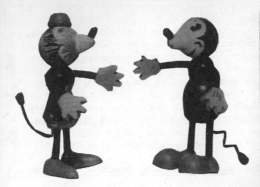

American Mickey and Minnie Mouse, two Fune-Flex painted wooden toys, circa 1931, 6¾in. high. $300

Walt Disney's 'Alice in Wonderland' Punch-Out Book, 1955. $25

Walt Disney rug in tufted cotton, showing characters from his films, 1950's, 104 x 70in. $600

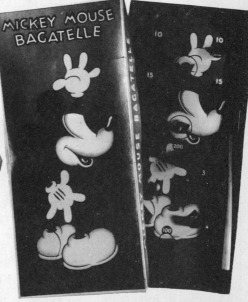

'The Three Caballeros', three plaster figures of Disney characters, circa 1950. $200

Mickey Mouse Bagatelle by Chad Valley Co. Ltd. $60

DOLLS

From the 17th to the early 19th century, ownership of fine looking dolls expensively dressed in silks was generally the prerogative of fashionable society ladies. Some even had two; one clad in the latest haute couture while the other sported a risque negligee. Most children, on the other hand, had to be content to play with dolls made of simply painted wood or rags, very few of which have managed to survive all the loving care lavished upon them.

It wasn't until the mass production methods of the Victorian age that young girls were provided with something a little more lifelike, with bisque china head and limbs and hair that you really could comb. No doubt their popularity was partly brought about by Queen Victoria, who was an avid collector of dolls, dressing many of them herself.

A bisque headed doll with composition body, marked Porzellan Fabrik Burggrub Daslachende Baby, 1930/3/ Made in Germany DRGM, 18in. high. (Dacre, Son & Hartley) $750

A Scottish boy doll in Highland dress, with bisque head, in original box marked 'Kelly Boy 306', 12in. high. (Lawrence Fine Art) $220

A bisque headed autoperipatetikos doll with painted blue eyes and brown kid arms, 10in. high. (Christie's) $300

Early 20th century German character doll by Kathe Kruse, 17in. high. (Bermondsey) $500

A William and Mary wooden doll with a wisp of real auburn hair and nailed-on stitched linen wig, English, circa 1690, 16¾in. high. $30,000

A bisque headed bebe with papier mache jointed body, marked 12 by Steiner, 29in. high. (Christie's) $4,000

168

A jointed wooden doll with painted features and real blond hair wig, circa 1845. (Christie's) $400

A bisque headed clockwork walking, talking bebe petit pas, marked BRU Jne R 11, 24in. high. (Christie's) $4,000

A bisque headed doll with jointed composition body, marked Armand Marseille, Germany A9M, 24in. high. (Dacre, Son & Hartley) $380

An American 'Shirley Temple' personality doll, 21in. high, circa 1935. (Bermondsey) $800

A bisque headed child doll, marked SFBJ Paris 14, 32in. high, original box marked Bebe Francais. (Christie's) $1,400

A Bru Teteur bisque doll, French, circa 1875, 19in. high. (Lawrence Fine Art) $7,500

An English mid 19th century vendor doll of wood and cloth, under glass dome with turned walnut base, 16in. high. (Robt. W. Skinner Inc.) $3,500

A bisque two-faced doll with original blonde wig and with jointed composition body, 11in. high. (Christie's) $1,400

A Franz Schmidt bebe doll with sleeping brown eyes, open mouth and composition body, 9in. high. (Hobbs & Chambers) $250

A bisque headed character child doll with blue sleeping eyes, marked K*R SH115/A 42, 16½in. high. (Christie's) **$3,750**

A cloth doll painted in oils with gray eyes and blonde painted short hair, 23in. high. (Christie's) **$900**

A painted wooden Grodenthal type doll with gray curls, circa 1835, 12½in. high. (Christie's) **$1,100**

A painted felt doll modeled as a young girl, marked on the feet Lenci, 25in. high. (Christie's) **$340**

An early 19th century group of painted wooden headed dolls, 'There was an old woman who lived in a shoe', 5in. long. (Dacre, Son & Hartley) **$240**

Late 19th century German bisque headed novelty doll, 13in. high. (Bermondsey) **$500**

A fine German character doll by Kestner, with original clothes, 13in. high, circa 1915. (Bermondsey) **$2,500**

A bisque headed character baby doll with open closed mouth, marked 211 J.D.K., 17in. high. (Christie's) **$650**

A painted cloth doll with brown painted hair, the stuffed body jointed at hip and shoulder, by Kathe Kruse, 17in. high. (Christie's) **$600**

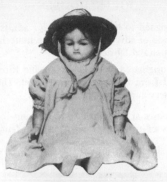

A china doll of an Irish gentleman, with gusseted kid body and china lower limbs, 13in. high. (Lawrence Fine Art) $240

A poured-wax child doll with fixed pale blue eyes, 20in. high, in box. (Christie's) $600

A Jumeau bisque doll, French, circa 1880, 15in. high. (Lawrence Fine Art)

$2,500

A bisque headed doll with moving eyes, marked on head A.M. 4DEP, Made in Germany, 19in. high. (Dacre, Son & Hartley) $360

A clockwork toy of a bisque headed doll pulling a two-wheeled cart, marked 1079. Halbig S & H 7½, by Toullet Deeamps. (Christie's)

$900

A bisque headed bebe with five upper teeth, fixed brown eyes and pierced ears, 18½in. high. (Christie's) $1,300

A bisque headed doll with tinted complexion and kid covered body, 21in. high. (Dacre, Son & Hartley) $500

A Dep Tete Jumeau bisque headed doll, impressed DEP 8, with jointed wood and composition body, 19in. high. (Lawrence Fine Art) $700

A George II wooden doll with blonde real hair nailed-on wig, English, circa 1750, 16in. high. $20,000

DOLLS' HOUSES

Early 'baby houses' were designed to be a plaything for adults. They were furnished with precious miniature pieces made of silver and other fine materials. Many contain examples of early hand blocked wallpaper and fabrics.

They were thought to have originated from Germany and kitchens complete with all the utensils were being exported from there as early as 1660. The dolls' house, as a toy for children, was kept in the nursery and furnished for play.

A catalogue of the Dolls' Houses at Bethnal Green Museum in London, illustrates houses from 1673 to 1921 and offers an invaluable insight into contemporary life of the times.

The outside of some houses also give a good idea of the lifestyle with carriages, carts and trains set in the landscape.

Large doll's house in the form of a two-storey suburban house, English, circa 1930, 45in. high. $1,000

19th century wooden Mansard roof doll's house with painted brick front, 23¾in. high. $400

Early 20th century American wooden gabled roof doll's house with glass windows, 24¾in. high $600

A wooden doll's house painted to simulate stonework of five bays and three storeys, 46in. wide. $7,600

A custom crafted Colonial-style doll's house, circa 1980, with ten rooms of furniture, 28in. high. $2,400

American diorama of an early 19th century hallway, made circa 1950, fitted with dolls and furniture, 19½in. wide. $300

DOORSTOPS

Such is the multitude in variety and composition of door stops, particularly from the 19th century, that one is left to wonder why the Victorians were so keen to keep all their doors ajar.

Due to their function, they are usually heavy and made of cast iron, lead or brass in many forms such as animals, fruit, flowers, fish or in representations of famous people of the day; Wellington, Albert or Victoria. Even Jumbo the notable elephant from London Zoo was immortalized after he was transported to the famous Barnum & Bailey's Circus where he met his untimely death trying to charge a steam train.

Doorstops are also found made of green glass in the shape of a beehive or of Nailsea glass from Bristol with air bubble decoration.

Victorian brass dog door stopper, 9in. high. $50

'Lion-Tamer' cast iron doorstop, 10in. high, circa 1850. $160

Heavy cast iron door stop of a zebra, circa 1820, 10½in. long, 8in. high. $80

Napoleon and Princess Eugenie cast iron door stop, 12in. high. $120

19th century cast iron Toby figure, 14in. high. $465

A 19th century brass dolphin door stopper. $95

A solid cast brass standing plaque, stamped on back 'Crowley & Co., Manchester', circa 1860, 9in. long, 7in. high. $40

Victorian cast iron door stop of a Highlander, 9in. high. $50

Victorian cast iron door stop of a horse, on a stepped base, 11¼in. long, 10in. high. $80

DOULTON

So prolific and varied was the output of the Doulton factory in the late 19th century that most households could boast an example of their work, be it a utilitarian piece of stoneware in the bathroom or a fine pair of vases well able to grace any mantelpiece.

Of particular interest, and value, are the works of Hannah Barlow and her sister Florence whose forte was drawing animals and birds freehand onto the wet clay on a wide variety of wares. Musicians and chessmen in the form of mice and frog cricketers by George Tinworth are also well worth looking for.

The most interest recently however, has centered on the Doulton character jugs produced from the 30's to the present day. Find one depicting Sir Francis Drake without a hat and we're talking $3,000 plus, a clown with red triangles on his cheeks is near to $2,000, but the real jewel in the crown is a jug featuring Winston Churchill. Uncolored, apart from two black handles, this little gem, produced in 1940 and withdrawn because Sir Winston didn't approve of the design, is now worth $12,000 plus.

A large character jug modeled as Mephistopheles, D5757, designed by H. Fenton, issued in 1937, withdrawn 1948.

$1,350

A large character jug modeled as Churchill, (white) D6170, designed by C. Noke, issued in 1940, withdrawn 1941.

$12,000

A large character jug modeled as Drake (hatless) D6115, designed by H. Fenton, issued in 1940, withdrawn 1941.

$3,000

A large character jug modeled as Mae West, D6688, designed by C. Davidson, issued in 1983, withdrawn 1985. $100

A large character jug modeled as the Maori, designer unknown, issued circa 1939.
(Pilot issue) $12,000 plus

A large character jug modeled as John Barleycorn, D5327, designed by C. Noke, issued in 1934, withdrawn 1960.

$90

A large character jug modeled as Parson Brown, D5486, designed by C. Noke, issued in 1935, withdrawn 1960. $90

A large character jug modeled as the Gondolier, D6589, designed by D. Biggs, issued in 1964, withdrawn 1969. $300

A large character jug modeled as the Gladiator, D6550, designed by M. Henk, issued in 1961, withdrawn 1967. $405

A large character jug modeled as Jimmy Durante, D6708, designed by D. Biggs, issued in 1985, withdrawn 1986. $100

A large character jug modeled as Old King Cole (yellow crown) D6036, designed by H. Fenton, issued in 1939, withdrawn 1940. $1,200

A large character jug modeled as Robinson Crusoe, D6532, designed by M. Henk, issued in 1960, withdrawn 1983. $45

A large character jug modeled as Ronald Reagan, D6718, designed by E. Griffiths, issued in 1984. $375

A large character jug modeled as a Clown (red-haired) D5610, designed by H. Fenton, issued in 1937, withdrawn 1942. $1,875

A large character jug modeled as the Ugly Duchess, D6599, designed by M. Henk, issued in 1965, withdrawn 1973. $345

'Myfanwy Jones', HN39, designer E. W. Light, issued 1914-1938. $1,500

'Mendicant', HN1365, designer L. Harradine, 8¼in. high, issued 1929-1969. $125

'Prudence', HN1883, designer L. Harradine, issued 1938-1949. $300

'Bo-Peep', (style one) HN1327, designer L. Harradine, 6¾in. high, issued 1929-1938. $600

'Promenade', HN2076, designer M. Davies, issued 1951-1953. $1,200

'One of the Forty', HN665, designer H. Tittensor, issued 1924-1938. $720

'Jovial Monk', HN2144, designer M. Davies, 7¾in. high, issued 1954-1976. $165

'Rhythm', HN1904, designer L. Harradine, 6¾in. high, issued 1939-1949. $450

'Gainsborough Hat', HN705, designer H. Tittensor, issued 1925-1938. $525

'Pirate King', HN2901, designer W. K. Harper, 10in. high, issued 1981-1986. **$135**

'Sonia', HN1692, designer L. Harradine, 6¼in. high, issued 1935-1949. **$410**

'Bather', (style two) HN 773, designer L. Harradine, 7½in. high, issued 1925-1938. **$450**

'Ermine Muff', HN54, designer C. J. Noke, issued 1916-1938. **$675**

'Wandering Minstrel', HN1224, designer L. Harradine, 7in. high, issued 1927-1938 **$1,200**

'Blithe Morning', HN2021, designer L. Harradine, 7¼in. high, issued 1949-1971. **$135**

'Alchemist', HN1259, designer L. Harradine, 11½in. high, issued 1927-1938. **$600**

'Coming Of Spring', HN1723, designer L. Harradine, 12½in. high, issued 1935-1949. **$1,200**

'Aileen', HN1803, designer L. Harradine, 6in. high issued 1937-1949. **$375**

'Carolyn', HN2112, designer L. Harradine, 7in. high, issued 1953-1965.
$180

'Blacksmith of Williamsburg', HN2240, designer M. Davies, 6¾in. high, issued 1960-1983.
$90

'Marianne', HN2074, designer L. Harradine, issued 1951-1953. $330

'Fruit Gathering', HN562, designer L. Harradine, issued 1923-1938. $1,125

'Madonna of the Square', HN2034, designer P. Stabler, issued 1949-1951.
$675

'Centurion', HN2726, designer W. K. Harper, 9¼in. high, issued 1982-1984. $100

'Carmen', (style two) HN2545, designer E. J. Griffiths, 11½in. high, issued 1974-1977. $110

'Butterfly', HN1456, designer L. Harradine, 6½in. high, issued 1931-1938. $600

'Beggar' (style one) HN526, designer L. Harradine, 6½in. high, issued 1921-1949. $300

Toby XX D6088, designer
H. Fenton, 6½in. high,
issued 1939-1969. $105

Squire D6319, designer
H. Fenton, 6in. high, issued
1950-1969. $135

Cliff Cornell (blue suit),
designer unknown, 9¼in.
high, issued 1956 in a
limited edition of 500.
                    $525

Sairey Gamp D6263, small,
by H. Fenton, issued 1948-
1960. $100

Charlie Chaplin, designer
unknown, 11in. high,
issued circa 1918. $6,000

Sam Weller D6265, small,
by H. Fenton, issued 1948-
1960. $100

George Robey, designer
unknown, 10½in. high,
issued circa 1925. $5,250

The Best Is Not Too Good
D6107, designer H. Fenton,
4½in. high, issued 1939-
1960. $60

Old Charley D6030, designer
H. Fenton, 8¾in. high, issued
1939-1960. $80

FAIRINGS

If you had gone to a traveling fair in the 1860s and had proved your prowess on the hoopla stall, chances are that you would have returned home the proud owner of a small china figure bearing a humorous and probably slightly risque legend on the base. These are referred to nowadays as "fairings".

Most are about 4in. high and stand on rectangular bases measuring 2in. by 3in. Subjects include themes like courtship, marriage, politics, war, childhood and animals behaving as people. In all, there are over 400 different types.

With something so typically English as fairings, it comes as a surprise to learn that most were made in Germany, and the two main manufacturers were Springer and Oppenheimer of Elbogen, and Conte and Boehme of Possneck. Of course, it was all a matter of getting down to a price, for the same objects could be bought in the shops for a copper or two, and the German manufacturers had perfected cheap mass production methods without losing on quality.

The manufacturers have obviously borrowed many of their ideas for fairings from such printed materials as sheet music covers. Two, entitled 'Pluck' and 'The Decided Smash' are copies from the cover of a popular song sheet of the time called 'Full Cry Gallop'. In the case of 'Slack' and 'How's Business', these are very good copies of each side of a Staffordshire mug. 'Champagne Charlie is my name' represents George Leybourne making popular the song 'Champagne Charlie' in the 1860s. There are also a few scenes of the Franco-Prussian War which include 'English Neutrality attending the Wounded'.

'Hit Him Hard'. $300–$500

'The Surprise' (Also captioned 'Wet Reception'). $300–$500

'When A Man's Married His Troubles Begin'. $50–$90

'Vy Sarah You're Drunk'.
$90–$150

'The Orphans'. $90–$150

'Shamming Sick'. $150–$200

'English Neutrality 1870/71
Attending The Sick And
Wounded'. $300–$500

'Happy Father. What Two? Yes
Sir. Two Little Beauties'.
$90–$150

'God Save The Queen'.
$150–$200

'Twelve Months After Marriage'.
$30–$50

'All Over'. $500–$1,500

'His First Pair'. $90–$150

FANS

It is known that Elizabeth I had an interesting collection of fans, as did the richest and most sophisticated ladies of that day, but it was not until the eighteenth century that they became more fashionable, less expensive and more plentiful.

Most eighteenth century fans are either delicately hand painted or those referred to as brise fans, which are composed of overlapping sticks radiating from a pivot and joined with ribbon threaded through slots at the top.

Many of the fans seen today date from the 19th century and, as a rule, do not fetch the very highest prices unless they are made from the finest of materials, incorporate precious metal and stones or are connected with the Empress Eugenie, who was partly responsible for their return to fashion in the Victorian era. Fans became such an important fashion feature that no expense was spared in their design and decoration.

Lace fans with mother-of-pearl mounts were popular from about 1860, until the vogue for all things Oriental popularized large silk fans decorated with birds and flowers in the Japanese style. These were followed by sequinned fans of black and white lace, and large Spanish types with ebony sticks.

The fan, originally a simple and effective gadget, was often modified to incorporate functions other than its original cooling system, e.g. a concealed mirror, peep holes, eyeglasses and even a weapon for self defence — a stiletto!

Particularly popular now are those rich plume fans of Art Deco design made during the brief fan revival of 1925-30.

A late 19th century French fan with gilded ivory sticks, 35cm. long. (Phillips) **$600**

Late 19th century silver filigree mounted gold lacquer fan, 39.5cm. high. (Christie's) **$3,675**

Mid 18th century German ivory fan, the leaf painted with the Continence of Scipio in the manner of Pietro da Cortona, 11in. long. **$1,585**

Mid 18th century European framed fan, gouache on skin, on foiled pearl sticks, guard length 11¾in. (Robt. W. Skinner Inc.) **$485**

European 18th century folding fan with pierced and painted ivory sticks, guard length 11.1/8in. (Robt. W. Skinner Inc.) $220

Late 19th century lace fan, fine needle lace on pierced, gilded pearl sticks, guard length 10¾in. (Robt. W. Skinner Inc.) $655

Framed fan, gouache on paper, pearl sticks with multicolor foil floral decoration, France, circa 1880's, guard length 12¾in. (Robt. W. Skinner Inc.) $415

Folding fan, depicting Rebecca at the well, gouache on vellum, circa 1740, guard length 11½in. (Robt. W. Skinner Inc.) $310

19th century Chinese fan with sticks of stained and pierced ivory decoration. $65

Late 19th century framed fan, Louis XVI style, with pearl sticks, guard length 10½in. (Robt. W. Skinner Inc.) $380

French double-sided fan with tortoiseshell guardsticks, circa 1880, 7in. $320

French fan with mother-of-pearl sticks, circa 1760, 7in. $800

Film Fun, September 1923. $15

From its early years to the present day the cinema has had its magazines. In the beginning, and indeed up until the post war period these magazines tended to be of two types. The professional magazine aimed at the distributor or cinema owner who needed to be informed as to what was coming onto the market, and by advertising, persuaded to rent the films for showing. The other type are the most common being addressed to the cinema audience. These range from the straight forward reviews and news of new films such as Picturegoer to magazines such as the American Film Fun which is more concerned with photos of leggy starlets.

Persons with an interest in individual stars collect copies of magazines featuring them or the films they appeared in. Particularly collected are Marilyn Monroe and James Dean and mags featuring them rate about twice the normal price while a magazine with a Monroe cover will fetch up to $10 each.

Also collected are magazines reviewing or featuring Walt Disney movies for the market is universal and enthusiastic and will always command a higher price.

In recent years as the cinema has sought recognition as a legitimate art form a more serious approach is reflected in magazines such as Films and Filming and the French Cahiers du Cinema.

Cinemonde, Grand Format, December 1948 $5

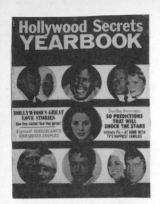

Hollywood Secrets Yearbook, 1968. $2

Fans' Star Library, Marilyn Monroe. $16

Screen Parade, August 1968. $2

The Cinema, 1947. $2

Picturegoer, Annual Awards, March 1952. $1

Picture Show and Film Pictorial, Christmas Edition, 1942. $3

Real Screen Fun, June 1937. $15

The Independent Film Journal, October 1953. $2

Weekly Film News, April 1950. $2

Screen Secrets, 1940's.
$3

Screen Annual, June
Allyson, 1946. $4

**The Anglo-American Film
Book,** 1940's. $4

Almanach Cinemonde,
1949. $6

Film Pictorial, Christmas
Extra, 1935. $8

Motion Picture Magazine,
March 1946. $4

Kinematograph Weekly,
Sept. 1952. $2

Movie Life, February
1938. $5

The Cinema, July 1942.
$2

FINGER PLATES

Of all door fittings, the finger plate offers the greatest scope for decoration and throughout the ages they have reflected fashionable taste and current architectural design.

The early examples were made from solid brass, steel, cut glass or fine quality porcelain and many were very ornate indeed. As a general rule, the earlier, the better the quality.

Around the mid 1920's finger plates came into more common use and there are some fine Art Deco designs made from bakelite, tin or perspex.

It is clearly demonstrated, by price alone, that the colorful enamel advertising finger plates are the most popular of all. These were designed to be affixed to the outside door of the dealer's shop and, some are still to be found on older properties, often under many layers of paint.

There was also a version made for use inside the shop and, wherever appropriate, this incorporated a match striker.

Spratt's Bird Seeds, match striker and plate. $100

Art Nouveau style pressed brass plate. $10

Player's Navy Cut, match striker and plate. $100

Mid 19th century pressed brass plate. $16

Green's Lawn Mower, 'For British People'. $90

French ormolu finger plate, circa 1860. $30

Sunlight Soap, 'Less Labour, Greater Comfort'. $60

Victorian solid brass cupid finger plate. $25

Thomson's Dye Works Perth. $40

Morris's Blue Book Cigarettes, match striker and plate. $150

FIRE IRONS & FENDERS

An open fire burning brightly in the hearth will tend to monopolize attention in any room and a great deal of expense and attention to detail went into the design and production of the focal point — the fireplace.

Catering for the practicalities of keeping a good fire going without razing the house to the ground led to the production of such necessary tools and accessories as Fire dogs, Fire irons and Fenders. These were produced mainly in materials such as brass, steel, wrought iron, cast iron or copper and fashioned in a variety of designs according to the period and fashion of the day.

A typical set of fire irons may include a shovel, brush, tongs, poker and some sets even incorporate bellows. Long handled irons were produced from the mid 19th century and these were displayed either resting on fire dogs or, where provision was made, in specially designed notches agains the fender. The principal function of the fender was to give protection against burning logs and hot coals tumbling from the hearth but the beautiful designs and good quality materials used in their production soon assured that the fender also became an important feature of the room. One of the most impressive examples, introduced to Britain around 1860, is the Club Fender which apart from a practical function offers quite comfortable seating with its broad, upholstered top running the full length of the hearth.

In recent years there has been something of a revival in the popularity of the open fire with resulting demand for all fireplace furnishings and, while the value of examples once on the market is quickly recognized, these are just the type of pieces that get stashed away in the attic when central heating is installed or the old fireplace removed. They are well worth resurrecting.

An early set of steel and brass fire irons, 32in. long, circa 1810. $220

An Edwardian brass companion set, 21in. high. $75

A fine set of Georgian steel fire irons, 32in. long. $290

A heavy set of Victorian brass fire irons, 32in. long. $170

Victorian brass barley twist fire irons, 30in. long. $180

Four-piece Edwardian brass companion set, 30in. high. $170

An ornate Victorian brass fender, 51in. long, circa 1870. $300

Victorian brass fender with scroll ends, 48in. long. $280

Victorian brass rail fender, 40in. long, circa 1870. $330

19th century polished steel fender with copper relief, 36in. long. $250

An early 19th century polished steel fender, 46in. long. $280

A Welsh steel fender, 48in. long, circa 1880. $95

Mid 19th century brass rail fender, 54in. long, circa 1850. $440

A finely pierced early 19th century polished brass fender, circa 1810. $380

A fine quality pierced brass fender, 50in. long, circa 1870. $400

Georgian serpentine-shape steel fender with cast brass embellishments, 60in. long. $590

Victorian brass bobbin fender, 46in. long.
$370

An early Victorian brass fret fender, 66in. long. $750

A copper and brass Art Nouveau style fender, 42in. long. $350

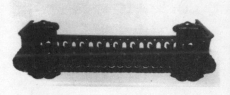

A small Victorian cast iron fender, 24in. long. $120

Brass Art Nouveau style fender, 46in. long.
$250

Deep brass fret fender, 56in. long, circa 1830. $400

FIREMARKS

In Britain, prior to about 1830, those in the unfortunate position of having their 'one up and one down with outside loo' burst into flames would have been at the mercy of the private fire brigades employed by the insurance companies.

If the outside of your house did not display the firemark of the first brigade to arrive, legend has it that their first priority was to sell policies to the neighbors and to blazes with you! It is also rumored that particularly unscrupulous companies sent runners to impede the progress of rival brigades.

The earliest firemarks were of lead, often bearing the policy number, and these are naturally rare, for I assume they melted if a fire occurred. Later firemarks were of copper, tin or zinc and occasionally of terracotta or porcelain.

Liverpool Fire Office, lead, liver bird and torse raised on circular section, 'Liverpool' raised on panel below and impressed with policy no. 426. (Phillips) $1,600

Royal Exchange Assurance, lead, raised Royal Exchange building, policy no. 570 on panel below, issued circa 1721. (Phillips) $6,350

Hercules Fire Insurance, cast iron, 'Hercules Fire Office' raised on ornate shield. (Phillips) $300

Berkshire, Gloucestershire and Provincial Life and Fire Assurance, 1824-31, copper, castle raised on oval. (Phillips) $250

Westminster Insurance, lead, open portcullis with Prince of Wales' feathers above, policy no. 20867 on panel below. (Phillips) $505

Aberdeen Fire and Life Insurance Co., stamped lead, oval, raised arms of the city with motto 'Bon Accord'. (Phillips) $2,160

North British Insurance, copper, St. Andrew and saltire cross raised in center, 'North British' raised on panel below. (Phillips) $300

Dundee Assurance, lead, raised arms of the city, impressed policy no. 3294. (Phillips) $1,150

Scottish, Commercial Fire and Life Insurance, copper, oval, raised figure of Caledonia. (Phillips) $315

Hampshire and South of England Insurance, 1841-47, copper, rose and crown raised on center. (Phillips) $275

Eagle Insurance, stamped lead, raised with eagle standing on rock, 'Safety' raised on panel below. (Phillips) $1,180

Edinburgh Friendly Assurance, heavy lead, policy no. 1805 pierced through panel below. (Phillips) $1,584

The General Insurance Company of Ireland, lead, rectangular, raised phoenix, torse and borders, policy no. 2036 on panel below. (Phillips) $1,150

London Assurance, lead, seated figure of Britannia with shield, spear and harp, 'London' raised on panel below, issued cira 1805-07. (Phillips) $600

Bristol Crown Fire Office, lead, crown raised in high relief, 'Bristol' raised on panel below. (Phillips) $500

FISHING REELS

The sport of angling has been a rich source for the collector ever since the days of dear old Isaac Walton. Be it salmon flies, plugs, spoons, spinners, floats, gaffs or even weights there are specialist collectors for all.

Most of the early tackle available dates from the 19th century and certainly very little was made before 1800.

The most notable makers of fine quality fishing tackle was the firm Hardy Brothers of Alnwick, established in 1872, but other well-known makers include Allcocks of Redditch, Farlows of London and Mallochs of Perth all of whom made excellent equipment.

With the exception of lightweight split cane trout rods and other useable items, rods are, in general, not considered to be very much in demand. They tend to deteriorate rapidly, and examples in poor condition are of little value. Rods also have the disadvantage of being difficult to display.

A Hardy Bros. 1896 pattern all brass 'Perfect' reel with ivorine handle, 4¼in. diam. (Christie's) $900

A Malloch's Patent spinning reel with horn handle, 4¼in. diam. (Christie's) $100

An Allcock's 'Aerial Popular' reel, solid front rim, adjustable drag and optional check, circa 1935, 3in. diam. (N. J. Marchant Lane) $40

A Hardy Bros. Ltd. 'Sea Silex' alloy reel with smooth brass foot, ebonite handles and ivorine check handle, 7in. diam. (N. J. Marchant Lane) $400

A Hardy Bros. all brass 'Perfect' reel with horn handle, smooth foot and oval logo, 2.3/8in. diam. (Christie's) $695

Brass salmon reel with ivory handle and ventilated drum, by Broddell of Belfast, circa 1900, 4¼in. diam. (N. J. Marchant Lane) $160

A Hardy Bros. Ltd. The 'Perfect' alloy reel with ivorine handle and smooth brass foot, 4in. diam. (Christie's) $240

A Dreadnought Casting Reel Co. Ltd. alloy reel with ivorine handle brass check-nut, 3¼in. diam. (Christie's) $60

A Hardy Bros. Ltd. 'St. George' multiplying alloy reel with ebonite handle and ribbed brass foot. (Christie's) $240

A Hardy Bros. Ltd. The 'Longstone' alloy reel with ebonized wooden handles, 4¼in. diam. (Christie's) $90

A Malloch's Patent bronze reel. (Woolley & Wallis) $130

An A. C. Farlowe & Co. Ltd. brass faced alloy reel with ebonite handle, 4.3/8in. diam. (Christie's) $195

A Hardy Bros. Ltd. The 'Perfect' alloy reel with ebonite handle, 4¼in. diam. (Christie's) $260

A Hardy Bros. Ltd. 'Silex' No. 2 alloy spinning reel with ivorine handles, 4½in. diam. (Christie's) $105

A Hardy Bros. 'Perfect' brass reel with ivorine handle, 4in. diam. (Christie's) $695

A Hardy Bros. Ltd. The 'Perfect' alloy reel with ebonite handle, 3.7/8in. diam. (Christie's) $120

A Julius Vom Hofe salmon fly reel, circa 1896, 4½in. diam. (N. J. Marchant Lane) $260

A Hardy Bros. Ltd. 'St. George' multiplying alloy fly reel, 3¾in. diam. (Christie's) $735

The 'H.J.S.' multiplying reel, blacked alloy with grooved alloy foot and nickel-plated thumb bar, 2.1/8in. diam. (N. J. Marchant Lane) $450

An Ocean City 'Automatic Go' (Philadelphia, USA) alloy reel with ivorine handles, 3½in. diam. (Christie's) $26

A brass reel with foliate engraved band to the front plate, horn handle, 4in. diam. (Christie's) $70

A Victorian gilt brass reel with ivory handle, with spring and cog mechanism, 3in. (Christie's) $3,400

A Hardy Bros. Ltd. large alloy sea-fishing reel with 'ship's wheel' tension nut, 9in. diam. (Christie's) $625

A Hardy Bros. Ltd. The 'Silex' No. 2 alloy sea reel with wooden handles, 7in. diam. (Christie's) $175

FURNITURE

The dictionary defines the word 'furniture' as the means of decorating and embellishing and since time began people have wanted to surround themselves with items that please them. Even cavemen painted on the ceilings of their caves.

Everyone collects furniture up to a point but discrimination begins when they look for satisfaction in the design of a piece as well as worrying about how well it carries out its function.

A rococo Revival laminated rosewood settee, attributed to John Henry Belter, New York, circa 1855, 66in. wide. (Robt. W. Skinner Inc.) $8,000

The field of furniture for the collector ranges from chairs and sofas to bookcases, armoires, chiffoniers and cabinets, Canterburys to tables of all types ranging from Pembrokes to peg-top. Special designers of furniture have been sought out by buyers of taste and men like Chippendale, Hepplewhite, Sheraton and Pugin greatly influenced the living conditions of their day even among people who never heard of them.

The materials used to make furniture range from papier mache, much loved by the Victorians for drawing room pieces, to rare woods like rosewood, tulip wood, satinwood or, more practical and hard wearing, oak, mahogany and teak. Pieces were painted, gilded, upholstered and polished. They were inlaid with marquetry and mounted in ormolu, covered with leather or tapestry and trimmed with tassels but each item of furniture reflects the taste of its time and the skill of its creator which is why we still admire them today.

A rococo Revival laminated rosewood lamp table, by J. B. Belter, New York, circa 1855, 26in. diam. (Robt. W. Skinner Inc.) $23,000

A Louis XVI style ebonized sideboard with bronze and ormolu mountings, America, 1865-70, approx. 69in. wide. (Robt. W. Skinner Inc.) $1,800

An Edwardian mahogany display cabinet, inlaid with checkered boxwood lines and harewood, 52in. wide. (Christie's) $2,400

A William IV rosewood veneered circular snap-top breakfast table, 4ft.3½in. diam. (Woolley & Wallis) $1,400

A Regency rosewood work table by Gillows of Lancaster, 35½in. wide, open. (Christie's) $1,500

An early Georgian oak bureau with double half round moldings, 38in. wide. (Lawrence Fine Art) $1,700

A George III mahogany breakfront bookcase with molded dentilled cornice, 95½in. wide. (Christie's) $7,500

A 17th century oak four-poster bed with paneled headboard, 64in. wide, 93in. high. (Christie's) $4,500

A mahogany latticework waste-basket on bracket feet, feet, 14½in. wide. (Christie's) $5,500

Late 19th century Moorish inlaid occasional table. (British Antique Exporters) $80

A fine quality late 18th century mahogany tray top commode, complete with bowl, 20½in. wide. (Bermondsey) $1,000

A 19th century Dutch walnut and marquetry cylinder top bombe-shaped bureau, 36in. wide. (Dacre, Son & Hartley) $2,300

A Federal mahogany Pembroke table with two drop leaves, Penn., 1800-10, 49¾in. wide, open. (Christie's) $1,850

Oak twin pedestal roll-top desk, 1900. (British Antique Exporters) $1,250

A French gold and parcel gilt armoire on squat cabriole feet. (Christie's) $2,600

A late 18th century Anglo-Indian engraved ivory and tortoiseshell veneered table cabinet, 19in. wide. (Christie's) $5,500

A George III two-tier mahogany dumbwaiter with molded circular shelves, 37in. high. (Christie's) $1,400

A late 19th century black and gold lacquer four-leaf screen, 77 x 26in. (Christie's) $2,750

A Chippendale mahogany blockfront secretary desk, circa 1780, 42in. wide. (Robt. W. Skinner Inc.) $50,000

A mid Victorian walnut and inlaid side cabinet with glazed door, 34½in. wide. (Dacre, Son & Hartley) $1,000

A Victorian mahogany canterbury. (John Hogbin & Son) $1,000

A Georgian secretaire bookcase with glazed doors enclosing brocade lined shelves. (Worsfolds) $2,250

Early 19th century fruitwood center table, Austrian or North Italian, 37in. diam. (Christie's) $1,250

A 19th century Louis XV-style commode with molded breccia marble top, 40¼in. wide. (Robt. W. Skinner Inc.) $1,500

A Charles II black and gold lacquered cabinet on stand, 45in. wide. (Christie's) $17,500

A Regency calamander wood davenport, the turned feet with brass castors, 21¼in. wide, circa 1820. (Woolley & Wallis) $1,850

A William and Mary black and parcel gilt stool with four S-scroll legs, 20in. diam. (Lawrence Fine Art) $11,000

A mid 18th century oak dresser, the three drawers with brass knobs, 69in. wide.(Dacre, Son & Hartley) $1,750

A George III brass bound mahogany cellarette with lead lined interior retaining tap beneath, 19in. wide. (Christie's) $4,000

GLAMOR POSTCARDS

When compared to the standard of todays equivalent, these glamor postcards represent a return to an earlier age of innocence.

Glamor cards, always a keenly collected subject, were particularly popular with soldiers of the 1st World War who carried the cherished pin-up into the trenches with them.

The French, as always, were much bolder and their more permissive attitude is demonstrated by the disproportionate number of cards of French origin currently available.

It is difficult to imagine that contemporary collections were kept hidden in secret places and, for obvious reasons, a card which has successfully passed through the postal system would be an extremely rare item.

Glamor is still an inexpensive collectible with an appeal which lies mainly in the nostalgia content.

French Bondage Study, 1920's. $8

Le Bain De La Parisienne by Suzanne Meunier. $14

1930's French Nude Study. $5

Fantasy/Glamor 'Light-prayer', photographic, German. $9

Brigitte Bardot, 1st Series, 50's, 60's, color. $6

Parisienne Stocking Study with Pierrot doll. $6

French Bathing Beauty,
Fabrication Francaise.
$2

Glamor/Fantasy, Girl in Bubble, NPG Series. $18

Les P'tites Femmes, by F. Fabiano, No. 39. $15

German Bathing Beauties 1903, S. Hildeshiemer. $6

Paris Series postcard No. 1445, **silk stockings and frilly knickerbockers, partially dressed study.**
$6

Marilyn Monroe, (printed in Germany). $15

GLAMOR POSTCARDS

Paris Series postcard No. 1519, **lingerie study**. **$7**

Art Deco Glamor, by Marte Graf, **'Falto'** Series, **'Getting It Through The Gate'**. **$15**

Paris Series postcard No. 1831, **a temptatious study in silk**. **$8**

Gestes Frivoles, by Suzanne Meunier. **$15**

Diabolo?, Fantasy Head, Printed in Prussia. **$16**

French Bathing Beauty, Fabrication Francaise. **$4**

French **'Bathing' Glamor**, hand-tinted photo type. **$3**

Art Deco Glamor, by Marte Graf, **'Falto'** Series, **'The Monkey and the Hoop'**. **$15**

Jayne Mansfield, 1st Series 50's and 60's, color. **$7**

GLASS

Glass is made primarily from a combination of silicic acid and an alkali, potassium or sodium. Added ingredients make possible the huge variety in glass – for example lead, calcium, metallic oxides or gold. Since the Middle Ages people have been collecting glass and today it is one of the most interesting of the collecting categories.

The Venetian glass making industry dates back to the 11th century and in the 13th century the glassmaking ovens were removed to Muran. From the beginning Venetian glass makers delighted in displaying their workmanship by intricate designs, elaborate decorations and coloring.

It was the German glassmakers who developed the skill of cutting glass which was practised with much success in Bohemia. Ruby glass Bohemian goblets are today highly prized by collectors.

Throughout the centuries and in every country there have been skilled and experimental glassmakers. In the late 19th and early 20th centuries, the Art Nouveau and Deco periods produced artists like Galle, Daum, Tiffany and Lalique whose work changes hands today for astronomical prices. Lalique in particular brought the craft of glass molding to a high art and he did not only create very expensive objects but also produced utilitarian objects like bottles for perfume manufacturers which made his art accessible for a wide range of people and greatly influenced public taste. Collectors also seek out pewter mounted glass articles produced for the London store Liberty's under the trade name of Tudric.

Glass is essentially a utilitarian material and therefore can be found in many guises – flagons, figurines, plates, beakers, goblets and ewers, chandeliers, vases, perfume bottles and of course paper weights. Those made by Baccarat, St Louis and Clichy are among the most beautiful.

Four Lobmeyr beakers, the bowls fluted, enameled with cartouches portraying ladies and gentlemen in 18th century costume, 4in. high. (Christie's) $500

Bohemian gold decorated cobalt blue glass punch set, late 19th century, 9½in. high. (Robt. W. Skinner Inc.) $1,100

A set of three Bristol green spirit bottles and stoppers, with cut shoulders and canted corners, gilt with Rum, Shrub and Brandy, 20cm. high. (Lawrence Fine Art) $800

GLASS

A Venini handkerchief vase in blue with a white interior, 9½in. high. (Christie's) $220

'Three Dahlias', a Lalique blue opalescent circular box and cover of clear and satin finished glass, 20.9cm. diam. (Christie's) $650

One of a pair of Portland clear overshot glass compotes, late 19th century, 8¾in. high. (Robt. W. Skinner Inc.) $675

A baluster goblet, the thistle bowl supported on a cushion above a drop knopped section, circa 1700, 15.5cm. high. (Christie's) $1,515

An oak bottle box with thirteen blown glass bottles, late 18th/early 19th century, 13½in. wide. (Christie's) $1,500

A Nailsea jug, dark green splashed with white, with flared neck, 23cm. high. (Lawrence Fine Art) $155

A Stourbridge olive-green opaline vase on four gilt feet detailed in white and black enamel, 12¾in. high. (Christie's) $320

A large Regency ormolu and cut glass vase, the urn-shaped body set with faceted cabochons in latticework frame, 22in. high. (Christie's) $17,500

A double eagle historical pint flask, GII-40, bright green, sheared mouth-pontil scar, Kensington Glass Works, 1830-38. (Robt. W. Skinner Inc.) $385

204

A Steuben crystal-footed bowl and cover, 'The Plains', designed by Lloyd Atkins, 33cm. high. (Christie's) $2,750

A stained glass panel with scene of medieval punishment, 18¾ x 15in. (Capes Dunn & Co.) $3,800

'Figurines Avec Bouchon', a Lalique frosted glass bottle and stopper, 11½in. high. (Christie's) $1,750

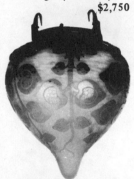

A Le Verre Francais cameo glass hanging lamp shade in the form of a strawberry overlaid in orange and blue, 30.9cm. high. (Christie's) $1,500

A Bohemian dated, double overlay, gilt metal mounted, rectangular casket for the Persian market, circa 1848, 15cm. wide. (Christie's) $4,000

A Guild of Handicrafts silver and glass box and cover, designed by C. R. Ashbee, with London hallmarks for 1900, 21cm. high, 16oz. 15dwt. gross weight without cover. (Christie's) $8,000

A Bohemian lithyalin, flaring cylindrical beaker, 4¾in. high. (Christie's) $440

A Lalique opalescent glass dish, 'Sirene', signed, circa 1925, 14½in. diam. (W. H. Lane & Son) $1,300

A Bohemian transparent-enameled chinoiserie beaker, circa 1835, 12.5cm. high. (Christie's) $2,000

GLASS

Mid 19th century Bohemian overlay and enameled casket, the body in opaque white, 5¼in. wide. (Bermondsey) $600

A Bohemian ruby overlay engraved tumbler of flared form, circa 1860, 12.5cm. high. (Christie's) $750

A Baccarat close millefiori wafer dish, the base with a cane inscribed 'B1848', 10cm. high. (Christie's) $1,500

A Daum limited edition pate-de-verre and fiber glass surrealist sculpture by Salvador Dali, depicting a soft clock slumped on a coat hanger. (Christie's) $3,500

Pair of 19th century cut glass lusters, 11½in. high. (Du Mouchelles) $700

A Hukin & Heath electroplated metal mounted glass claret jug, designed by Dr. C. Dresser, with registration lozenge for 12th November 1879, 23.7cm. high. (Christie's) $10,500

A Galle enameled and green oviform single-handled glass jug, 8½in. high, inscribed. (Christie's) $400

A glass vase designed by Koloman Moser, the clear glass with gilt loop decoration and iridescent red tears, 17.1cm. high. (Christie's) $2,500

A Lalique opalescent tapering cylindrical glass vase, 'Rampillon', 5in. high. (Christie's) $600

A Galle cameo vase, the flattened globular body on splayed foot, 23.5cm. high. (Christie's) $2,250

An opalescent 'Ondines' dish, engraved R. Lalique, France, 8in. diam. (Capes, Dunn & Co.) $620

A Baccarat molded enameled cylindrical tumbler, decorated in color on gilt foil, 9cm. high. (Christie's) $375

A baluster candlestick, the stem with true baluster section above a beaded knop and triple annulated basal knop, circa 1745, 19.5cm. high. (Christie's) $1,000

A pair of 19th century, blown, colorless glass hanging lamps, approx. 15in. high. (Christie's) $1,500

A 19th century glass drug jar with a lid, 24in. high. (Lots Road Chelsea Auction Galleries) $280

A bell-shaped mug with gadrooned lower part and everted folded rim, mid 18th century, 11cm. high. (Christie's) $260

A Vienna Secession glass goblet attributed to Moser and the design to J. Hoffmann, circa 1915, 12.8cm. high. (Christie's) $400

A Ver Centre vase, elongated ovoid shape enamel painted in various colors over a green ground, signature Ver Centre 1927, 29cm. high. (Christie's) $1,750

GOLDSCHEIDER

The Goldscheider factory of Vienna was founded in 1886 by Friedrich Goldscheider.

Production continued after his death in 1897, under the supervision of his widow and his brother Alois until 1920, when his two sons Marcel and Walter took the business over. Marcel left in 1927 to start the Vereinigte Ateliers fur Kunst and Keramic.

The Art Nouveau and Art Deco figures produced from the turn of the century, always incorporate the human form and are the pieces most desirable to collectors.

There are several marks for Goldscheider most including the name and another shows the Imperial Eagle along with the initials F.G.

A Goldscheider pottery bust of a young woman in the Art Deco style, signed F. Donatello, 23½in. high. (Outhwaite & Litherland)
$600

A pair of Goldscheider pottery figures of a young girl and a young man, made in Austria, 15in. high. (Christie's) $650

A Goldscheider pottery figure of a woman wearing a beaded costume, on a black oval base, 18in. high. (Christie's)
$2,500

A china Art Deco figure of a woman by Goldscheider, Vienna, 12½in. high. (Robt. W. Skinner Inc.) $300

A Goldscheider pottery mask of a girl looking down, Made in Austria, circa 1925, 23cm. high. (Christie's)
$600

A Goldscheider pottery figure modeled as a naked young girl with her arms crossed in front of her, 14¼in. high. (Christie's)
$750

GOLFING ITEMS

Almost everything to do with the sport of golf is enthusiastically collected; from bags, which made their first appearance around the 1880's, to trophies and other commemorative pieces. Even the most ordinary artefacts, when related by design to golf (like a hatpin in the form of a club), will fetch a much higher price than could otherwise be expected.

The earliest golf balls were made of leather and filled with a concoction of boiled feathers. They were then hammered to a round shape and painted white. In time, these were followed by the 'gutta-percha' balls which were of smooth appearance and patented by a Dr. Paterson of St. Andrews. The balls came into common usage by 1850 and were superseded by the mass produced molded 'hammered' ball used today.

Golfing items have a particularly strong following for it is a sport with international appeal and early clubs will often obtain hundreds of dollars at auction.

Historical Gossip about Golf and Golfers, Edinburgh, 1863. (Phillips) $17,920

A brass Gutta golf ball mold for the Trophy golf ball, bramble pattern No. 11917, by J. White & Co., Edinburgh. (Christie's) $650

A bronze figure of Harry Vardon by H. S. Ludlow, cast by Elkington & Co., circa 1900, on oak base, 5in. high, 7½in. overall. (Christie's) $1,750

A Royal Doulton two-handled vase printed and colored with two golfers and a caddie below a landscape of a golf course, 8in. high. (Christie's) $455

A composition painted caricature figure carrying a golf bag of clubs advertising the 'Dunlop' golf balls, 17in. high. (Christie's) $455

A Royal Doulton Kingsware mug, the raised decoration of a golfer and his caddie, circa 1910, 5¾in. high. (Christie's) $435.

A scared head wooden putter by Robert Forgan, with Prince of Wales feathers, circa 1875. $500

A scared head putter by Auchterlonie, circa 1900. $175

One left-handed cleek by John Gray, circa 1875. (Christie's) $280

One right-handed cleek by Nicholson of Pittenweem, circa 1890. (Christie's) $280

A mallet headed 'cross-head' club, owned by Sir G. Alexander, circa 1900. (Christie's) $600

A scared head longnosed baffing spoon by W. & G. Ashford, stamped. $500

A scared head longnosed driver by J. Moore. $600

A scared head longnosed driver by James Anderson, circa 1880. $1,000

A scared head longnosed middle spoon golf club by Tom Norris, circa 1870. $750

A scared head longnosed driver by Jack Morris, with greenheart shaft. (Christie's) $1,000

A scared head longnosed grassed driver by Wm. Park, Snr., circa 1870. (Christie's) $1,250

A Carrick rut iron, the shaft stamped John Wisden, London, circa 1870. (Christie's) $1,300

A scared head longnosed short spoon by Tom Morris, circa 1875. (Christie's) $1,400

A Hickory shafted roller headed club, the nose stamped patented July 1907. (Christie's) $520

A scared head longnosed spoon by W. D. Day. (Christie's) $500

A scared head putter by Jackson of Perth, circa 1870. (Christie's) $1,750

A scared head longnosed spoon by McEwan, the head so stamped, circa 1875. (Christie's) $1,750

A scared head wooden putter by Tom Morris, regripped. (Christie's) $975

GOSS

Had you been a holidaymaker in Britain at the turn of the century, the chances are that among your souvenirs you would have carried home an example of the work of William Henry Goss.

A Londoner, born in 1833, he started business in 1858 producing fine china in the Copeland style. He might have gone on forever as just another china man had he not been interested in heraldry, and had his eldest son, Adolphus, not had a passion for archaeology. By combining his manufacturing talent and those two great interests, Goss hit upon a unique and highly successful formula for the holiday trade.

The best china shops of the time had shelves crammed with his miniature models of Roman vases, tombs and lighthouses, together with detailed replicas of famous buildings, which are amongst the most sought after pieces of Goss available today.

He made models of 51 cottages between 1893 and 1929, all of which (bar the Massachusetts Hall and Holden Chapel) were British. The two exceptions, having been made specifically at the request of his Boston (U.S.) agent, are rarely found outside America.

The firm traded under the name of W.H. Goss & Sons and later W.H. Goss Ltd. Printed marks include W.H. Goss, with goshawk, wings outstretched.

A number of factories, well aware of the success of Goss china, went into production with similar models but these are generally of inferior quality but do change hands for the same high price as Goss. Other manufacturers' pieces are quite clearly marked so there need be no confusion between the two.

Charles Dickens' house, Gads Hill. $210

Ellen Terry's farm Tenterden, Kent. $550

Wordsworth's home, Dove Cottage. $750

Shakespeare's home. $100

A triple bag centrepiece, 200mm. high. (Goss & Crested China Ltd.) $200

Manx cottage nightlight, fully coloured, 122mm. long. (Goss & Crested China Ltd.) $230

The Veiled Bride, on socle plinth, 270mm. high. (Goss & Crested China) $1,000

Parian bust of Charles Swain, a colleague of W. H. Goss, 283mm. high, first period. (Goss & Crested China) $1,200

Goss doll, made during the Great War when German products were unavailable. (Goss & Crested China) $600

Kirk Braddon Cross in brown washed parian. $120 Unusually, the white parian example is more valuable at $350

Ribbed jug with black transfer view of 'Bamburgh Castle'. (Goss & Crested China) $60

Angel's head wall vase. $300

A Windsor kettle, the favorite of Queen Charlotte, 170mm. high. (Goss & Crested China Ltd.) $175

GRAMOPHONE NEEDLE TINS

There are many collectors of needle tins throughout the world as the collecting of gramophones and phonographs is a well established international hobby and the collecting of tins developed from this.

The City of London Phonograph and Gramophone Society caters for all those collectors from Australia, America, Holland, Germany and the United Kingdom. There are now many auction houses throughout the world who hold sales of all relevant items including tins.

It is only in the last few years that collecting gramophone needle tins, as a distinctly separate hobby from collecting gramophones and phonographs, has developed. The tins used to be found inside the machine or in the lid, so that many machine collectors already had some tins, and these made an ideal side collection as did the cutters, sharpeners and the record cleaning pads.

In their heyday, there were many hundreds of different brands produced and, because initially, each needle was only used once and then thrown away, the need arose to keep buying tins of 100 or 200 needles. The machines had no volume control, the tone being set by the needle, and most popular tones were medium, loud and extra loud.

The common brands were HMV, Songster, Columbia, Decca, Embassy and Edison Bell.

It is possible to build up a collection of 200 tins easily just by collecting variations of these six, and its an ideal start for novice collectors.

Collecting these tins has many advantages: their small size, ease of storage, relative cheapness, so the hobby is growing in popularity all the time.

Aeolian Vocalion – blue, pale blue and gold tin, large as it held 1000 needles, possibly German, 8cm./5cm./1.5cm. Very rare and attractive tin. **$14–$20**

Embassy 'Gramotube' – green and white tube 9cm. long with nozzle at end to dispense needles one at a time. Full instructions on the side of tin. Comes in different colors and tones, 200 or 150 needles, 200 extra loud needles from Redditch. **$24–$35**

Columbia Triple Tin – orange and gold tin, a round tin of 8cm. diam. and 1.5cm. deep. 3 compartments each of 200 needles of soft, medium and loud tones. A sliding top reveals the 3 sections. **$10–$18**

GRAMOPHONES & PHONOGRAPHS

The earliest record player, a phonograph, was invented by Thomas Alva Edison around 1877. This consists of a box structure housing the works, surmounted by a spindle, a needle lever and a horn. The record in the form of a cylinder is fitted to the spindle and when the works are cranked up, upon release of a catch the cylinder begins to turn, the needle moves onto the cylinder and the sound issues from the horn. It must have seemed like magic

The gramophone operating a sound system with flat discs followed in 1887, developed by Emil Berliner in America.

From the simple Pixie Grippa to the rare examples of early phonographs, this field of collection offers a vast range with something to suit whatever your budget.

Academy 78rpm gramophone with bell-shaped horn, circa 1930, 13in. square.　**$485**

Edison diamond disc phonograph, model C19, American, circa 1915, in mahogany cabinet.　**$440**

Gramophone Co. Ltd. Junior Monarch horn gramophone with Exhibition soundbox, circa 1910.　**$750**

Edison Amberola 1A phonograph in mahogany cabinet, circa 1909, 49½in. high.
$2,000

Edison opera phonograph with self-supporting Music Master laminated horn, circa 1912.　**$4,250**

Edison Amberola Bi phonograph, Serial No. 4384, circa 1911, 50½ x 21½in.
$2,400

Gramophone Company Style No 6 gramophone, circa 1900, in ornate oak cabinet.
$1,500

Modern reproduction of a Berliner gramophone, Type B, in oak cabinet. **$440**

Edison Business phonograph, Model C, Serial No. 6421, in oak case, circa 1908.
$530

Junior Monarch tin or brass horn, oak case, by Gramophone & Typewriter Co., 1904. (Capricorn Curios) **$600**

Zonophone gramophone in oak cabinet, 1912. (Capricorn Curios) **$100**

Aeolian-Vocalion gramophone in D-shaped sideboard, circa 1930, 47in. wide. **$800**

Gramophone & Typewriter Ltd. double-spacing Monarch gramophone in oak case, circa 1906. **$1,000**

Gramophone & Typewriter Ltd. Junior Monarch horn gramophone, circa 1904, in carved oak case. **$600**

HMV table grand, 109 Model, 1925. (Capricorn Curios) **$120**

Edison Home phonograph, Model A, Serial No. 6221, circa 1898. **$700**

Gramophone Company Style No. 5, trademark gramophone with Clark Johnson soundbox. **$1,430**

Edison Amberola 30 phonograph, Serial No. 12866, circa 1915, 15½ x 15in. **$485**

HAIR COMBS

Stage shows in the 19th century had, in much the same way as films and television do today, an incredible influence on fads and fashions of the period.

A prime example in Victorian times was Bizet's opera Carmen which opened in 1875 and prompted the popularity of large tortoiseshell combs worn in the Spanish style. They continued in fashion, although often of much smaller design, until the end of the century when the hair comb again received a boost in popularity as a result of the new designs created by the Art Nouveau movement.

Although most of those found today are plain tortoiseshell examples, costing a few pounds at the most, occasionally they can be seen decorated with gold and silver, or even semiprecious stones. These will obviously cost a lot more, depending on the design, with exceptional examples fetching a few hundred as opposed to a few pounds.

Pacific North-West coast wood comb, possibly Salish, 15cm. high. $2,000

Japanese blonde tortoiseshell hair comb ornament and pin, inlaid with gold, silver and mother-of-pearl. $500

Mid Victorian tortoisehsell comb decorated with metal lover's knots. $30

A 9kt. gold engine-turned comb by Dunhill, hallmarked Birmingham 1922. $150

Victorian horn comb decorated with ivy leaves in blue and green enamel. $40

An early 16th century boxwood double-sided comb, 6¾ x 4¾in. $1,980

A late Gothic period ivory comb of French or North Italian manufacture. $9,000

Art Nouveau style tortoiseshell hair comb. $50

A rare hair comb of tortoiseshell surmounted by French jet, circa 1830. $2,500

HANDKERCHIEFS

The use of handkerchiefs originated in Italy then, gradually, the custom spread throughout Europe.

At first, any old shape was considered suitable and it was only later that the traditional square shape was adopted. It was, actually, more by proclamation than adoption, for it was Marie Antionette, Queen of France, who first suggested the traditional shape and on 2nd January, 1785, a royal decree was announced to the effect that 'Henceforth, all handkerchiefs will be square in shape'.

A collection may follow one of a dozen or more themes such as heraldic, comic, silk, lace, initialed etc., and the price range is wide enough to cater for everyone.

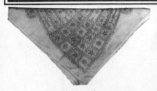

Late Victorian embroidered handkerchief with floral designs. $10

Late 19th century handkerchief with central medallion and all-over floral pattern. $8

Souvenir of Ypres embroidered handkerchief. $10

A printed George Washington handkerchief, probably England, circa 1800, 12½ x 11½in. (Robt. W. Skinner Inc.) $655

Royal Corps. of Signals silk and satin handkerchief. $16

Early 19th century printed handkerchief, printed in red on linen, 32 x 25½in. (Robt. W. Skinner Inc.) $1,100

'The Reformers attack on the Old Rotten Tree — of the Foul Nests of our Morants in Danger', handkerchief printed in color on silk, circa 1830. (Christie's) $440

Early 19th century printed handkerchief apotheosis of George Washington, England, 26 x 19½in. (Robt. W. Skinner Inc.) $1,250

HATPINS

Hatpins have been in use to some degree since the 1880's. Originally sold in pairs, or in sets of three or four, they are usually from five to twelve inches long with tops of silver, enamel, glass or semi-precious stones. Designs include butterflies, teddy bears, thistles, flowers, sporting themes, birds, shells and clusters of jewels. Some tops are hinged to give a snug fit close to the hat.

The original function of the hatpin was to anchor hat to hair and as hats got bigger, so did the hatpin. They began to look suspiciously like a dangerous weapon — resulting in a bill being read in America, proposing that, anyone wearing a hatpin more than 9in. in length would be required to carry a licence.

When very short hairstyles became fashionable in the 1920's the hatpin suffered something of a decline in popularity and those made after that date are generally of poorer quality.

Fine hand-painted porcelain hatpin, early 20th century. $60

Very unusual Victorian hatpin, a bird's wing in burnished metal set with purple Vauxhall glass. $45

Silver tennis racket hatpin, 1912. $45

Satsuma hatpin, early 20th century. $70

Unusual large and fine silver bear (a popular figure), 1911. $65

Very fine gold and silver pique hatpin, early 20th century. $100

Unusual double-faced pierrot on long pin. $90

Silver butterfly, set with garnets, circa 1900. $70

Silver gilt 'Trembler', which nods as the wearer walks, Victorian. $55

HATPINS

Edwardian hatpin in pale blue and green enamel.　$25

Silver and imitation amethyst hatpin by Charles Horner, 1912.　$35

Silver hatpin in the form of a Welsh hat, 1912. $30

Late 19th century cloisonne enamel hatpin.　$20

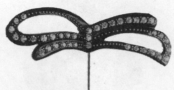

Art Deco jet and diamante bow, circa 1918.　$35

9kt. gold hatpin set with an amethyst in each side, 1905.　$55

Carved ivory hatpin in the form of a dragon, circa 1890.　$60

Pewter stag-beetle hatpin, circa 1918.　$60

Edwardian painted glass hatpin.　$6

Edwardian silver hatpin, dated 1906.　$30

Cut steel swallow with glass eye, on swivel, circa 1900.　$35

Delicate silver hatpin with marcasite decoration, circa 1900. $35

221

HATS

Anyone who has become interested in hats can look forward to forming a thoroughly fascinating collection.

Most hats on the market today date from no earlier than the middle of the 19th century, however, this offers a range including, beautiful Victorian silk bonnets and little richly trimmed hats which were worn perched on top of the head, monumental Edwardian straw extravaganzas, and all of the attractive hats of the 20's, 30's and 40's.

Men's hats also make a marvelous collection and offer examples of the 18th century tricorne which was followed by the top hat made of beaver or felt, then the bowler, checked woollen caps, the summer straw boater and the trilby.

An enthusiastic collector may even attempt to determine the name of the original owner in the knowledge that the hats of the famous can be real collector's items.

Iroquois beaded velvet cap with floral designs on black velvet. (Robt. W. Skinner Inc.) $330

A black satin bonnet trimmed with pleating, circa 1880. (Christie's) $40

An early 18th century cord quilted linen gentleman's cap. (Phillips) $600

A top hat of black beaver, with black silk ribbon, 7in. high, circa 1840. (Christie's) $485

A mourning bonnet of black crepe, circa 1830. (Christie's) $220

A top hat of brown felt, with black ribbon, by A. Giessen, Delft, circa 1870. (Christie's) $675

A Nazi Panzer NCO's peaked service cap with dark green band. (Wallis & Wallis) $220

1930's lady's felt hat with satin band. $6

A post war U.S. Naval officer's peaked cap with gilt and silvered badge and gilt side buttons. (Wallis & Wallis) $24

A child's or young lady's hat of ivory silk quilted with a scale design and trimmed with a rosette of ivory ribbons, circa 1820. (Christie's) $1,000

A top hat of gray beaver, possibly 1829, labeled M. Strieken, 8in. high. (Christie's) $1,100

A lady's flat wide-brimmed hat of black figured silk laid over plaited straw, circa 1770, 15¼in. diam. (Christie's) $1,200

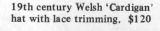

A bonnet of brown striped plaited straw trimmed with brown figured ribbons, edged with a fringe, circa 1850. (Christie's) $100

19th century Welsh 'Cardigan' hat with lace trimming. $120

A straw bonnet with deep brim, trimmed later with satin with chine silk ribbon and artificial flowers, circa 1830. (Christie's) $320

A 16th century man's embroidered cap embellished with sequins and gold lace trim, England, 8in. high. (Robt. W. Skinner Inc.) $10,000

A bonnet of black satin trimmed with a large bow and rouleaux, circa 1830. (Christie's) $360

Stovepipe bearskin hat belonging to Abraham Lincoln. $9,000

HELMETS

It is apparently untrue that Viking warriors wore horned helmets when they went into battle but nonetheless helmets were used to terrify the enemy as much as to protect the head of the warrior. Magnificent helmets have turned up in burial sites as far apart as Greece and northern Scotland and the workmanship and design of them all testify to their function and status.

It is possible today to buy fairly cheaply, simple helmets with nose guards such as were used by troopers in the wars between the Cavaliers and the Roundheads and which used to hang on the walls of large houses for the men to grab when an alarm sounded. Border reivers were recognizable by their curved 'iron bonnets' and the collecting field extends to recent times with Nazi helmets or war-time 'tin hats' used to protect air raid wardens during bombing raids.

Some of the most impressive helmets, however, are those made by Eastern craftsmen, particularly the Turks and Persians and, even more frightening, the armor helmets turned out by German armorers for mounted knights. The hideously grimacing faces on front of them must have filled the knight's adversaries with terror.

An other rank's composite metal helmet of the Prussian Line Cuirassier Regt. (Christie's) $750

A Victorian officer's lance cap of The 17th (Duke of Cambridge's Own) Lancers. (Wallis & Wallis) $1,250

A late 16th century morion, brim with band of foliate decoration and roped edge. $2,750

A U.S. Military Academy shako with gilt helmet plate, numeral 5 within garter, circa 1900. (Wallis & Wallis) $200

A late 16th century cabasset with brass plume holder. $1,750

An embossed and parcel gilt helmet, together with two arm guards, Persia, 19th century. (Robt. W. Skinner Inc.) $850

A German burgonet, one-piece skull with tall comb and pierced hinged ear flaps, circa 1600. (Wallis & Wallis) $900

A Prussian Garde du Corps trooper's helmet, with parade eagle to crown. (Wallis & Wallis) $2,000

An Artillery officer's busby by Hawkes & Co., the metal case inscribed Earl of Chester's Rifles. (Christie's) $350

The Blandford Yeomanry Cavalry black japanned metal helmet of early 19th century Roman style. (Christie's) $1,250

An 18th century Prussian miter cap, Fusiliermutze, circa 1740-56. (Christie's) $3,500

A 4-plate folding buff, top plate with roped border and pierced sights, circa 1600. (Wallis & Wallis) $1,000

HORN

Horn is one of those materials which people seem either to dislike intensely or to collect avidly.

The range of objects of horn is almost limitless from spoons to mirror frames, from snuff boxes to chairs, from drinking vessels to chandeliers, and it is in this tremendous versatility that the chief attraction of the material lies.

Dividing horn into three categories we have articles made from treated horn (spoons, combs, shoehorns, snuff boxes, carved drinking vessels), those made of untreated — usually stags' — horn (chairs, tables, chandeliers, cutlery handles) and the grotesquely decorative (heads and skulls with antlers attached which adorn the walls of a few hunters' homes and those of many more would-be hunters).

Combs, spoons, fans, boxes, shoehorns and buttons are fairly widely available at reasonable prices, though spoons dating from the 16th and 17th centuries are rather more desirable and will fetch considerably more. Those having whistles incorporated in their handles are the best.

Powder horns make interesting collections, since many are finely carved and engraved with everything from flowers to coats of arms and hunting scenes.

It is not only the small objects to look for, however, for tables, chairs and chandeliers can also be found, their curiosity value ensuring a ready market.

Victorian horn and brass gong. (British Antique Exporters) $150

A 17th/18th century rhinoceros horn libation cup with pierced pine handle, 13cm. wide. (Christie's) $4,000

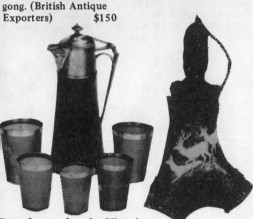

Part of a set of twelve Victorian silver mounted horn beakers, maker's initials H.W.D., London, 1877, together with a horn claret jug, 11½in. high. (Christie's) $1,346

A Bohemian carved staghorn powder flask with silver mounts. (Bermondsey) $1,600

A late 18th century Scottish horn snuff mull carved with the profile of the Old Pretender, 4¼in. high. (Christie's) $650

A 17th century pressed horn plaque with the Raising of Lazarus, 6 x 5cm. $705

The magazine devoted to that sub-species of popular fiction, the horror story, originated in the USA in the early twenties. Various titles were published and easily the most popular at the time, and most collected today is 'Weird Tales'. This included original stories by all the masters of the genre and in particular the stories of H. P. Lovecraft.

These early magazines now sell for high prices but they can still be found in general book shops for a few dollars or less. Unfortunately if buying from the specialist one can expect to pay the going rate and they will cost up to $40 each.

True Strange Stories, Vol. 1, No. 1, March 1929. $30

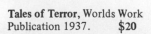

Tales of Terror, Worlds Work Publication 1937. $20

Strange Tales, by Hugh B. Cave, January 1933. $30

Tales of Magic and Mystery, March 1928. $30

The Witch's Tales, Vol. 1, No. 2, Dec. 1936. $30

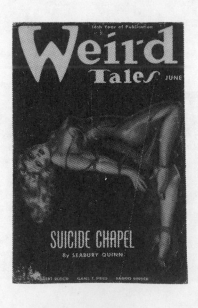

Ghost Stories, Uncanny, Spooky, Creepy
Tales, July 1929. $16

Weird Tales, H. P. Lovecraft Stories, June
1938. $40

HORSE BRASSES

Horse brasses were thought to have originated over 4000 years ago in the near east and their symbolic designs to have evolved from the heraldic emblems on early horse armor. These decorative amulets were thought to have the power to deflect the gaze of the 'evil eye' from the wearer.

Handmade by gypsies and tinkers from sheet brass and sold at fairs up and down the country in the early 19th century they soon became very popular and were often awarded as prizes at agricultural shows and fairs. Demand eventually became so great that a more commercial method of production was sought resulting in the cast brass version making its first appearance around 1830 followed by a mass produced stamped brass as demand reached a peak at the end of Victoria's reign.

Early designs show acorns, flowers, wheatsheaves, trees, stags and fox masks with the later versions of 1840-1860 depicting portraits, county symbols, events and a variety of geometric designs. Of particular interest to collectors are those issued to celebrate Queen Victoria's Jubilee. A most attractive display can be made with Martingales, horse lames and even straps and buckles from Victorian harness.

It is something of a bonus if the brasses are still mounted on their original leather straps.

There is now almost a glut of modern horse brasses on the market but once you have handled and studied early brasses it will become easier to distinguish between the old and the new. As a broad rule, the modern version is much lighter in weight and shows no signs of rubbing on the reverse side.

Victoria 1870, a rare cast brass. $120

Cast steam locomotive brass. $60

Stamped brass of horse pasant, showing a well worn hanger, a good sign of an old brass. $30

ICONS

Russian icons dating from the 10th to the 17th century are extremely rare and precious works of art. However, examples from a later period are more common and the high standard of their workmanship has guaranteed their continuing popularity with collectors.

Usually worked in tempera on wood, the subject is always of a religious or mystical nature showing representations of Christ, The Virgin, The Saints or scenes from a religious life. The majority of icon painters were monks and this work was often produced as part of the discipline of a life of contemplation.

Icons were sometimes set in a folding frame so that they could be carried from place to place. These frames are often of exquisite design and craftsmanship. A three-fold panel is called a triptych.

The Sainted Hierarchs of Rostov, James and Dimitre, late 18th century, 34.5 x 27.5cm. $835

The Virgin Hodigitria, Cretan, 1480-1520, 40.5 x 32.5cm. $10,000

The Tikhvin Mother of God painted on a gold ground, maker's mark A.V., Moscow, 1790, 30.2 x 26cm. $2,200

The Hodigitria Mother of God, inscribed 'through the hand of Nicholas Lamboudi of Sparta', 15th century, 67 x 47.5cm. $35,000

Saints Zosima and Savatii, the oklad with a silvered metal revetment, 18th century, 32 x 26.7cm. $2,250

Early 17th century icon of St. Onouphrios The Great, signed by E. Lambardos, 55.5 x 36.5cm. $75,000

Saint Nicholas, probably Byzantine, early 15th century, shown bust length. 36.5 x 27.5cm. $4,000

An ivory plaque carved in low relief with twelve Festivals, early 16th century, 6.1 x 5.7cm. $1,600

An icon painted in two registers with the Mother of God and the Beheading of John the Baptist, circa 1700. 31.8 x 27cm. $1,100

The Saviour, shown head and shoulders, 18th century. $3,500

The Mother of God of the Sign, St. Petersburg, 1826. $2,000

Christ Pantocrator, encased in a silver oklad, Moscow, 1880. $2,250

The Mother of God of Life-Giving Source, probably Constantinople, dated 1778, 52.8 x 39.3cm. $1,600

An icon painted in two registers, contained within a repousse and silver gilt oklad, late 18th century, 48.5 x 39.5cm. $4,500

Late 17th century icon of St. Nicholas, 31.2 x 26.6cm. $1,100

Christ Pantocrator painted in traditional manner, Moscow, 1819. $2,000

St. Nicholas, naturalistically painted and encased in a parcel gilt oklad, Moscow, 1899-1908.
$2,500

The Kazan Mother of God painted on a gold ground, Kostroma, 1857. $1,600

Saints Zosima and Savatti founders of the Solovki Monastery, 17th century. $2,000

18th century Russian iconostasis panel, 'The Evangelist St. Matthew', 53.5cm. high. $2,000

The Doctor Saints Cosmas and Damian, late 17th century.
$2,500

The Kursk Mother of God, naturalistically painted, 1899-1907. $1,250

The Mother of God of the Sign, undated Moscow, early 19th century. $1,000

Christ Pantocrator, naturalistically painted, 1899-1907. $1,250

INHALERS

Collectors of medical antiques and memorabilia will be aware of the compulsive interest in health held by the more affluent of our forefathers. This led to an expansive and profitable market for the manufacturers of medications and medical equipment.

Hockin's Acme Inhaler with all-over floral design in sepia and blue coloring. $100

The Bournemouth Inhaler, sepia printed with floral decoration. $120

Although relief from coughs and bronchial troubles could probably be obtained effectively by simply inhaling some of the vapor straight from a bowl of boiling water containing some of the prescribed preparation, manufacturers produced a variety of inhalers, some boasting various claims and other bearing attractive motifs.

Small portable inhalers were designed specifically for use when traveling and for convenience, the medication could be introduced beforehand and hot water added when required.

Today, although some searching must be done for the more desirable examples, inhalers can provide a varied and unusual theme for the collector, offering a range from the bizarre to quite beautiful.

Dr. Nelson's Improved Inhaler, circa 1880. $20

The Simplex Inhaler with white body overprinted with directions in black. $80

The Westminster Inhaler, sepia printed with floral decoration. $120

Improved Earthenware Inhaler by S. Maw Son & Thompson with attractive marbled effect. $50

INK BOTTLES

Ink was expensive in the 19th century and to keep the price of their product down in a very competitive market, ink manufacturers made every effort to market it as cheaply — but as eye-catchingly — as possible.

Ink bottles can be found in glass, saltglaze pottery and occasionally porcelain. Among the rarest examples are 'sheered lip' glass bottles in which the glass bottle openings were not polished but only broken off and sealed with a cork and sealing wax.

There were ink bottles in the shape of turtles, cottages, locomotives, Bonaparte, Mr Punch, igloos, bird cages and grimacing clowns. Today there is a strong American interest in ink bottle collecting.

Staffordshire ceramic clown head ink bottle, the open mouth providing access to the ink reservoir and with a quill holder on top of the head. $120

An extremely rare circular cottage inkwell in aqua glass with Registry of Designs diamond embossed on the base for August 1968, 6cm. high. $400

Mid 19th century 'Bonaparte' ink bottle, the hollow body forming the reservoir while the front hole acts as a quill holder and the rear hole as access to the ink. $300

'Mr. Punch', one of the most sought after salt-glaze ink bottles, incised on the back 'Gardeners Ink Works', 1851, 4½in. high. $250

American red and blue ceramic bottles known as 'Ma' and 'Pa', with removable heads forming the cork stoppers, patented by C. H. Henkels of Philadelphia for Carter's Ink Co. of Boston. $200

A Whitefriar's paper-weight inkwell, from the Bacchus period, circa 1840, 7in. high. $560

INROS

Most Japanese inros take the form of a decorative slim rectangular lacquered box. They will usually divide up into three to five sections slotting neatly together and strung on a cord threaded through slots in the sides.

They were used, by men, from the 16th to the 19th century for carrying the family seal, medicine or tobacco and were worn hanging from the belt alongside the sword.

The cords of the inro are secured by a bead (ojime) and attached to the girdle by a netsuke carved in wood or ivory.

A 19th century Tamenuri three-case inro, with cornelian glass bead ojime. (Christie's) $850

A 19th century four-case Kinji inro, signed Hasegawa saku above a red tsubo seal and Shibayama on a shell tablet. (Christie's) $1,500

Early 19th century four-case Nashiji inro, unsigned. (Christie's) $500

A small three-case Ginji inro, decorated in gold hiramakie, with wakasa-nuri bead ojime. (Christie's) $2,500

A 19th century three-case silver inro, with attached silver filigree bead ojime and lightly stained ivory netsuke. (Christie's) $11,000

An 18th century four-case Nashiji inro, decorated in gold hiramakie, takamakie and hirame, unsigned. (Christie's) $1,250

INSTRUMENTS

If ever there was an age of discovery, it must have been the second half of the 19th century when new theories and inventions were being created daily. It would appear that the whole populus was fascinated by science, with hardly a magazine or newspaper not devoting acres of column inches to the likes of Darwin, Eddison and Bell. This has left a legacy of finely made instruments with many, such as the microscopes and telescopes, adequately fulfilling today, the function for which they were designed.

It is not only the scientific instruments such as circumferentors, theodolites, equitorial dials and graphometers which are sought after but domestic instruments as well, such as telephones, typewriters and telegraphs.

All, when cleaned and polished make an interesting display, a tribute to fine 19th century craftsmanship and inventiveness.

A 16th century gilt brass miniature armillary sphere, probably German, 55mm. diam. (Christie's) $4,500

A small 2½in. reflecting telescope, signed J. Watson, London, circa 1800, on folding tripod base, 235mm. long. (Christie's) $1,500

A brass transit on circular foot with focus leveling screws, signed Troughton & Simms, London, 39cm. high. (Christie's) $800

A small Zoetrope optical toy on wood stand with several picture strips, diam. of drum 5¼in. (Christie's) $200

An English Withering type botanical microscope and case, circa 1800, with box, 10.5cm. high. (Christie's) $600

A brass circular protractor with box, signed Blunt, London, circa 1800, 78mm. radius. (Christie's) $500

A German cube dial, the wooden cube with five printed scales, signed D. Beringer, 7in. high. (Lawrence Fine Art) $950

A 17th/18th century brass graduated circle, probably French, 13.7cm. diam. (Christie's) $1,000

A two-day marine chronometer, the dial signed by Dobbie McInnes Ltd., Glasgow, no. 9615, dial 10cm. diam. (Christie's) $1,000

A brass Culpeper-type monocular microscope on three scrolled legs, 10¼in. high, contained in its mahogany case. $880

An Ive's Kromskop color stereoscopic viewer, in wood carrying case. (Christie's) $1,100

An American brass and plated brass compound monocular microscope, signed E. Gundlach, pat. Sept. 14, 1878, 29cm. high approx. (Christie's) $500

Late 18th century brass transit instrument, signed Lenoir (Paris), on circular base with three leveling screws, the telescope 53.5cm. long. (Christie's) $3,500

A gilt brass pedometer, German, possibly Augsburg, circa 1700, 65mm. long. (Christie's) $1,250

A cradle-mounted stereographoscope in black ebonized finish with lens panel, 16in. high. (Christie's) $350

A French 19th century brass orrery on stand depicting the asteroids, 23cm. diam. (Christie's) $1,500

A mahogany folding Cuminoscope concave mirror photograph/print viewer, by The Cuminoscope Patent Brevetes, S.G.D.G. (Christie's) $300

A large brass mounted lodestone with bail handle, 20.5cm. high. (Christie's) $4,250

Late 18th century sand clock, the two sand glasses mounted in a brass frame, 5½in. high. $850

An 18in. Malby's celestial globe on stand, 45in. high. $2,000

A cast iron sundial by E. T. Hurley, circa 1900, 10¼in. diam. (Robt. W. Skinner Inc.) $500

An 18th century brass analemmatic and horizontal inclining dial, signed J. Deens, Vienae, 113mm. long. (Christie's) $1,000

A brass and mahogany 4in. refracting telescope, signed Steinheil in Munchen, no. 2811, the sighting telescope, no. 2886, 171cm. long. (Christie's) $2,000

A London Stereoscopic Co. Brewster-pattern stereoscope with brass mounted eye pieces, in fitted rosewood box, 13in. wide. (Christie's) $600

An 18th century signed brass and wrought-iron wall spitjack, England, 11in. high. (Robt. W. Skinner Inc.) $750

A 19th century English brass universal equatorial dial with three leveling screws, 11.5cm. diam. (Christie's) $700

A chased silver universal equatorial dial with perpetual calendar, signed Jean-David Beyser, Augsburg, circa 1750, 80mm. long. (Christie's) $1,250

A Regency mahogany library globe, 28in. diam. (Christie's) $27,500

A Henry Crouch brass binocular microscope, No. 2092, of Lister limb construction. (Lawrence Fine Art) $1,000

A brass Martin type orrery with tellurium of American interest, signed T. Blunt, London, 22cm. diam. (Christie's) $17,500

Late 18th century brass protractor, signed Lenoir a Paris, 13cm. radius. (Christie's) $250

A cased set of Jacobus Listingh coin weights, Dutch, dated 1659, 3½ x 6¼in., in leather slip case. $5,000

A small brass sextant of T-frame style signed Berge, London, in fitted shaped mahogany case, circa 1800. (Reeds Rains) $2,250

Early 18th century boxwood nocturnal, the shaped and pierced handle stamped 'Both Bears', 8½in. long. $1,850

Late 17th/18th century South German steel lock and key, 6½ x 3.5/8in. $2,000

An early 19th century American set of brass parallel rules with protractor, signed S. Dod, Newark, 30.5cm. long. (Christie's) $880

A. T. Cooke & Sons brass transit theodolite, 15½in. high. $500

A 2¾in. pocket terrestrial globe, English, circa 1770, 3¼in. diam. $1,000

A terrestrial globe on a mahogany stand, globe printed by J. & W. Cary, London, 1818, 24¾in. high. (Christie's) $1,650

A two-day marine chronometer by Morris Tobias No. 794, diam. of bezel 115mm. $2,000

A lacquered brass compound monocular microscope, by Powell & Lealand, 1901, 49cm. high, in case. (Phillips) $4,650

An orrery on turned mahogany stand with three scroll feet, French, circa 1810, 53cm. high. (Christie's) $2,420

IRONS

A wise buy for those with the collecting urge, would be old irons. They are comparatively cheap, fairly plentiful, and will form an interesting collection which is sure to increase in value. The variety of different types is staggering; from tiny curved 4in. lace irons to the enormous, professional Tailors Goose which can weigh anything up to 30lb.

It would appear that the practice of ironing clothes was known to the Chinese in the eighth century and introduced to Britain by the Viking invaders, who used a massive smooth stone resembling an inverted mushroom known as a 'sleek'.

Early flat irons were sold in pairs so that one could be reheating either on the stove or placed directly against the fire while the other was in use. They were heavy and the handles hot and awkward to manage. A set of irons with exchangeable handles was patented in America by a Mrs Potts in 1871.

In the 18th century, it was not uncommon for a household wash to be tackled only once every two or three months — an event presenting many challenges with fabrics requiring pleating, crimping, ruffling, goffering and finishing so that by the Victorian period every housekeeper worth her salt was armed with a battery of irons designed to cope with every conceivable task, even one with a tiny base and long handle for ironing hats.

If you keep your eyes open you can find old irons just about anywhere and, a few pounds will buy a simple cast flat (or sad) iron. Raise your sights and you can become the proud possessor of an interesting gas or methylated spirit model — or even a hollow iron complete with heating stone.

A leaf iron in two parts in which silk is placed to receive an impression. $80

19th century Continental brass charcoal iron. $140

Velvet iron complete with stand. $45

A small wood fluter with a flat base and rolling-pin top. $30

Scottish box iron with ornate brass supports. $130

Crimping machine with adjustable corrugated rollers, various types. $80→$160

IVORY

Ivory has been recognized as a perfect material for carving since ancient times and the art of the skilled carver has always been well appreciated.

Craftsmen used several kinds of ivory including, elephant tusks (the hard white ivory comes from the African elephant and the yellower from the Indian), and hippopotamus or walrus tusks to produce boxes, jewelry, knife handles, combs, buttons and statuettes and ornamental groups of particular beauty.

Ivory inlaid with designs in fine materials is known as Shibayama, named after the Japanese family Shibayama who excelled in this style of decoration.

There are many well produced fakes made of plastic on the market, but close examination of the surface may show a lack of the characteristic streaking or flecking of ivory. A test, which should be undertaken entirely at your own risk, is to place a hot needle pressed flat against the base of a suspect piece. Plastic will melt!

Late 19th century ivory carving of Kannon, signed Shunyosai Nobuyuki, 13.9cm. high. (Christie's) $900

A 19th century ivory okimono of a human skull, signed Shosai to, 13cm. long. (Christie's) $6,000

Late 19th century sectional ivory okimono of a basket weaver and his wife, signed Eitoku, 10cm. high. (Christie's) $1,000

A mid 19th century decorated ivory ink stand, Europe, 3in. high, 5in. diam. (Robt. W. Skinner Inc.) $350

Late 19th century ivory carving of a basket seller, signed Jogyoku, 25cm. high (Christie's) $2,250

A German 17th century ivory plaque carved with half length figures, 11.5 x 9.7cm. (Lawrence Fine Art) $750

A carved ivory tray of finger citron form with shallow rounded sides, 8in. long, Qianlong. $750

A Japanese ivory model of a boat with an exotic bird's head figurehead, 17in. wide. (Christie's) $1,250

An ivory okimono of Hotei, signed Munetak, Meiji period, 14.7cm. wide. (Christie's) $700

A large, late 19th century, Continental silver mounted ivory tankard and cover, 16in. high. (Christie's) $12,000

A 18th century inlaid ivory brushpot, 5in. high. $1,000

Late 19th century ivory tusk vase inlaid in Shibayama style, signed, overall height 42.7cm. (Christie's) $900

A Japanese carved ivory figure group, signed on inset red lacquer panel, 19.5cm. high. (H. Spencer & Sons) $375

An ivory 'Washington' chess set, stained red and natural, king 8.5cm., pawn 3.8cm., circa 1880, in tortoiseshell veneered box. (Phillips) $1,350

A 17th century carved ivory figure of Buddha, seated cross-legged, on wood stand, 4¾in. high. $1,000

IVORY

Late 19th century ivory box and cover carved as Benkei seated on top of the great bell of Miidera, signed Takayuki, 24cm. high. (Christie's) $1,000

An early ivory rectangular plaque, Yuan/Ming Dynasty, 9cm. wide. (Christie's) $2,000

Late 19th century sectional ivory okimono of Daikoku, signed Gyokuyu, 13.8cm. high. (Christie's) $625

A Dieppe carved bone wall mirror, 84cm. high. (H. Spencer & Sons) $500

Late 19th century ivory group of a farmer with his wife and son, 18cm. wide. (Christie's) $2,650

An 18th century ivory brushpot of irregular section, 6in. high, with wood stand. $3,100

A 17th century ivory figure of the infant Buddha, 5¼in. high. $1,000

Late 17th/early 18th century ivory portrait roundel, attributed to Jean Cavalier, 3¼in. diam. $800

A 19th century French or German ivory group of a medieval woodsman and a court jester, 20cm. high. (Christie's) $7,500

JADE

There are three materials which are called jade — JADEITE, the finest, is white with a purple tint or emerald green; NEPHRITE, which has been known and used since ancient times and CHLOROMELANITE, which is so dark a green that it almost looks black.

These varieties of jade are found in Upper Burma, Central India, Turkestan, Siberia, New Zealand, Silesia and Alaska. Although the people who have always been most fond of jade are the Chinese, none occurs naturally in that country. Chinese jade had to be imported and it was carved into beautiful and delicate objects ranging from religious objects, seals and boxes to vases and jewelry. The skill of the carvers is breathtaking and many beautiful jade pieces can be seen in museums everywhere.

A pale celadon jade figure of a recumbent horse, Yuan Dynasty, 4.6cm. long. (Christie's) $2,500

A celadon jade brush washer modeled as a pressed hollowed melon, 3in. wide. (Christie's) $1,000

A jade figure of a recumbent horse, Tang/Song Dynasty, 6.5cm. long. (Christie's) $1,500

A large celadon jade peach-shaped brushwasher, late Qing Dynasty, 19.5cm. wide. (Christie's) $2,750

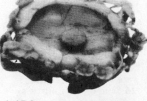

A 17th century jade brush-washer, the stone of grayish-celadon color, 6¼in. wide. $1,900

An 18th century spinach green two-handled bowl, 26cm. wide, with fitted box. (Christie's) $6,000

A mottled grayish jade square seal carved in the archaic taste, probably Qing Dynasty, 9.5cm. square. (Christie's) $1,400

A brown and pale celadon jade leys jar, zhadou, Ming Dynasty, 13.1cm. diam. (Christie's) $3,400

A pale celadon jade model of two mythical birds feeding from a branch of peaches, 6¾in. wide, on wood stand. (Christie's) $4,500

Dark green spinach jade covered urn of bronze form, on giltwood base. (Stalker & Boos) $1,200

A gray and green jade carving of a striding dragon, Six Dynasties or later, 11cm. long. (Christie's) $2,300

An early celadon jade circular disk, bu, Han Dynasty, 10.7cm. diam., in fitted box.(Christie's) $4,250

A Mogul dark celadon jade ewer of oval octafoil cross-section, 17th/18th century, 15.5cm. high. (Christie's) $10,000

A Longquan celadon yanyan vase, early 14th century, 26.5cm. high. (Christie's) $5,000

A small Longquan celadon jarlet and lotus-molded cover, 13th/14th century, 7.5cm. high. (Christie's) $2,000

Late 18th century celadon jade group formed as a hollowed section of bamboo beside a gu-shaped quatrefoil vase, 16cm. high, with wood stand. (Christie's) $855

A pale celadon and brown jade vase, 17th/18th century, 12.5cm. high, with wood stand. (Christie's) $8,500

An 18th century pale celadon jade rectangular table screen carved with the eight Daoist Immortals, 29 x 19cm., with wood stand. (Christie's) $7,000

The forerunner to the modern jigsaw puzzle was invented by a map maker in London during the 1760's and designed to facilitate the teaching of geography.

The puzzle was referred to as a 'dissecting map' and was hand made by mounting a map on a sheet of mahogany which was then cut by a fine marquetry saw. Lines were cut to define areas and the pieces fitted together to form a fairly accurate map. The puzzles were presented in a wooden box with a sliding lid bearing an engraved label.

Early puzzles were hand made and therefore expensive to produce, but their popularity with both adults and children soon led other manufacturers to appreciate their market potential as a learning aid and the range of subjects widened to encompass history, the three R's, religion, mythology and so on. Manufacturers best known during this period were J. Wallis, W. Darton, J. W. Barfoot, W. Peacock, Dean & Son and J. Betts and puzzles by these names are eagerly sought after.

Towards the end of the nineteenth century, boxes began to bear hand-colored pictorial labels and these have now become collectible in their own right.

The 20th century saw the introduction of mass production techniques and the use of plywood and motorized fretsaws with hundreds of manufacturers responding to the jigsaw 'craze' of the 1920's and 30's. Notable British firms producing during this period are Raphael Tuck (Zag Zaw), Chad Valley (GWR, Cunard/White Star Line), Fredrick Warne (Chandos, Bedford), Victory (Supercut, Artistic), Holtzapffel (Figure-it-out), Salman (Academy), Delta fine cut, Zig Zag, Huvanco and A.V.N. Jones.

Snow White, Walt Disney, 1938. $15

'The Milkmaid', 1930's 'Chandos' puzzle by F. Warne, it has a distinctive and easily recognizable style of cut which can make it awkward to assemble, 7 x 9in. $20

The Piglets, Beatles Take-Off, Waddington's, 1964. $6

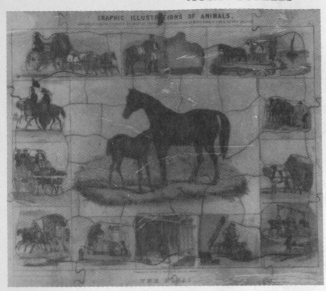

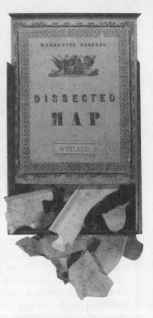

'The Horse', one of a series of 'Graphic illustrations of animals showing their utility to man', by Roake & Varty, circa 1840, 12 x 15in. $140

Dissected Map of Scotland, by Peacock, 19th century. $70

A rare Barfoot puzzle, a double-sided map dissection, showing the Eastern and Western hemispheres, 12 x 8in., circa 1855. $440

'First Whiff', a Lawson Wood cartoon made into a puzzle, probably by an amateur, 1930's. Humor was always a popular subject for amateurs (who often cut to professional standards, and usually with an interpretive flair) and Lawson Wood has become highly collectible now, 10 x 8in. $30

'Sporting Days', a 1920's Raphael Tuck 'Oilette' picture puzzle by H. Drummond, 6 x 9in. $35

Double-sided puzzles became very popular during the inter-war jigsaw 'craze' years; they were mass produced on a large scale, since they offered 'two for the price of one'. This one has a typically sentimental subject for each side, 7 x 10in. $15

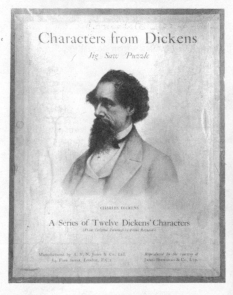

'A Welcome Intrusion', a 1930's Chad Valley puzzle with its characteristic patented— 'book-box' design of container with guide picture, 10 x 14in. $25

'Captain Cuttle', one of a series of twelve Dickens characters made into puzzles and issued by A. V. N. Jones in the 1930's, 10 x 8ih. $40

'The Victory', one of The Delta Fine Cut 'National' Series of puzzles from the 1930's. The box lid bears a traditional design that has a family resemblance to the Victory box, 13 x 18in. $40

KEYS

These fine old keys come from lock sets which were designed to be both functional and attractive.

The old locks come on the market less frequently than the keys, most remaining united with their original door or chest, but keys are more plentiful and offer an interesting variety of designs.

They are most commonly made of steel, iron and brass though some unusual examples are in gilded wrought iron or pinchbeck. Great attention was given to the design of the 'bow', many are intricately designed and decorated with figures, birds, cherubs and heraldic motifs.

It will add interest to the collection if you know a little about the history of a key and obligingly, they occasionally have faded, written labels attached.

A 15th/16th century Venetian key, 6in. long. $200

A large iron key converted into a corkscrew. $40

Late 17th century French Renaissance key, the bow cut as two stylized dolphins, 6in. long. $440

Late 18th century iron door key, 5in. long. $15

Early 18th century French iron masterpiece lantern key, 5¾in. long. $5,250

Italian 18th century iron casket key, 4¼in. long. $6,500

Early 17th century Italian steel key, the bow pierced and cut with scrolling foliage, 3¾in. $400

A North Italian key, the bow cast and chiseled with scrolls, circa 1600, 8¼in. long. $615

17th century French Renaissance key, the bow cut with adorned griffins, 5½in. long. $770

An all steel patent safe key, 3in. long, 'Climax Detector Birmingham'. (Christopher Sykes) $70

An 18th century French casket key, the gilt bow cast and chased in the form of entwined dolphins. $170

KINGSWARE

In 1899 a new method of stoneware production was introduced at Burslem which involved applying color slips of subdued greens, yellows and reddish browns to the interior of plaster molds in which a design was impressed. When another brown slip was poured in the colors fused to give a deep and soft effect to the embossed design.

Kingsware was mostly used for the production of pottery flasks to hold whiskey and they were produced in enormous quantities, usually in editions of 1,000, for firms like John Dewar and Sons of Perth; Bulloch Lade; Greenlees and Watson and the Hudson's Bay Company.
The glaze was most commonly a dark treacle brown but more unusual was a paler yellow called the 'Kingsware yellow glaze'.

Royal Doulton Kingsware tobacco jar decorated in relief with a gentleman smoking, 8¼in. high. $100

The Leather Bottle, a Royal Doulton Kingsware flask, circa 1918, 6¼in. high, 6in. long. $520

Squire, a Kingsware Toby jug, hallmarked silver rim, 6½in. high. $500

The Alchemist, a Royal Doulton Kingsware clock, 7½in. high, circa 1913. $640

Dickens' Characters, a Royal Doulton Kingsware water jug, 7in. high. $170

Pied Piper, a Royal Doulton Kingsware water jug with hallmarked silver rim and lid, 8½in. high. $220

KITCHEN EQUIPMENT

Times change, and fashions with them, but one branch of the antiques business which goes on forever is that dealing in kitchenware – particularly from the Victorian period.

It all began as a reaction against the vogue, some years back, for plastic laminated antisepsis in the kitchen. Doubtless influenced to some extent by the country-kitchen full-color photographs on the cookery pages, people began to react quite strongly against the characterless rooms in which they were expected to create culinary marvels. Storage jars, pestles and mortars, the odd copper saucepan or two, gradually the demand grew from a trickle to a steady stream.

For centuries, the kitchen in upper and middle class houses was a purely functional room used only by servants for the preparation of their masters' meals. No attention was paid to comfort, decor or labor saving.

As the years passed, meals were no longer prepared by servants but by the mistress of the household who became not only the cook, but nanny and bottle washer into the bargain. And now the wheel has turned still further; the kitchen has become a fashionable room. Food is not only cooked here, but often eaten too, and the kitchen is becoming one of the main living rooms of the house – often being recreated as a place in which to relax and sometimes even entertain.

For this reason alone, the utensils of the great kitchens of the past are much sought after for their decorative qualities. The Victorian kitchens with their copper and brass, their intricately carved wooden implements and their stone and steelware have a lot to offer, particularly since all these things were made in the days when mass production was in its infancy and individual artisan skills were given full rein.

19th century wooden malt shovel used in brewery. $40

A 19th century steel and beechwood meat cleaver, stamped W. & O. Wynn, 11in. long.
$100

White glass rolling pin painted with sailing ships. $40

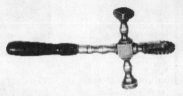

A 19th century brass and ebony pastry wheel, 8½in. long. $200

A set of four late 19th century copper plated tin molds. $30

Late 19th century tin scoop.
$15

Victorian wooden handled tin scoop. $6

Twin handled steel chopper.
$18

Late Victorian chopper with turned wood handle. $15

Victorian turned wood crumpet pricker with steel spikes.
$15

Late 19th century cast iron mincer 'Rollman Food Cropper', No. 15.
$6

Set of six late 19th century shaped pastry cutters. $36

Victorian cased set of icing bag barrels. $36

An early bentwood quart measure. $36

Early 19th century American wire potato boiler, body diam. 11in. (Robt. W. Skinner Inc.)
$415

One of two 19th century copper jelly molds of castellated form, 4in.
$245

Lister ball bearing cream separator. $30

Plated tin tongue press, circa 1900. $30

Toleware spice box complete with contents and central nutmeg grater, circa 1835. $55

Spong & Co. metal coffee grinder. $30

Sheet tin bread board and rolling pin, 11 x 18½in. (Robt. W. Skinner Inc.) $450

Farmhouse individual butter churn, late 19th century. $25

Early 19th century japanned tin plate warmer with cast metal carrying grips, 27in. high. (Lawrence Fine Art) $2,860

Late 19th century plated tin milk can, ½ gallon.$16

Kitchen grater of tin with three variations, circa 1900. $8

LABELS

With many items it is the impact of the label upon the customer which sells the product. Labels are, therefore, usually handsomely produced and eye catching. Collectors with an interest in a particular subject find that these items, though inexpensive, are not easy to find but if you just want a few for decorative purposes many ephemera dealers carry a small stock.

The labels used on fruit boxes and textile bales are particularly impressive simply because of their size and these are in demand.

Most label collectors however, tend to specialize in such as beer, whisky, perfume, cheese or wine labels, adding to their collections with a keen eye on the weekly shopping, for it is surprising how quickly labels date and acquire a 'period' charm.

Squaw Brand, Petit Pois, Centerville Canning Co., 1910. (Dodo) $8

Buy-Rite Sliced Pineapple, 1925. (Dodo) $4

Hula Apples, U.S.A. $5

Late 19th century American **Trick Pony and Punch & Judy** lithographic labels, the larger 5½ x 3½in. $395

Late 19th century American **Speaking Dog and Stump Speaker** lithographic labels, the larger 5 x 3¼in. $530

Extrait Concentre Aux Fleurs. (Dodo) $2

Orisia Lotion, Paris, 1920's. (Dodo) $8

Wide Awake, Nunca
Dormimos. $2

Cordial, Lake County Citrus Sales.
                                    $4

Nehesco Textile Label.
                     $3

American late 19th cen-
tury 'Mason' toy savings
bank lithographic label,
5½ x 3¼in.   **$245**

Golden Sceptre, Orange Crate Label,
1920. (Dodo)   **$15**

Late 19th century Ameri-
can **Humpty Dumpty**
lithographic label,
5½ x 3½in.   **$200**

Roulette. $3

Nuchief, Washington Apples, 1950's.
                                    $5

Titania Textile label.
                     $2

LAMPS

Although early lamps were operated on little more than an oil supplied candle, by about 1860, the wick and paraffin burning table lamp had been perfected and was in common use. Another popular type was the acetylene lamp, which has a small reservoir of water placed above a container at the base, filled with calcium carbide. Drops of water released onto the carbide would produce acetylene gas which, in turn, produced a brilliant white flame. While most people have some idea of the value of a Victorian brass oil lamp there is a possibility that some of the old brass carbide lamps and tilley lamps may be overlooked. These are collected today and have some monetary value.

A long way away from the basic function of providing a source of light, are the shimmering Art lamps of the late 19th and early 20th century. Lamps are often signed and the names to look for are Daum, Emile Galle, Gustav Gurschner, Handel, Lalique, Loetz and many more. These lamps are traditionally made with a cast bronze stem.

A Tiffany Studios favrile glass and bronze ten-light lily lamp, 19½in. high. (Woolley & Wallis) $7,500

A Daum Art Deco table lamp, frosted glass with wrought iron, engraved with cross of Lorraine, circa 1925, 46cm. high. (Christie's) $6,000

'Nymph among the bull-rushes', a bronze table lamp cast after a model by Louis Convers, 28.1cm. high. (Christie's) $1,000

A Galle blowout lamp, varying shades of red on an amber ground, signed, circa 1900, 44.5cm. high. (Christie's) $60,000

A Tiffany Studios gilt bronze and glass table lamp, stamped Tiffany Studios New York 590, 48cm. high.(Christie's) $3,250

An early 20th century Handel lamp on Hampshire pottery base, with Mosserine shade, 20in. high. (Robt. W. Skinner Inc.) $1,000

LAMPS

A Louis Comfort Tiffany bronze leaded glass and favrile glass two-light table lamp, 56cm. high. (Christie's) $6,300

A Victorian three-branch brass light fitting, 1880. (British Antique Exporters) $210

A patinated bronze and ormolu baluster vase, with ivory silk shade, 24½in. high. (Christie's) $2,350

Victorian brass desk lamp, 1900. (British Antique Exporters) $100

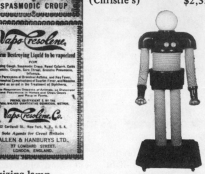

A medical vaporizing lamp to destroy germs, together with instructions 'printed in U.S.A.'. (Christopher Sykes) $175

Rudolph, a robot light fitting, designed by Frank Clewett, 149cm. high. (Christie's) $3,500

A lampe bouillotte with three candlebranches and pleated green silk shade, 20in. high. (Christie's) $2,200

A Gustav Stickley hammered copper lamp with willow shade, circa 1905, signed, 22in. high, 20in. diam. (Robt. W. Skinner Inc.) $1,500

A Legras etched and enameled glass table lamp with mushroom shaped shade, 50.6cm. high. (Christie's) $2,350

A Doulton Flambe figure by Noke, modeled as a seated Buddha, mounted as a lamp, circa 1930, 57.5cm. high. (Christie's) $1,250

A plated two-branch student's oil lamp with green tinted shades. (Peter Wilson & Co.) $340

A tole urn decorated in lacquer with flowers and with pleated silk shade, 27½in. high, including shade. (Christie's) $1,800

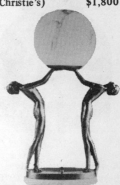

A bronze, marble and glass lamp cast after a model by M. Le Verrier, signed, circa 1925, 86.2cm. high. (Christie's) $2,000

A Galle double overlay cameo glass lamp, circa 1900, 32.4cm. high. (Christie's) $11,000

An Art Deco bronzed electric table lamp on oval base with onyx stand, 20in. high. (Anderson & Garland) $450

Early 20th century Tiffany blue iridescent candle lamp, signed, 1924, New York, 12¼in. high. (Robt. W. Skinner Inc.) $950

A Fulper pottery 'Vase-Kraft' table lamp, circa 1915, 18in. high, 16½in. diam. (Robt. W. Skinner Inc.) $5,600

A carved cameo helmet shell lamp, probably Italy, depicting Homer and nine muses dancing, 11½in. high. (Robt. W. Skinner Inc.) $250

LEACH

The English potter Bernard Leach was born in 1887. He spent his early years both in Japan and England, returning to Japan to teach engraving and design. His work was influential in the development of the Japanese folk art movement which gained recognition in 1929. In 1920 he started work at St. Ives in Cornwall, producing stoneware from local materials and re-introducing the art of marbled slip decoration.

The work of Bernard Leach and his pupils is noted for the vast range of decorative techniques. Marks include initials BL impressed within rectangle or painted and the work of the Leach pottery at St. Ives is marked with S and I crossed, with two dots, enclosed in circle or square, impressed.

While this is undoubtedly an expensive field of collecting it is one in which knowledge will be rewarded, for the reason that, the work of Leach is not immediately recognizable to the general public as a piece of such potential value.

A stoneware tea caddy, Bernard Leach, circa 1970, 16cm. high. (Christie's) $440

A stoneware teapot with cane handle by Bernard Leach, circa 1920, 17.2cm. high. (Christie's) $1,250

A stoneware flattened rectangular slab bottle by B. Leach, impressed BL and St. Ives seals, circa 1960, 20.2cm. high.(Christie's) $2,250

A tall stoneware jug, by Bernard Leach, with ribbed rim and strap handle, 28.8cm. high. (Christie's) $600

A slip-trailed soft raku bowl by Bernard Leach, impressed BL and St. Ives seals, circa 1920, 23.2cm. diam. (Christie's) $1,350

A stoneware large oviform vase by Bernard Leach, impressed BL and St. Ives seals, circa 1958, 34.3cm. high. (Christie's) $1,250

LEAD SOLDIERS

In 1893, with the British Empire at its height, the firm of William Britain introduced a series of toy soldiers representing the regiments of the British army.

These were an immediate success and Britain's went on to increase their range, producing an abundance of military models including armies of other nations, tanks, gun units and army bands. Britain's continued to produce new models up until the time of the Coronation of Elizabeth II in 1953.

Early models fixed to a round base are more valuable than those on a rectangular base, and the stamp on the bottom will help to date the pieces. 'Copyright Wm. Britain' was used before 1912, and 'Britains Ltd.' before 1937. After this 'Made in England' was added. Although most sets change hands at less than $200, a set of Salvation Army Bandsmen recently made nearer $2,000 and the largest set ever made by Britains sold for over $15,000.

Britains Foreign Legion, set of No. 1711, in original box, 1950's. (Robt. W. Skinner Inc.) $55

Britains set No 1470, The Coronation State Coach, including eight Windsor grays, four outriders, H.M. Queen Elizabeth II and Prince Philip, in gold painted state coach, in original box. $320

Britains set No. 37, Band of the Coldstream Guards. $400

Britains set of South African Mounted Infantry in its original box. (Phillips) $780

Heyde 30mm. hand-painted Indian elephant, with howdah, containing Maharajah and bower, an Indian lancer, 5 palm trees, six 54mm. scale figures and six other figures. $200

Elastolin 100mm. scale hand-painted composition soldiers, Coldstream Guards, marching at slope arms in full equipment. $1,100

LEAD SOLDIERS

Britains set No. 315, 10th Royal Hussars, Prince of Wales' Own, at the halt with swords, and bugler, in original box. (Christie's) $500

Britains Attendants to the State Coach, including walking outriders, footmen of the Royal Household and Yeomen, in original box. $370

Part of a set of Britains 21st Lancers, Royal Scots Greys (2nd Dragoons), and The 9th Queen's Royal Lancers, No. 24 $150

Two Whistock boxes of Britains King's Royal Rifle Corps, No. 98, each box containing eight figures, circa 1905. $400

Britains extremely rare display set 131, the largest set ever made by Britains, consisting of 281 figures including cavalrymen, infantrymen, bandsmen, sailors and Camel Corps soldiers, circa 1905. (Phillips) $15,000

Eight British Boer War soldiers wearing tropical helmets, in their original box. (Wallis & Wallis) $85

A Britains set No. 434, R.A.F. Monoplane, with two pilots and four R.A.F. personnel, in original box. (Christie's) $1,400

Britains set No. 1634, The Governor-General's Foot Guards, marching at the slope arms, with officer, in original box. (Christie's) $150

Britains early set No. 211, 18in. Howitzer No. 2, with ten horse team, in review order with No. 2 Howitzer and limber, in original box. $1,500

A Britains boxed set of The Royal Horse Artillery gun team. (Phillips) $10,000

Two Whistock boxes of Britains Bluejackets, No. 78, each box containing eight figures, circa 1905. $350

A Britains R.A.M.C. 4-horse covered ambulance waggon, in original linen cover, with 2 A.S.C. drivers and 2 seated R.A.M.C. orderlies, all full dress, and R.A.M.C. officer, nurse and stretcher. (Wallis & Wallis) $250

Twelve German made solid pewter model Boer soldiers, 45mm. high, circa 1900, in their original red box. (Wallis & Wallis) $100

Part of an eighteen piece set of Britains model hunt, unboxed. (Hobbs & Chambers) $75

LIBERTY

In 1875 Arthur Lazenby Liberty was the manager of Farmer & Rogers, a London firm specializing in Oriental imports, when he plucked up the courage to open his own shop in Regent Street.

He commissioned works from many of the designers associated with the Arts and Crafts movement and within five years had established himself as the leading purveyor of goods in the avant garde style. His enthusiasm embraced not only furniture and fabrics but pottery, silver, pewter and jewelry.

Noted among the pewter designs are those marked TUDRIC, which date from 1902, and among the silver articles those marked CYMRIC, a range launched in 1899.

A Liberty & Co. walnut 'Thebes' stool, the square seat strung with brown hide. (Christie's) $1,250

A Liberty pewter and enamel table clock designed by Archibald Knox, circa 1900, 14.2cm. high. (Christie's) $1,850

A Liberty & Co. silver and enamel wine coaster, Birmingham hallmarks for 1905, 9.5cm. diam., 2oz.14dwt. gross wt. (Christie's) $700

A Liberty & Co. Tudric pewter 'Architectural' mantel clock, circa 1920, 7¼in. high. (Robt. W. Skinner Inc.) $1,000

A Liberty pewter and Clutha glass dish on stand, designed by A. Knox, 6½in. high. (Christie's) $600

A Liberty silver coffee pot, designed by A. Knox, Birmingham, hallmarks for 1906, 21.6cm. high. (Christie's) $675

LIGHT BULBS

One Otto Von Guericke, a contemporary of Robert Boyle, is generally regarded as producing the first light from electricity back in the 17th century when he discovered that by holding the hands firmly against a revolving ball of sulphur, the friction produced a dull glow.

It wasn't, however, until the electric arc was discovered early in the 19th century by Sir Humphrey Davy, that a practical source of artificial light was established.

Light bulbs themselves date from about 1841 when an American inventor named Starr found that a bright light could be produced by sending an electric current through a piece of carbon.

The first successful incandescent electric lamps produced in the U.K. were made by J.W. Swan of Newcastle and subsequently by several other inventors and pioneers including St. George Lane Fox, while in America the market was dominated by T.A. Edison.

All of these manufacturers used carbonized material as the filament, such as a cotton thread (Swan), a fibre of grass (Lane Fox) or a sliver of bamboo (Edison). Such light was regarded with fascination and carbon filament lamps were tremendously popular from 1880 until the turn of the century.

The big breakthrough came in 1906 when the General Electric Company found that by using a tungsten filament sealed in a glass bulb, it not only produced a clear white light but used very little electricity as well.

This revolutionized the whole industry and created a massive demand, though doubts were expressed at the time as to the adverse effect all this powerful light would have on the eyesight of future generations.

Swan 'Pipless' circa 1882. $600

'Bottom Loop' bulb probably by Swan Lamp, circa 1884. $300

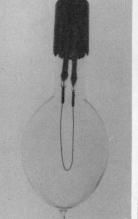

English light bulb by Lane Fox, circa 1881. $500

Nernst Lamp, circa 1900, 6in. high. $75

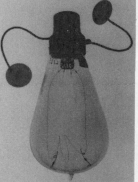

Dual Carbon Filament (dim/bright), circa 1905. $50

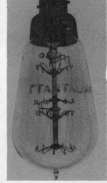

Tantalum Lamp, probably German, circa 1906. $75

MAGAZINES

There seem to be magazines on every conceivable subject possible, and there seem to be collectors for all of them. Some, such as The Electrical Times, obviously have only a limited appeal and can be bought for $1 or less, while others have a wider collecting public because of the more general nature of their content.

Who can resist a forty year old copy of a pictorial magazine with its superb studies of the way we used to live. Magazines are often bound up in annual sets and these often had covers and adverts removed, this seriously devalues them.

In fact it is the adverts which often dictate the value of many magazines for usually they are more suited for framing than the general contents.

Fun, Magic, Mystery, May 1935. $10

The Ring, Exclusive Annual Ratings, February 1958. $2

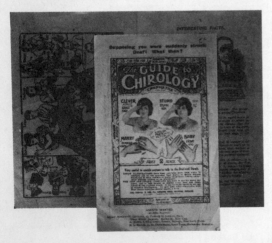

The Guide to Chirology. $4

Electrical Times, August 1937. $1

Children's Magazine 1912. $3   Catalogue of Free Gifts given with Watson's Soap. $3   My Magazine 1920.$3

World Radio, Christmas 1930. $4   Physical Culture, For Mind and Body, December 1930. $3

Child's Companion and Juvenile Instructor 1890. $4   Canadian Colored Concert Co., 1890. $5   The Red Arrow Series 1932 No. 1 of the Swift Story Paper. $2

The Saturday Evening Post, April 1958. **$5**

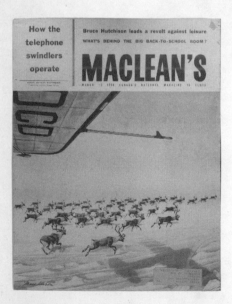

Maclean's, Canada's National Magazine, March
1958. **$1**

August 1971 issue of **'Playboy'** Entertainment
for Men. **$3**

MAPS

The enthusiasm shown by maps and atlas collectors has guaranteed the continuance of sales held specifically for them with the big map names of Ortelius, Speed, Jansson, Valk and Sanson well to the fore.

A travel book with maps is even more sought after than one with only prints and plates and books of maps alone can make hugh prices. A Mercator atlas worth over $300,000 turned up not long ago on a Belgium roadside bookstall.
More common maps are those produced for various religious and missionary organizations and maps made for Victorian cyclists, railway maps and even stagecoach maps. There are more of those still about than may be imagined.

Map of New York by The Society for the Diffusion of Useful Knowledge, 1844.
$650

Travels Through The Counties of England by Reuban Ramble, 1845.
$1,150

Town Plan of Bruges from the Braun and Hogenburg Civitates Orbis Terrarum, 1612.   (Phillips) $4,200

Bedfordshire from Christopher Saxton's Hartfordiae Comitatus, 1579.   (Phillips) $3,000

Abraham Ortelius, 'Theatrum Orbis Terrarum', 112 double-page maps, Anvers, C. Plantin, 1584. (Christie's)   **$22,000**

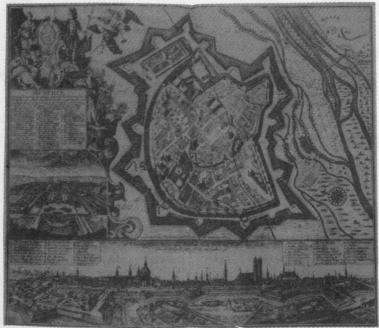

J. B. Homann, 'Atlas Novus', 3 volumes, pictorial engraved title and 367 engraved plates, Nuremberg.   **$76,000**

Noronha Freyre, 'Istoria delle Guerre del Regno del Brasilie', 2 volumes in one, 26 engraved folding maps, plans and views, Rome 1700. (Christie's)　　**$4,000**

Claudio Duchetti, 'De Minorica Insula', engraved map, attractive pictures of buildings, hills etc., Rome 1570.　　**$420**

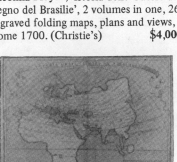

John Knapton, 'Geographia Antiqua', maps linen backed, extra illustrations with 8 maps, Joseph Priestley's copy, 1800. (Robt. W. Skinner Inc.)　　**$620**

Ignace Pardies, 'Globi Coelestis . . . Opus Postumum', 2nd Edition, 6 double page star maps and large folding engraved table, French Jesuit inscription, very rare, Paris, 1693.　　**$1,300**

Nicolaus Visscher, 'Atlas Minor sive totius orbis terrarum', 36 hand-colored double page engraved maps, Amsterdam, after 1705. (Christie's)　　**$4,800**

MARBLE

The name 'marble' means shining stone and it is a term applied to any limestone or dolomite which is sufficiently close in texture to allow it to be polished.

Greek sculptors worked in marble from their own islands, particularly Paros. The Venus de Milo is a prime example of their art, but the stone most used by the Romans and up to the present day is Carrara marble which is found in northern Italy. India's Taj Mahal is a miracle in marble and the stone for its delicate pierced screens was quarried in Ulwar.

Objects made of marble have always been much coveted and they range from fountain heads to religious objects, fireplaces, vases and statuary. The French were very keen on marble during the 19th century and ormolu mounted vases made at that time fetch high prices.

Fine French marble bust, 1870. (British Antique Exporters) **$550**

One of a pair of Verde di Prato models of lions, 21¼in. wide, 16½in. high. (Christie's) **$4,000**

Marble copy of head of Apollo Belvedere, 19in. high, on fitted stand. (Robt. W. Skinner Inc.) **$1,700**

A pair of Breccia and black marble obelisks, 15in. high. (Christie's) **$750**

A marble relief of a Roman Emperor on a blue ground, in giltwood frame, 8½ x 7in., and another similar. (Christie's) **$2,650**

A Venetian white marble wellhead, the Lion of St. Mark sculptured in relief, dated 1394. (Crowther, Syon Lodge Ltd.)**$10,000**

MARBLE

One of a pair of gilt metal mounted Breche Violette marble vases with fruiting finials, 19in. high. (Christie's) $3,675

Pair of 19th century carved Carrara marble sphinxes, 2ft.5in. high. (Crowther, Syon Lodge Ltd.) $8,750

A white marble relief of a Roman Emperor in white and gold oval frame, 7½in. high. (Christie's) $750

Late 14th century white marble head, possibly of Frederick II, 17¾in. high. (Robt. W. Skinner Inc.) $1,000

A late George III white and sienna marble mantelpiece with breakfront stepped top, 62in. high. (Christie's) $1,300

A 15th century Italian carved marble head of a king, mounted on a wooden base, 14½in. high. (Robt. W. Skinner Inc.) $1,000

A white marble group of a mother and child with a deer, inscribed G. Geefs Premier, Statuaire de S.M. le Roi, 42in. high. (Christie's) $1,200

A white marble sculpture of a standing naked Venus, 26in. high. (Lots Road Chelsea Auction Galleries) $650

Marble bust of Apollo, head turned down gazing to the right, 18¾in. high. (Robt. W. Skinner Inc.) $3,500

MARTINWARE

Robert, Walter and Edwin had all, at one time or another, worked at the Doulton factory in Lambeth but they eventually got together and opened their own workshop at Southall in 1877. It was run by the fourth brother, Charles, who also ran a retail shop in Holborn to sell the wares the brothers produced.

Most of the leering birds and other animal models were made by the eldest brother, Robert, while Walter prepared the clay and made vases, leaving the youngest brother, Edwin, to do all the fancy decoration and, doubtless, make the tea, run round the corner to get the paper and all the other things youngest brothers do. They also produced candlesticks, jugs, clock cases and goblets until the eventual close of the factory in 1914.

A Martin Bros. oviform single-handled pottery jug, in an uneven gray glaze with deeper brown patches, 9¼in. high. (Christie's) $325

A Martin Bros. stoneware jug, the bulbous body suggesting a sea-creature, 21.8cm. high. (Christie's) $750

A Martin Bros. stoneware tobacco jar and cover, modeled as a grotesque grinning cat, 1885, 22cm. high. (Christie's) $12,500

A Martin Brothers stoneware vase with incised decoration of flowering lilies and a dragon-fly, London & Southall 18.7.84, 20.5cm. high. (Christie's) $550

A Martin Bros. stoneware 'judge' bird tobacco jar and cover, London & Southall 4-1889, 25.8cm. high. (Christie's) $4,000

A Martin Bros. face flask with two handles, incised marks dated 1901, 8in. high. (Christie's) $1,250

A Martin Bros stoneware model of a bird, 36cm. high, the head only dated 1898. (Phillips) $4,900

A large Martin Bros stoneware jardiniere of tapering cylindrical shape, 32cm. high. (Christie's) $960

A Martin Bros stoneware two-handled spirit flask, 9½in. high, London and Southall, 1901. (Reeds Rains) $1,100

A Martin Bros stoneware spherical vase, London Southall, 1892, 9in. high. (Christie's) $600

A Martin Bros stoneware grotesque, double face jug with strap handle, 1897, 22.8cm. high. (Christie's) $2,600

A Martin Bros stoneware jug painted with fish and sea monsters on mottled blue ground, 10¼in. high, London and Southall 1897. (Reeds Rains) $1,100

A Martinware gourd single-handled lobed pottery jug, London Southall, circa 1900, 10in. high. (Christie's) $650

A Martin Bros stoneware slender oviform vase, London Southall, 1889, 13in. high. (Christie's) $400

A stoneware Martin Bros jug in dark brown and blue glazes, circa 1900, 21cm. high. (Christie's) $250

MARY GREGORY

One of the most distinctive styles of glasswork is that known as Mary Gregory.

Although most of the glass in this style seen today was manufactured during the second half of the 19th century at Jablonec, Czechoslovakia, by the firm of Hahn, the original Mary Gregory worked as an enameler at the Boston & Sandwich Glass Company in the U.S.A.

There she decorated inexpensive blown and tinted glass decanters, jugs and vases with pink or opaque white figures, usually of playful children frolicking, flying kites, fishing, trundling hoops or picking flowers.

The base colors are likely to be red, green, blue, pink, amber or even turquoise, with the earlier examples tending to be slightly 'softer' than pieces made at the turn of the century.

All Mary Gregory glass however, from wherever the provenance, is now eagerly sought after for its appeal is much wider than that normally attributed to glassware.

Cranberry glass, inexpensively produced in Britain in the late 19th century, was often engraved with Mary Gregory style figures. This is a clear pinkish-red glass originally produced for use in the manufacture of chemists' bottles and then adopted in the production of vases, bowls and dishes. A characteristic of Cranberry glassware is the applied clear glass frilled rim.

Mary Gregory amber glass pin tray depicting a boy with a butterfly net. $170

Mary Gregory glass jug, 8in. high. $100

Mary Gregory green glass decanter. $60

Pair of Mary Gregory green glasses depicting a boy and girl. $120

Mary Gregory hand-painted glass cream jug. $50

Mary Gregory enameled dish with everted rim, circa 1880, 13¼in. diam. $300

MATCH CASES

Matchboxes have not always been the simple card, wood or plastic containers we know today. Originally, they were known as fire boxes, match safes or safety boxes.

Owing to the fact that early matches were liable to flare into life at the slightest knock, or with exposure to not very great heat, it was felt necessary to keep them in containers which, in the event of accidental combustion, would restrict the fire.

As far as is known, the first friction matches were produced in about 1827 and were sold in a tin case to a Mr. Hixon by their maker, John Walker of Stockton-on-Tees. By 1850 the different types of fire boxes were almost limitless, often taking the form of soldiers, historical figures or animals made of iron, brass and other metals. Usually, the heads of the figures were hinged to allow matches to be stored in their hollow interiors.

Very often, there was a small hole somewhere in which a single, lit match could be placed – possibly for reasons of economy in that this allowed the full length of the wooden shaft to burn, and possibly as a means of holding the flame steady when it was being used to melt sealing wax.

In addition to the metal fire boxes, some quite beautiful examples were made of ceramics or wood. Many of these had different provisions for igniting the various kinds of matches. Some merely had roughened patches, others had two roughened disks between which the match head was sandwiched before being sharply withdrawn to effect ignition. There was also a type of match which consisted of a small wooden splint tipped with chlorate of potash. This was lit by dipping the tip into sulphuric acid. Containers for these usually took a cylindrical form, in the center of which stood the small bottle of acid surrounded by the potash-tipped matches.

Vesta match case showing King Edward, 1901. $150

Vesta match case advertising Otto Monsteds Margarines. $260

Silver vesta case inscribed Bryant & May's Wax Vestas. (Phillips) $110

Silver match case with floral decoration. $70

A gold match safe, 19th century, with floral and scroll motifs and a gem set clover in central cartouche. (Robt. W. Skinner Inc.) $510

Oval Vesta case in the form of a creel, by T. Johnson, London 1883, 5.7cm. long. $1,500

Metal match case in the form of a Gladstone bag. $100

A Victorian brass matchbox holder in the form of a book. $20

MATCH STRIKERS

Before the widespread use of matches in boxes there were numerous little containers designed to house them. Made from a variety of materials including wood, bone, glass, papier
mache, Tunbridgeware, enamel, stone and china, their common feature is a lidless compart-
ment for the matches and a grooved or roughened striking surface.

The most numerous and generally regarded as most appealing specimens are those made of
porcelain by the German firm of Conte and Boehme, who were also responsible for producing most of the 'fairings' which are so eagerly sought after today.

Many bear a humorous or slightly risque inscription on the base often borrowed from a
popular song of the day.

'Match, Sir' (also captioned
'Any Lights Sir'). $90—$150

'I Am Going A-Milking Sir,
She Said'. $90—$150

'Daily News Sir'. $150—$200

'A Copper Sir?'
$30—$50

'Peau D'Lapin Chiffons'.
$90—$150

'Sweet Violets, Sir'. $90—$150

MEDICAL ITEMS

When one surveys the array of medical instruments the Victorians had to endure, it seems a miracle that so many survived at all. And this is the fascination which has given all redundant medical items a ready and eager market.

Cased sets of surgical instruments are particularly sought after by makers such as Hutchinson, A. & S. Maw, J. Milliken and William Pepys. As a rule, wooden, ivory and bone handled instruments are made prior to 1870 and are much more desirable than the later chromium plated examples.

Amputation sets, leech jars, medicine chests and microscopes are all very collectible and can obtain astronomical money for early examples.

Beware, however, of some of the Victorian electrical appliances offered as 'cure alls', for which they had a fascination — try them at your peril.

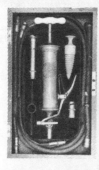

Mid 19th century S. Maw, Son & Thompson enema or stomach pump apparatus, English, 12½ x 7½in. $350

A Keratometer, an instrument for measuring the curvature of the cornea of the eye, made of brass on a cast-iron stand, circa 1910, 24in. long. (Christopher Sykes) $770

French mid 19th century Charrier amputation set, in fitted walnut case, 16 x 9½in. $1,210

An all brass medical ear syringe with a three-finger pull one end and the hollow tube the other, 9½in. closed, circa 1870. (Christopher Sykes) $100

Dr. Macaura' 'Blood Circulator' complete with attachments and original box. $25

An 18th century set of surgeon's instruments, engraved Ambulance de S M. L'Empereur. (Christie's) $16,200

MEDICAL ITEMS

A late 19th century mahogany medicine chest, 32cm. wide. $600

A Simpson part amputation set, in a fitted mahogany case. $1,150

A surgeon's instrument by 'Weiss, London', 7½in. long. (Christopher Sykes) $95

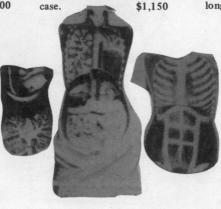

A dental spittoon in black and gilt metal, mid 19th century. $400

A 19th century four-part model of an anatomical torso. (Phillips) $1,750

A fine toothed bone saw with steel blade and ivory handle. $700

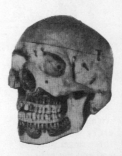

An anatomical model of the human dentition, with fourteen porcelain teeth, circa 1900. $500

A Czermak's demonstration laryngoscope by John Weiss & Son, circa 1870. $500

A student's demonstration human skull with hinged jaw. $300

MEISSEN

The manufacture of china in the Saxon town of Meissen near Dresden began in 1710. During the Napoleonic Wars, the industry suffered a decline but with the appointment of H. G. Kuhn as Director in 1849, its fortunes revived and many of the successful 18th century models were revived as well as new ones being introduced.

Among the most popular pieces of Meissen china are children and the mythological groups produced between 1860 and 1890 as well as models of soldiers and figures in contemporary costume which appeared after 1870. The Meissen mark is a device of crossed swords with the addition of dates in some cases. A dot appears between the sword blades on pieces made between 1924 and 1934.

A Meissen group of a scantily draped woman at her toilet, blue crossed swords marks and incised numerals, circa 1880, 15.5cm. high. (Christie's) $650

A Meissen bullet-shaped vase and cover in blue with decorated panels, on stand. (F. H. Fellows & Sons) $750

A Meissen figure of a jay modeled by J. J. Kandler, circa 1745, 39cm. high. (Christie's) $17,500

A Meissen hot water jug and cover, decorated in cisele gold, 17.5cm. high, red luster mark 11, 1725. (Lawrence Fine Art) $10,000

One of a pair of Meissen pug dogs modeled by J. J. Kandler and P. Reinicke, one with blue crossed swords mark on base, circa 1745, 15cm. high. (Christie's) $5,000

A Meissen rectangular tea caddy and cover, traces of blue crossed swords mark on base, circa 1770, 12.5cm. high. (Christie's) $1,750

281

A Meissen bombe-shaped snuff box with contemporary silver mounts, scroll thumbpiece, circa 1745, 7cm. wide. (Christie's) $2,250

A Meissen figure of a rhinoceros modeled by J. J. Kandler after Albrecht Durer, 1735-40, 17cm. long. (Christie's) $2,300

A Meissen chinoiserie dish, the center painted by C. F. Herold, blue crossed swords mark, circa 1734. (Christie's) $18,400

A Meissen group of a peasant woman, modeled by P. Reinicke, circa 1745, 15cm. high. (Christie's) $1,150

A Meissen two-handled quatrefoil tray and four cups, blue crossed swords marks and Pressnummer 24 and 26, circa 1740. (Christie's)$10,000

A Meissen circular snuff box and cover painted by B. G. Hauer, the interior of the base solid gilt, 1725-30, 7.5cm. diam. (Christie's) $27,500

A Meissen group of Die Polnische Verlobung modeled as a sultan with his Polish bride and Polish soldier servant, circa 1745, 15cm. high. (Christie's) $9,200

One of two Meissen figures of seated cats modeled by J. J. Kandler, circa 1740, 17.5cm. high. (Christie's) $9,200

A Meissen oval bombe-shaped snuff box and cover, 1725-28, 7cm. wide. (Christie's) $13,800

MINIATURES

These miniature pieces fall into three main categories. Dolls' house furnishings, apprentice pieces and simply miniature items which have been crafted to as small a scale as possible in perfect replica of full size objects.

Apprentice pieces, unlike dolls' house furnishings designed specifically for play, were made, as the description implies, by an apprentice, as perfectly as his talents would allow, as part of his final exam before graduating as a fully fledged craftsman. Although most of the furniture today dates from the 19th century, this is a practice which has been in operation since furniture was first made on a commercial scale, with early pieces obtaining the highest prices. It is a practice which would seem to have been fairly widespread for apprentice pieces can be found in all European countries as well as in America.

An American late Federal mahogany miniature chest of drawers, 10in. wide. (Christie's)　$1,500

An Empire mahogany miniature sofa, American, circa 1840, 19in. wide. (Christie's)　$2,000

Miniature 19th century banquet lamp with brown glass shade, 3in. high.$120

Miniature wicker fernery with high woven handle, 7in. high.　$40

An early 19th century miniature Dutch marquetry and mahogany bureau. (Woolley & Wallis)　$800

A miniature apprentice made marquetry top table.　$300

MINIATURES

Miniature Biedermeier nightstand with marble top and tiny oval mirror, 1 in. scale. (Theriault's) $155

Group of 19th century miniature furniture of a cupboard and three chairs, cupboard 7½ in. high. (Christie's) $130

Set of tableware in wooden case with red suede lined interior, 1 x 2 in. (Theriault's) $130

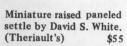

Miniature raised paneled settle by David S. White. (Theriault's) $55

Miniature Napoleonic-style bed and chairs, 4½ x 4 in. (Theriault's) $320

A Federal mahogany miniature chest of drawers, 1790-1810, 14½ in. wide. (Christie's) $1,245

19th century tin piano, 3½ x 4 in., in excellent condition. (Theriault's) $120

Part of a set of 19th century miniature maple wood furniture of a Gothic style settee and a set of shelves. (Theriault's) $140

Miniature contemporary canopy bed in walnut with quilted cover, 7½ in. high. (Theriault's) $210

MINIATURES

Miniature Chippendale style wing chair and stool with walnut cabriole legs, chair 4½in. high. (Theriault's) $40

Set of 19th century miniature maple wood furniture including a writing desk and two chairs, desk 5½in. wide. (Theriault's) $160

Miniature 19th century Biedermeier type dressing table, 5in. long, trimmed in marble-like stripes. (Theriault's) $260

Contemporary silver cash register in 19th century style, 1¼in. high. (Theriault's) $30

Miniature Austrian set of porcelain and silver cutlery of nineteen pieces in excellent condition. (Theriault's) $290

19th century miniature maple wood piano with functioning keyboard, 5in. wide. (Theriault's) $40

19th century hanging wall clock, 3½ x 1½in., with brass clock frame. (Theriault's) $90

19th century miniature maple dining-room set with carved legs and leather seats. (Theriault's) $80

Charles I miniature oak cupboard with diamond-inlaid panels, circa 1640, 2ft.7in. wide. $6,000

MINTON

This Staffordshire pottery began in Stoke on Trent in 1793 and produced a wide range of high quality items including Parian ware, vases in the Sevres style, painted plates, domestic earthenware, tiles, decorated panels and garden ornaments in terracotta and majolica.

Some of the famous names to look out for in Minton ware include T. Allen who painted panels and vases; T. Kirkby who decorated items with flowers and fruit; H. Mitchell, painter of animals and R. Pilsbury who painted flowers. Tiles by W. Crane, J. Moyr-Smith and E. J. Poynter are also highly sought after as are the earthenware vases in the Art Nouveau style produced by L. V. Solon between 1897 and 1909.

A Minton 'Christmas Jug', the handle modeled as entwined holly branches, impressed Minton 580 (circa 1870), 22.5cm. high. (Christie's) **$1,400**

A Minton jardiniere and underdish with molded decoration overall of rambling flowers, date code for 1858 on jardiniere, 37cm. high. (Christie's) **$2,750**

One of a pair of Minton pedestal form garden seats, naturalistic polychrome coloring on an olive ground, 43cm. high. (Christie's) **$3,000**

A Minton honeycomb dish modeled as a beehive, impressed Minton 1499 and date code for 1877, 18cm. high. (Christie's) **$3,250**

A pair of Minton full figure Toby jugs, impressed Minton 1104 and 1140 and with date stamps for 1867, restored, 28cm. and 28.4cm. high. (Christie's) **$950**

A Minton 'Perforated Garden Pedestal', impressed Minton 451 and date code for 1865, 80.5cm. high. (Christie's) **$900**

A Minton figure, 'Seahorse with Shell', after Carrier-Belleuse, impressed Minton 326 and with date code for 1872, 41.5cm. high. (Christie's) $1,900

A Minton figure, 'Vintager with basket in each hand', impressed Minton. (Christie's) $1,300

A Minton majolica jardiniere embossed with foxgloves and ferns, 1ft.7in. wide over the handles, 13in. high, date marked for 1871. (Hobbs & Chambers) $875

A Minton vase and cover, painted by H. Boullemier, the reverse by W. Payne, 18cm. high, mark in gold. (Lawrence Fine Art) $95

One of a pair of garden seats modeled as crouching monkeys holding coconuts and supporting cushions on their heads, 46.5cm. high. (Christie's) $16,000

One of a pair of Minton 'moon' vases with gilt loop handles, 26.5cm. high. (Lawrence Fine Art) $670

A large Minton 'moon flask' vase with two lug handles, circa 1890, 43.2cm. high. (Christie's) $700

A Minton aquarium hexagonal plate, decorated in polychrome colors with three frogs resting, impressed date marks for 1882, 37.6cm. diam. (Christie's) $500

A Minton 'Palissy' vase formed as a ewer, impressed Minton 900 and date code for 1872, 37cm. high. (Christie's) $650

MIRRORS

Since Narcissus admired his own reflection in a pool of water, people have wanted to see themselves as others see them but till the end of the Middle Ages they could only do this in hand mirrors of polished metal.

In 1507, however, the Venetian glassmakers at Murano acquired a monopoly on making mirrors of plain glass backed by an amalgam of mercury and tin. These mirrors were spotted and distorting but the quality improved after 1615 when an Englishman called Sir Robert Mansell patented his mirrors backed by mercury and tinfoil. His factory had over 500 employees and they exported mirrors all over Europe.

The earliest mirrors were small and hand held but when the Duke of Buckingham established a glass works at Vauxhall which could produce mirrors up to three and a half feet long, a revolution in interior decoration was on its way. Owners of fine houses bought mirrors to put on walls between windows and over chimney pieces.

Decorative mirrors are still hugely popular and antique examples fetch high prices. They are found not only as wall hangings but as dressing table and cheval mirrors and come in a variety of styles ranging from the rococo of the mid 18th century to elegant Chippendale gilded pine. This gave way to Chinese Chippendale and the more stately Adam style. Regency oval mirrors still go well with modern decorating schemes as do the larger Victorian gilt gesso framed mirrors.

A Regency giltwood and ebonized overmantel in the manner of Thomas Hope, 58½ x 50in. (Christie's) $9,400

An Irish, George III giltwood overmantel with shaped divided plates, the upper panel painted with a Venetian scene. (Christie's) $23,500

A mirror attributed to Bugatti, various woods decorated with beaten copperwork and copper and pewter inlay, circa 1900, 66 x 61.8cm. (Christie's) $2,000

Victorian mahogany marble top toilet mirror, 1860. (British Antique Exporters) $230

A Federal gilt convex mirror, circa 1820, 27½in. high. (Robt. W. Skinner Inc.) $500

A 19th century birchwood toilet mirror, the oval plate in Gothic arched frame, 29in. wide. (Christie's) $1,100

A Queen Anne giltwood mirror, 47 x 27½in. (Christie's) $4,320

A 17th century Spanish parcel gilt and grained mirror, 40½ x 28½in. (Christie's) $760

A Chippendale inlaid mahogany mirror, possibly N.Y., 1760/80, 43½in. high. (Christie's) $1,800

A George III giltwood mirror with later rectangular plate, 64 x 42in. (Christie's) $15,000

An early 18th century William and Mary walnut veneered mirror, 20in. wide. (Robt. W. Skinner Inc.) $1,400

A German Art Nouveau bronze domed mirror, 21in. high. (Christie's) $600

An 18th century giltwood
mirror with oval beveled
plate, 39 x 36in. (Christie's)
$3,420

A William and Mary oyster
walnut cushion-framed wall
mirror, 1ft.6in. high, circa
1700. $730

Late 18th century courting
mirror, North Europe, 23in.
high. (Robt. W. Skinner
Inc.) $3,100

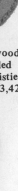

An 18th century Queen
Anne wall mirror, walnut
veneer on pine, 17¼in. high.
(Robt. W. Skinner Inc.)
$700

An Italian carved giltwood
and gesso decorated rococo
frame triptych dressing
table mirror, 3ft.5½in. high.
(Woolley & Wallis) $500

Late 18th century decora-
ted Chippendale mirror,
possibly America, 41½in.
high. (Robt. W. Skinner
Inc.) $3,000

A late 18th century Anglo-
Indian vizagapatam toilet
service veneered with engraved ivory. (Christie's)
$6,000

Late 18th century Chinese
mirror painting of a lady
seated under a tree, 14.5 x
11.7in. (Woolley & Wallis)
$3,250

A George II giltwood mirror
with rectangular beveled
plate, 46 x 25in. (Christie's)
$5,130

MODEL BUSES

Collecting toys and models has become increasingly popular over the past ten years and collectors today tend to specialize in a particular area of interest such as buses and trams. No model is too large or small, old or modern, for a good representative collection will cover items ranging in size from 1 in. to 8 ft. in length like the miniature 1945 Renault and 1949 Harrington coaches.

Prices vary considerably according to condition and while there are many expensive items it is still possible for a new collector to make a start for a comparatively modest outlay. Enthusiasts are well catered for with Collectors Fairs & Swopmeets. It is also worth looking in antique shops, secondhand shops and even in the long established toy shops for old stock. When buying for investment do look out for any signs of metal fatigue on early diecast models and also learn to distinguish between the many replica models being produced today and an authentic item.

Tootsietoy Greyhound bus (U.S.A.), diecast, circa 1940. **$70**

Wells Brimtoy (Great Britain) tinplate buses and coaches, circa 1950. Value **$60 to $120**

Tippco (German) tinplate clockwork streamline coach, circa 1950. **$90**

Rico (Spain) tramcar with cut out tin figures in the windows, circa 1910. **$400**

Siku (W. Germany) one and a half deck coach, circa 1950. **$90**

Siku (W. Germany) Bussing coach, circa 1950. **$70**

Siku (W. Germany) Riveria coach, circa 1950. **$55**

Wells Brimtoy Greenline tinplate coach, 1950's. **$100**

All Metal Toy Co. (U.S.A.) tinplate coaches, 1940's. **$80**

Betall tinplate trolleybus, circa 1950, 220mm. long. **$120**

Betall (Great Britain) tinplate trolleybus, 1950's, 175mm. long. **$80**

Guntermann (W. Germany) tinplate General Bus, 1920's. **$600**

Guinness tinplate bottle crate, 1964. **$120**

C.I.J. (France) postwar Renault coach. **$80**

C.I.J. (France) prewar Renault coach. **$120**

MODEL PLANES

Die-cast model toy aeroplanes have been made in numerous countries and have proved to be very popular and highly collectible. Examples made by companies such as Dinky, Corgi, Lone Star (U.K.), Tootsie Toys (U.S.A.), Tekno (Denmark), Schuco (Germany), Solido and Dinky (France), Mercury (Italy), C.I.J. (France), Aeromini and Tomica (Japan) are particularly popular.

Probably the most sought after model to any Dinky collector is number 992 Avro Vulcan. This model of the most famous of the R.A.F. V-Bombers, was produced between 1955 and 1956. The model is quite large and finished in silver. Although it was given the number 992 it carried the number 749.

An original mint and boxed Dinky Vulcan could reasonably be expected to fetch between $2,000 and $2,800 at auction. The original box is extremely rare and adds a great deal to its value.

Frobisher Class Air Liner No. 62R, 1939-41.
$90

Vautoor No. 60B, French Issue, 1957-63.
$40

Mayo Composite Aircraft No. 63, 1939-41.
$180

Tomica (Japanese) F-14A Tomcat, 1978-80.
$30

Avro Vulcan No. 992, issued 1955, (not issued in U.K., unknown number released in Canada). $2,400

Bloch 220, No. 64BZ, French made Dinky, sold in U.K., 1939-40. $90

A pre-war Empire Flying Boat No. 60R, 1937. $90

Nord Noratlas No 804, 1960-64. $200

A pair of Fairey Battles, known as the Mirror Image Pair, 1939-40. $200

Flying Boat Clipper III, No. 60W, 1938-41. $90

Imperial Airways Liner No. 60A, 1934-40. $150

The first Dinky boxed set, No. 60, issued in 1934 to 1940. $600

Flying Fortress No. 62G, 1939-41. $100

Lockheed Constellation No. 60C, produced by Meccano France, 1957-63. $200

MODEL SHIPS

Many of the model ships found today could well have originated from a market stall such as that set up on the Esplanade outside Edinburgh Castle by prisoners of the Napoleonic War. They sold wonderfully detailed model ships made largely from left-over bones from the cookhouse, embellished with scraps of ivory, wood and metal bought with the proceeds of other sales. Needless to say, these model ships varied somewhat in size and skill of execution, from two foot long models of 100 gun men o' war now costing many thousands of dollars, to quite small examples.

The Victorians, too, were enthusiastic makers of model ships, particularly those which could be put into glass cases.

A shipbuilder's model of the schooner yacht 'America', American, circa 1850, 28in. long. **$4,750**

Mid 19th century English contemporary model of a sailing ship hull, 9in. long. **$270**

A carved and painted model of ocean liner 'Liberte', executed for the Companie Generale Transatlantique, circa 1950, in wooden and plexi-glass case, 54in. long. (Christie's) **$6,000**

Early 20th century shipbuilder's model of the turret deck steamer 'Duffryn Manor', English, 44in. long, in glazed mahogany case. **$3,200**

An early 20th century American steamship model, diorama scene in mahogany case, 48in. wide. (Robt. W. Skinner Inc.) **$600**

A 20th century carved and painted model of the paddle steamer 'City of Key West', American, in wooden and glass case, 38in. long. (Christie's) **$1,250**

A late 19th/early 20th century ships model of a harbor dredger, 78in. long. (Boardman) **$960**

A builder's mirror back half model of a single screw cabin motor cruiser built by John I. Thorneycroft & Co. Ltd., London, 6 x 26in. (Christie's) **$2,000**

A 20th century American model of the extreme clippership 'Cutty Sark', on a walnut base, fitted in a glass case. (Christie's) $1,320

A contemporary early 19th century French prisoner-of-war bone and horn model man of war reputed to be the French ship of the line 'Redoubtable' of 74 guns, 20½ x 26¾in. (Christie's) $11,600

Late 18th century prisoner-of-war carved ivory ship, with rigging and thirty-four gun ports, Europe, 13½in. long. (Robt. W. Skinner Inc.) $800

A planked and rigged model of a Royal Naval Cutter built by I. H. Wilkie, Sleaford, 36 x 42in. (Christie's) $500

A planked and framed fully rigged model of the Royal Naval armed brig H.M.S. 'Grasshopper' of circa 1806, built by R. Cartwright, Plymouth, 32 x 41in. (Christie's) $940

Early 19th century prisoner-of-war bone model of a ship-of-the-line, 7¾in. long. (Christie's) $3,200

A 20th century American model of a fishing schooner, 'Kearsar', fitted in a glass case, 33½in. long. (Christie's) $935

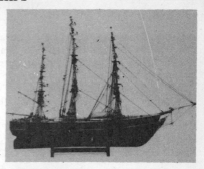

A 19th century three-masted ship model, sails furled, approx. 36in. long. (Robt. W. Skinner Inc.) $500

A detailed ¼in.:1ft. model of a twelve gun brig of circa 1840 built to the plans of H. A. Underhill by M. J. Gebhard, Tottenham, 36 x 47in. (Christie's) $4,350

A 19th century carved bone model of a frigate, probably French, 16½in. long. (Christie's) $3,000

An early 19th century French prisoner-of-war bone model of a ship-of-the-line, 8½in. long. (Christie's) $2,500

Early 19th century prisoner-of-war bone model of a First Class ship-of-the-line, 21in. long. (Christie's) $10,000

MODEL TRAINS

Model trains tend to fall into two distinct collecting fields. Those designed as toys, and these have been made since the last quarter of the 19th century mainly by the German firms of Bing and Marklin, and those superb scale models occasionally as large as 10ft. long, by firms such as Bassett-Lowke.

One of the most prolific British makers was Hornby and occasionally a complete set can be found in its original cardboard box. This adds greatly to the value as does the condition of the train; those with original paintwork and livery obtaining a premium.

Carriages, tenders, stations, bridges and all landscaping features are also eagerly sought after.

Marks to look for are G.B.N. for Bing, G.C. and Co. for Carette and G.M.C. for Marklin.

An exhibition standard 5in. gauge model of the Great Western Railway Dean Single 4-2-2 locomotive and tender No. 3012 'Great Western', 14 x 61in. (Christie's) $10,000

An exhibition standard 5in. gauge model of the William Dean diagram 21 Brake Composite twin bogie passenger coach No. 3391 of 1897, 13 x 57in. (Christie's) $2,600

A gauge 0 live steam spirit-fired model of the S.E.C.R. steam railcar, by Carette, circa 1908. (Christie's) $1,450

A 3½in. gauge model of the 4-4-0 locomotive and tender No. 573 built to the designs of 'Virginia', 11½ x 45in. (Christie's) $1,305

A 7¼in. gauge model of the Great Western Railway 4-6-0 locomotive and tender No. 1011 'County of Chester' rebuilt and reboilered by F. West, 21¾ x 10in. (Christie's) $17,400

A gauge 0 (3-rail) electric model of a Continental Doll BLS electric engine, with overhead pantograph, by Bing, circa 1930. (Christie's) $260

A 5in. gauge model of the London Midland and Scottish Railway re-built Scot Class 4-6-0 locomotive and tender No. 6154 'The Hussar' built by K. Edge, Peterborough, 15½ x 70in. (Christie's) $4,350

A gauge 0 clockwork model of the London Midland and Scottish Railway 4-4-0 locomotive and six-wheel tender No. 5320 'George V', by Bing for Bassett-Lowke. (Christie's) $220

A rake of three fine gauge 1 Great Western Railway twin bogie passenger coaches, by G. Carrette. (Christie's) $435

A gauge 1 clockwork model of the London and and North Western Railway 4-6-2 'Bowen-Cooke' tank locomotive No. 2663, in black livery, by Marklin for Bassett-Lowke, circa 1913. (Christie's) $1,260

An early Bing 2½in. gauge II live steam spirit fired Midland Railway 4-4-0 locomotive, with a six-wheel tender and a six-wheel carriage, the locomotive 14in. long, circa 1902-06. (Lawrence Fine Art) $980

A gauge 0 clockwork model of the North Boarder Railway 4-4-0 pannier tank locomotive, by Bing for Bassett-Lowke, and a Bassett-Lowke clockwork mechanism. (Christie's) $220

A fine gauge 1 clockwork model of the London and North Western Railway 4-4-2 'Precursor Tank' locomotive No. 44, in black livery, by Bing for Bassett-Lowke, circa 1810. (Christie's) $560

A rake of three gauge 1 Midland Railway twin bogie passenger cars, including two first class coaches and a 3rd class brake car, by Bing for Bassett-Lowke, circa 1927. (Christie's) $530

Two gauge 1 Great Northern Railway, teak, 1st/3rd class twin bogie passenger cars, Nos. 2875, by Marklin, circa 1925. (Christie's) $385

A gauge 3 live- steam spirit-fired model of the London and South Western Railway 4-4-0 locomotive and tender, by Bing for Bassett-Lowke, circa 1904. (Christie's) $4,150

A contemporary mid 19th century 4½in. gauge brass model of the 2-2-2 locomotive 'Apollo' of 1844 built by Franklin & Co., Manchester, 9¾ x 14¼in. (Christie's) $4,640

A Marklin 3RE 20 volts 4-4-0 LMS locomotive and four wheeler tender, the first/third class carriages and brake van, Bing controller. (Phillips) $650

Two gauge 0 C.I.W.L. twin bogie passenger coaches, restaurant car, Ref. No. 1746/GJ1, and sleeping car, Ref. No. 1747/GJ1, by Marklin. (Christie's) **$100**

A 3½in. gauge model of the London and North Eastern Railway Class V2 2-6-2 locomotive and tender 'Green Arrow' built by A. Ficker, Radlett, 10½ x 53in. (Christie's) **$2,175**

A 5in. gauge model of the London and North Eastern Railway Class J39 0-6-0 locomotive and tender No. 2934, built by K. Edge, Peterborough, 13¾ x 59in. (Christie's) **$3,625**

A Bing spirit fired 0-4-0 LNWR locomotive and tender No. 1942 with separated lamps and a Bing gauge 1 signal. (Phillips) **$400**

A gauge 1 (3-rail) electric model of a Continental 4-4-0 locomotive and tender, by Bing, circa 1910. (Christie's) **$465**

A gauge 0 (3-rail) electric model of the 0-4-0 locomotive, Ref. No. RF66/12920, by Marklin. (Christie's) **$315**

A 7¼in. gauge model of the Hunslet 0-4-0 contractor's locomotive designed by M. R. Harrison and modeled by J. Maxted, Ramsgate, measurements overall 33½ x 98in. (Christie's) **$4,000**

'Juliet', a 3½in. gauge live steam coal fired 0-4-0 tank locomotive, together with a trailer, 20in. long overall. (Lawrence Fine Art) **$300**

A gauge 1 London and North Western Railway twin bogie 3rd class brake car, by Bing for Bassett-Lowke, circa 1922. (Christie's) **$190**

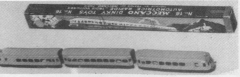

Pre-war French Factory 16Z diesel streamlined train by Dinky. (Phillips) **$500**

MODELS

The thing which sets models apart from other 'toys' is that most are hand crafted by skilled individuals and in some cases, as with scale model traction engines, this can mean thousands of hours of work involved. As such, it is not unreasonable when some of these intricate models sell for thousands of dollars at auction. The same applies for model steam trains by Bing, Carette and Marklin and some of the magnificent sailor made shipping dioramas from the 19th century.

They are generally found to be in good condition for they were constructed as an adult hobby and never intended for play as with more commonplace toys.

Engineering models of steam and traction engines tend to obtain the highest prices, but the award for charm must go to the Victorian models of butcher's shops complete with sides of mutton, ribs of beef and a rosy cheeked butcher with striped apron and boater.

An exhibition standard 2in. scale model of a Burrell 5 N.H.P. double crank compound three shaft, two speed Showman's Road Locomotive, 20 x 30½in. (Christie's) $8,415

An unusual model of a steam driven 19th century twin bore Deep Well Engine House and Pump, built by R. J. Sare, Northleach, 16½ x 18½in. (Christie's) $300

Late 19th century model of the three cylinder compound vertical surface condensing mill engine 'Asia', 16¼ x 13¼in. (Christie's) $3,000

A well presented approx. 1:20 scale model of the Weatherhill Pit Winding Engine of 1833, built by W. K. Walsam, Hayes, 19 x 14½in. (Christie's) $1,200

A late 19th century glazed and cased model of M. Osborne's — The Butcher's Shop, 46.5 x 43.5cm. (Phillips) $1,500

A model of a hall with marquetry floor dividing at the landing into stairs on either side going up to a galleried landing, 26in. wide. (Christie's) $600

A 1½in. scale model of a spirit-fired Shand-Mason horsedrawn fire engine of 1894. (Phillips) $1,175

A scale model of a Ferguson TE20 tractor and plow, 15¾in. long overall. (Lawrence Fine Art) $420

An exhibition standard model of the three cylinder compound surface condensing vertical reversing marine engine fitted to the Cunard Liner S.S. 'Servia' and modeled by Thos. Lowe, 1907, 14½ x 12½in. (Christie's) $5,000

A fine contemporary late 19th century small, full size, single cylinder horizontal mill engine, measurements overall 18 x 25in. (Christie's) $970

A well engineered 3in. scale model of a Suffolk Dredging tractor, built by C. E. Thorn, 27 x 30in. (Christie's) $700

A 2in. scale model of a single cylinder three shaft two speed Davey-Paxman general purpose agricultural traction engine built by A. R. Dyer & Sons, Wantage, 23½ x 38in. (Christie's) $2,600

A finely engineered, exhibition standard 1in. scale model of the single cylinder two speed four shaft general purpose agricultural traction engine 'Doreen', built to the designs of 'Minnie', by H. A. Taylor, 1980, 11½ x 18in. (Christie's) $1,650

A 1½in. scale model of a Burrell single crank compound two speed three shaft general purpose agricultural traction engine, built by J. B. Harris, Solihull, 15½ x 25in. (Christie's) $3,190

A finely engineered and well presented model 'M E', center pillar beam engine, built by K. R. F. Kenworthy, measurements overall 13 x 17½in. (Christie's) $1,190

A detailed steam driven model of a Bengali Die Mixing plant, built by A. Sare, Northleach, measurements overall 18½ x 24in. (Christie's) $1,000

An exhibition standard 2in. scale model of the Burrell 5 n.h.p. double crank compound two speed three shaft 'Gold Medal' tractor, engine No. 3846, Registration No. AD7782 'Poussnouk-nouk', built from works drawings by P. Penn-Sayers, Laughton, 19¾ x 27¼in. (Christie's) $10,875

An early 20th century model single cylinder surface condensing 'A' frame beam engine, 19½ x 24in. (Christie's) $2,500

MONEY BANKS

Most of the early money banks we see today are made of metal, many have a mechanical function and most still work. One of the earliest patents for a cast iron mechanical money bank was taken out by J. Hall on 21st December, 1869, for his 'Excelsior' bank.

Magic banks always have a mechanical function. A typical example is where a coin is placed under a magician's hat which, when lowered, causes the coin to disappear. The Trick Dog bank is activated by a lever which causes the dog to leap through a hoop and deposit the coin from its mouth into a barrel. These mechanical banks are fascinating but most are a bit pricey.

Special note: look out for a mechanical bank featuring a young girl skipping. Only recently 'A Girl Skipping Rope' mechanical bank from the late 19th century, sold at auction for $15,000

A cast iron novelty bank, by J. & E. Stevens Co., the building with front door opening to reveal a cashier, American, late 19th century. $375

An unusual wind-up drummer boy money box, 6in. high. $80

Late 19th century American cast iron 'Punch & Judy' mechanical bank, by Shepard Hardware Co., 7½in. high. $675

A late 19th century cast iron 'Girl Skipping Rope' mechanical bank, 20cm. wide. $15,000

Late 19th century American 'Uncle Sam' mechanical bank, by Shepard Hardware Co., 11½in. high. $325

Late 19th century American cast iron 'Santa Claus' mechanical bank, 6in. high. $750

American late 19th century Paddy and the Pig cast iron mechanical bank, 8in. high. $900

A cast iron 'Always Did 'Spise a Mule' money bank, American, circa 1897, by J. Stevens & Co., 10in. long. $1,050

A tinplate monkey mechanical bank, German, circa 1930, 6½in. high. $450

'World's Fair' cast iron mechanical bank, J. & E. Stevens, Co., pat. 1893, 8¼in. long. (Robt. W. Skinner Inc.) $600

Oliver Hardy money box, late 1950's. $20

A mechanical cast iron money box, as a football player with articulated right leg, causing the player to shoot a coin into a goal and ring a bell, circa 1890, 10½in. long. (Christie's) $825

Late 19th century cast iron 'Speaking Dog' mechanical bank, by J. & E. Stevens Co., 7¼in. long. $1,200

A 20th century English cast iron 'Dinah' mechanical bank, by John Harper & Co. Ltd., 6½in. high. $175

A cast iron mechanical bank, 'Trick Pony', by Shepard Hardware Co., American, circa 1890, 7in. long. (Christie's) $450

MOORCROFT POTTERY

When some bright spark at James Macintyre and Co. decided in 1913 to switch production from pottery to the new-fangled electrical goods, their pottery designer, William Moorcroft, was left a little short of work, to say the least.

So with 15 years of experience behind him, and bearing in mind that life begins at 40, he took the plunge and established his own pottery works at Cobridge, near Stoke-on-Trent, employing many of his former colleagues from Macintyres.

Without any restraints he could give full reign to his ideas leaving a legacy of distinctive pottery now eagerly sought after today.

All his products bear his signature, W. Moorcroft, usually in green until 1920 and thereafter mainly in blue, together with the impressed mark Moorcroft or Moorcroft Burslem.

A Moorcroft Macintyre two-handled vase, design no. 360574, signed in green W. Moorcroft, 19cm. high. (Lawrence Fine Art)· $550

A Moorcroft two-handled box and cover, decorated in the 'Claremont' pattern, 6½in. high. (Christie's) $690

One of a pair of Moorcroft Dawn pattern vases of ovoid form, 18.5cm. high. (Lawrence Fine Art) $750

A William Moorcroft grape pattern vase of ovoid form, 16in. high. (Capes, Dunn & Co.) $400

A Moorcroft circular pottery dish painted in the Leaf and Berry pattern, 11½in. diam. (Christie's) $170

A Moorcroft pottery oviform vase made for Liberty & Co., in the Toadstool pattern, 10in. high, signed in green. (Christie's) $1,250

MOTTOWARE

One day in 1867, when a certain Mr. G.P. Allen was dutifully digging in his back garden at Watcombe House, he unearthed, not gold, but what was regarded at the time as the finest red clay in England.

Recognizing the potential value of his find he enlisted the aid of Charles Brock, an experienced potter from Hanley. Within two years they had established the Watcombe Pottery, engaging many imported Staffordshire craftsmen.

Most of their products were designed specifically for the souvenir trade, the most popular proving to be modest earthenware pieces with a decoration on one side and a motto on the other — now referred to as Devon motto ware.

The early mark was simply 'Watcombe Pottery' or 'Watcombe Torquay' and from 1875 incorporated a woodpecker seated upon a branch with the sea in the background.

Aller Vale Art Potteries, established in 1865, was a similar firm to Watcombe Pottery, and eventually they amalgamated in 1901. The combined factory prospered until 1962 under the trade name Royal Aller Vale and Watcombe Art Pottery.

Originally the Aller Vale pottery, situated near Newton Abbot, manufactured drain pipes and roof tiles but after the works were severely damaged by fire, John Phillips the owner re-opened and began to produce the popular Art Pottery.

The output from both firms was prolific and, because their products were bought primarily by tourists, pieces can be found in almost all parts of Britain at moderate prices in antique shops and auctions.

An Aller Vale pottery teapot bearing the legend, 'Ye may get better cheer, But no' wi' better heart'. $30

An unmarked pottery hot-water jug. $25

A Watcombe pottery tile decorated with leaf and flower swirls. $25

A Dartmouth pottery jug, inscribed 'No Road is long with Good Company'. $8

An unmarked earthenware coffee pot, the motto cut through the white slip to the brown clay. $25

Torquay Ware shaving mug in brown and cream bearing the motto 'Better do one thing Than dream all things!' $30

MUSICAL BOXES

Music in the home was as common during Victorian times as it is today — the difference being that, in those happy days, at least one member of most families was a more or less accomplished musician who would be happy to entertain the rest of the household at the slightest nod from Papa.

If, however, the said accomplished being was unavailable to perform, the neighborhood would not necessarily be plunged into an abyss of silent gloom for there was a multitude of cabinets and boxes ready to spring into melodious life at the wind of a handle and the touch of a lever.

Although musical boxes had been fairly widely available during the 18th century, they had been extremely small affairs; novelties produced by ingenious clockmakers who, with wonderful precision, had fitted their tiny mechanisms into small boxes, seals, watches, and even into the handles of walking sticks.

The more widely accepted form of musical box, the antecedent, in its way, of the family record player, didn't put in an appearance until the early 19th century when it was introduced by David le Coutre.

It comprised of a clockwork mechanism powered by a coiled spring. This causes a cylinder, studded with steel pins, to rotate, the pins, pinging against a steel comb with teeth of different lengths to create the different notes.

Other still more exotic examples have drums, flutes, whistles, and even castanets to add a spot of excitement to their tunes.

An interchangeable cylinder mandolin musical box on table with six eight-air cylinders, 47in wide overall, the cylinders 11in. (Christie's) $6,200

A clockwork barrel-organ, by Flight & Robson, 66½in. wide, the barrels 35 x 8in. diam., and a discus electric suction unit. (Christie's) $8,500

A rosewood cased standing cylinder music box, by B. A. Bremond, Switzerland, 41½in. wide. $4,000

A Euphonika 'Herophon' organette with twenty-four reeds, German, circa 1905. $580

Late 19th century singing bird music box, Switzerland, with bird-shaped key, 4in. wide. (Robt. W. Skinner Inc.) $2,220

A Czechoslovakian late 19th century 12-key serinette with 18cm. pinned wooden barrel playing six tunes on wooden pipes. $580

A lever wind musical box, by Nicole Freres, No. 51725, playing 4 overtures, with tune sheet and rosewood veneered case, 27½in. wide. (Christie's) $3,750

A 9½in. Symphonion disk musical box, 11in. wide, together with one metal disk, German, circa 1900. $400

German Troubadour disk musical box, no. 1615, with coin chute and winding handle, circa 1900, 38½in. high. $780

A Schmidt & Co. 'Ariosa' organette, for use with annular disks, with eighteen reeds, German, circa 1904. $500

A 15½in. polyphon disk musical box, number 84941, together with eight disks, 21½in. wide. $1,800

A musical box, by Baker-Troll, playing eight airs accompanied by drum, castanet and six-engraved bells, 23½in. wide. (Christie's) $3,000

A late 19th century J. M. Draper 'English' cardboard strip organette with fourteen reeds. $500

A 19th century Swiss musical box, the movement playing twelve airs, striking on six bells and a drum, 25½in. long. (Woolley & Wallis)
$1,300

Late 19th century French key-wind singing bird automaton, 4in. wide. (Reeds Rains) $600

An automatic barrel piano, the 48-note coin operated movement playing from a 33in. pinned wooden cylinder, 49½in. $1,570

A Celstina paper roll 'orguinette', No. 8425 with twenty reeds, together with eighteen paper rolls, American, circa 1890. $855

A 19th century square section bird cage of wire and turned wood, the base containing a musical box, 17in. high. (Peter Wilson & Co.)
$200

A changeable cylinder overture box by Nicole Freres, with five cylinders each playing four tunes, 38in. wide. (Christie's) $5,750

A musical box playing 12 sacredains accompanied by 9 bells with bee strikers, 31in. wide. (Christie's)
$2,500

A gilt metal and enamel singing bird box, decorated with Watteauesque scenes. (Christie's) $1,000

NAUTICAL ITEMS

If seafaring is your bag, then it would be easy to turn your home into a veritable nautical paradise – cash permitting.

Items you will find among the many splendid instruments of superb quality and precision are, sextants, log screws, compasses, telegraphs, octants, astrolabes, theodolites, telescopes, and nocturnal dials – any of these items will contribute to an agreeable collection. If it is possible to house something a bit larger, there are binnacles, ship's figureheads or wheels. Nautical furniture will also make an excellent theme for a collection for, almost without exception, all pieces are well proportioned and made from the finest wood set with sunken brass handles.

In fact, one of the main attributes of all nautical items is the quality of the materials used in their production for they were designed for a hard life on the high seas.

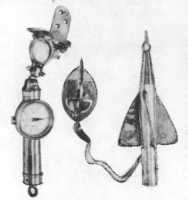

An eight-day marine chronometer by Hatton & Harris No. 570, diam. of bezel 133mm. $10,000

Early 20th century Thos. Walker 'Harpoon' depth finder, English, 6½in. long. $330

Early 20th century Davey & Co. starboard lamp in copper casing. $100

A Siebe, Gorman & Co. brass and copper diver's helmet, English, circa 1920, 19in. high. (Lawrence Fine Art) $1,000

Early 20th century White Thompson & Co. ship's binnacle compass, 54in. high. $1,100

Mid 19th century English ship's wheel with ten turned mahogany spokes, 68cm. diam. $1,500

A 16th/17th century Italian ship's drycard compass, 11cm. diam. (Phillips) $6,200

A 19th century anodized brass Troughton & Simms double frame sextant, the index arm with 8in. radius. (Phillips) $800

Brass ship's barometer, circa 1860. (British Antique Exporters) $75

A Kelvin & Hughes Ltd. ship's binnacle compass, English, circa 1940, 53in. high. $1,500

A Cary brass sextant with gold scale, numbered 3856, 11¾ x 11¼in. (Lawrence Fine Art) $3,200

Early 20th century Kelvin & White Ltd. ship's binnacle, 53in. high, together with a Brown Brother's ship's wheel, circa 1920. $1,500

A James Ayscough mahogany Hadley's quadrant, English, circa 1760, 17½in. radius. $3,190

An early marine chronometer by John Arnold & Son, with 4½in. circular silvered dial, in mahogany box. (Phillips) $11,600

A mariner's brass astrolable, the scale divided from 0° to 90°, with rising loop handle, 23.5cm. diam. (Christie's) $1,450

NETSUKE

As the traditional national costume of Japan, the kimono, didn't have pockets, objects such as an inro, purse, drinking gourd or tobacco pouch were usually hung from a cord at the waist. The cord was attached to a netsuke (pronounced netski) which was simply slipped under the sash (obi) which fastened the kimono and was held in place by pressure. Originally netsuke were simple wooden toggles but as attention was given to them they became elaborately carved reaching a sustained peak by the end of the 18th century. They were usually made of either wood or ivory but can be found of bone, rhino, buffalo and stag horn, coral, jet, turtle shell, amber or even metal. The subjects carved are more numerous than the carvers (of whom over 3000 have been identified) but two of the main groups are those depicting characters from Japanese folk history (Mukashi – Banashi) and Sugata – depictions of various craftsmen. Eroticism was also a popular subject and examples not infrequently took the form of young ladies indulging – or being indulged by – sea monsters and mythological characters.

Most netsuke originate from the large areas of population such as Osaka, Nagoya, Kyoto and Edo where the carvers could make a good living. Their popularity declined when Japan ended her seclusion with the Meija restoration in 1868 and western style dress with pockets became popular. The influx of tourists however, eager for souvenirs of old Japan became a major market for netsuke and vast numbers, of a poor quality compared to earlier ones, were exported to Europe and America.

An early/mid 19th century ivory netsuke of a professional sneezer, signed Ryuko, and kao. (Christie's) $675

A boxwood netsuke study of an Oshidori, by the Kyoto School artist Masanao.
$52,800

Early 19th century ivory netsuke of a sumo wrestler, unsigned. (Christie's) $2,150

A 19th century ivory netsuke of a cicada, signed Masatsugu. (Christie's) $6,000

313

A 19th century stag-antler style manju netsuke of Raiden, signed with the seal of Hoshunsai Masayuki. (Christie's) $1,470

A 19th century ivory netsuke of a Temple horse being groomed, signed Kigyoku, Edo School. (Christie's) $660

Late 18th century wood netsuke carved as a group of five clam shells, signed Sari, Iwashiro School. (Christie's) $735

Late 19th century ivory okimono style netsuke of two seated Manzai dancers, signed Fujiyuki. (Christie's) $310

A 19th century wood and ivory manju-type netsuke in the form of a gourd, signed Yamahiko. (Christie's) $515

Early 19th century ivory netsuke of Kanzan and Jittoku reading a makimono, unsigned. (Christie's) $515

A carved ivory netsuke of two playful Karashishi, signed Shoko, 18th century, with an ivory ojime signed Naokazu.(Christie's) $1,760

Mid 19th century boxwood netsuke of Ono No Komachi, unsigned. (Christie's) $700

A 19th century ivory netsuke of three karako playing beside a tsuitate, unsigned. (Christie's) $320

A 19th century wood net-suke of a cicada on half a walnut, unsigned. (Christie's) $530

A late 19th century ivory netsuke of a coiled snake, inscribed Toshitsugu. (Christie's) $615

A 19th century ivory netsuke of a dove on a group of three lotus leaves, the eyes inset in dark horn. (Christie's) $675

A boxwood netsuke of two monkeys, by the Tamba School artist Toyomasa. $36,000

Late 18th century ivory netsuke of a stylized goose preening, unsigned. (Christie's) $1,175

Late 19th century ivory net-suke of a monkey and her two young, signed Masatami (Shomin), Yamada School. (Christie's) $1,400

Early 19th century wood netsuke of a rat, eyes inset in translucent horn. (Christie's) $1,030

Mid 19th century stained ivory netsuke of the Sambo Kojin, signed Ono Ryomin, Edo School. (Christie's) $880

Early 19th century ivory netsuke of a green frog sitting on an awabi shell, unsigned. (Christie's) $500

Most novelty books are designed for children and because they are usually intended to do something they tend to receive more handling and wear than ordinary children's books. Older items in fine condition are therefore quite rare, and this combined with their current demand among collectors means that they command high prices, with Victorian moveables generally rating over $200.

Novelty books for adults are unusual. Among the most interesting are the Dennis Wheatley Crime Dossiers which are facsimile police files with documents, photos, actual clues— the object being to solve the crime.

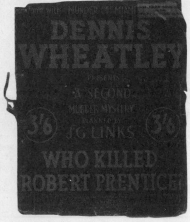

'Who Killed Robert Prentice?', by Dennis Wheatley, 1936. **$60**

'My First Jig-Puz Book', Five Jigsaws. **$60**

Dean's Home Stencil Book, No. 1, by Dean & Son, 1930's. **$10**

'No doubt my wife has something nice and warm for me this cold night'. **$40**

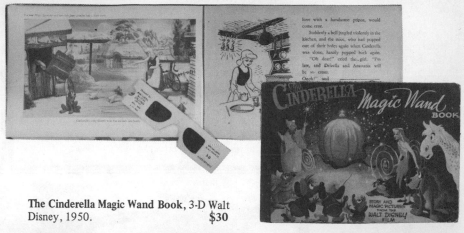

The Cinderella Magic Wand Book, 3-D Walt
Disney, 1950. **$30**

Sewing Pictures 1940's. **$5**

The Big Book Of Shops, fold-over book, 1930's.
$50

NUTCRACKERS

It was a Victorian tradition to serve fruit and nuts in their shells towards the end of a meal and predictably, these gadget conscious people had to have the proper tools for the job.

It was not, however, considered sufficient to provide a simple and effective appliance, for, like the nutmeg grater and any other implement which had to be used in the presence of company, a pair of nutcrackers had to compliment the tableware and reflect the status of the household.

For practical purposes, nutcrackers had to be made from a fairly sturdy metal and the focus of attention centered on design. The handles were often decorated with ivory or bone and some were fitted with a scalpel shaped pick, designed to help winkle the kernel from the shell.

Finer examples in silver plated or gilt metal rarely survive intact.

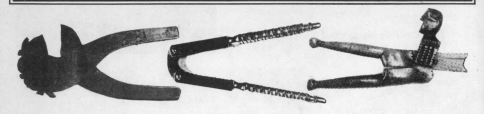

A pair of finely carved Scandinavian treen nutcrackers, circa 1880, 6¼in. long. (Christopher Sykes) $70

A 19th century pair of steel nut and also lobster shell crackers, circa 1870, 5in. long. (Christopher Sykes) $30

An 18th century yewwood nutcracker of hinged form carved with a man's head, 6¾in. $615

A late 18th century wood figure of a sailor his mouth operating as a nutcracker, 9½in. high. (W. H. Lane & Son) $115

A pair of cast brass 19th century nutcrackers, the top in the form of a cockerel's head, circa 1800, 5¾in. long. (Christopher Sykes) $95

An 18th/19th century walnut nutcracker in the form of an old woman seated, 7¾in. $220

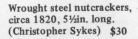
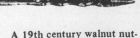

Victorian steel nutcrackers with 'barley sugar' handles, circa 1860, 6in. long. (Christopher Sykes) $36

Wrought steel nutcrackers, circa 1820, 5½in. long. (Christopher Sykes) $30

A 19th century walnut nutcracker of screw type, 8½in. $175

As more and more people become aware of the power of advertising and the influence it has upon their lives, it becomes obvious that, by looking back at company images created at a time when the publicity men must have been more or less working in the dark, some got it right. Shell, Castrol and Mobiloil did-some were not so successful, B.P. and Pratts for example. So, as we move into the present day and take a look at these old pieces of functional advertising in the form of oil cans and pourers, it is the Shell and Castrol examples which are the most sought after and the High Performance Oil containers of these companies 'Aeroshell' and 'Castrol R' which are the most popular.

The Shell company used a variety of shaped enamel signs which now fetch a considerable amount of money.

The Castrol company passed through four distinct design periods. The first can be seen in the Castrol R tin, followed by the style used on the quart Oil Power. There are examples of a pourer in the first style having been repainted and a transfer from the later style applied to bring the pourer up to date. The subsequent style which was employed up to the 1950's can be seen on the quarter and half pint pourers. It was at this time that the present style came into use with the loss of the lower arm on the logo. As time goes by, these modern pieces will almost certainly be collected but as yet they do not really interest collectors.

Remember, you will not be able to find any early Esso items, for the Anglo-American Oil Company used the name of Pratts and, demonstrating the march of progress, all Esso stations are now Exxon in the U.S.A.

Texaco enamel sign made by The Texaco Company, U.S.A. $40

Mobiloil poster 'Give Me Mobiloil'. $30

Aeroshell Lubricating oil pourer with winged Shell emblem. $40

Castrol motor oil enamel sign. $60

Castrol motor oil quart pourer. $40

An unusual combined Shell motor oil and petrol can. $70

'Shell' motor oil enamel sign by Shell-Mex Ltd. $160

Castrol one pint motor oil tin of conical form. $30

A 2 gallon Adcoids tin by Alexander Duckham & Co. $40

Castrol 'R' motor oil can. $20

Brass oil spraying container with plastic handle. $30

Designed as a cheap alternative to the hardback book the paperback only came into its own as a collectible item in the last decade. While there were earlier publishers, indeed Tauchnitz started publishing in 1837, it was not until the advent of Penguin books in 1935 that the paperback became 'respectable'.

Today the collector of paperback books appears in many forms. Some people seek the first 1,000 Penguin books of which No. 1, Ariel, by Maurois sells for around $60. Others may collect a favorite author in paperback first editions where the original hardback 'firsts' are outside their price range, while yet others collect subjects which were often only published in paperback such as the range of teenage gang and drugs novels of the 1950's and 1960's.

Detective and Science Fiction paperbacks also have their enthusiastic collectors while many only have eyes for Mills and Boon romantic novels and those of Barbara Cartland of which there are over 300.

A further field of collecting is based upon the cover art work. Look for American Signet and Bantam books with covers by Avati, the Pocketbook series with McKnight Kauffer art work and the 1950's pulp novels with the lovely ladies by Heade.

Most paperback collectors find the bulk of their books on the shelves of conventional bookdealers who haven't yet realized the desirability of certain paperbacks.

Charity shops and rummage sales are also a happy hunting ground, and even from the specialist paperback dealer most titles are no more expensive than new paperbacks today.

The Brigitte Bardot Story, U.S. Belmont Books, 1961. $6

Waterfront Blonde, U.S. Intimate Novels, 1953: $4

Ariel, by Andre Maurois, No. 1, 1935. $60

Germany Puts The Clock Back, 1st Special 1937. $7

The Mark of Zorro, Dell, 1951. $6

Marihuana, by William Irish, Dell, 1951. $100

PAPERBACKS

Gulliver's Travels, 1938, wood engravings by T. Naish.　**$6**

The Terror of the Leopard Men, Avon, 1951.　**$6**

The Diary Of A Nobody, Pan Books, 1945-47. **$6**

Young, by Miriam Colwell, Ballantine Books.　**$10**

Reform School Girl, by Felice Swados, Diversey, 1948. **$200**

A Tangled Web by L. G. Moberly, Ward Lock, 1931. **$5**

Nigger Heaven, by Carl Van Vechten, Avon Books. **$40**

Immortality, 1919, 1st Cheap Edition.　**$2**

Rumble, by Harlan Ellison, Pyramid, 1958. **$35**

Strange Ritual, Compact '64' Series.   **$5**

Mrs Miniver, by Jan Struther, Pocket Books.   **$5**

Marijuana Girl, U.S. Publication.   **$15**

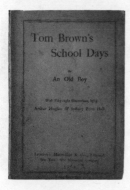

Tom Brown's School Days, Macmillan, 1904.   **$3**

Naked On Roller Skates, by Maxwell Bodenheim, Diversey 1949.   **$40**

Sweeney Todd, The Demon Barber, Hellifont Press, 1920's.   **$6**

Tarzan and the Lost Empire, Dell, 1951.   **$5**

The Bride Wore Weeds, Gaywood Press, Heade Cover.   **$7**

All Over But The Shooting, Popular Library.   **$3**

Love Me To Death, Phantom Books, 1956. **$3**

Death Hitches A Ride, Tracked Down, Ace Double, 1954. **$4**

Too Busy To Die, Dell 1947. **$10**

The Postman Always Rings Twice, by James M. Cain, Pocket Books. **$5**

Verity, Corpse in Lovers Lane, Herrett Publications, 1940's. **$3**

Thin Edge of Violence, Phantom Books, 1956. **$3**

Six Nights Of Mystery, by William Irish, Popular Library. **$6**

The Four of Hearts, by Ellery Queen, Pocket books. **$4**

Tiger Standish Does His Stuff, Hodder & Stoughton, Yellow Back, 1952. **$3**

Into The Alternate Universe, Coils Of Time, Ace Double, 1964. **$6**

The Time Traders, Ace Books, 1958. **$6**

I Am Legend, Corgi Books, 1956. **$5**

Freaks Against Supermen, Laywood Press, 1951. **$8**

Tales Of Tomorrow, Spencer Publications, 1940's. **$6**

The Weird Shadow Over Innsmouth, Bart House. **$60**

Into Plutonian Depths, Avon Books. **$45**

Fight For Life, Crestwood U.S.A. 1947, Murray Leinster, 1st Edition. **$12**

Projection Infinity, Badger Books, 1960's. **$4**

Although glass paperweights are reputed to have been used in ancient Egypt, the earliest dated examples of the now familiar shape came from France and Venice in 1845.

They were developed as luxury additions to the popular writing boxes of the period, and the most sought after were produced in vast numbers by three French firms, Baccarat, Clichy and Saint Louis.

American and English glassworks such as the Boston and Sandwich Glass Co. and Bacchus and Sons followed suit a few years later, but their work is somewhat over-shadowed by the charisma attached to the weights produced in the first ten years by the French firms.

While the majority of paperweights consist of a heavy clear glass dome, enclosing multi-colored glass rods designed to represent fruit or flowers, weights produced by the French glass artists such as Daum, Almeric Walter, Lalique and Baccarat are to be found in many different shapes including dragonflies, frogs, snakes, birds and nymphs.

It is worth noting that many weights are signed with an initial and a date but usually these marks are so cleverly incorporated into the design as to make them difficult to spot.

Examples by important French makers will naturally be expensive, anything from a few hundred to thousands of dollars but a start can be made with the cheap English variety produced at the end of the 19th century. These usually depict such scenes as 'The Esplanade at Hastings' simply stuck beneath a glass blob, but for all their simplicity they do have a certain charm.

A large Paul Ysart garlanded flat bouquet weight, 9.5cm. diam. (Christie's) $925

A Baccarat snake weight, the pink reptile with green spine markings, 7.9cm. diam. (Christie's) $4,750

A St. Louis small crown weight, 5.5cm. diam. (Christie's) $850

A St. Louis pink ground pompom weight, 7cm. diam. (Christie's) $2,250

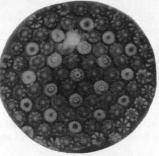

A Clichy blue ground scattered millefiori weight, 8.5cm. diam. (Christie's) $1,000

A Clichy flat bouquet weight, 7cm. diam. (Christie's) $15,000

A Clichy swirl weight, with alternate turquoise and white staves radiating from a central claret, green and white cane, 8.2cm. diam. (Christie's) $1,000

A Paul Ysart garlanded bouquet weight, with PY initials included in the bouquet, 7.5cm. diam. (Christie's) $475

A French scramble paperweight with blue, green, white and red canes, 3in. diam. (Robt. W. Skinner Inc.) $500

A Clichy blue and white dahlia weight, 7.2cm. diam. (Christie's) $9,250

A Baccarat mushroom weight on a star-cut base, 8cm. diam. (Christie's) $2,800

A St. Louis faceted concentric millefiori mushroom weight, 8cm. diam. (Christie's) $550

PARIAN

The art of parian statuary was first introduced around 1840 and almost simultaneously produced by Copeland & Garrett and Minton; followed in 1848 by Wedgwood.

Parian is a slightly translucent, silky textured, matt white porcelain bearing a strong resemblance to marble but, unlike marble which requires carving, this material could be molded to reproduce copies of famous pieces of sculpture scaled down to a more practical size for the average home. Manufacturers also commissioned models for their statuary products.

Initially used for the manufacture of figures, groups and applied decoration, the range widened as the production process improved and includes vases, jugs, tea services and other tableware.

A Minton Parian group of a nude female figure seated on the back of a lion, circa 1847-48, 1ft. 3½in. high. (Hobbs & Chambers) $100

A Goss Parian bust of Queen Victoria, for Mortlock's of Oxford Street, 236mm. high. (Phillips) $320

A colored Parian group modeled as a young girl on rockwork, entitled 'You can't read', 12¼in. high, possibly by Robinson & Leadbetter. (Christie's) $300

A Copeland Parian group, entitled 'Go To Sleep', impressed Art Union of London, J. Durham Sc 1862, 26in. high overall. (Anderson & Garland) $740

A pair of Royal Worcester glazed Parian figures of Paul and Virginia, circa 1865, 33cm. high. (Christie's) $950

One of a pair of glazed Parian figure brackets, allegorical figures in rock-like niches, 9½in. high. (Capes, Dunn & Co.) $220

PENKNIVES

Single bladed pocketknives were originally designed for the purpose of trimming and cutting the quill pen; thus the common name penknife. A knife with both a large and a small blade can usually be dated from about 1850 onwards.

Small silver bladed fruit knives, with bone or ivory handles, date from the 19th century. Traditionally used for peeling and cutting fruit, the silver blade left no nasty aftertaste and some better examples have a little silver fork attachment.

The Victorian capacity for invention was given full rein in developing gadgets for the popular multi-purpose knives with features such as scissor blades, button hooks, corkscrews and other gadgets; some exhibition pieces incorporate blades for hundreds of different functions.

Although many of these functions are obscure and difficult to identify one of the more obvious mechanisms is that for a boxlock percussion pistol, only 4in. long.

Late Victorian miniature knife with steel blade, 1in. long. $5

Miniature double bladed mother-of-pearl handled penknife, 2in. long. $7

Miniature bone handled knife, 1in. long. $6

A Belgian boxlock percussion combination knife pistol, barrel 4in., Liege proved, folding blade 4in. (Wallis & Wallis) $460

Unmarked gold miniature knife with one steel blade and one gold blade, 1½in. long closed. $25

A World War II O.S.S. Special Forces combination clasp knife. (Wallis & Wallis) $640

Late 19th century miniature penknife with mother-of-pearl handle, 1½in. long. $5

Victorian pocket fruit knife and patent orange peeler with mother-of-pearl handle. $200

Silver penknife with mother-of-pearl handle, dated 1897. $40

PENS

A potted history of pens would take us from the stylus used in ancient times by scribes scratching away on tablets of wax to the quill and stalk pens of the 6th century A.D.; from the nib and penholder, to the fountain pen invented in the 1880's; the ball point pen introduced in 1944, to the myriad designs on the market today.

The earliest type of fountain pen was the Vulcanite which was filled with ink from a glass tube fitted with a rubber bulb on the end. Many patented designs exist, but it was from the Vulcanite that we see the transition to the rubber ink holder, sometimes with a lever action, followed by the screw top plunger and eventually the cartridge.

There are many fine examples for the collector and some are worth a considerable sum of money. It is worth looking out for pens which were either the property of a well known personality or used at the signing of significant documents. In either case, some authentication is necessary if the top price is to be achieved.

A good quality 1950's Parker pen with 14kt. gold nib. $25

Early 20th century bone handled silver pen with chased barrel. $20

A Swan fountain pen No. 4662, with gold plated nib. $15

A silver cased Swan fountain pen with chatelaine attachment. $30

1940's Sheaffer 'Snorkel' with 14kt. gold nib, in original box with instructions. $36

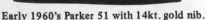

Early 1960's Parker 51 with 14kt. gold nib. $15

A gold and enamel calendar fountain pen by Cartier, circa 1925, 10.5cm. long. $2,660

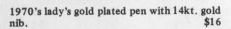

1970's lady's gold plated pen with 14kt. gold nib. $16

A Swan fountain pen in chased silver case. $40

Late Victorian silver cased fountain pen by Swan of London. $25

Indian silver quill pen. $80

Swan pen with plated lapel clip, circa 1905. $8

1930's desk pen mounted on an onyx base. $16

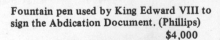

Fountain pen used by King Edward VIII to sign the Abdication Document. (Phillips) $4,000

Late 19th century silver cased housekeeper's fountain pen. $40

Hallmarked silver ruler pen by Asprey, London. $90

PEWTER

Pewter is an alloy based on tin with the addition of other metals which may be lead, brass or copper. It is thought to have been made by the Romans but was most popular in Europe during the 16th century when it was employed for church vessels, domestic purposes and civic functions.

Pewter began to be used for church vessels in the early Middle Ages when it replaced wood for the chalices. Until the 15th century it was customary to bury a pewter chalice with the priest. Pewter chalices, flagons, alms dishes and collecting plates can still be found in many church vaults.

Generally speaking pewter was a makeshift substitute for silver and it was worked in the same patterns and styles as the more precious metal. Some pewter, particularly from Germany, was intricately decorated and cast in relief but such items are rare and pewter is generally spare and workmanlike in design. Artists continue to work in pewter and it appears very successfully in Liberty's Tudric and Clutha designs for serving flagons.

A coffee pot of tapering, cylindrical form, by Israel Trask, Mass., circa 1825-35, marked with Jacobs touch 262, 11½in. high. (Christie's) $420

A coffee pot of baluster shape with a hinged lid, by Daniel Curtiss, 1822-40, 11in. high. (Christie's) $300

A pewter covered Church tankard of lighthouse shape with C-scroll handle, circa 1766. (Robt. W. Skinner Inc.) $700

One of a pair of mid 19th century pewter lanterns. (Robt. W. Skinner Inc.) $600

A WMF electroplated pewter drinking set with shaped rectangular tray, circa 1900, tray 48 x 34cm. (Christie's) $1,100

A lighthouse shaped flagon, by Thos. D. Boardman, marked with eagle touch, name touch and Hartford touch on base, 13¼in. high. (Christie's) $2,000

An apple-shaped teapot, by Roswell Gleason, Mass., 1821-71, 7½in. high. (Christie's) $245

A WMF silvered pewter jardiniere cast as a conch shell with a salamander, 32cm. high. (Christie's) $800

A pewter bedpan, by Thos. D. and S. Boardman, Hartford, 1810-50, initial touch struck once on base, 17½in. long, overall. (Christie's) $450

A pewter porringer, by Wm. Billings, Providence R.I., circa 1791-1806, marked on handle with Laughlin touch 346, 4.1/8in. diam. (Christie's) $425

A Jugendstil polished pewter triptych mirror in the style of P. Huber, 32.2 x 53.4cm. (Christie's) $700

A covered pitcher, by Boardman, Boardman & Hart, 1828-53, marked on bottom, 7¾in. high. (Christie's) $725

A 19th century pewter leech jar, the pierced lid with carrying handle, 7in. high. (Christie's) $450

A WMF rectangular shaped pewter mirror, 14in. high, stamped marks. (Christie's) $800

A tapering, cylindrical cann, by Robt. Palethorp, Phila., 1817-22, marked inside, 4.1/8in. high. (Christie's) $2,250

PEWTER

A pyriform teapot, by Thos. Danforth, Conn., 1805-50, marked on bottom, 7in. high. (Christie's) $1,000

One of two similar Italian, late 18th/early 19th century, pewter flagons, 14¼in. high. (Christie's) $650

A 17th century pewter charger with reeded rim, 22in. diam. (Woolley & Wallis) $2,250

One of two pewter beakers, by James Weekes, New York City, 1820-35, 3.1/8in. high. (Christie's) $350

A Kayersinn pewter jardiniere, stamped Kayersinn 4093, 29.8cm. high. (Christie's) $425

An electroplated pewter mirror frame attributed to WMF, circa 1900, 50cm. high. (Christie's) $725

A tankard with a domed lid and scrolling thumbpiece, late 18th/early 19th century, unmarked, 6¼in. high. (Christie's) $1,700

A pair of pewter fluid lamps, by James H. Puttnam, Mass., 1830-55, 7¾in. high. (Christie's) $700

A water pitcher, by Roswell Gleason, circa 1830, 11½in. high, together with a coffee pot and a water cooler. (Christie's) $500

PHOTOGRAPHS

The photographs most popularly collected today fall into two main categories. Those of historical significance in the development of the art and those photographs which are the work of a recognized master. Occasionally the two are combined in one photograph.

Notables of the early days are, William Fox Talbot who patented the Calotype in 1841 and, Louis-Jacques Mande Daguerre who invented the Daguerreotype which, in its early stages of development required over thirty minutes of exposure time. Other early photographers of note are Frances Frith, J.D. Edwards, Roger Fenton, Gustave Le Gray, F.R. Pickersgill and Henry Peach Robinson.

Photographers of importance in more modern times are Man Ray, Bill Brandt and Weegee amongst others.

'City Hall and Police Office, New Orleans', by J. D. Edwards. $1,200

'River Front, New Orleans', by J. D. Edwards. $1,550

Two studies of New Orleans, by J. D. Edwards, numbered '85 and '87. $2,000

'The Mosque of Kaitbey', by Frances Frith, signed and dated 1858, 391 x 465mm. $395

'Foret de Fontainebleau', albumen print, by Gustave Le Gray. $3,500

Xie Kitchin in bed, albumen print by Lewis Carroll, 1870. $2,000

The photographer's son 'Hans', by Heinrich Kuhn, 1907. $925

Florence Maude and her sister posed beside a window, by Lady Clementina Hawarden. $4,850

Study of a church by Frederick Scott Archer, 1860. $570

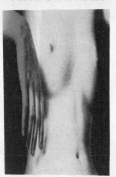

A sixth-plate daguerreotype portrait of a man with a white hat and a rifle, American, 1850's. **$220**

'**Distortion no. 6**', silver print by Andre Kertesz, 1933. **$615**

A good Le Blondel Freres large half-plate daguerreotype group of two young girls, 1855. **$660**

'**Hypatia**' portrait of Marie Spartali, albumen print, 300 x 345mm., circa 1870. **$1,500**

Sir Henry Taylor, albumen print, 252 x 202mm., circa 1865. **$1,540**

'**The Flower Peddler**', silver print by Weegee, circa 1940. **$310**

Boy seated on a Bench, by J. Whistler, salt print, 259 x 217mm., circa 1855. **$350**

Setting Up The Bow Nets, by P. H. Emerson, platinum print, 120 x 174mm., 1886. **$485**

Newhaven Fisherman, calotype, by R. Adamson and D. O. Hill, 155 x 116mm., circa 1845. **$835**

PHOTOGRAPHS

Study of a woman in Eastern costume by Roger Fenton, late 1850's. **$1,145**

'International Exhibition', albumen print, 430 x 388mm., 1862. **$570**

Miss Kitchin seated in profile by Lewis Carroll, 1870. **$1,100**

Study of a young woman in striped Eastern costume, albumen print, late 1850's. **$2,200**

Young Girl Amongst Hollyhocks, by Eva Watson Schutze, circa 1910. **$310**

Study of a couple in opulent Eastern costume, albumen print, late 1850's. **$440**

Architectural study attributed to Friedrich Von Martens, 1860's. **$1,000**

Portail Meridional De L'Eglise De Notre Dame, by Henri Le Seq, 1851. **$1,000**

Le Printemps, copy of Manets portrait by Chas. Cros, 1881-82. **$660**

Miss Matilda Rigby, calotype, circa 1845.
$840

A Claudet half-plate daguerreotype portrait of **A. Hewat**, after 1851.
$240

Gerhardt Hauptman, silver print by Edward Steichen, 1932.
$400

Mrs Arthur Gordon Bowman, by Edward Steichen, 1933.
$935

A Reedcutter at Work, platinum print by Peter Henry Emerson, 1886.
$770

The Duncan Dancers from Moscow, silver print, by Steichen, 1929.
$485

Diana Wynyard in Surreal Setting, by Angus McBean, 1940's.
$375

Saratoga Springs Hotel Courtyard, by Walker Evans, 1933.
$485

Seated Nude, silver print, by Bill Brandt, 1950's.
$440

PHOTOGRAPHS

Henry Taylor by Julia
Margaret Cameron, 1869.
$600

Two Girls Reclining In A Bed,
by F. Seidenstucker, 1930's.
$150

Village Street Scene, by
Bertram Cox, 1920's.
$150

**Employment Agency on
6th Avenue,** by Adreas
Feininger, 1940. **$160**

Portrait Of A Man, 1975, by
Ralph Gibson. **$200**

Charles Darwin, an albumen
print by Julia Margt. Cameron,
1868, 12½ x 10½in. (Christie's)
$150

**Cecil Beaton in the Sailor's
Return, 1947,** by Hills &
Saunders. **$250**

**Brunnen In Stadtpark Von
Barcelona** by Bill Brandt,
1930. **$350**

Marilyn Monroe by Lawrence
Schiller, 1962. **$1,000**

PIN BOXES

These novel little porcelain boxes were designed to sit on the dressing table and, although referred to as pin boxes, they were suitable for a multitude of small things such as cufflinks, studs and buttons.

They are made of a similarly hard paste porcelain to that used in the production of fairings and match strikers and were, in fact, made by the same manufacturer, Conte & Boehme of Possneck, in Germany.

Some of the boxes are captioned and have a figure on the lid identical to those on fairings. They were clearly intended for the same market — as prizes at the hoop-la or as a cheap souvenir.

All are of fairly crude manufacture with bright enamel coloring.

'Swansea To Bristol'.
$50–$90

'Pins Madame?'
$50–$90

'Caernarvon To Liverpool'.
$50–$90

'Cousin And Cousine'.
$300–$500

'Lor Three Legs! I'll Charge 2d.'
$50–$90

'After The Race 1875'.
$50–$90

'Anti Vivisectors'.
$50–$90

'The Model Of Laxey'.
$50–$90

'Missus Is Master'.
$50–$90

PIN-UP MAGAZINES

From the naughty art work of the Victorian era's 'La Vie Parisienne' to the center-fold lovelies of this month's 'Playboy' magazine the pin-up and glamor magazine has been ever popular. While the early magazines relied upon drawings it was not long before the reproduction of photographs was cheaply available.

Some collectors still prefer the art work pin-up and look for the superb covers of the pre-war American magazines by artists like Dryben and Bolles. Others like the photographs and the candid lingerie shots found in Spick, Span and Silky but almost all collectors agree that the true pin-up has no need for full frontal explicitness and do not collect beyond the magazines of the late 1960's.

Although a relatively new field of systematic collecting, four main areas of interest have emerged . They are artists and their artwork, photographers, specific models and subsequent matter.

A magazine to look out for is London Life from the 1920's and 1930's. This apparently innocent journal is devoted to all manner of fetishes, in a very restrained manner of course. Also popular are the works of Pett, the artist who created Jane his journals turn up from time to time and are very collectible.

Most book shops are a little shy about handling pin-up items, while for adult book shops these magazines are a little tame. However, they do turn up from time to time, and there are a few mail order dealers who issue catalogues.

Penthouse Magazine, Volume 1 Number 1. **$15**

La Beaute, Vol. 3, Paris 1926.　　　　**$50**

La Vie Parisienne, January 1906. **$12**

Silk Stocking Stories,
November 1937, Dryben
Cover.   **$17**

Movie Merry-Go-Round,
July 1937.   **$15**

High Heel Magazine,
November 1937, Dryben
Cover.   **$15**

Breezy Stories, July 1936.
        $10

The Winning Post, 1919,
Cover by Rene Bull.
        $9

Breezy Stories, Feb. 1937,
Fire of Spring.   **$9**

Bits of Fun and Fashion,
Fads & Fancies, 1920. **$12**

Midi Paname, 1950's. **$3**

Movie Humor, Hollywood
Girls and Gags, March 1938.
        $15

Gay French Nights, 1940's.
$3

The Kirchner Album, Sketch Publications London. $50

French Frolics, Spicy Story Magazine, 1940's. $3

Paris Sex-Appeal, August 1935. $7

Life, 1910. $12

Paris Magazine, February 1932. $7

Flirty, Daring, Thrilling, Exciting, 1940's. $4

l'Amour, August 1902, French. $9

Hollywood Frolics, Spicy Stories, American, 1940's. $3

PIPES

The earliest European pipes were made of clay and, because tobacco was so expensive, fitted with a small bowl. The stem of the early pipe was short in length, as in the Cutty, which was followed by a longer stemmed pipe known as the Churchwarden. During the reign of George I the Churchwarden pipe was adapted to accommodate a red wax tip to the mouthpiece and was then referred to as the Alderman.

The best English pipes were made at Winchester and Bronseley. Brier pipes made from the root of the brier shrub are well collected, but the most popular of all is still the Meerschaum. Meerschaum is a material ideally suited to carving and has the added attraction of turning the most beautiful mellow color with use.

One of the most important, but lesser known pipemakers was Bambier of Paris. His work includes pipes in the form of stylized animals, satirical caricatures of prominent figures and some quite macabre subjects.

Late 19th century German Meerschaum figural pipe with amber stem, 12¼in. long. (Robt. W. Skinner Inc.) $1,000

Silver mounted cast iron pipe bowl, probably German, circa 1840, 3¾in. high. $575

A Zulu wood pipe with a carved female figure. (Christie's) $600

Late 19th century Meerschaum pipe, carved with a lion's head, 7½in. long. (Robt. W. Skinner Inc.) $500

A 19th century Meerschaum pipe, modeled with a figure of a bearded gentleman, 19cm. long. (H. Spencer & Sons) $480

Plain Meerschaum pipe with curved bowl and white metal mounts, carved in high relief with coat-of-arms. (Christie's) $200

A 17th century Dutch fruitwood pipe, 3.3/8in. long. $4,000

A Staffordshire pottery curled pipe painted with blue and yellow dashes. $440

Carved burl Civil War pipe bowl, American, circa 1862-63. (Robt. W. Skinner Inc.) $1,185

PISTOLS

Antique pistols are particularly popular with collectors and investors for, as they disappear into collections, their scarcity naturally pushes the value up.

Flintlocks and percussion weapons are straightforward enough, but before purchasing those with a pinfire mechanism, check with the police as they could be regarded as firearms and then certain legislation comes into force.

Always try to buy weapons in pristine condition with no missing or replaced parts, keeping a particular eye for makers such as Nock, Manton, Twigg, Egg, Kuchenreuter and Lepage. Also be on the lookout for pairs of pistols, as they are worth at least three times that of a single — even more if they are in a box complete with accessories.

A 6-shot .36in. model 1851 third type Colt Navy single action percussion revolver, 13in., blued octagonal barrel 7½in. (Wallis & Wallis) $5,600

A 14-bore flintlock holster pistol, 14in., barrel 8½in., Birmingham proved. Fullstocked, with stepped lock and steel furniture and rounded checkered butt. (Wallis & Wallis) $540

A 26-bore all steel Scottish flintlock belt pistol by Murdoch of Doune, circa 1770, 12in., barrel 7¾in., foliate engraved, reeded breech, faceted muzzle. Steel fullstock, stock and rounded butt. (Wallis & Wallis) $2,200

A .15in. Continental enclosed action percussion target pistol, 12¾in., tip down smooth bore octagonal barrel 7½in., secured by side lever and opening merely for capping. Steel furniture and fluted walnut butt. (Wallis & Wallis) $460

A .48in. boxlock sidehammer Continental needle fire holster pistol, 12½in., right octagonal barrel 7in., released by underlever. Scroll engraved frame, side cocking lever and steel furniture, checkered saw handled walnut butt. (Wallis & Wallis) $460

A double-barreled percussion coaching pistol with 8½in. barrels fitted with spring bayonet and wooden ramrod, the lockplates engraved Enty, London. (Christie's) $600

PISTOLS

A 5-shot .38in. Tranter's patent double action percussion revolver, 10in., octagonal barrel 4½in., London proved. (Wallis & Wallis) $666

A double barrel silver-mounted flintlock boxlock pistol, breeches struck with London proof marks and I G, circa 1760, 11¼in. long. $3,460

A 6-shot .44in. Magnum Ruger Super Blackhawk single action revolver, 13½in., barrel 7½in., with sidegate loading and ejection. (Wallis & Wallis) $132

A .455in. Webley Mark I double action center fire revolver, no. 1676, 9in., barrel 4in., molded bakelite grips. (Wallis & Wallis) $166

A 6-shot .31in. self-cocking transitional percussion revolver, 11in., barrel 5½in. Cylinder roll engraved with dogs and deer. Foliate engraved brass backstrap, one-piece checkered walnut grips. (Wallis & Wallis) $680

A 28-bore back-action percussion traveling pistol, by Burnett, 10in., octagonal barrel 5in., with engraved steel furniture and brass tipped wooden ramrod. (Wallis & Wallis) $210

An 18-bore brass barreled flintlock holster pistol, by J. Harding & Son, for the protection of Mail Coach operatives, 14½in., brass barrel 9in., London and military proofs. (Wallis & Wallis) $1,250

A 16-bore New Land pattern flintlock holster pistol, 15½in., browned barrel 9in., Tower proved. (Wallis & Wallis) $925

PISTOLS

A .41in. rimfire National Arms Co. derringer, 5in. overall, barrel 2½in., silver plated scroll engraved brass frame with sheath trigger. (Wallis & Wallis) $300

A 6 shot .44in. Smith & Wesson Russian Model single action revolver, 12¼in., barrel 7in., patent dates to 1869, spurred trigger guard, two-piece wooden grips and steel lanyard ring. (Wallis & Wallis) $240

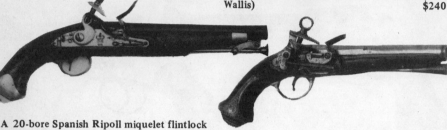

A 20-bore Spanish Ripoll miquelet flintlock belt pistol, circa 1780. (Wallis & Wallis) $700

A 16-bore New Land pattern flintlock holster pistol, 15in., browned barrel 9in. (Wallis & Wallis) $700

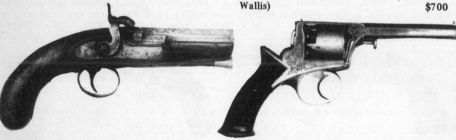

A 24-bore percussion Police pistol of The Cheshire Constabulary for the Wirral Hundred. (Wallis & Wallis) $500

A 5-shot 120-bore Adam's patent model 1851 self-cocking percussion revolver. (Wallis & Wallis) $600

A brass barreled flintlock blunderbuss pistol by Jackson, circa 1795. (Wallis & Wallis) $450

A 5-shot .32in. extra short rimfire Remington-Rider magazine pistol. (Wallis & Wallis) $325

PLAYING CARDS

The origin of playing cards is still a subject for speculation, the most widely held view being that they probably originated both in the East and the West independently and simultaneously. The earliest record in Europe is a decree of 23rd May, 1376, issued in the City of Florence, prohibiting their use.

The earliest decks, now of course out of reach of most collectors and to be found only in museums, were hand-drawn and painted packs commissioned by Royalty and the wealthy aristocracy of the period. The earliest pack a collector can hope to possess dates to the end of the 17th century when a series of playing cards in England were used as general information for the public. These early engraved packs are priced at around $1,000 and above. The range for the collector is otherwise very wide indeed. Cards of the last century can vary dramatically in price range with rarer packs fetching as much as $2,000 whereas some of the common ones are priced at below $20. There also is a very wide range of modern cards with unusual designs produced in the past decade which are priced well below $10 per deck and are undoubtedly the collectors pieces of the future.

Collectors will only be interested in 'non-standard' decks, that is ones that have unusual designs, mainly of the Court card and in game packs which are card decks without suit signs. The English suit signs of spades, hearts, diamonds and clubs (which are derived from the French packs) are not universally in use and even today, the Germanic countries still use the hearts, leaves, dumb-bells and acorns and the Spaniards and Italians still use the coins, cups, swords and sticks. The subject matter of Tarot and fortune-telling cards is an additional and effectively separate branch within the overall picture of playing cards.

Marlborough's Victories — 52 engraved cards each with scene relating to War of the Spanish Succession, captions below, 92 x 61mm., Christopher Blanchard, circa 1708. $6,000

A complete set of 52 playing cards, illuminated on pasteboard, each card made up of 4 layers of paper pasted together, South Flanders, possibly Lille, circa 1470-85. $145,000

Question and Answer Cards — 40 engraved cards of 50 each with a question or answer, 55 x 45mm., Germany, circa 1700. $300

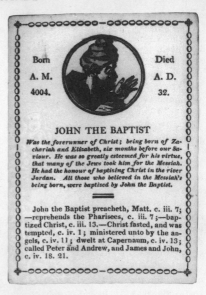

Italy — A single-suited French deck produced by Viassone in Turin, circa 1820, 52/52. $160

England — Biblical educational cards by J. Wallis, circa 1800, 32/32. $170

Iran — Persian 'Asnas' deck, circa 1860, 25/25, hand-painted and lacquered. $560

France — The 'Four Seasons' designed by J. P. Le Doux, published by Draeger, Paris 1961. $50

Belgium — The 'Dilkhus' playing cards, makers unknown, circa 1920, Indian ethnic pack. $70

Italy — 18th century 'Cucu' deck 38/38. $600

France — 'Cartes a Rire' — transformation pack attributed to Baron Louis Atthalin 1819 (Courts represent Paris newspapers). $1,900

England — Victoria Diamond Jubilee deck by Goodall & Son, London 1897, all portraits of British Royalty. $170

Russia — A Slavic costume deck unknown maker, circa 1935. $120

Popish Plot 1679 by R. Walton, London. $1,600

England — Transformation pack by Maclure, Macdonald and Macgregor, Manchester, circa 1870. $440

Italy — Playing cards by E. Dotti, Milan, circa 1870, hand-coloured. $320

POISON BOTTLES

Poison bottles were produced in distinctive shapes, designs and finishes so that they were instantly recognizable and could not be confused with other medicine bottles by someone who may be dosing themselves in the night or in dim light. The first English poison bottle was patented in 1859 and during the rest of the century, hundreds of thousands of them were produced in a staggering variety of designs. Most of the bottles were made of glass colored cobalt blue, green or amber. Cobalt glass disappeared as the usual container for poison in the 1950's when it was replaced by plastic.

Bottles with embossed labels are the most valuable and among the rarer items are those shaped as skulls, wasp waisted bottles, six sided bottles, bottles shaped like binoculars, submarines or with a sharp U-bend in their necks.

Very rare 'Wasp Waist' Poison with rows of diamond points embossed on the front and side panels, patented 1894.
$900

Skull Poisons, Patented by Carlton H. Lee, 1894, in America, cobalt blue glass.
$700

Quine's Patent, aqua glass bottle with 'Poison' embossed on the side, patented 1893.
$150

American, 'Quilt Poison', with cross hatching around the sides of the bottle. $200

O'Reilly's Patent, known as Binoculars Poison, embossed on the base 'O'Reilly's Patent 1905', only two of these bottles are known. $1,600

Wilsons Patent emerald green, triangular bottle with notched edges, patented in 1899.
$150

POLYPHONES

Polyphones are basically a development of the conventional musical box and are credited to the ingenuity of Paul Lochmann who founded the Symphonion Company in Leipzig in 1885. It was he, together with Gustav Brachhausen (founder of the Polyphon Company), who is responsible for the production of most of these delightful machines. Brachhausen in fact, emigrated to America in 1894 where he started the Regina Company in New Jersey.

The music is produced by projecting pegs cut into a metal disc which ping the teeth of a steel comb as the disc revolves to produce a Gilbert and Sullivan aire or the latest singalong from the Music Hall.

The discs themselves range from 8in. on the small portable machines meant for home entertainment, to over 24in. diameter on the grander coin-operated varieties.

Polyphon disc musical box, German, in walnut veneered case, 12in. wide, circa 1910. $800

A 19.1/8in. upright Symphonion disc musical box with 'Sublime Harmony's combs and six disks. (Christie's) $2,500

Polyphon disc musical box, Style No. 45, German, circa 1900, 21½in. wide. $2,000

Polyphon disc musical box in oak and beechwood case, circa 1895, 50in. high. $4,000

A 14in. Stella disc musical box with twin-comb movement in walnut case with disk storage drawer, and 13 disks. (Christie's) $1,750

Late 19th century German polyphon disc musical box, in coin-operated box, 34in. high. $2,000

POP-UP BOOKS

It is little wonder that generations of adults and children have fallen under the spell of these enchanting books with their superb color illustrations, intricate designs and exciting constructions.

The very best examples not only pop-up but incorporate some mechanically operated action and these are highly prized indeed, but even the simplest of these characteristically beautiful productions is worthy of a place in any collection.

The firm Bookano published a whole series of pop-up books and many of those dating from the 30's and 40's are specimens of their work.

Original 19th century copies are very, very rare, often incorporating ingenious mechanisms and are worth in the region of $200.

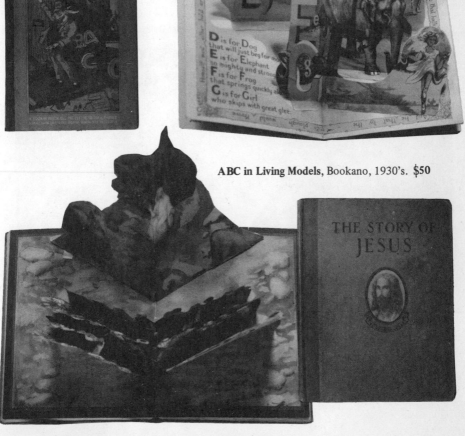

ABC in Living Models, Bookano, 1930's. $50

The Story of Jesus, Bookano, 1938. $15

Bookano Stories, 1940's. $50

Hans Andersen's Fairy Stories, Bookano. $50   Into Space with Ace Brave!, 1950's. $15

PORTRAIT MINIATURES

Before the days of photography, the only way to carry a true likeness of someone was in the form of a miniature portrait, an artform which reached its peak in Europe in the last quarter of the 18th century.

Even small towns boasted their own miniaturist and fashionable resorts supported whole colonies

Their charges varied from a couple of guineas up to twenty-five guineas for the work of a master such as John Smart. Other names to look for are Richard Cosway, Henry Spicer, Horace Hone, Richard Crosse, Ozias Humphrey, Jeremiah Meyer, Charles Bestland and George Engleheart. Most miniatures from this period are painted on ivory with watercolors used to produce flesh tones and opaque color for dress.

More reasonably priced examples can be found from the 19th century, though the skills involved seem to decline with the onset of the camera.

Francois Courtier, later Madame Navarre, by Jean Marie Voille, signed and dated l'an 1e (1793), oval, 2.5/8in. high. (Christie's) $4,000

A Lady called Elizabeth, Lady Willoughby D'Eresby, by Isaac Oliver, 2.1/8in. high. (Christie's) $6,500

A gentleman facing left in blue coat, by Sampson T. Roche, signed and dated 1811, oval, 3in. high. (Christie's) $325

A lady facing right in decollete white dress, Circle of Engleheart, signed with monogram, 3in. high. (Christie's) $725

Frederick V, Elector Palatine, King of Bohemia, enamel, by Henry Pierce Bone, 3.5/8in. high. (Christie's) $700

A girl facing left in a white dress, the reverse with locks of hair, by Andrew Plimer, oval, 3in. high. (Christie's) $2,000

A nobleman by Francisek Smiadecki, circa 1650, oil on copper, oval 2in. $1,250

James Hannen full face in dark gray coat and waistcoat, by Stephen Poyntz Denning, oval, 5½in. high. (Christie's) $1,500

Charlotte Anne Freill, by John Smart, signed with initials and dated 1788, oval 2¾in. $10,500

A gentleman, by the artist signing V ., circa 1785, 2½in. oval. $475

Charles James Fox and Lord North, enamel, oval, 1.7/8in. high. (Christie's) $625

A gentleman by Rosalba Carriera, circa 1710, 3¼in. $4,150

A nobleman in crimson coat and lace jabot, by Christian F. Zincke, 1.5/8in. high. (Christie's) $1,500

A gentleman facing right, by Wm. Marshall Craig, the reverse with gold monogram HW on plaited hair, oval 2.5/8in. high. (Christie's) $800

Maria Pavlovna, by Alois G. Rockstuhl, after Lampi, signed and dated 1864, 4in. high. (Christie's) $3,000

PORTRAIT MINIATURES

Master James Parke, by Andrew Plimer, gold frame with split pearl border, 3in. high. (Christie's) $6,750

Christiane Lichnowsky in white dress and pink stole, by Heinrich F. Fuger, 3in. high. (Christie's) $14,500

An 18th century miniature on ivory of a young lady, 1½in. high. (Robt. W. Skinner Inc.) $500

Fanny Elssler facing left in white off the shoulder dress, by Aime Zoe Lizinka de Mirbel, signed and dated 1838, oval, 3¾in. high. (Christie's) $4,665

James II, signed on reverse James 2nd/London, June 1845/painted by H. P. Bone/ enamel painter to Her Majesty H.R.H. Prince/Albert, after Lely, oval 1.7/8in. high. (Christie's) $450

Mid 17th century miniature on ivory, said to be Nell Gwynn, 1.7/8in. high. (Robt. W. Skinner Inc.) $250

The Stolen Kiss, Circle of Claude Jean Baptiste Hoin, oval, 2¾in. high.(Christie's) $925

A Young Clansman, English School, circa 1790, 2¼in. oval. $3,300

Etienne Francois, Marquis D'Aligre by Augustus Dubourg, after Van Loo, signed and dated 1789, 2¾in. diam. $1,750

POSTAL SCALES

The earliest postal scales were made by the manufacturers of scientific instruments such as S. Morden and Co. who had a tradition of using fine wood and brass. As a result many of the early scales are true works of art with mahogany and ebony bases and fine fret cut brasswork. Later models are often made of cast iron and are purely functional items with little aesthetic appeal.

Apart from the weight most scales also display the actual postal charges, enabling the collector to date them fairly accurately for there were frequent changes by the Post Office.

Painted metal scales by Salter, 1940-52, 7½in. high. **$30**

Brass and mahogany scales by S. Morden & Co., 1906-15, 15in. wide. **$300**

19th century painted tin scales, 9in. high. **$40**

Salter parcel scales with cast iron frame, 1957-61, 11in. high. **$15**

Brass and painted metal scales, 1906-15, 11in. high. **$40**

Painted metal and brass scales by Triner Scale Co., Chicago, made for the U.K. market, 1935-40, 8in. high. **$40**

POSTCARDS

When one postcard, delivered on September 20th, 1902, after a trip from Manchester to Haslingden by Balloon Post, sells for $2,500 at auction, postcard collecting needs no further justification for its popularity.

The world's first postcard was issued in Austria on October 1st 1869 and proved to be so popular that many other countries followed suit — Britain 1870, Canada 1871 and America 1873. Early American postcard publishers such as Ettlinger, Photocraft Co., Hugh C. Leighton Co., W. B. Hale, Theochrom and Rotograph had many of their cards produced in Germany for the chromo lithographic work was considered to be of a superior quality than the home produced product.

The first British postcards issued by the General Post Office in 1870 were designed to take the address only on one side and the message alongside the illustration on the other side. This card came complete with a printed half penny stamp and it was not until 1894 that independent companies issued postcards for use with an adhesive stamp. An Act of Parliament in 1902 allowing the message and address to be written on the same side leaving the other side free for a picture gave rise to the popular trend as we know it today. There is absolutely no limit to the variety of themes from which a collection can be formed and special interest areas include cards depicting Film Stars, Glamor Girls, Humor, Advertising, Transport, Topography and many more subjects.

Some sets of cards are particularly pleasing such as those by C. W. Faulkner and the Tucks Record Card demonstrates the high popularity of cards with some special feature. These always get between $10 and $20 although the record itself is usually disappointing. Cards incorporating moving parts will also get between $10 and $20.

'California Honeymoon', color photolitho, by Edward H. Mitchell, San Francisco, 1910. $25

Sing Fat Co. Inc., the famous Oriental bazaar in Chinatown, Los Angeles. $8

'Bottle', printed in Germany for Hugh & Leighton Co., Portland Maine, 1909. $20

'Flying High in Kansas City', real photograph. $16

Broncho Billy, official Film Co. issue, made by the Garraway Co., Rutherford, N. Jersey. $8

Nancy's Lawn Sale, by Art Strader, 1982. Comic caricature of the President's wife. $3

Anita 'The Living Doll', aged 30 years, the smallest adult the world has ever seen (signed postcard).$12

Concours De Byrrh, one card by Maurice Denis, in good condition. $200

Wilfred Westwood, tallest, heaviest boy in the world, aged 11 years, weight 20st. 6lb. $3

James Cagney, Warner Bros. $8

Gibbs Dentifrice, with Tucks Record Card. $15

Mae West, Paramount Pictures. $8

'Hold to Light' card, illuminates holly, berries, moon and windows when held to light, **'Tobogganing in the Snow'**. $8

Moge alles dir stets glucken, Novelty Postcard. $12

Embossed chromo litho postcard with real velvet applied to figures' clothes, Novelty **'Applique'** card. $8

'Lady with Sunburst', 1905. **$65**

Lifeboat Saturday, a card delivered by air from Manchester to Haslingden on Sept. 20th 1902. **$2,500**

'That's what keeps me awake at night', circa 1930. **$6**

Postcard decorated with the head of a horse, by Pablo Picasso, 1923. **$1,100**

'The Tie that Binds', Photocraft Co., Newark, New Jersey, 1912. **$20**

'Fancy Free', by Philip Boileau. **$10**

A saucy German postcard, 1904. **$18**

Loretta Young, born in Salt Lake City, Jan. 6th 1913. Her films include 'Caravan', 'Clive of India' and 'Heroes for Sale', 20th Century Fox printed postcard. **$5**

Melox Marvels, Advertising Card. **$9**

'Sperry Flour Mills',
Washington. $2

'Howdy from New York.
                        $4

'Boston Beans'. $5

Boston Floating Hospital.
                        $7

'Barely Able to Write'. $5

'Kodak Park Works'. $2

Greetings from 'Dothan,
Alabama'. $4

Greetings from 'Beaver
Falls!' $4

POSTERS

Originally designed to be displayed in public places the function of the poster was to inform by advertising goods or publicizing events. Competition in the market place led to a high standard of art work and the production of beautifully colored and highly decorative items which, unlike some printed collectibles acquiring significance to the collector only with the passing of the years, have been enthusiastically collected since their introduction at the end of the 19th century.

In fact, a monthly magazine 'The Poster', which gave information on how to keep abreast of the trend became an instant bestseller.

The now famous Alphonse Mucha poster announcing Sarah Bernhardt in the new play 'Gismonda' demonstrates the quality of early productions. He went on to design all her publicity material on an exclusive basis for a period of six years and any of his works will command the highest of prices today.

Subjects most favored by collectors include Motoring, Theater, Circus and, of course, posters in the Art Nouveau style from that period.

Film posters too have their devotees with Humphrey Bogart, Mae West, Greta Garbo and James Cagney all keenly sought as are the early Rock 'n Roll posters particularly of Elvis and 'super groups' such as the Beatles and the Stones.

While condition and rarity factors are important when evaluating investment potential a collection may be gathered around the work of a particular artist, style, period, range of goods or a specific product with examples spanning a price range from only a few dollars to many thousands.

Late 19th century hand-colored lithograph, 'P. T. Barnum's New and Greatest Show On Earth Coming By Four Special Trains', 17¼ x 25½in. (Robt. W. Skinner Inc.) $500

Steinhardt, Unter Den Linden, by Hans Lindenstaedt, lithograph in colors, 1912, on wove paper, 710 x 945mm. (Christie's) $600

A Belgian poster, Anvers — New York, designed by Henri Cassiers. (Christie's) $800

G. B. Borsalino, FV. Lazzaro & Co., Fabbrica di Cappelli by Simonetti, lithograph printed in colors, on wove paper, 1345 x 955mm. $300

Femme au Carton a Dessins, lithograph printed in colors 1898, on wove paper, 595 x 505mm. by Alphonse Mucha. $4,400

Ansaldo, Torino, Italia. (Yesterday's Paper) $130

Normandie, by Adolphe Mouron Cassandre, lithograph printed in colors 1935, 972 x 602mm. $2,800

Solanis, Le Magicien Moderne, by Conde, 1940. $70

Anchor Line Glasgow & New York via Londonderry, by K. Shoesmith. (Onslow's) $527

La Raphaelle, by Rossetti, 1908, 62½ x 46½in. $100

David Hockney at the Tate Gallery, lithograph in color, 1980, on wove paper, signed in pencil, 760 x 505mm. (Christie's) $90

G. Marconi, Le Maitre De La Radio, by Paul Colin, lithograph in colors, printed by Bedos & Cie, Paris, 1578 x 1130mm. (Christie's) $440

Pierre Stephen, lithograph in colors, on wove paper, printed by Bauduin, Paris, 1538 x 1175mm. (Christie's)$840

Absinthe Robette, by Privat Livemont, lithograph in colors, 1896, on wove paper, printed by J. L. Goffart, Bruxelles, 1105 x 806mm. (Christie's) $1,500

The Dreadnoughts, 1920, 53 x 39in. $120

La Revue Des Folies Bergere, by Jules Alexandre Grun, lithograph in colors, 1905, printed by Ch. Verneau, Paris, 1246 x 880mm. (Christie's) $300

Cunard, Europe America Berengaria, by Odin Rosenvinge. (Onslow's) $1,000

Thompson's Bread, 1930, 39 x 30in. $90

Cowgirl Circus Poster, 1920. $60

Camp Romain, Vin Rouge, Rose, Blanc, by L. Gadoud, lithograph in colors, on wove paper, 1600 x 1200mm. (Christie's) $320

Cyclistes !!! Attention, by Tichon, 1890, 51 x 37in. $150

Job, by Alphonse Mucha, lithograph in colors, 1898, on wove paper, printed by F: Champenoise, Paris, 1500 x 1010mm. (Christie's) $6,000

Nord Express, by Adolphe Mouron Cassandre, lithograph in colors, 1927, on wove paper, 1048 x 752mm. (Christie's) $2,500

Alcazar Royal, by Adolphe Crespin and Edouard Duych, lithograph in colors, 1894, 1010 x 775mm. (Christie's) $500

XXVI Ausstellung Secession, by Ferdinand Andri, lithograph in colors, circa 1904, on wove paper, 920 x 602mm. (Christie's) $14,000

Framed circus advertising poster, Walter Main, 3 Ring Shows, Riverside Print Co., Chicago, 27 x 41in. (Robt. W. Skinner Inc.) **$400**

Les Petites Barnett, lithograph printed in colors on wove paper, printed by Ch. Levy, Paris, 570 x 777mm. **$400**

POWDER FLASKS

A 17th century German powder flask made from an antler horn, the surface engraved with foliage, could cost hundreds of dollars but the metal variety by Batty, Hawkins, Ames, Dixon, or The American Flask & Cap Company among others, are fairly plentiful and therefore more reasonably priced. Most are decorated in some form, from simple fluting or basket weave designs to Coats of Arms, deer or even horrendous battle scenes. Of particular interest are the Old Colonial powder horns, which are nearly all engraved or carved by the owners themselves, often complete with personal mottos and beliefs.

An early 19th century engraved powder horn, the body incised with a thistle encircling John Davis Royal Mail 1815, 12in. overall. **$440**

A German flattened cowhorn powder flask with Boche charger, 13in., brass mounts and horn nozzle. (Wallis & Wallis) **$160**

A large 19th century engraved powder flask made from the shoulder blades of an ox, 16in. overall, probably by Ernst Schmidt of Munich. (Wallis & Wallis) **$1,000**

A Scottish silver mounted dress powder horn, circa 1850, 15in., oval Cairngorm stone mounted in thistle embossed silver cap. (Wallis & Wallis) **$400**

A 17th century powder horn, body of flattened cowhorn, 11cm. **$1,475**

A cowhorn powder flask for the Baker rifle issued to the Percy Tenantry, 13in. (Wallis & Wallis) **$100**

A late 16th century South German powder flask of triangular form with incurved sides, 5.5/8in. high. $7,800

An 18th century Persian priming powder flask, 5in. overall. $975

A copper three-way powder flask, 3½in., stamped Sykes, with common-brass top with blued spring. (Wallis & Wallis) $90

An early 18th century Arab silver mounted powder flask Barutdan, 8in., of iron in coiled horn form. (Wallis & Wallis) $75

A gun sized fluted copper powder flask, 7¾in., patent brass top stamped James Dixon & Sons, Sheffield. (Wallis & Wallis) $70

A 17th century powder horn, body fashioned from section of antler, 12½in. $600

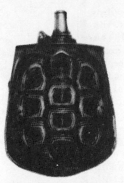

Late 16th/early 17th century powder horn with four small suspension rings, 23cm. $450

A silver mounted tortoise-shell powder flask, 4in., with silver spout and sprung lever. (Wallis & Wallis) $100

A mid 19th century powder flask with measuring cup, 4¾in. $80

PRAMS

The earliest known baby carriage in Britain was made in 1730 (for the children of The 3rd Duke of Devonshire), and designed to be pulled along by a small animal. The first of the baby carriages manufactured for public use was made in 1840. This was a three wheeled version with iron tyres and it still had to be pulled along. About the mid 19th century, a handle was fitted to the back so that the pram could be pushed and this version was called the perambulator. The three wheeled perambulator remained in popular use until about 1880 when it was displaced by the new four wheeled bassinette. The early four wheeled prams were, at first, categorized by the authorities as road vehicles but as they became more popular, this was rescinded.

The pram has always been something of a status symbol and the early prams were no exception. They were coachbuilt with bodies made of wood, sometimes of leather, and dressed with fittings of brass. They were lavishly trimmed and the interiors were often upholstered in soft skins or a leatherette, some deep-buttoned for effect. Safety features such as brakes and strappings were not introduced until after 1900.

An early safety feature perhaps worth noting, is the pram fitted with two handles, one at each end. This was not merely a fashionable 'extra' but a necessity for the safe-keeping of the infants who were trundled around the treacherous roads of the early perambulating days. Pavements were either very narrow or non existent and traffic regulations for coaches and carriages still a bit sketchy, which made turning a pram for the return journey, a hazardous business. With a handle fitted at both ends, the prampusher only had to pass alongside the pram to reverse direction in safety.

Wooden 'mail cart' pram with carved sides, leather hood and brass trim. $600

1930's German wickerwork pram with alloy wheel arches and bumpers. $120

1920's Acme pram with wooden body and 'C' springs, reg. no. 465485. $160

1930's simulated leather doll's pram with folding hood and brake. $70

1930's Stella doll's pram with plywood body, leatherette hood and umbrella holder. $80

An early Star Manufacturing Co. round-head pram with leather trim and porcelain handle. $500

Country style 'mail cart' push-chair with iron wheels. $200

A rare T. Trotmans patent 1854 folding pram with carpet back seating and wood and brass wheels. $800

The 'London' baby coach with wooden body and fabric cover. $110

Country style oak framed back to back twin pram with brass hubs. $360

A rare Bassinett two-handled double pram with painted leather body, circa 1860. $500

A large 1960's Silver Cross pram with metal body and fabric and leatherette upholstery. $70

Silver Cross 1930's twin hood doll's pram with metal and wood body and leatherette and fabric hood. $100

1930's Pedigree pram by A. J. Dale & Son, Warminster. $110

Tan-Sad wartime Cot-Kar pram, No. 3214, with wooden body and leatherette hood. $170

PRATTWARE

The term Prattware is generally associated with the transfer printed pot lids of the Victorian period manufactured by F. & R. Pratt & Co., of Fenton, England.

Much of the success of this firm was due to their engraver Jesse Austin who was a master of the art of transferring the works of Landseer, Gainsborough and Mulready onto lids, plates and other tableware, using a multi-color printing process made up of small dots.

Many of his engraved plates were rediscovered and subsequently revived at the turn of this century. Articles from this period often bear fine cracks all over the glaze, a process known as crazing.

An earlier member of the Pratt family however, also shares the term Prattware for his Toby jugs, some bearing the portraits of Nelson or Admiral Vernon. He also made a variety of figures and a distinctive type of earthenware of Italian influence, with either orange, green, blue or yellow panels.

A Prattware cottage money box in the form of a two-storeyed house with blue tiled roof, 12.5cm. high. (Phillips) $650

A Prattware pot lid depicting Strathfieldsay, 5in. diam. (Christie's) $75

A Prattware jug of slightly flattened baluster form with angular handle, circa 1780, 18.5cm. high. (Christie's) $300

A large Prattware two-handled loving cup, bearing the Jolly Topers, malachite ground, gold line decoration. (Phillips) $675

A Pratt type Toby jug modeled as a rotund gentleman seated, entitled 'Tobey', 9¾in. high, circa 1790. (Christie's) $930

A Pratt type pearlware group, circa 1790, 15cm. high. $1,200

PRINTS

One of the attractions of collecting prints is that apart from there being the range to suit all pockets there is always the chance of coming across a real treasure. This is a classic example of where acquiring knowledge could yield a fortune.

On a more moderate level prints by Le Blond, Baxter, Icart and Cruikshank are always worth seeking.

Look for clear impressions, preferably in color, with good margins and no damage and also keep an eye open for limited editions which will always command a premium.

'The Great Bartholdi Statue, Liberty Enlightening The World', published by Currier & Ives, 1885. (Robt. W. Skinner) $1,200

Campbell's Soup, by Andy Warhol, screenprints in colors, 1969, on wove paper; 907 x 957mm., and album. (Christie's) $6,000

Plakat Muim Institut, by Ernst Ludwig Kirchner, woodcut printed in blue and black, 1911, on rose laid paper, 728 x 492mm. (Christie's) $8,000

L'Artisan Moderne, by Henri de Toulouse-Lautrec, lithograph printed in colors, 1894, on cream wove paper, 923 x 648mm. (Christie's) $12,000

Melancholisches Madchen, by Ernst Ludwig Kirchner, woodcut printed in three colors from one block, 1922, on soft Japan, 752 x 445mm. (Christie's) $65,000

Kasimir Malevich: Patriotic Poster against the Germans, lithograph printed in colors, 1914-15, on wove paper, 516 x 340mm. (Christie's) $4,000

'The Darktown Yacht Club — On The Winning Tack', published by Currier & Ives, 1885, small folio. (Robt. W. Skinner Inc.) $335

'The Great Fire at Boston', published by Currier & Ives, 1872, small folio. (Robt. W. Skinner Inc.) $575

The actor Asao Gakujuro as Mashiba Hisatsugu, a poem by Enjyaku above. (Christie's) $1,800

La Baie des Anges, by Marc Chagall, lithograph printed in colors, 1962, on wove paper, 777 x 575mm. (Christie's) $375

Vor dem Spiegel, by Max Beckmann, drypoint, 1923, on laid paper, 227 x 172mm. (Christie's) $2,400

'The Rights of Women' published by D. Bogue. (Yesterday's Paper) $30

'The Champion in Luck', published by Currier & Ives, 1882, small folio. (Robt. W. Skinner Inc.) $110

'The Accommodation Train', published by Currier & Ives, 1876, small folio. (Robt. W. Skinner Inc.) $350

'Notice To Smokers And Chewers', published by N. Currier, 1854, small folio. (Robt. W. Skinner Inc.) $900

'Rysdyk's Hambletonian', published by Currier & Ives, 1876, large folio. (Robt. W. Skinner Inc.) $1,800

'The Celebrated Horse Dexter, 'The King Of The World' Driven By Budd Doble'', published by Currier & Ives, 1867, large folio. (Robt. W. Skinner Inc.) $2,250

'The Trotting Mare Goldsmith Maid, Driven By Budd Doble', published by Currier & Ives, 1870, large folio. (Robt. W. Skinner Inc.) $1,350

PURSES & HANDBAGS

Apart from any natural deterioration resulting from the passage of time, an attack of moths or storage in a damp place, evening bags and purses are generally found to be in fair condition; used mainly on special occasions they were rarely subjected to the rigors of everyday use.

The body of the pouch was produced in a number of materials including leather, beadwork, tapestry, embroidered silks and a chain mail of gold, silver or steel links. The clasps, and mounts too, were sometimes made of precious metals inset with gem-stones, gilt, silver or silver filigree but more commonly of tortoiseshell.

All types of old handbags are now being appreciated for their 'period' styling and this includes handbags produced up until the 50's and, in cases like the Cartier, to the present day.

Edwardian snakeskin clutch bag with silver mounts.
$200

Mid 18th century Louis XV gold mounted black leather purse from the collection of Madame de Pompadour, 11cm. $2,500

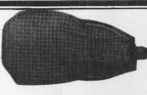

An Art Deco suede evening bag encased in a mesh of pearls with an onyx and diamond set frame. (Phillips) $7,000

Plains beaded buckskin tipi bag, 20 x 13in. (Robt. W. Skinner Inc.) $1,200

A 19th century beadwork and mother-of-pearl button decorated purse. $15

A fine late 19th century beadwork purse with plated mounts. $45

A 20th century French hallmarked 18kt. gold mesh evening bag, 192.8gr. (Robt. W. Skinner Inc.) $2,135

A large Berlin woolwork bag with leather clasp and brass handle, circa 1860. (Christie's) $235

A painted silk purse, inscribed in ink 'Judith N. Peaslee, painted under the care of Miss C. Gage, Bradford Academy, 1812', Mass. (Robt. W. Skinner Inc.) $695

QUACK MEDICINE BOTTLES

The Victorians swallowed an amazing quantity of quack medicines and the gullibility of the public seems to have known no bounds if the claims on the bottles are to be believed.

The most popular medicines were those which advertised themselves as having been used by royalty and bottles embossed with such claims are now prized by collectors. Some of the rarer and more interesting glass medicine bottles contained materials which cannot be obtained over the counter today like Elixir of Opium or the strangely named Mouse Ear Syrup. There was also Extract of Mistletoe Druid Cure and Seaweed Extract in a green glass bottle. Medicines were produced for babies — Croup Mixture was popular — and for nervous ladies who might have taken Miss Pike's Powders for Fits and Nervous Complaints.

Holden's 'Tommy' bottle, Cures Sprains and Sore Throats, aqua glass. $60

Dr. Wartburg's Fever Tincture, Tonic Medicine, in aqua molded bottle. $100

Pre 1850 Ruspinis Styptic in cobalt blue pontilled bottle. $200

Miss Pikes Powders for Fits and Nervous Complaints, in a lead glass bottle, circa 1800. $200

Dalby's Carminative, in a cone-shaped aqua bottle. $60

Dr. Lobb's Blob Lipped, cylindrical clear glass bottle with an embossed humanoid face on the reverse. $280

'By the King's Patent', True Cephalic Snuff, in a crudely blown pontilled bottle of light green glass. $200

True Daffys Elixir, in a lime green pontilled bottle. $200

Dr. Solomon's Cordial Balm of Gilead, in molded aqua glass bottle. $300

QUILTS

Bedcovers and quilts, many of very humble origin indeed, are now most enthusiastically collected in all parts of the Western world.

They are treasured for their intricate designs, colorful patterns and, perhaps more important still, the skill demonstrated in the fine hand stitching. Some examples are considered to be so rare and valuable that they hang, framed and under special glass to prevent fading. The original concept was a simple one — to make use of odd scraps of fabric in producing a bedcovering with a practical function. As many more women became proficient in the art, traditional patterns developed, but even these formal designs show much individual style.

In setting out the pattern for a quilt, a paper pattern was cut, often from whatever bits and pieces were to hand; letters, household accounts and other documents were used. The paper pieces were sometimes stitched into the backing of the quilt and may provide a clue in dating a piece.

A 19th century patchwork cotton quilt, with unusual tulip border motifs, America, 92 x 92in. (Robt. W. Skinner Inc.) $2,250

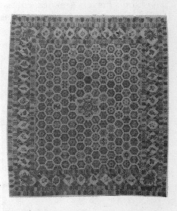

An early 19th century patchwork coverlet in plain and colored printed glazed cotton, circa 1830, 2.70 x 2.24m. (Christie's) $1,000

An appliqued coverlet with pineapple pattern, America, circa 1840, 82 x 98in. (Robt. W. Skinner Inc.) $2,250

An applique album quilt, New Jersey and Pennsylvania, 1853, 7ft.9in. x 8ft.7in. (Robt. W. Skinner Inc.) $3,500

QUILTS

Late 19th century crazy quilt with The Lord's Prayer, America, consisting of velvets, brocades and cottons of varying shapes, 69in. wide. (Robt. W. Skinner Inc.) $450

A patchwork quilt, Penn., signed and dated in ink on the back, 'Phebeann H. Salem's(?) Presented by her Mother 1848', 8ft.11in. x 9ft. (Robt. W. Skinner Inc.) $2,000

A pieced and quilted cotton coverlet, lily pattern, American, circa 1900, approx. 84in. long, 80in. wide. (Christie's) $800

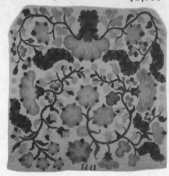

A wool bed rug, worked with a darning stitch in a tree-of-life pattern on a natural wool foundation, dated 1773, 84 x 85in. (Christie's) $11,000

An appliqued quilt with attached label 'Made by Mrs. J. Walter Marshall of Old Frankport Rd., Lexington, Kentucky', circa 1860. (Robt. W. Skinner Inc.) $2,250

An applique quilt signed and dated 'Sarah Ann Wilson - 1854', consisting of thirty appliqued squares of floral and animal design, 7ft.1in. x 8ft.4in. (Robt. W. Skinner Inc.) $35,000

Early 19th century red and blue patchwork Calamanco coverlet, America, 108 x 100in. (Robt. W. Skinner Inc.) $1,300

A 19th century cotton piecework quilt, American, with a center star motif, 90 x 91in. (Christie's) $1,500

A 19th century American appliqued quilt, 7ft.1in. x 6ft.2in. (Robt. W. Skinner Inc.) $1,300

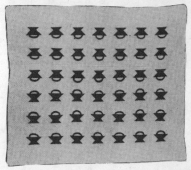

A Maryland pieced applique quilt of 'Basket' pattern, circa 1860. $1,250

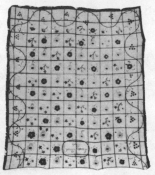

An embroidered blanket, probably New York, 'Lucretia Brush(?) Busti, 1831', large blue and white check, 6ft.4in. x 7ft.4in. (Robt. W. Skinner Inc.) $6,000

A patchwork cover worked with hexagonal pieces of mid/late 19th century printed and plain colored cotton, 2.50 x 2.34m., lined. (Phillips) $450

A wool and cotton jacquard coverlet,
Pennsylvania or Ohio, 1830-50, 82 x.70in.
(Christie's) $1,250

An American patchwork and applique
quilt, 'Stars and Stripes', 87 x 80in.
(Christie's) $800

American 19th century cotton applique
quilt, 88 x 86in. (Christie's) $1,900

Early 20th century American pieced
and quilted coverlet with sixteen blazing
stars, 97 x 95in. (Christie's) $700

Victorian crazy quilt and two pillow shams,
American, circa 1870, 61 x 61in. (Robt. W.
Skinner Inc.) $615

A bed rug with reddish tan background,
inscribed 'HH-1770', American, 4ft.6in. x
6ft.10in. (Robt. W. Skinner Inc.) $5,500

RACKETANA

Lawn tennis is the most popular ball game in the world and it has its roots in games played in Persia and Egypt in 500 B.C. From these early games a variety of other racket games evolved ranging from battledore to ping pong and today there is a strong interest in collecting the bats, rackets, balls and shuttlecocks used in those games.

One of the earliest tennis rackets dates back to 1880 but shuttlecocks from as early as 1840 can be found. Early rackets were strung with gut or wire and a few were made of vellum sheets. There were even bats with delicate wooden fretwork faces. Ping pong bats were often also vellum sheeted in the 19th century and the first wooden ones appeared in America in 1900.

Long-headed lawn tennis racket with 'fish-tail' grip by G. G. Bussey & Co., circa 1900. $150

Lawn tennis racket with steel head and strung with wire, circa 1925. $80

'Lop-sided' lawn tennis racket, maker unknown, circa 1885. $350

Pair of wooden 'Ping-Pong' bats by Parker Brothers U.S.A., circa 1900. $50

De Luxe 'Ping-Pong or Gossima' set in wooden box, by J. Jaques & Son, circa 1900. $400

Table tennis battledore with single vellum sheet in bamboo frame, circa 1900, made by J. R. Mally. $80

Miniature battledore and shuttlecock set, the battledores faced with vellum and only 8in. overall. $100

Table tennis bat, circa 1900, delicately cut out in fretwork. $80

Pair of table tennis rackets, 16½in. overall, by G. G. Bussey & Co., circa 1900. $100

RADIOS

Put an old 78 record on an old wind up gramophone and the atmosphere of a bygone era bursts forth from the elegant horn. It therefore comes as something of a surprise, to find todays national news emitting from a 30's bakelite radio, when Al Jolson might be more appropriate.

Radios have come a long way since Mr. Marconi harnessed the transmission of electro magnetic waves back in 1894 and this is the fascination for collectors.

From Catswhisker and crystal to three valve battery sets in kit form, the plug in coils, grid leaks and flexi valve holders, hold all the magic of a pioneer world in which the reward is a signal from far away places – if assembled in the right order.

'Celestion' Speaker, wood cabinet 1928. (Capricorn Curios) **$100**

'Vulcan' All Battery Set SG3, J.G. Graves 1935. (Capricorn Curios) **$100**

'Kolster Brandes' Straight 3 1928. (Capricorn Curios) **$100**

'Ekco' AC Mains model A22 round, bakelite 1938. (Capricorn Curios) **$200**

'Marconi', 1923, V2 Long range wireless set in a walnut case, 10in. high. **$900**

'Amplion' Moving iron speaker, wood petal horn, brass base, 1927. (Capricorn Curios) **$150**

'Freed Eiseman' Junior Bedside AC-DC U.S.A. Line Cord Set 1935. (Capricorn Curios) **$125**

Crystal Set with Earphones 1922. (Capricorn Curios) **$75**

'Bestone' Clock Radio, U.S.A., oak cabinet 1934. (Capricorn Curios) **$150**

'Fellophone' Super 3 Bright Emitter battery set, 1922-24. **$250**

'Phillips' Mains AC 'Super Inductance' model 830A, 1932. **$200**

'Ultra' AC Mains '3', wood cabinet 1932. (Capricorn Curios) **$125**

'Ekco' AC Mains model AC74 bakelite, 1939. **$125**

'Gecophone' 3 Valve All Battery Set 1928. (Capricorn Curios) **$125**

'Ekco' Mains AC Radio model 830A bakelite 1932. (Capricorn Curios) **$125**

RATTLES

Since the beginning of time it has been a tradition to present a young child with a rattle of sorts. Examples exist from the simplest dried gourd with rattling seeds to the most elegant of Georgian rattles crafted by leading silversmiths and decorated with coral. Coral rattles were the most highly prized for the substance was thought to contain medicinal properties beneficial to the child.

As a rule, Georgian rattles are plain and Victorian rattles fussier; having bunnies, elves and other sentimental characters introduced into their design.

One of the most attractive designs was created for the older child. It is known as a poupard and consists of a doll's head and body placed upon an ivory stick incorporating a whistle. When the stick is turned a small musical box within the body of the doll plays a melody.

Victorian silver rattle with ivory teether and whistle.　　$180

A Victorian silver rattle dated 1886.　　$70

Northwest coast polychromed carved wood raven rattle, carved in two sections, 12¼in. long. (Robt. W. Skinner Inc.)　　$5,555

18th century child's rattle and whistle by Shem Drowne , Boston,1749.　$440

Early 18th century child's silver rattle, 5¼in. long, circa 1700.　　$720

Georgian silver baby's rattle and comforter, maker's mark GU on whistle mouthpiece, Sheffield, 1818, 5in. long.　　$250

A 20th century baby's plated rattle.　　$20

Sterling silver baby rattle with sliding monkey, Birmingham, circa 1905, 6½in. long.　$630

An Edwardian plated baby's rattle.　　$8

17th century child's rattle bearing the Edinburgh date letter for 1681.　$2,500

RAZORS

Razor collecting is still a fairly new field and exceptionally fancy specimens can still be bought.

The vast majority of plain black and white.handled cut-throat razors are too plain and recent to interest many collectors and these are worth less than one dollar each.

Items at a premium are; perfect pearl-handled razors, preferably Sheffield, with carved pearl panels — $30-$40; and Sterling silver handled razors, preferably solid and engraved, though silver on ivory are also desirable at $40-$60.

Good, uncracked 1800 period razors with straight handles are generally more collectible than later items and German razor sets, and imitation ivory sets are always worth less than the equivalent Sheffield made ivory sets.

Mid 19th century razor with one-piece pearl handle and silver pins. $40—$60

19th century German razor with three-piece pearl handle. $40—$60

Mid 19th century razor with simple ivory handle. $120—$160

Mid 19th century razor, the ivory handle carved in the form of a fish. $120—$160

Ivory handled razor engraved with the image of George III, silver pins. $120—$160

19th century English razor with plain tortoise-shell handle with silver mounts. $30—$40

Mid 19th century hollow ground razor with stipled black horn handle. $20—$25

Mid 19th century razor with inlaid black horn handle. $20—$25

Mid 19th century gambler's traveling razor with dice designs on the handle. $120—$160

Mid 19th century razor with pressed black horn handle. $20—$25

A possibly unique set of six razors with silver gilt handles, by Paul Storr, with matching strap, 1834. $3,000

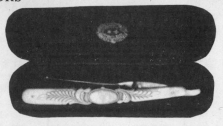

Mid 19th century pearl handled razor, in its velvet lined case. $80—$100

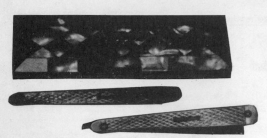

A pair of checker carved pearl handled razors with solid gold pins, contained in a mother-of-pearl case, by I. H. Farthing, circa 1805. $350

A good late 18th century French, mahogany case necessaire de voyage in silver gilt, including razors. $5,400

A rare sailor's twin-bladed razor, with penwork handle, engraved 'Plymouth'. $200

Pair of mid 19th century razors with embossed silver handles. $200

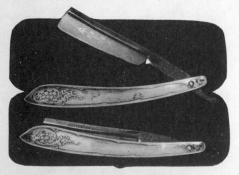

A pair of Swedish steel razors marked Dannemora Gjutstahl, with silver handles, contained in a black leather case, 1874. $170

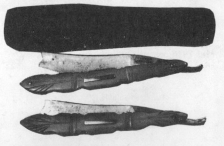

Pair of late 18th century razors by Johnson, with pressed horn handles. $40—$60

RIFLES

The making of weapons, particularly guns, has always been a highly skilled craft. Today there are still master gun makers like Scotland's David McKay Brown whose output is not more than five or six weapons a year but who can demand five figure prices for each of them. These rifles instantly become collectors' items and join the weapons which are eagerly sought after by the world's richest connoisseurs.

The earliest long barrel guns were simply iron or brass tubes fitted to a stock of wood and they first appeared in the late 15th century. A cock was fitted slightly later but the German invention of the wheellock in 1517 gave us the origin of the rifle as we know it today.

Gunsmiths always sought for elegance in their products which went on to include the flint lock, the matchlock which was used by Wellington's armies and the English 'Brown Bess' which first appeared during the reign of William IV. By the early 19th century England had become the center of the gun making industry and pioneered or developed all significant advances including the invention of the double-barreled shotgun which had first appeared as a novelty in 1784.

Guns to look out for include military firearms produced by gunmaker Robert Murden during the English Civil Wars and 'dragon' carbines from the same period which have long barrels, bellied muzzles and full stocks with flat sided butts on which dragons' heads were carved. From these dragon guns the term 'Dragoon' appeared. Rifles made by London gunsmiths J. Purdey and Sons have been famous for over a century and some collectors specialize in weapons from various campaigns and wars, including those used in the gun battles of America's Wild West.

A 5-shot .56in. Colt's Patent single action revolving percussion rifle, 43in., barrel 24in, Patented Sept. 10th 1850. (Wallis & Wallis) $3,400

An early 18th century Spanish miquelet flintlock musketoon, 41in. overall, half octagonal swamped twist barrel 26in. (Wallis & Wallis) $1,500

A .40in. circa 1800 pump-up reservoir butt tap loading air rifle by Bate, 47½in., octagonal barrel 31½in. to tap. (Wallis & Wallis) $900

A 12-bore screwless lock military flintlock carbine, by H. Nock, 44in., barrel 28in. (Wallis & Wallis) $2,500

A .44in. rimfire Winchester model 1866 factory engraved underlever repeating rifle, 44in., barrel 24in. (Wallis & Wallis) $8,200

A small brass barreled flintlock blunderbuss, circa 1675, three stage swamped barrel 13½in., the octagonal breech with raised band and sighting groove. (Wallis & Wallis) **$900**

A 16-bore and 6.5mm. snap action drilling combined hammer gun and rifle, 42½in., barrels 26½in., engraved Aug Luneburg Kile with sight mounts, back-action locks, underlever snap action, set right trigger and checkered pistol grip. (Wallis & Wallis) **$310**

A brass barreled Irish flintlock blunderbuss with spring bayonet, 30¾in., half octagonal barrel 14½in., triangular bayonet 11½in., with roller bearing spring released by top thumb catch. (Wallis & Wallis) **$760**

An 18th century Persian miquelet flintlock gun, 42½in. octagonal barrel 28¾in., with chiseled ribs to swollen muzzle, fullstocked with external mainspring. (Wallis & Wallis) **$265**

A Moroccan snaphaunce gun Kabyle, 65in., barrel 50in., with traces of silver inlay at breech. Fullstocked, stock with fish tail butt, iron trigger guard, and fish tail butt cap. (Wallis & Wallis) **$305**

A double barreled 16-bore percussion sporting gun by George & John Deane, No. 516, 47in., browned damascus barrels 30in., engraved George & John Deane, on top rib, in its tooled pigskin lined close fitted brass bound mahogany case. (Wallis & Wallis) **$1,100**

A 20-bore Bavarian percussion rifle built in the form of a wheellock 39½in., rifled octagonal barrel 26in., probably from an earlier weapon. (Wallis & Wallis) $470

A .56in. flintlock birding gun by Wilson, circa 1760, with take-down barrel and extending butt, 53¼in., swamped barrel 41in., London proved. (Wallis & Wallis) $1,530

A late 17th century Continental wheellock sporting rifle, 43½in., octagonal barrel 31½in., with eight-groove rifling. Fullstocked, carved cheekpiece and engraved steel trigger guard. (Wallis & Wallis) $2,610

An Irish military style brass barreled flintlock blunderbuss, 30½in., half octagonal barrel 14¼in., with bell mouth. (Wallis & Wallis) $530

A .65in. Paget's pattern military flintlock carbine 32in., barrel 16in., proved with crowned MR, with regulation brass mounts, steel ramrod, saddle bar, sling swivels lanyard rings. (Wallis & Wallis) $630

A 10-bore Brown Bess military flintlock musket 62½in., with 46in. barrel, Tower proved, complete with its triangular socket bayonet. (Wallis & Wallis) $2,150

ROBOTS

Toyland was first invaded by robots in the 1950's and, as you might have guessed, over 90% were made in Japan.

These colorful tinplate mechanical men and other related space toys with their numerous battery operated talents were an immediate success. They were able to perform hitherto undreamed of feats, many combining more than one action i.e., walking, talking, turning, shooting, flashing lights while rotating at a dizzying speed and so on.

Demand was high in the 1960's and the manufacturers entered a 'golden age' of production. In 1970, however, production of the well-loved tinplate models was abandoned in favour of the use of plastics but these were not nearly as pleasing, nor as popular.

As an indication of the current interest in collecting robots of the 50's and 60's, note that Mr Atomic Robot, made in the early 1960's, is now valued at over $800.

Marx wind-up 'Buck Rogers' space ship, New York, 1927, 12in. long. (Robt. W. Skinner Inc.) $600

'Planet Robot', 1960's Japanese plastic. $120

'Astronaut', Japanese 1960, battery operated robot. $120

A Marx 'Buck Rogers' spaceship, Pat. 1927, lithographed tin, 12in. long. (Robt. W. Skinner Inc.) $270

'Dino Robot', 1970, Japanese tin and plastic robot whose head opens to reveal a dinosaur's head. $200

'Space Explorer', Hong Kong plastic battery operated 1960's robot. $50

'Last in Space Robot', 1970 American, plastic battery operated robot. $160

ROCK 'N' ROLL MEMORABILIA

It would appear that inside many a sober suited pillar of society there still lurks a 'Rocker' at heart judging by the very healthy market for all material relating to the rock 'n' roll era. Be it psychedelic rock, rhythm and blues, punk, reggea or soul, you can be sure of an enthusiastic demand.

Anything to do with the early stars, no matter how tenuous the connection, is being collected but it is the items more personally identified with our idols which really fetch big money — Paul McCartney's upright piano, circa 1902, $15,000; Elvis's watch $4,000; a Sgt. Pepper gold disc, dated 1967, $20,000.

At first thought to be 'just a flash in the pan', the market in rock 'n' roll memorabilia is now well established with frequent sales by all the major auction houses.

One of eight Jimi Hendrix photographs, together with twenty-two negatives and eleven color transparencies, sold with copyright. $1,000

A radio telephone once the property of Elvis Presley, contained in a leather brief-case with initials E.A.P. beneath carrying handle. $1,500

George Benson, a presentation 'Platinum' disc, 'Breezin', the album mounted above a reduction of the L.P. cover, and a plaque. (Christie's) $275

An Elvis Presley wristwatch, by M. Tissot, 'Elvis Presley' in raised letters, circa 1970. $4,000

A 1960's Fender Tremolux amplifier and 2 x 10in. speaker cabinet in light colored Tolex vinyl, used on the set of the Paul McCartney Film, 'Give My Regards to Broad Street'. (Christie's) $734

A limited edition resin bronze G.R.P. bust of Jimi Hendrix, circa 1985, by J. Somerville, no. 5 of an edition of 20, 24in. high. (Christie's) $600

Jimi Hendrix, one of four unpublished black and white photographs taken at The Round House, Chalk Farm, London, in Feb. 1967, 14 x 9in. (Christie's) $575

Dire Straits, a presentation 'Platinum' disc, 'Brothers In Arms', the album mounted above a reduction of the L.P. cover and a plaque. (Christie's) $490

A colored screen print portrait of Mick Jagger, by Andy Warhol, number 176 of 250 copies, 44 x 29in., 1975. (Christie's) $840

A 'Presentation' 'Gold' disc of '(I Can't Get No) Satisfaction' by the Rolling Stones. $2,200

John Lennon, a self portrait with Yoko Ono in black felt-tip pen, autographed by John and Yoko beside each appropriate caricature, 7½ x 10½in., 1969. (Christie's) $1,800

An unusual paper collage by John Lennon in the form of cuttings from newspapers and magazines, 1966. $6,600

John Lennon 'Starting Over', the paper sleeve to the single bearing signatures of John Lennon and Yoko Ono.   • $770

John Lennon, detail from hand-drawn Christmas card in wax crayon, 1968. $4,400

Eric Clapton platinum disc for 'Backless' presented by RSO Records Inc. for the sale of one million copies, circa 1978. $1,540

Original etching and aquatint of 'The King', by David Oxtoby, signed by the artist, 27 x 21½in. (Christie's) $380

Dire Straits, a presentation 'Platinum' disc, 'Brothers In Arms', the album mounted with a 'platinum' cassette above a reduction of the album cover. (Christie's) $615

A promotional postcard for the release of The Move album, 'Flowers In The Rain', circa 1967. (Christie's) $300

A 1966-69 Vox Mando 12 String Guitar in sunburst, serial no. 74309. (Christie's) $300

George Harrison, the original artist's proof for an un-issued album cover, 'Somewhere in England', Dark Horse Records, 1981, 18½ x 26in. (Christie's) $1,000

A quantity of autograph material from Pink Floyd, The Who, Marvin Gaye and 'Auf Wiedersehen Pet'. (Christie's) $300

Pete Townshend's pound note suit worn in 'Tommy', circa 1975, with label 'Bermans & Nathans'. (Christie's) $2,750

Paul McCartney's Chappell & Co. Ltd. upright piano, 50 x 50 x 24½in., English, circa 1902. $15,000

One of three Dezo Hoffman portrait photographs of The Rolling Stones, 8 x 12in., 9 x 12in. and 12 x 9½in. (Christie's) $170

Eddie Cochrane and Gene Vincent photographed in 1960 on a British tour. $200

An acetate of John Lennon unreleased composition, 'God Save Oz', on Apple label, 1971 $1,320

John Lennon original drawing in black felt-tip pen on yellow lined foolscap paper. $2,850

A 1976 Portative Organ by N. P. Mander Ltd., custom made for David Palmer of Jethro Tull, used on tour between 1976-80 and on the album 'Songs From The Wood'. (Christie's) $1,530

'The Motley Bunch', a pen and ink drawing by John Lennon, circa 1965. $4,800

A Mark Smith Custom electric guitar, the body and sides in mahogany with a two-piece bird's-eye maple top. (Christie's) $765

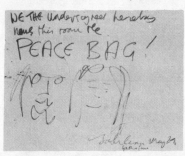

'Old Wrecked Car — Portugal', circa 1977, a silk screen print of a color photograph taken by Linda McCartney, no. 5 of a limited edition of 150, 18¾ x 13in. (Christie's) $380

John Lennon, an original drawing in black felt-tip pen of portraits of John and Yoko entitled, 'We The Undersigned Hereby Name This Room Peace Bag'. $4,400

Elvis Presley, a portrait of the singer executed in black ballpoint pen, signed and dated 24 December 1973. $990

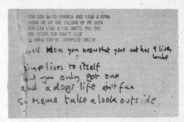

John Lennon, a photocopy of the three first verses of 'One Thing You Can't Hide' with added fourth verse in Lennon's hand, 1971. $1,500

A good bronze bust of John Lennon, by K. Carter, 15½in. high. $6,000

An Audiotek/Cadec mixing console used by John Lennon to record the 'Imagine' album, together with a letter of authenticity, circa 1970. $11,000

Dire Straits, gold disc for the LP 'Making Movies', with presentation, 16 x 14in., 1981. $925

Buddy Holly and the Crickets, photographed in England during 1958. $180

Series of twenty-four photographs of The Rolling Stones in the early stages of their career. $770

ROOKWOOD POTTERY

Established in 1880 at Cincinnati, Ohio, by Maria Longworth Nichols, the Rookwood Pottery at first relied mainly on manufacturing unfired blanks for outside decorators. They gradually developed their own Art Pottery however and from 1883 produced finished work initially with Japanese motifs and later naturalistic plants and animals under a variety of tinted glazes.

William Taylor, who had been manager since 1883, took over the business in 1900 and greatly increased the production of Art Pottery with a variety of new lines and finishes including Cameo, Iris, Sea Green and Aerial Blue. They also produced articles featuring portraits of American Indians and Negroes together with images of paintings by Rembrandt and Frans Hals. New lines continued to be created in the Art Nouveau style or incorporating the incised designs of Indian Pottery until the company ceased trading in 1941.

A Rookwood standard glaze pottery Indian portrait vase, decorated by Grace Young, date cypher for 1905, 30.5cm. high. (Christie's) $4,620

Rookwood standard glaze ewer with sterling silver overlay, Ohio, 1892, 10¼in. high. (Robt. W. Skinner Inc.) $2,800

A Rookwood pottery iris glaze vase, initialed by Olga G. Reed, circa 1902, 7¼in. high. (Robt. W. Skinner Inc.) $380

A Rookwood silver overlay vase, impressed artist's monogram SS, 12.5cm. high. (Christie's) $790

One of a pair of Rookwood stoneware bookends, modeled as sphinx holding books, light brown glaze, 18cm. high. (Christie's) $190

A Rookwood pottery Indian squaw portrait vase, circa 1899, 11in. high. (Robt. W. Skinner Inc.) $650

ROYAL DUX PORCELAIN

This most distinctive porcelain was produced at the Royal Dux factory established in 1860, in Dux, Bohemia.

The factory quickly gained a reputation for beautifully fashioned portrait busts and ornate vases but the most sought after pieces around today are the scantily clad nymphs of flowing form, more often than not seductively draped around shell-shaped bowls or curved mirror frames.

The most noticeable characteristic of this unglazed porcelain is the color tones of soft pastel beige, pink and green.

Marks include an embossed pink triangle stamped Royal Dux Bohemia or E (proprietor: E. Eichler) in an oval surrounded by Royal Dux Bohemia.

Dux figures were exported in considerable quantities to America and Australia establishing a lasting international popularity.

A large Royal Dux figure of a peasant boy leaning on a wooden pitcher, 59cm. high.
$750

Large Royal Dux group with camel and Bedouin seated on its back, 19¾in. high. (Reeds Rains)
$1,160

A Royal Dux porcelain group of classical figures, the boy in wolf-skin, and girl wearing a gown, 26in. high. (Dacre, Son & Hartley)
$1,520

A Royal Dux porcelain group of a peasant man and woman, on leaf decorated base, 22¾in. high. (Dacre, Son & Hartley)
$600

A Royal Dux Art Nouveau conch shell group with three water nymphs in relief, 17½in. high. (Reeds Rains)
$940

A Royal Dux bust, the young Art Nouveau maiden gazing to the left, raised pink triangle mark, 20in. high. (Christie's)
$1,320

ROYAL DUX PORCELAIN

A Royal Dux porcelain group of a lion, lioness and dead gazelle on rustic base, 19in. wide, no. 1600. (Dacre, Son & Hartley) $260

A Royal Dux group of a flute player and dancer both wearing Orientally inspired costume, 12in. high, raised pink triangle mark. (Christie's) $260

A fine Royal Dux group of a classical Grecian horseman with his charges, 43cm. high, circa 1900. $625

A Royal Dux centerpiece with figure of a water nymph kneeling on an abalone shell, 15½in. high. (Reeds Rains) $390

An Art Nouveau Royal Dux figural vase modeled as a tree trunk with a maiden draped around the side, 46cm. high. (Phillips) $540

Pair of small Royal Dux figures. (Cooper Hirst) $530

A Royal Dux figure of a young girl, naked, seated on a rock, 54cm. high. (Lawrence Fine Art) $430

A fine pair of Royal Dux figures of a Shepherd and Shepherdess, 79cm. high. $1,560

A Royal Dux gilt porcelain figure of a girl bather seated on a rock, 19in. high. (Dacre, Son & Hartley) $720

RUGS

Traditionally, in the east, Oriental carpets have always performed a dual role:

Firstly, as furnishings they have been used not only as floor coverings but also wall hangings, divan covers, and in decoration generally. In Turkey and Iran in particular they satisfy an aesthetic need which, in the west, paintings have fulfilled.

Secondly, in countries where governments and currencies were unstable they performed the function which stocks and shares perform here — a reserve of wealth to fall back upon in bad times.

As an investment in present day Europe and America they similarly should fill both roles — for those who take household furnishings seriously they may combine profit and pleasure.

Remember that, unlike paintings, the value of a rug is more in proportion to its size and type. This is because the intrinsic value of a rug depends upon months or even years of hand knotting.

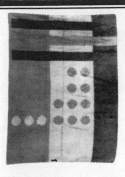

An Art Deco hand-made tufted wool carpet by Terence Prentis, 363 x 263cm. (Christie's) $2,160

An Isfahan pictorial rug with beige and floral meander border with dark blue guard stripes, 3ft. x 2ft.6in. (Capes, Dunn & Co.) $725

A hand-knotted woollen rug, the design possibly by A. Knox, with Celtic motif in pink and blue on a white ground, 153.5 x 86cm. (Christie's) $530

An Isfahan rug, the ivory field with three flower vases and flowering trees, 6ft.11in. x 4ft.10in. (Christie's) $6,050

Eastern Caucasian/Kuba rug, dated H1322, the dark blue field with ivory, blue green and red Leshgi stars, 4ft.3in. x 5ft.4in. (Robt. W. Skinner Inc.) $1,800

Late 19th century Eastern Caucasian/Kuba rug, woven in the afshan or 'crab-kuba' design, 3ft.5in. x 4ft.10in. (Robt. W. Skinner Inc.) $760

Late 19th century South Caucasian Karabagh rug, 4ft. 4in. x 7ft.11in. (Robt. W. Skinner Inc.) $3,300

A Jules Leleu circular woollen rug, 188cm. diam. (Christie's) $1,250

A Ziegler carpet, 17ft.10in. x 12ft. (Christie's) $10,960

Late 19th century Northwest Persian carpet, the yellow field woven in all over Mina Khani floral trellis, 10ft.5in. x 14ft. 7in. (Robt. W. Skinner Inc.) $4,100

Late 19th/early 20th century 'Eagle' Kazak rug, Southwest Caucasus, 5ft. 11in. x 7ft.7in. (Robt. W. Skinner Inc.) $2,900

Late 19th century Northwest Persia, Serapi carpet, with a 'turtle' border, 9ft. 6in. x 13ft.4in. (Robt. W. Skinner Inc.) $4,200

A Navajo pictorial rug, 9ft.11½in. x 5ft.5½in. (Robt. W. Skinner Inc.) $2,500

A Modernist rug in shades of brown and beige, 231 x 173cm. $600

A Kashan carpet, the light blue field with palmettes, trees and floral sprays, 11ft. 3in. x 6ft.4in. (Christie's) $5,640

Early 20th century Heriz
Area carpet, 9ft.8in. x 13ft.
(Robt. W. Skinner Inc.)
$4,250

Late 19th/early 20th century
S.W. Persian Qashqai bag face,
1ft.1in. x 1ft.3in. (Robt. W.
Skinner Inc.) $325

Late 19th/early 20th cen-
tury Kazak rug, the red field
with concentric hooked
medallions, 4ft.6in. x 7ft.
(Robt. W. Skinner Inc.)
$2,200

Early 20th century Kurdish
Kelim rug, the ivory field
with red and blue forked
medallions, 6ft.1in. x 8ft.4in.
(Robt. W. Skinner Inc.)
$275

Late 19th/early 20th cen-
tury N.W. Persia, Soumak
bag face, the dark blue field
with medallions of various
colors , 2ft.1in. x 2ft. (Robt.
W. Skinner Inc.) $1,500

A Kashan embossed part
silk pictorial rug, 35½ x
24½in. (Capes, Dunn & Co.)
$865

A J. J. Adnet wool pile carpet in
tones of russet, black, brown
and beige, circa 1930, 156.5 x
144.4cm. (Christie's) $1,340

A Modernist carpet, 327 x
267cm., 1930's. $1,430

Late 19th century Kuba mat,
E. Caucasus, the blue field
with flowerheads of blue and
red, 2ft.8in. x 2ft.9in. (Robt.
W. Skinner Inc.) $800

An Eastern Caucasian/Shirvan prayer rug, 3ft.7in. x 5ft. 3in. (Robt. W. Skinner Inc.) $6,100

Early 20th century American calico cat hooked rug, 15½ x 32in. (Robt. W. Skinner Inc.) $450

A Southwestern Caucasus Kazak rug, 8ft. x 5ft. (Robt. W. Skinner Inc.) $8,000

A 19th century Spanish Aubusson part metal thread Entre Fenetre, 3.26 x 1.88m. (Phillips) $3,600

Early 20th century N.W. Persia, Soumak bag face with white field, 1ft.8in. x 1ft.8in. (Robt. W. Skinner Inc.) $175

A Bessarabian Kilim, the mottled ivory field with two large floral sprays, 6ft.6in. x 5ft. (Christie's) $550

A tufted wool rug designed by Marion Dorn, 1930's, 195 x 140cm. $1,650

Cotton Disney characters scatter rug, 1950's, 45 x 59in. (Robt. W. Skinner Inc.) $35

Late 19th century Soumak bag, 1ft.8in. x 1ft.9in. (Robt. W. Skinner Inc.) $2,000

One of two India Drugget scatter rugs, designed by Gustav Stickley, circa 1910, 38in. wide. (Robt. W. Skinner Inc.) $650

An early 19th century American hooked rug, 34in. deep, 53in. wide. (Christie's) $660

Early 20th century Kazak prayer rug, S.W. Caucasus, a red field with ivory medallion, 4ft.2in. x 6ft.11in. (Robt. W. Skinner Inc.) $2,425

A Shirvan rug with multiple floral decoration on indigo field, 80 x 51½in. (Reeds Rains) $1,000

An early 20th century reverse Soumak animal trapping, one bag, 1ft.3in. x 1ft. 4in., flanked by two small bags, 7 x 8in. (Robt. W. Skinner Inc.) $850

Late 19th century Northwest Persian landscape carpet, 10ft.8in. x 13ft.3in. (Robt. W. Skinner Inc.) $17,000

20th century Trans-Caucasian rug, the abrashed dark blue field featuring three Lesghi stars. (Robt. W. Skinner Inc.) $245

Late 19th/early 20th century Kurdish Soumak salt bag, 1ft.1½in. x 1ft.6in. (Robt. W. Skinner Inc.) $350

Serapi carpet, madder rust field with all over floral design, 9ft.3in. x 11ft.7in. (Robt. W. Skinner Inc.) $7,250

SAMPLERS

Samplers were produced from early in the 18th century right through until after the First World War as a means of showing how adept a young girl could be at the useful art of embroidery, as well as knowing her alphabet.

A variety of colored silks were worked, most popularly in cross-stitch, on a canvas backing to incorporate the name and age of the exponent, the date, numbers one to ten together with the alphabet, a hymn or a poem and a multitude of designs depending on how clever our young needlewoman was.

Examples include such worthy subjects as a documented family register but, above all, these charming pieces reflect a refreshing simplicity of style.

An American needlework sampler, signed Jane Littlefield, circa 1810, worked in silk threads on a dark green canvas, 24in. high, 15½in. wide. (Christie's) $3,740

Needlework sampler 'Ann Major her work 1812', Philadelphia School. (Robt. W. Skinner Inc.) $5,000

Late 18th century needlework sampler, worked in silk yarns of gold, light blue, red, brown, ivory and black on natural linen, 7 x 10½in. (Robt. W. Skinner Inc.) $3,300

A George IV needlework sampler, by E.H., 1826, 17 x 12½in. (Graves, Son & Pilcher) $550

Early 19th century needlework sampler, 'Phebe L. Slessor work aged 11 years', New England, 16 x 16in. (Robt. W. Skinner Inc.) $1,250

Needlework sampler, 'Sally Butman her work in the 11th year of her age, 1801', Marblehead, Mass., 10.3/8 x 12½in. (Robt. W. Skinner Inc.) $15,000

Late 18th century needlework sampler family record, 10½ x 16in. (Robt. W. Skinner Inc.) $4,305

An early 19th century needlework sampler, 'Jane Slessors work aged 13 years January 16', New England, 17 x 17½in. (Robt. W. Skinner Inc.) $500

Early 19th century woolwork sampler, worked by Elizabeth Shufflebottoms 1841, 23½ x 23¾in. (Reeds Rains) $600

A Boston School needlework sampler, made by Sarah Henderson in 1765, aged 12, 21 x 18½in. (Robt. W. Skinner Inc.) $25,000

An 18th century needlework sampler well decorated in colored silks, 17 x 12½in. (Graves, Son & Pilcher) $700

Needlework sampler marked 'Wrought by Sally Alden June 14 1811', Mass., 16 x 21in. (Robt. W. Skinner Inc.) $3,750

A sampler by Charlotte Way, Portland, 1841, worked in pale brown silk, 14 x 11½in. (Christie's) $200

Mid 18th century Boston School, Adam & Eve sampler, 6¾ x 11½in. (Robt. W. Skinner Inc.) $7,000

A needlework sampler, 'Emily Furber her sampler aged 10, wrought March 16, 1827', 23 x 26in. (Robt. W. Skinner Inc.) $2,400

SATSUMA

Satsuma is a type of Japanese pottery which derives its name from Kagoshima, formerly known as Satsuma, the prefecture of Japan in which it was produced. The production of Satsuma ware began in the late 16th century but it was not introduced to the West until it was exhibited at the Universal Exhibition in Paris in 1867. The earliest examples were copies of Korean and Chinese pottery pieces and they were mainly tea ceremony ware in a hard grayish white or parchment colored faience with a crackle glaze. In the mid 18th century lavishly enameled and gilded pieces began to be made and these are highly prized by collectors.

A 19th century Satsuma shaped oval box and cover, signed Tokozan, 24cm. wide. (Christie's) $1,500

Late 19th century Satsuma model of a recumbent karashishi, 34cm. long. (Christie's) $1,850

A 19th century Satsuma bowl, signed on the base Gyokushu, 15.5cm. diam. (Christie's) $1,100

A Satsuma large lidded jar, gilded figures on black ground, 13in. high. (Barber's Fine Art) $1,240

Late 19th century Satsuma teapot and cover modeled as a stylized bird, 18cm. long. (Christie's) $1,500

A 19th century large Satsuma oviform vase, signed Satsuma Tansai above an iron-red Shimazu mon, 50.2cm. high. (Christie's) $1,350

Late 19th century Satsuma model of a recumbent caparisoned elephant, signed, 25cm. long. (Christie's) $1,750

A Satsuma pottery pot pourri bowl on three feet in the form of grotesque heads, 8½in. diam. (Capes, Dunn & Co.) $190

A Satsuma pottery cylindrical box, the cover painted and gilded with geishas, 3in. diam. (Reeds Rains) $400

SCENT BOTTLES

Throughout the 18th and 19th centuries, it was customary to carry a container of insoluble crystal salts blended with aromatic essence purchased from a chemist or perfumier.

It was not until the 20th century that perfume was sold in ready filled bottles, and of these, the bottles made by Lalique for Coty and Nina Ricci are particularly sought after. Examples by Daum, Galle and Webb also fetch good prices but a start can be made with Victorian overlay scent bottles, often double ended, and far more reasonably priced.

Scent bottles can be found made in a number of materials including, silver, gold, enamel and porcelain, but the vast majority are made of glass with a variety of decorations.

A cameo glass swan's head scent bottle in yellow and white, with silver cap marked Chester, 1884, 22cm. long. **$2,400**

A Franchini gilt metal mounted scent bottle, the hinged cover with ring and bead chain attachment, 7.5cm. long. (Christie's) **$520**

Victorian silver scent phial, Birmingham, 1892, 8in. long, 5oz., in case. (Hobbs & Chambers) **$520**

 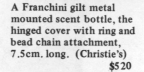 

An Apsley Pellatt sulphide and cut glass scent bottle and a stopper, 9.5cm. high. (Christie's) **$550**

One of a pair of Edwardian cut glass cologne bottles, by Wm. Comyns, London, 1905, 5½in. high. (Christie's) **$1,400**

A Lalique glass perfume bottle, flattened, square body with central oval depression, 1930's, 12.75cm. high. **$600**

19th century cameo glass salts bottle with silver screw top, in case, 4in. long. (Capes, Dunn & Co.) **$350**

A ruby glass scent bottle of tapering elongated form, with hinged silver cap marked Birmingham, 1880's, 24.5cm. long. **$1,500**

A Franchini silver gilt mounted millefiori scent bottle, the base with a cane dated 1847, 7.2cm. long. (Christie's) **$400**

SCENT BOTTLES

'Amphyrite', a Lalique perfume bottle and stopper, the blue tinted frosted glass molded as a snail shell, 9.5cm. high. (Lawrence Fine Art) $625

Late 18th century Spanish opaque opaline scent flask, in the form of a bird, painted in colors and enriched in gilding with flower sprays, 20cm. wide. (Christie's) $1,100

One of a pair of Lalique glass perfume bottles, molded as sea urchins, 9.5cm. high, 1930's. $300

A Clichy cut glass and patterned millefiori scent bottle and stopper, 18cm. high. (Christie's) $1,500

A glass scent bottle and stopper, inscribed 'Cigalia, Roger et Gallet, Paris', 13cm. high, in original box. (Phillips) $450

A Marinot scent bottle and stopper, with enamel painted decoration, circa 1920, 17cm. high. (Christie's) $1,750

'Worth', a Lalique glass scent bottle, with original Worth paper label, 24.5cm. high. (Christie's) $450

Galle cameo glass perfume bottle and mushroom stopper, 4½in. wide, 3¾in. high. (Capes, Dunn & Co.) $725

A Baccarat enameled cut glass scent bottle with gilt metal screw cover, 9.5cm. long. (Christie's) $1,500

SCIENCE FICTION MAGAZINES

'Amazing Stories' the first all science fiction magazine was published in April 1926, the brainchild of one Hugo Gernsbach who could, with some reason, lay claim to being the guru of science fiction.

He had been publishing such stories as 'The Scientific Adventures of Baron Munchhausen' since 1911 in the magazine Modern Electrics of which he was the editor. Strand Magazine and Pearsons Magazine also carried a few sci fi stories but Gernsbach was the first to see the full market potential.

Also worthy of note is the British magazine 'New Worlds' published from 1947 and edited by John Carnel. Michael Moorcock editor from 1967 adopted a policy of making sci fi respectable in a literary sense and did much to advance its popularity.

Startling Stories, July 1939. $20

Yankee Science Fiction, No. 3, 1940's. $10

Marvel Science Stories, November 1938. $30

Wonder Stories, 'The Best' In Science Fiction', August 1935. $25

Science Fiction, Vol. 1, Number 1, March 1939. $50

Astounding Stories, August 1934. **$30**

Amazing Stories, Vol. 1, No. 1, April 1926. **$90**

Galaxy, 'Science Fiction', No. 27. **$3**

Fantastic, Vol. 1, No. 7, 1954. **$3**

Super Science Stories, No. 14. **$5**

Unknown, 'Fantasy Fiction', July 1940. **$8**

Thrilling Wonder Stories, October 1938. **$20**

SCISSORS

Scissors at first took the form of sheep shears with no central pivot, the cutting action being performed by compressing together the naturally sprung open arms.

Examples found in medieval graves are pivoted, but have finger loops set centrally on the arms. It wasn't until the 18th century that the finger loops generally became set on the outside edge of the arms much in the style of modern scissors.

As with many tools, scissors have been adapted for the specific tasks demanded from an individual trade or need and a fascinating collection can be built up of just grape scissors or those for surgeons, hairdressers or dressmakers.

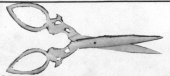

Pair of Edwardian bone scissors with peacock handles, circa 1910. $15

A large pair of shears for cutting sheet metal, 18in. long. $35

A pair of early 20th century steel folding scissors, 3½in. long. $8

An unusual pair of 19th century steel scissors. $12

A pair of French silver gilt grape scissors, by Alexandre Lefranc, Paris, 1819-38, 6oz. 7dwt. (Christie's) $500

Tang silver gilt scissors, 7½in. long. $16,000

19th century steel wick trimmers. $16

Combination scissors incorporating a file, screwdriver, wire cutters, glass cutter and glass snapper, 4in. long. $10

Pair of miniature scissors, 1¾in. long. $10

Late 18th century pair of Spanish engraved steel tailor's shears, dated 1791, 14in. long. $1,000

SCRAPS

Originally from Germany , scraps or oblaten, are highly colored, stylized paper cut-outs. They became popular and were used throughout Europe and America for decorative purposes on gift boxes, greetings cards, furniture and on the packaging of many products. Victorian ladies devoted much of their time to forming album collections and the themes vary widely. There are flowers, animals, children at play, beautiful ladies, Christmas, hunting and circus scenes, cherubs, fruit clusters, Royalty, castles, cavalry and scraps designed for educational purposes with alphabetical characters. Very large scraps were often pasted onto room dividing panels to form the Victorian Scrap Screens so desirable today.

Finally, one must not forget to mention the skill and inventiveness of the unknown artists who designed these delightful little works of art.

Black and White Retriever, 2in. high.
$2

Children With Flower Baskets, 4in. high. $12

Eggs In A Basket.
$2

Love Birds, 3in. high.
$2

Floral Bells, 4½in. across. $5

Child With Hat, 5in. high. $6

Girl In Yellow With Songbird, 4in. high.
$5

Victoria Cross by Harry Payne, 6in. wide. $10

Shaggy Haired Dog, 2½in. wide. $2

Cherub on a Cloud.
$2

Newman Noggs and Nicholas Nickleby's Children. **$10**

Gabriel Varden and Sim Tappertit, **$10**

Victoria Cross Gallery, Serg't. Joseph Malone. **$10**

Father Christmas with Presents. **$5**

Mr Tupman, Miss Wardle and the Fat Boy. **$10**

Old Mr Turveydrop and Peepy and Guppy. **$10**

Girl in Red Dress, 5in. high. **$5**

Joe Gargery and Pip. **$10**

SCRIMSHAW

Scrimshaw work was a popular pastime for sailors aboard the big whaling ships of the 19th century. The work can best be described as extremely fine engraving on bone or ivory, the incised detail darkened down with black ink or soot.

Usually working on a whale's tooth, though sometimes on whalebone, the sailors most commonly chose a theme relating to life at sea but, just occasionally, one may come across a mildly erotic design.

Scrimshaw work is often mounted for display or used to embellish objects such as gongs, inkstands and a variety of small boxes.

A mid 19th century decorated panbone, 10in. wide. $1,200

The Unicorn Crimper made of scrimshaw. $22,500

Mid 19th century English whale's tooth scrimshaw decorated with a schooner in choppy seas, 6½in. long. $615

Mid 19th century American whale's tooth scrimshaw decorated as an eagle's head, 5in. long. $420

Mid 19th century well-scrimshawed whale's tooth 8½in long. $1,300

Mid 19th century whale's tooth scrimshaw, 6in long. $880

A pair of 19th century scrimshaw candlesticks, America, 4¾in. high. (Robt. W. Skinner Inc.) $1,215

A pair of mid 19th century scrimshawed walrus tusks, English, 48cm. high. $1,500

An unusual pair of scrimshawed whale's teeth, circa 1840, 8in. high. $1,400

SEALS

There are three main types of seal. A desk seal, a fob seal and a seal, or signet, ring.

Early desk seals of the late 17th and early 18th centuries were shaped rather like a mushroom, with a bulbous wooden handle, and a carved silver seal set into the end of the stem. Over the years the shape was modified to slimmer proportions and the handles made of precious materials set with stones.

Fob seals were made of gold, silver and silver gilt, with ornate handles and seal matrices cut in gemstones, steel and a variety of materials. Around the middle of the eighteenth century it was considered fashionable to wear not one, but a cluster of fobs, hanging from the fob pocket of the breeches.

Although designs are numerous and elaborate it may still be possible to identify and date a sealing instrument from the print. Many bore coats of arms, self portraits or initials. From 1791 the law required gold and silver seals to be hall-marked.

An English gold fob seal with pendant ring and the chalcedony matrix engraved with armorials, 3.2cm., circa 1835. $225

A two-color gold and hardstone articulated triple desk seal by Faberge, St. Petersburg, 1908-17, 9.1cm. $5,250

An early 19th century English three-color gold fob seal, 5.3cm. $650

An English gold double-sided swivel fob seal with ribbon-bound reeded pendant, 4.6cm., circa 1790. $425

An early 19th century two-colored gold fob seal, matrix detached, 2.9cm. $250

Late 18th century English gold double-sided swivel fob seal of oval form, 5.3cm. $650

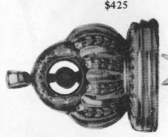

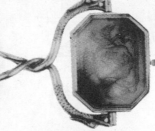

Early 19th century Swiss gold and enamel musical fob seal, 4.2cm. $1,200

A gold double-sided swivel fob seal with scrolled wirework mount in the form of two serpents, 5cm., circa 1810. $1,650

Mid 18th century English gold fob seal with smoky-quartz matrix, 3.2cm, $475

SERIES WARE

"Adorn yet serve some useful purpose" was the reasoning behind the very successful introduction of Series Ware which was the brain child of Charles J. Noke who joined Doulton's in 1889.

He realized that standard pottery shapes could be decorated with popular images and sold as 'novelty art wares' to the general public who were not able to afford the more expensive creations of individual artists.

Designs, many of them by Noke himself, were transfer printed onto plates, jugs, bowls, mugs and teasets. Refined earthenware or bone china was used and the transfer prints were handcolored which gave the technique the name of 'print and tint'.

The first series issued was the 'Isthmian Games' in 1889 and it was followed by a new theme almost every year until the late forties.

Willow Pattern Series jar and cover, 6½in. high, circa 1912. **$135**

The Gleaners, Series ware sandwich tray. **$60**

Sir Roger de Coverley Series teapot, 5in. high, circa 1911, depicting Sir Roger in the garden, **$110**

Oliver Twist tankard in low relief, designed by C. J. Noke, issued 1949-1960. **$120**

Rural England (Welsh) Series, two-handled vase, 12½in. high, circa 1907, depicting a woman in traditional dress. **$115**

'Nightwatchman', a Series ware jug by C. J. Noke, 8½in. high, D1198, 1903. **$75**

SEVRES

King Louis XV established and partly financed the Sevres pottery factory at Vincennes in 1756. They produced a soft paste porcelain as well as hard paste imitation Chinese Ming dynasty eggshell porcelain which was a great success when it was shown at the Great Exhibition in London in 1851.

In 1876 the factory was removed to St Cloud and a great deal of experimentation was done in formulae and pastes which resulted in the discovery of a kaolin based paste which resembled the original Chinese formula and a silicate paste which provided a wide range of colors for decoration of the pieces.

Among the modelers employed by Sevres was the great sculptor Rodin and A. Leonard who made unglazed figures at the turn of the 20th century.

One of a pair of late 19th century Sevres pattern metal mounted turquoise gound oviform vases, 84cm. high. (Christie's) $9,000

A Sevres biscuit group of The Judgement of Paris, circa 1781, 41cm. high. (Christie's) $2,250

A Sevres-pattern porcelain and ormolu mounted mantel clock, imitation interlaced L and initial marks, circa 1880, 61.5cm. high. (Christie's) $4,250

A Sevres bleu nouveau baluster milk jug, blue interlaced L mark enclosing the date letter q for 1769, and painter's mark B, 12cm. high. (Christie's) $700

A Sevres bleu nouveau cylindrical coffee cup and saucer, blue interlaced L marks enclosing the date letters EE for 1782. (Christie's) $850

A Sevres ornithological circular sugar bowl and cover, blue interlaced L marks enclosing the date letter U for 1773 and painter's mark of Evans, 11.5cm. high. (Christie's) $850

SEVRES

A Sevres pattern gilt bronze oval two-handled jardiniere, circa 1860, 44.5cm. wide. (Christie's) $1,380

A Sevres teacup and saucer, blue interlaced L marks, enclosing the date letters ii for 1786 and painter's mark of J. Fontaine. (Christie's) $355

A Sevres green ground deep bowl, blue interlaced L marks enclosing the date letter q for 1769, and painter's mark of Nicquet, 23.5cm. diam. (Christie's) $1,500

A pair of large documentary Sevres seaux a bouteille with gilt-edged shell and scroll handles, blue interlaced L marks and with incised marks 7, nu and C 6, 18.5cm. high. (Christie's) $22,500

A Sevres bleu nouveau cylindrical cup and saucer, blue interlaced L marks, and painter's mark C.D. and incised 40, circa 1780. (Christie's) $600

A pair of Sevres pattern square bottles and stoppers decorated with portraits of Louis XIV and Me. de Lamballe, circa 1880, 15.5cm. high. (Christie's) $1,750

A Sevres Art Deco porcelain figure of a lady in evening dress designed by Odartchenko, 28cm. high. (Christie's) $550

A First Empire Sevres porcelain two-handled cup and cover, 6½in. high. (Geering & Colyer) $235

A Sevres bust of Napoleon as First Consul, dated 1802 29cm. high. (Christie's) $1,100

420

SEWING MACHINES

The first practical sewing machine was patented in America in 1845 by a machinist named Elias Howe. In the following years up to 1900 rival manufacturers produced many unusually shaped and interesting machines and these are the ones to collect. If the machine looks ordinary, it will be! The Singer Sewing Machine Company produced ten million machines by 1890 and many are still in use. A credit to Victorian technology but not always the most desirable of objects to collectors.

Appearances can be deceptive for some machines of the 1890's copied ideas patented in the 1860's. So be careful and look at machines in collections, read up on as much information as you can find and seek the unusual.

Beware of chipped paint and worn decoration as this is difficult to restore. Light rust however, is not a problem and neither is oily dirt, as both can be removed.

Chain-stitch machine by **Willcox and Gibbs**, U.S.A., with patent dates to 1864. Hand-wheel support made at Coalbrookdale and marked with Registration Mark of 1869. **$150**

A Grover & Baker hand sewing machine, the brass Patent plaque with patents to 1863. (Christie's) **$1,750**

'Prima Donna' lock-stitch machine with brass face-plate and slide-plates. Made by **Whight and Mann** of Ipswich but not so marked. No patent dates, circa 1875. **$300**

'Princess of Wales' lock-stitch machine by **Newton Wilson** of Birmingham. Elaborate gilded cast-iron frame with Prince of Wales' feathers and exotic decorations, circa 1880. **$350**

'Howe' lock-stitch machine with rubber belt drive and lovely hand-painted floral and gilt decorations. No maker's address nor patent dates, but presumed by Howe Sewing Machine Co. circa 1876. **$350**

'Gresham' lock-stitch machine by **Gresham & Craven**, Manchester. Has rudimentary reverse and cloth-guide, and original receipt of 1871. Elaborately gilded and decorated. **$300**

Un-named lockstitch machine with patent date of 1868 and others up to 1865, of type made by the **Gold Medal Sewing Machine Co.**, Mass., U.S.A. Hand-painted floral and gilt decoration, circa 1870. **$250**

'Advance' lock-stitch machine, made in Germany and imported by **J. Collier & Son**, Clapham Road. Based on the 'Howe' machine and found under several trade names. Gilt transfer decoration, circa 1880. **$125**

'The Challenge' lock-stitch machine made by the **Imperial Sewing Machine Co.** of Birmingham. Bears a registration mark of 1871 and a patent of 1874. Elaborately decorated with gilt and with elaborate brass face-plate, circa 1875. **$200**

'Original Express' chain-stitch machine by **Ghul & Harbeck**, Germany. No patent dates, but Liverpool importer's name on cloth plate. Gilt floral decoration. **$125**

'Wanzer A' lock-stitch machine made in Canada by the **Wanzer Sewing Machine Co.** Patent dates up to 1875. Gilt transfer decoration, circa 1880. **$200**

SHOES

In the past, collectors have followed the history of footwear through collections of highly detailed replica boots and shoes originally designed as containers and made of silver, pewter, brass, porcelain and glass.

Today they are looking for the 'real thing'. Early or unusual examples are being snapped up at auction sales and more antique shops are making space to display footwear from all periods up to the 1940's.

Prices range from a few dollars to a thousand and more, depending on the appeal, rarity and condition of the goods. Late Victorian shoes and little satin low heeled slippers are fairly common and will cost about $50, and Edwardian leather strap shoes about $30.

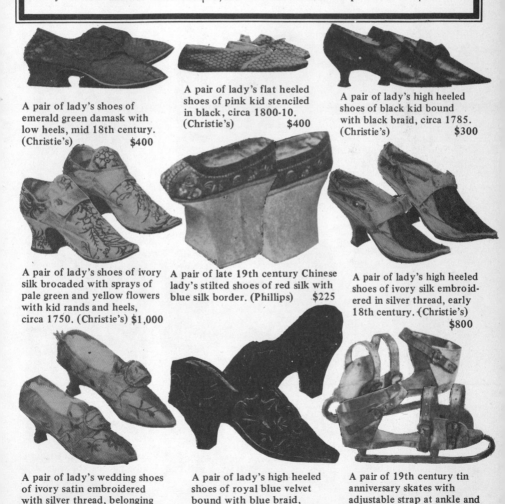

A pair of lady's shoes of emerald green damask with low heels, mid 18th century. (Christie's) $400

A pair of lady's flat heeled shoes of pink kid stenciled in black, circa 1800-10. (Christie's) $400

A pair of lady's high heeled shoes of black kid bound with black braid, circa 1785. (Christie's) $300

A pair of lady's shoes of ivory silk brocaded with sprays of pale green and yellow flowers with kid rands and heels, circa 1750. (Christie's) $1,000

A pair of late 19th century Chinese lady's stilted shoes of red silk with blue silk border. (Phillips) $225

A pair of lady's high heeled shoes of ivory silk embroidered in silver thread, early 18th century. (Christie's) $800

A pair of lady's wedding shoes of ivory satin embroidered with silver thread, belonging to Margaret Gladstone, circa 1784. (Christie's) $700

A pair of lady's high heeled shoes of royal blue velvet bound with blue braid, English, circa 1640. (Christie's) $12,500

A pair of 19th century tin anniversary skates with adjustable strap at ankle and foot, 9in. long. (Robt. W. Skinner Inc.) $650

SIGNED PHOTOGRAPHS

Collecting signed photographs on a limited budget is still possible and may even prove to be a profitable experience.

A new collector would be well advised to start at the lower end of the market, buying and selling in a comparitively safe area until he has made a few contacts, acquired some knowledge of the subject and learned to identify the mass produced machine signed copies circulating within the market. Many stars of the early cinema, music hall performers, even some of yesterdays' pop idols signed photographs which now change hands at between $2 and $200.This is an interesting area and valuable experience may be gained before moving up into a league where a fine photograph of Tchaikovsky, signed and inscribed by the composer, will fetch over $2,000.

Charles Chaplin, good photograph in black and white signed in black ink. 10 x 8in. $280

Robert Browning: Cabinet photograph of Browning, signed and dated 5 May 1886. $900

'Nelson Eddy', signed photograph together with original envelope. $30

Johann Strauss, The Younger, carte de visite photograph, signed with an autograph musical quotation of four bars from 'The Blue Danube', framed and glazed. $1,650

Greta Garbo, Metro Goldwyn Mayer, 1931. $80

Victoria, the official Diamond Jubilee photograph, signed and dated by the Queen, inscribed on the reverse by her secretary, Sir A. Bigge, to the photographer Downey, 13 x 7½in., April 1897. $1,240

Virginia Woolf, leaf extracted from her passport bearing her photo and signature, both overstamped by the Foreign Office, 18th April, 1933. $340

Piotr Ilyich Tchaikovsky, 1840-93, photograph, signed and inscribed in ink, in Russian, dated 2 May 1885, 159 x 102mm. $2,200

'Best Wishes Nelson Eddy', 1933. $50

'Yours truly, Willie Edouin', $6

Mae West, photograph signed, inscribed 'To John Best Wishes Mae West', 10 x 8in. $40

'Vesta Tilley', male impersonator. $12

Ronald Reagan, 40th President of the U.S.A., photograph of Reagan when a film star, signed and inscribed 'Good Luck', postcard 5½ x 3½in. $110

'To Miss Rene Jones, Best Wishes from Florie Forde, 1936'. $20

'My Best Wishes to you, Gertrude Lawrence'.$16

SIGNED PHOTOGRAPHS

Joan Crawford, Metro Goldwyn Mayer, 1931. **$50**

Sir Winston Churchill, fine photograph of the young Churchill, signed on mount, 9 x 7½in. **$500**

Elvis Presley, photograph of Presley in military uniform in a car, signed in blue ball-point, with another, 5½ x 3½in. **$220**

Laurel and Hardy, good photograph of them in characteristic pose signed by both, 5 x 7in. **$160**

Pablo Picasso, full length photograph of Picasso in bathing trunks, signed in ballpoint, 7¼ x 5in. **$300**

Leo Tolstoy, postcard photograph signed in black ink in English script. **$400**

'To Irene Jones, My best wishes, Ben Lyon, Bebe Daniels'. **$25**

Marlene Dietrich, Paramount, 1932. **$70**

Field-Marshal Montgomery: photograph with Eisenhower, signed. **$110**

SIGNS

Stand in any main shopping centre today and one is confronted with the familiar shop signs of the multiple stores. Which is a shame, for shops are becoming so impersonal these days with individuality being a thing of the past.

Town planning is partly responsible for it has stifled the use of elaborate shop signs which used to boldly display the interests of the shopkeeper. Literacy is more the cause of their demise however, for graphic signs were often the only way many people could identify the trade.

Tobacconist shops seem particulary well endowed with signs, from magnificent life size blackamoors and Red Indians to a multitude of smaller figures and animals of carved wood.

Late 19th century American apothecary sign, 3ft. high. (Robt. W. Skinner Inc.) $1,300

A metal Kodak store sign, triangular with heavy metal bracket, 'Developing Printing Enlarging'. $120

American 19th century sheet metal hatter's sign, 14in. high. (Robt. W. Skinner Inc.) $1,200

The Spalding Co. Iron Advertising trade sign, the cast-iron pocket watch frame with zinc painted face, 22¼in. high, circa 1890. $400

A painted wooden hollow standing horse, American, circa 1850/90, 49in. long, possibly used as a harness-maker's sign. (Christie's) $3,500.

Early 20th century American carved and painted trade sign, 39¼in. high. (Christie's) $550

A giltwood medical shop sign carved as a carp with black lacquered eyes, Meiji period, 126cm. long. (Christie's) $3,300

'Flea Circus' stained glass window, circa 1900, 5ft. long. (Robt. W. Skinner Inc.) $775

A leaded glass pharmacy sign, America, 64½in. wide. (Robt. W. Skinner Inc.) $970

A carved and painted counter top cigar store Punch figure, by Chas. Henkel, Vermont, 1870, 26in. high. (Christie's) $19,800

'Cafe' leaded glass window, in metal frame, circa 1900, 4ft.4in. high. (Robt. W. Skinner Inc.) $475

Late 19th century wooden barber pole, polychrome decorated, America, 90in. high. (Robt. W. Skinner Inc.) $230

Victorian House Mover's sign made of well-cut letters, foliage, birds etc., circa 1880. $500

Early 20th century drug store Moxie sign, 23½ x 31¾in. $780

Kodak glass and celluloid store sign, 37 x 15in., in black frame, circa 1910, with 'Kodaks' in 8in. gold recessed letter on black background. $590

Early 20th century gilt wooden trade sign in the form of a fish, American, 57¼in. long, 17in. high. (Christie's) $4,400

SNUFF BOTTLES

Chinese snuff bottles usually resemble small vases about 6cm. (2½in.) high, and are made of a variety of materials including porcelain, ivory, jade, cloisonne, horn, agate, glass and bronze. Most sought after, and therefore most expensive are those made of porcelain from the late 17th and early 18th century, closely followed by carved hardstone such as agate, quartz and amethyst. A guide to quality, although it is not infallible, is the size of the hole in the neck (the smaller the better) and the degree of hollowing out — those with a large interior being the best. This also applies to glass bottles which were generally carved out of a solid piece as opposed to being blown.

A white jade rounded square snuff bottle and matching stopper, carved overall with bands of wicker work. (Christie's) $1,500

An inside painted glass rectangular bottle with two equestrian archers pursuing a deer, signed Chen Zhong-san. (Christie's) $375

An Imperial style ivory snuff bottle, four character Qianlong mark on the base, with matching stopper. $8,500

An agate rounded square snuff bottled carved in intaglio from a brown inclusion on one side, with stopper. (Christie's) $675

An agate flattened disk-shaped snuff bottle, carved from an area of darker inclusion as a sage sitting on rockwork. (Christie's) $2,150

A red lacquer spade-shaped snuff bottle, relief carved with two pairs of figures on fenced terraces. (Christie's) $1,000

An agate rounded square bottle with animal mask ring handles. (Christie's) $400

A mottled apple and celadon jadeite disk-shaped snuff bottle and stopper. (Christie's) $570

A plain amber flattened disk-shaped snuff bottle, with a dragon around the neck, with stopper. (Christie's) $225

An inside painted glass rounded square snuff bottle painted with a leopard beneath bamboo, signed Wang Bai-chuan, dated 1982. (Christie's) $325

A red lacquer spade-shaped snuff bottle, relief carved with two groups of children playing, with stopper. (Christie's) $425

An agate rounded rectangular snuff bottle carved on one side from a caramel shadow with three birds around a tree. (Christie's) $685

An agate flattened disk-shaped snuff bottle, banded with an irregular concentric panel, with stopper. (Christie's) $200

An agate rounded square snuff bottle of translucent grayish tone with gilt metal collared coral stopper. (Christie's) $2,150

An inside painted glass disk-shaped snuff bottle, dated 1981. (Christie's) $270

SNUFF BOXES

For many hundreds of years people have been taking snuff and, an indication of the popularity of this habit can be seen in the abundance of delightful snuff boxes we have to choose from.

They come in all shapes and sizes and made from many materials including gold, silver, tortoiseshell, papier mache, and enamel ware. Like the vinaigrette, many have gilt interiors. Generally the lids are decorated and here the variety is infinite. They may be painted, inset with semi-precious stones or inlaid with contrasting materials. Those ornamented with representations of the famous castles, 'castle-tops', are particularly desirable boxes, notably that of Windsor Castle by Nathaniel Mills.

Unusual examples have two compartments so that snuff can be separated into grades and a most uncommon box may have a watch inset in one section.

An early Victorian castle top snuff box, by N. Mills, Birmingham, 1838, 7.2cm. long. (Lawrence Fine Art) $700

A tortoiseshell pique snuff box, probably English, circa 1730, 3.1/8in. wide. $450

A shallow tortoiseshell snuff box, circa 1740, possibly French, 3.1/8in. wide. (Christie's) $1,400

A George IV tortoiseshell snuff box in the form of a tortoise, by T. Wallis & J. Hayne, London, 1820, 3¼in. long. $4,600

An early Victorian gilt lined, engine-turned box with applied cast floral thumbpiece, possibly by E. Edwards, London, 1839, 4¾in. long. (Christie's) $665

A late 18th century Italian silver gilt circular snuff box, Venice, circa 1770, 5.6cm. diam. (Phillips) $500

A mid 19th century Russian niello snuff box with foliate scroll decoration, maker's mark EE, Moscow, circa 1850. (Phillips) $450

A Continental silver and tortoiseshell snuff box, unmarked probably French, circa 1820. (Christie's) $170

A French 19th century oblong snuff box, the base and sides nielloed with a checkered effect, 3½in. long. (Christie's) $520

SNUFF BOXES

An Austro-Hungarian rectangular snuff box, Vienna, 1852, 9cm. long. (Christie's) $125

A French 19th century oblong gilt lined snuff box, the lid finely nielloed with 18th century hunting scene, with house and trees beyond, 3½in. long. (Christie's) $475

A George IV hunting scene snuff box, by John Jones III, 1824, 8.8cm. long. (Lawrence Fine Art) $820

An oval baluster form snuff box, by Charles Murray, Perth, circa 1830, 2¼in. high. $1,650

A George III silver gilt fox mask snuff box, by T. Phipps & E. Robinson, 1807, 3¼in., 3oz. 10dwt. (Christie's) $4,320

19th century circular snuff box set in the cover with a micro mosaic of Pliny's doves of Venus, 2.7/8in. diam.(Christie's) $1,400

A late 17th/early 18th century tortoiseshell snuff box inlaid in silver with a seascape. circa 1700. (Phillips) $325

An English gilt metal and aventurine snuff box, probably Birmingham, mid 18th century, 2½in. wide. $400

An Italian rectangular silver gilt mounted hardstone snuff box, by Giacomo Sirletti, Rome, 1811-36, 3½in. long. (Christie's) $6,250

A gilt metal and mother-of-pearl snuff box, probably German, 2¾in. wide, circa 1740. $475

A Scottish silver mounted cowrie shell snuff box, circa 1810. (Christie's) $175

A silver gilt cartouche-shaped snuff box, probably German, circa 1760. $1,000

SPECTACLES

Before 1880, spectacles were usually made of gold or steel, and later, of rolled gold or gold filled. Gold was preferred because it was acknowledged that it was the material less likely to cause any skin irritation.

Until recently, old spectacles were bought up for the scrap value of the gold content but now they are being collected out of an interest in their history and the development of the many different styles.

Written evidence dates 'eye glasses' to as far back as 1289.

Temple spectacles, with side pieces, were introduced by E. Scarlett in 1727 and, bi-focal lenses by Benjamin Franklin in 1785.

Sunglasses date from the 1880's.

Contact lenses were devised in 1887.

An 18th century pair of steel ring side spectacles with tinted lenses in a leather case, 5in. long. (Christie's) $230

A pair of 18th century burnished steel green tinted protective folding sides spectacles with circular lenses. (Phillips) $435

A pair of brass framed Chinese spectacles, with folding sides and quartz lenses. (Christie's) $260

A pair of Chinese brass framed turn-pin sides spectacles with brown tinted quartz lenses, in a brown stained sharkskin case, 6¾in. long. (Christie's) $185

A pair of 16th century leather nose spectacles, 9cm. wide. (Phillips) $2,480

A pair of silver turn-pin sides 'D' cup blue smoke lense spectacles. (Christie's) $220

9kt. gold 'nose grip' spectacles and case. $30

A pair of binocular spectacles with adjustable lenses. $20

A pair of 19th century brass and tortoiseshell folding-sides spectacles with deep clouded brown quartz lenses, in shagreen case, 6½in. long. (Christie's) $340

STAFFORDSHIRE POTTERY

If you stand in the car park in the center of Stoke and turn full circle, you will be confronted by numerous chimneys emblazoned with the household names of the most famous potteries. Drive a few miles and the road signs tell of Fenton, Longton, Hanley, Burslem, Tunstall and Burmantofts, all familiar names to collectors of Staffordshire pottery. At one time there were over four hundred factories going full blast to meet the insatiable demand of the Victorians to have a pottery figure covering every available surface.

Most are press molded and decorated in underglaze blue and black with touches of color in overglaze enamel and gilding. Early examples have closed bases or sport a small hole in the base, while 20th century pieces are usually slip cast in Plaster of Paris molds and are open ended.

Vast quantities of these earthenware figures were produced from around 1850 right up until the First World War. They are referred to as Staffordshire figures although many were produced at factories in the north of England and in Scotland.

Rare bust of Plato after a model by Enoch Wood, late 18th century, 13¼in. high. $500

Early 19th century Staffordshire pearlware mantel ornament of the Royal Coat-of-Arms, 22.5cm. high. $1,720

Staffordshire figure of Eliza Cook, 1860's, some crazing, 10¼in. high. $220

A Staffordshire Toby jug of conventional type, seated holding a frothing jug of ale, circa 1780, 24.5cm. high. (Christie's) $865

A money box modeled as a chapel, inscribed Salley Harper Hougate March 16th 1845, 6¾in. high. (Christie's) $900

Large Staffordshire pearlware figure of a dog, 42cm. high, circa 1830. $1,940

A pastille burner modeled as a cottage with an iron-red doorway flanked by flowers and trees, on an oval shaped base, 6in. high. (Christie's) $380

One of a pair of late 18th century Staffordshire pottery cow creamers, 6¼in. long. (Dacre, Son & Hartley) $2,300

One of a pair of Staffordshire lion and lamb groups, circa 1850, 4¾in. $2,200

Mid 19th century tobacco jar and cover, modeled as the head of a spotted dog, 6¾in. high. $530

A Staffordshire pottery mug commemorating the Coronation of Queen Victoria, circa 1838, 8.5cm. high. $750

A 19th century pottery 'Village Group' 19cm. $310

An Obadiah Sherratt group of Polito's menagerie, circa 1830, 29.5cm. high. (Christie's) $21,500

A Staffordshire portrait bust of General Booth wearing Salvation Army cap, circa 1900, 13in. high. $660

A Staffordshire blue and white cylindrical mug printed with equestrian figures of The Duke of Wellington and Lord Hill, 4¾in. high. (Christie's) $260

Early 19th century English figure of Britannia, with a lion at her side, 6¼in. high. $485

A Staffordshire saltglaze tartan ground Royalist teapot and cover with loop handle, circa 1750, 14cm. high. (Christie's) $15,335

A Staffordshire pottery figure of Samson and the Lion, 12¼in. (Dreweatts) $160

A Staffordshire pearlware box and cover modeled as a dog, the screw cover with the initials ET, circa 1815, 5cm. wide. (Christie's) $1,840

A pair of Staffordshire pugilist figures modeled as the boxers Mollineux and Cribb, circa 1810, 22cm. high. (Christie's) $2,730

A Staffordshire jug depicting Wellington at Salamanca, 5½in. high. (Christie's) $180

A group of Napoleon III and Empress Eugenie, the oval base named in gilt molded capitals, circa 1854, 12in. high. (Christie's) $320

A Staffordshire pearlware mug, printed with execution of Louis XVI picked out in enamels, 8.5cm. high, 1790's. $480

A Staffordshire pottery figure of Tom King, the highwayman, 11½in. high. (Dreweatts) $150

STANDS

If you are one of those happy souls whose habit it is to arrive home late on rainy evenings with muddy boots, library book in one hand, a walking stick in the other, rubber plant and fruitcake clutched to your chest and umbrella held aloft in a vain attempt to keep your new hat dry; and if, when you do arrive home so encumbered, you find that the power workers have called a lightning blackout and you have to grope your way about in candle-light — just relax. All you need is a collection of appropriate stands and your problems are over.

There are candlestands, plant stands, reading and music stands, cake stands, kettle stands, umbrella stands, hat stands, boot stands, shaving stands, even wig stands. Such was the ingenuity of past craftsmen and designers that there is a purpose built stand for just about everything from whips to cricket bats.

A Regency rosewood duet music stand, the pierced top filled with lyres. (Christie's) $1,400

An 18th century mahogany adjustable knee rest, 13¼in. $485

A 19th century mahogany whip and boot rack, 39½in. $220

A Swiss carved pine umbrella stand in the form of a stand-ing bear, 4ft.9in. high, circa 1900. $925

J. & J. Kohn bentwood coat stand, designed by Josef Hoffmann, circa 1905, 202cm. high. $705

Unusual Victorian music stand with papier-mache top inlaid with mother-of-pearl, circa 1850. $1,320

An early 19th century mahogany boot jack, 33½in. high. $500

A Chippendale mahogany birdcage candlestand with a dished and molded circular tilt top, 1760-90, 23½in. diam. (Christie's) $6,400

Gustav Stickley oak plant stand, circa 1903, 28in. high. (Robt. W. Skinner Inc.) $1,000

Victorian oak and cast-iron reading bracket and circular table. (Butler & Hatch Waterman) $190

Oriental carved teakwood stand, 16in. diam. (Stalker & Boos) $600

Late 18th century George III mahogany three-tier stand, 42in. high. (Robt. W. Skinner Inc.) $1,330

A late 19th century beechwood smoker's companion, 35in. high. $420

A late Federal pine stand, with single drawer above two cupboard doors, 1810-30, 22½in. wide.(Christie's) $530

A mahogany marquetry etagere by Louis Majorelle. (Christie's) $1,840

STEVENGRAPHS

When the government of 1860 removed the ban on imported silk goods, it had a disastrous effect on the weavers of Coventry, forcing many of them out of business. It did, however, spur on a certain Thomas Stevens to try out some of his new ideas. By adapting his looms to weave small, multi-colored pictures and bookmarks instead of the traditional ribbons, he found instant, overwhelming success. He also produced Christmas, birthday and Valentine cards, plus calendars, sashes and badges, all of which were offered to a totally new market, since they were sold through booksellers and fancy goods shops.

Stevens traveled to trade fairs all over Britain, Europe and America taking along with him portable looms so that visitors could watch the production at first hand and buy whatever took their fancy. The response in America was so favorable that he went on to export great quantities of pictures which explains why there are so many excellent collections in the U.S.A. today.

Although a variety of woven silk pictures can be found, those by Stevens usually bear the inscription 'woven in pure silk by Thomas Stevens, Coventry' printed on the front of the mount.

Thomas Stevens died in 1888, leaving the business to his two sons. Their products continued to be popular until the outbreak of the First World War but, although they continued to turn out a few portraits after that time, main production became geared to the manufacture of hatbands and the like. The firm survived until 1940, when the factory was completely demolished during an air raid.

'The Last Lap', pennyfarthing race, yellow axles, original mount. **$140**

'The Present Time 60 Miles An Hour', with two carriages. **$50**

'The Present Time', train emerging from tunnel, original mounts. **$80**

'The Death Of Nelson', deck of the Victory, remounted and framed. **$50**

'The Lady Godiva Procession', original mount, framed and glazed. **$120**

'Her Majesty Queen Alexandra', with the crests of England, Scotland and Ireland below portrait. **$50**

'Charles Stewart Parnell M.P.', with yellow harp and clover leaves below portrait. **$70**

'The Forth Bridge', a view of the bridge under construction. **$120**

'A Gentleman in Khaki', depicting a wounded soldier with rifle raised. **$40**

'The Late Earl of Beaconsfield', with black and white portrait facing left. **$40**

'A Present From Blackpool, a view of the town and piers. **$120**

'Ye Peeping Tom of Coventry', with brown window surround. **$80**

'The Good Old Days', original mount, framed and glazed. **$70**

'Sergt. G. H. Bates', the American Standard Bearer. **$120**

'Leda', a study of Leda and the swan.   **$140**

Windsor Castle', a view of the castle with the Thames in the foreground.   **$80**

'**Jake Kilrain**', study of notable American boxer.   **$80**

'**Called to the Rescue** ', original mount, framed and glazed.   **$50**

'**H.R.H. Prince of Wales**', facing left with flags below.   **$90**

'**Dick Turpin's Ride To York On His Bonnie Black Bess**', original mounts.   **$60**

'**Kitchener of Khartoum**', with head and shoulders above a Union Jack.   **$50**

'**Rt. Hon. W. E. Gladstone MP**', looking ahead with sprays of thistles and roses.   **$40**

'**Are you Ready** ', Boat Race, original mount, framed and glazed.   **$120**

'**Her Majesty Queen Victoria** ', Queen of a an Empire on Which the Sun Never Sets.   **$40**

STONEWARE

The production of saltglazed stoneware had been carried on at Lambeth in London for centuries when John Doulton first went into the pottery business there in 1815.

At first his firm continued the prevalent output of cheap mass produced items like bottles, jugs and barrels and it was not until John's son Henry joined the business that more complex modeling and detail began to be introduced.

It was Henry who diversified into architectural stoneware and who started to turn his Lambeth Pottery into a center for the production of decorative stoneware.

In 1866 he took into the company a group of students from the Lambeth School of Art and in the Paris Exhibition of 1867 their work was highly acclaimed.

The people who produced decorative stoneware at this time included the three famous Barlows, Frank Butler, George Tinworth and many others including women like Eliza Simmance.

A jug with incised green and yellow plants with blue flowers, c.m., 1878, 7¼in. high. $220

A cream jug and sugar bowl with an incised frieze of rabbits above green and blue leaves, c.m., 1880, 1886, 4½in. high. $760

A cylindrical jug with a dark brown glaze and applied flower heads, blue triangles and white beads, c.m., 1878, 6¾in. high. $170

A whist booby attributed to Leslie Harradine, molded with a skeleton, RDE, circa 1910, 4¼in. high. $200

A tyg with three incised groups of rabbits in a landscape, the handles with incised flowers, o.m., 1873, 5¾in. high. $340

A boy playing a fiddle supported on his foot, DLE, circa 1895, 4¼in. high. $1,240

A salt cellar by Hannah Barlow of hexagonal trencher type, o.u.m., circa 1872, 3in. diam. **$190**

A teapot with rough brown lace ground decorated with floral sprays, Slater's Patent 'Chine', r.m., 4¾in. high. **$70**

A match striker with Art Nouveau designs, DLE, 4in. high. **$40**

A water filter with incised, carved and applied decoration on a buff bround, DSL, 14½in. high. **$240**

A large pair of vases, each with an incised frieze of wolves and their cubs amongst foliage, r.m., 1885, 16½in. high. **$1,040**

A golfing jug, sprigged in white, with the panels of the 'Last Ball', 'Putting' and 'Driving', impressed Lambeth mark, circa 1880, 20cm. high. **$560**

A modeled owl with brown wings and feet, the detachable head and the body decorated with applied blue, green and white motifs, DSL, circa 1880, 7½in. high. **$585**

A monkey group inscribed 'A United Family', sitting on a bench and sheltering under an ocher umbrella, r.m. & e., circa 1892, 5in. high. **$1,700**

A biscuit barrel with plate cover and mounts, the sides painted in pate-sur-pate with four cockatoos, r.m., 1886, 5½in. high. **$260**

STONEWARE

A vase, the light buff body stenciled overall with impressed concentric circles, r.m., circa 1882, 12¼in. high.　$180

A large vase by Harry Barnard, the buff ground with incised foliage, r.m., 1881, 14¼in. high.　$1,915

A pepper pot by Alice Budden with incised leaves and bead work, c.m., 1880, 2½in. high.　$160

A mounted jug, the mottled brown ground with applied geometric and leaf patterns, c.m., 1878, 9½in. high.$160

A pair of candlesticks by Nellie Garbott with incised brown and blue leaves, c.m., 1879, 6¾in. high.　$585

A jug decorated with a shaped panel containing two pate-sur-pate black swans reserved on a buff ground, r.m., 1884, 7¾in. high.　$380

A mug by Constance E. Redford, the buff ground with white dots and incised blue scrolls, r.m., 1882, 5in. high.　$170

An early architectural clockcase glazed ocher and blue, with incised blue, green and purple leaves, o.m., 1875, 14½in. high.　$1,915

A small bowl by Emily Welch with impressed gilt concentric circles, r.m., circa 1888, 4in. high.　$325

SWORDS

From earliest times, a man's sword stood for a great deal. Not only was it used for protection but it signified his status and his pride. It is significant that the most popular item of booty has always been a sword and handing it over was symbolic of defeat. Mementos of campaigns far back in history can still be found hanging in the homes of the victors. Collectors today can buy Japanese swords taken during the 1939-45 war which have blades many hundreds of years old and prized by the owners' family so highly that they were passed down through the generations. These blades were often signed by the craftsmen who forged them.

There are swords in collections from Turkish campaigns, from the Crimea, from the Napoleonic Wars and the U.S. Civil War — in fact from almost any war since recorded history began. Warriors were buried with their swords and the engraving on a sword blade and the elaboration of its hilt gave a clue to the importance of the man who carried it. Recently the finely carved ivory lion's head hilt of a Shamsir sword ensured that it sold for $6,400 at auction.

A 19th century hunting sword, plain, single edged blade 13in., in its leather sheath, with provision for companion knife. (Wallis & Wallis) $120

A French transitional rapier, circa 1685, slim, straight, tapering, single edged blade 37in. (Wallis & Wallis) $800

A wakizashi, the red lacquered scabbard simulating cherry bark, fitted with a gilt kogai and shakudo-nanakoji kozuka, 16th century, 34.2cm. (Christie's) $6,500

A French Cavalry officer's sword of 1786 pattern type, straight, broad single fullered, single edged blade 38in., with false edge. (Wallis & Wallis) $380

A transitional dish hilted rapier, circa 1630, slender blade 41½in., stamped Sebastian Hernantis in the fullers. (Wallis & Wallis) $660

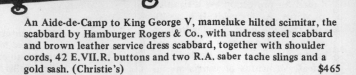

An Aide-de-Camp to King George V, mameluke hilted scimitar, the
scabbard by Hamburger Rogers & Co., with undress steel scabbard
and brown leather service dress scabbard, together with shoulder
cords, 42 E.VII.R. buttons and two R.A. saber tache slings and a
gold sash. (Christie's) $465

A Victorian mameluke hilted sword of General Officer's 1831 pattern,
in gilt mounted black leather scabbard, together with a gilt metal
scabbard to fit. (Christie's) $465

A Nazi Army officer's sword, slightly curved, plated blade 30½in.,
by Paul Weyersberg, the lion's head pommel inset with red glass
eyes, in its black painted steel scabbard. (Wallis & Wallis) $370

An early 17th century Northern European swept hilt rapier with long
double-edged blade and single fuller, 52.5/8in. long. $1,225

A daisho with fine Higo-style koshirae, probably by Bizen Kiyomitsu, with a date, Teiwa
ninen (1346), but 16th century, 71.5cm. long. (Christie's) $7,130

A mid 17th century Cavalry man's half basket hilted broadsword,
straight, double edged blade 33in. Brass hilt, stepped bulbous
pommel and leather covered grip. (Wallis & Wallis) $490

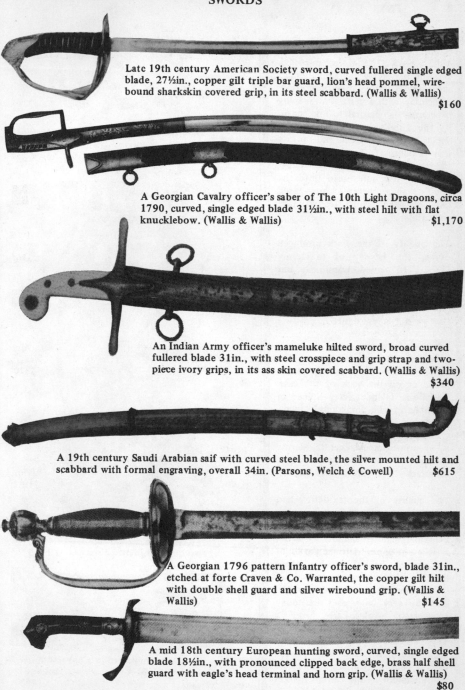

Late 19th century American Society sword, curved fullered single edged blade, 27½in., copper gilt triple bar guard, lion's head pommel, wirebound sharkskin covered grip, in its steel scabbard. (Wallis & Wallis)
$160

A Georgian Cavalry officer's saber of The 10th Light Dragoons, circa 1790, curved, single edged blade 31½in., with steel hilt with flat knucklebow. (Wallis & Wallis) $1,170

An Indian Army officer's mameluke hilted sword, broad curved fullered blade 31in., with steel crosspiece and grip strap and two-piece ivory grips, in its ass skin covered scabbard. (Wallis & Wallis) $340

A 19th century Saudi Arabian saif with curved steel blade, the silver mounted hilt and scabbard with formal engraving, overall 34in. (Parsons, Welch & Cowell) $615

A Georgian 1796 pattern Infantry officer's sword, blade 31in., etched at forte Craven & Co. Warranted, the copper gilt hilt with double shell guard and silver wirebound grip. (Wallis & Wallis) $145

A mid 18th century European hunting sword, curved, single edged blade 18½in., with pronounced clipped back edge, brass half shell guard with eagle's head terminal and horn grip. (Wallis & Wallis) $80

TAXIDERMY

Taxidermy was not perfected technically until the beginning of the 19th century. The interest in collecting and preserving birds and animals increased as the century progressed, coinciding with a general awakening of interest in natural history until, by the 1880's, almost every town could boast the great skill of its own taxidermist. The interest began to wane shortly before the Great War, and did not return until the 1960's, since which time cased taxidermy has become steadily more collectible.

The quality of the work produced during the heyday of taxidermy (1860-1914) varied enormously, but it is only the top quality work which has any real value today, and this represents perhaps less than 5% of all that was actually produced.

Although it is not essential, it is a good idea to look for the taxidermist's label which is usually placed inside or on the back of the case. Variations include Peter Spicer of Leamington who, for example, incorporated a signed pebble into the groundwork of his cases. Condition is of prime importance: taxidermy specimens are notoriously susceptible to attacks from moths and beetles.

The quality of the taxidermy and case setting is equally important: the bird or mammal must be mounted in a lifelike manner and be set in an artistic but appropriate simulation of its natural habitat. Within these limits, each taxidermist evolved his own particular and distinctive style, and the very best cases are today recognizable works of art.

The photographs chosen are mostly items from the top end of the market, and the prices, which are considered to be the current market values for each case, reflect this.

A Victorian ram's head snuff mull. $3,000

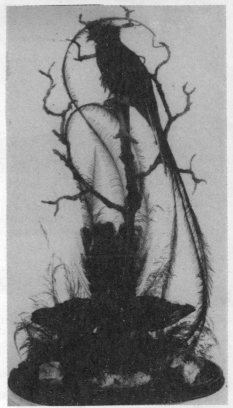

Two quetzals in oval dome, circa 1890. $400

A pike, 26lb., mounted in a bow-front display cabinet, 131 x 45 x 29cm. (Osmond Tricks) $400

Pair of pochard by Peter Spicer & Sons of Leamington, circa 1910. $400

Smew drake by Peter Spicer & Sons of Leamington, 1929. $300

Golden eagle by Macpherson of Inverness, circa 1900. $600

Pair of gray squirrels by Rowland Ward of London, circa 1900. $200

Barn owl by Allen of York, circa 1890. $200

Pair of albino pheasants by G. White of Salisbury, circa 1900. $200

Pair of great bitterns by T. E. Gunn of Norwich, circa 1890. $500

Badger by J. Gardner of London, circa 1880. $250

Pair of Arctic hares by J. Hutchings of Aberystwyth, circa 1905. $250

Pair of lesser birds of paradise, taxidermist unknown, circa 1880. $240

Pair of little bustards by Saunders of Great Yarmouth, circa 1910. $350

Fox and weasel in naturalistic setting contained in a glazed case. $200

Domestic pigeon in dome, 1922. **$100**

Three lapwings in case by T. E. Gunn of Norwich, circa 1890. **$200**

Pair of trout by J. Cooper of London, (who specialized in fish), in a bow-fronted case, 1920. **$300**

Fox mask on shield by Peter Spicer & Sons, circa 1920. **$100**

Group of wading birds by S. Hibbs of Ollerton, circa 1890. **$350**

Pair of red grouse by Peter Spicer & Sons of Leamington, circa 1905. **$300**

Of all boxes, chests, caskets and other assorted containers, tea caddies must surely be the most numerous and the most varied with regard to shape and style.

One reason for this is that tea has been drunk in Britain for some three hundred years, at prices ranging from £10 per lb. (at the beginning of the 17th century) down. Naturally, a commodity as expensive as this was neither served direct from the packet nor dumped in just any can on the kitchen shelf.

Early (i.e. 17th century) containers were usually of pottery or porcelain. As the cult of tea-drinking became more widespread during the 18th century, tea-containers of gold and silver began to appear, and these were housed in lockable chests or caddies (the word caddy is derived from the Malay "kati", a measure of tea weighing about 1¼lb.) The more widespread the tea-drinking habit became, the greater the variety of caddies to cater for the demand.

Chippendale, Sheraton and all the other designers and cabinet makers of note produced caddies in their characteristic styles, and ornamentation varied from the simplest, most elegant inlay work to encrustations of brass, ormolu, coloured straw, curled paperwork and every other possible decorative device.

Not too many years ago, it would have been easy to start a collection, for caddies could be picked up almost anywhere for only a few dollars — none but the very best reaching double figures. Nowadays, they are just as ubiquitous but the prices must warm the cockles of any heart who got a collection together at the right time.

They are to be found in a number of materials, including wood, ivory, papier mache, silver, copper, tortoiseshell, china, straw work, Tunbridgeware and with painted decoration.

A George III satinwood, marquetry and painted octangular tea caddy with hinged top, 6½in. wide. (Christie's) $1,250

A George III satinwood, rosewood and fruitwood tea caddy, the crossbanded lid with a silver plaque with initials J.E.R., 12¾in. wide. (Christie's) $2,500

Walnut tea caddy of hexagonal shape, each side with oval shell inlaid panel. (Butler & Hatch Waterman) $640

An 18th/19th century tea caddy in the form of a box-wood toadstool, 5in. high. **$1,500**

George III rectangular inlaid tea caddy on a brass edged base on bracket feet, 10in. wide. (Christie's) **$615**

An 18th century melon fruitwood tea caddy, England, 6in. high. (Robt. W. Skinner Inc.) **$3,000**

A George III oval tea caddy, the lid centered by a leaf-cast silver handle, circa 1795, 5in. high. **$5,720**

A pair of tea caddies, one in applewood, the other in pear-wood, 4¼in. and 6½in. high. **$7,920**

Chinese Peking, enameled, covered tea caddy, with multi-colored dragon reserve panel decoration, 4½in. high. (Stalker & Boos) **$290**

George III rolled paperwork tea caddy, dated 1799, panels inset with mezzotints, 7¼in. wide. **$1,870**

Three-color Wedgwood tea caddy, circa 1895, with domed lid, 6in. high. (Robt. W. Skinner Inc.) **$620**

An ivory veneered Georgian tea caddy with a brass handle and tortoiseshell decoration. (Martel Maides & Le Pelley) **$1,550**

TEAPOTS

Teapots dating from early in the 18th century will always command high prices for at first the famous leaf was an incredibly expensive luxury supped only by the very wealthy. Teapots of this period are accordingly very rare and of a high quality.

The duty on tea was reduced dramatically midway through the 18th century, considerably increasing its popularity which continued, unabated, throughout the 19th century.

Teapots have therefore been made in every conceivable shape, style and material for a very long time and as a result any would-be collector will need to be pretty discriminating, sticking strictly to a chosen type — be it Staffordshire barge teapots at under $200 to early saltglaze examples costing over $2,000.

A European silver mounted Arita teapot and domed cover decorated in iron-red, green and black enamels, circa 1700, 19.6cm. long. (Christie's) $860

An Abuja stoneware teapot with screw top, by Michael Cardew, circa 1958, 10cm. high. (Christie's) $630

A Wedgwood/Whieldon hexagonal teapot and cover in chinoiserie style, 16cm. high. (Phillips) $2,400

A Meissen teapot and cover, decorated in cisele gold, 12cm. high, red luster workman's cross mark, 1725. (Lawrence Fine Art) $9,000

A stoneware teapot and cover by Lucie Rie, covered in a matt manganese glaze, circa 1958, 15cm. high. (Christie's) $650

A Capodimonte oviform teapot with scroll handle and spout, blue fleur-de-lys mark, circa 1750, 14.5cm. wide. (Christie's) $1,290

TEAPOTS

A Minton teapot modeled as a Chinaman holding a mask from which the spout projects, circa 1875, 14.4cm. high. (Christie's) $1,080

A Royal Worcester aesthetic teapot and cover, modeled as the upper part of a body, 15.5cm. high. (Christie's) $1,500

A Wedgwood creamware globular teapot and cover, painted in the manner of David Rhodes, circa 1768, 15cm. high. (Christie's) $4,000

A Wedgwood green and white jasper cylindrical teapot and cover, circa 1800, 9.5cm. high. (Christie's) $540

A Satsuma miniature teapot, signed on base, 4in. high. (Reeds Rains) $650

An 18th/19th century Kakiemon type mokkogata teapot with shallow domed cover and arch-shaped handle, 19cm. long. (Christie's) $1,850

A Mennecy teapot and cover of globular shape with double ogee handle and flower finial, 9.5cm. high, incised DV mark. (Phillips) $1,100

A Linthorpe teapot, the design attributed to Dr. C. Dresser, 21.3cm. high. (Christie's) $240

A Vincennes bleu lapis conical teapot, blue interlaced L marks and painter's mark of Thevenet, circa 1753, 11cm. high. (Christie's) $1,750

TEDDY BEARS

President Reagan has one, so has Princess Anne, together with Enoch Powell and Pope John Paul, although his stays in the Vatican. Mrs Thatcher's is called Humphrey and he often raises money for charity and Lord Bath's friend called Clarence wears spectacles. Arctophily is the name of the game — they all have bears.

Margaret Steiff, a crippled dressmaker, is credited with making the first bear about 1900, but it wasn't until Teddy Roosevelt refused to shoot a bear on an organized hunt (it was, after all, tied to a stake by someone eager to please) that the Teddy Bear really took off in popularity.

Early bears have a hump on the back, jointed arms, head and legs and are generally stuffed with straw. The best have glass or button eyes, come complete with a growl and a Steiff metal tag in the ear. Most early bears are often described as 'well loved' which is why those in good condition will always command a premium.

A golden plush covered musical teddy bear, playing Sonny Boy by Al Jolson, 20in. high, circa 1930. (Christie's) $850

A golden plush covered teddy bear, the front unhooking to reveal a metal hot water bottle, by Steiff, 17in. high.(Christie's) $1,750

A tan mohair bear with wired limbs, blonde plush ears, snout and feet and glass eyes, Germany, circa 1930, 11in. high. (Robt. W. Skinner Inc.) $75

A Steiff pale plush teddy bear with black thread stitched nose and straw stuffed body, with button in left ear, 33cm. high. (Phillips) $850

German teddy bear by Steiff of pale plush color, renewed pads, snout and nose, circa 1909. (Phillips) $2,200

A teddy bear of gray plush with brown button eyes, embroidered nose, hump back and long paws, 13in. high. (Christie's) $500

TEDDY BEARS

Pre-war fur fabric teddy bear, 15in. high. (Reeds Rains) $40

A gold short plush covered teddy bear, slight hump, 15½in. high, circa 1926. (Christie's) $275

An orange plush teddy bear with smiling mouth, small hump back and swivel joints, 16in. high, circa 1930. $175

Late 19th century clockwork brown bear, real fur pelt, possibly France, 7in. high. (Robt. W. Skinner Inc.) $230

A long plush covered teddy bear with black button eyes, with Steiff button in the ear, 25in. high. (Christie's) $2,000

An R.D. France drinking bear, dark brown and white rabbit fur, glass eyes, electrical, 1930's, 14½in. high. (Robt. W. Skinner Inc.) $920

Blonde mohair jointed teddy bear, 1910, 17in. high. (Robt. W. Skinner Inc.) $275

A plush covered teddy bear with round ears, button eyes, pronounced hump and long paws, probably by Steiff, 21in. high. (Christie's) $500

A Steiff blonde plush teddy bear, with metal disk in left ear, 17in. high. (Lawrence Fine Art) $1,750

TELEPHONES

Hailed at the time as the Greatest Miracle of Human Achievement, early examples of the humble telephone are now ringing up good prices.

Although Alexander Graham Bell is credited with the invention of the telephone, an American, Elisha Grey, actually filed a patent on a similar machine exactly the same day as Bell but, unfortunately for him, a few hours later, so he lost his claim in an ensuing Supreme Court action. Surprisingly, the first telephonic contrivance was actually made 16 years before either Bell or Grey, by Professor Philip Reis of Friedrichsdorf. For the microphone, our ingenious friend hollowed out the bung of a beer barrel which he then covered with the skin of a German sausage to make a diaphragm. To this he attached a strip of platinum which vibrated with the diaphragm to form a make-and-break electrical circuit. Then he took a knitting needle surrounded with a coil of wire, which he attached to a violin to act as a sound box. This, unbelievably, reproduced the sound received by the bung covered with sausage skin – and gave rise to the first telephone.

Most of the older telephones found today are of the Ericsson type and emanate from Sweden, Denmark, France, Germany or Britain. There are particularly fine examples among these with their polished mahogany and walnut stands and brass and copper fittings.

Apart from those of a domestic nature there is also a ready market for military field telephones. The old red telephone boxes issued by the General Post Office in Britain are also sought after and are ideal for their original purpose or even as a novel shower unit.

An Ericsson table telephone with hand-set supported above a column on a circular metal base, French, circa 1920, 9in. high. **$150**

A Purcell Nobbs table telephone with Ericsson-type hand-set supported in a cradle, English, circa 1920, 13in. high. **$600**

A table telephone with black metal case, plaque initialed K.T.A.S., with magneto handle at side, 13in. high. **$450**

THIMBLES

Thimbles date back to Roman times and since then have been made of gold, silver, bronze, brass, pewter, iron, porcelain, enamel, ivory, bone, wood and leather.

Very early thimbles are rare and valuable and few on the market today date from earlier than the turn of the 18th/19th century. Up to the late 19th century silver thimbles were not always hallmarked but, it may be useful for identification purposes to note that, before the middle of the seventeenth century, thimbles were hand punched and show irregularity in the indentations.

The growing interest in thimbles has led to an escalation of current values but condition is all important if a high price is to be fetched. If the tops are perished to any extent this will detract from the value.

Goss china thimble 'Heckington'. **$30**

Chelsea thimble in hinged silver filigree case, circa 1700. **$2,400**

Near East, silver thimble, circa 1910. **$35**

Meissen thimble decorated in Schwarzlot and gold by I. Preissler. **$8,500**

A fine filigree silver thimble, circa 1800. **$500**

Filigree silver thimble, circa 1800. **$500**

Dorcas silver thimble, size 5, circa 1890. **$25**

Silver thimble containing a bottle, circa 1800. **$600**

Pewter thimble depicting the 'House of Commons' and 'Big Ben'. **$10**

Great Exhibition 1862 thimble. **$335**

Patent guard silver thimble. **$90**

Coral and silver thimble, circa 1880. **$95**

TOBACCO TINS

Cigarette and tobacco tin collecting has become very popular not only in America but also abroad, with collectors in Britain , Australia, and New Zealand. As a result, the varied and beautifully designed early tins, in good condition, are becoming increasingly scarce and consequently rising in price.

1880-1930 was probably the golden age for pictorial tins, as this period saw many tobacco companies, large and small, competing with one another in the tobacconist's window, trying to catch the eye of the smoker with their colorful tins ; a pretty girl, a man about town image or more popularly a naval theme.

Sadly most of these early tobacco companies have gone, never the less, the tins can still be found and what a thrill for the collector to spot a tin bearing the name of Taddy, Lusby or Kriegsfeld.

Hignett's 'Cavalier Bright Flake', circa 1900-20 **$30**

Hignetts 'Pilot Flake', circa 1900-20. **$40**

Lambert & Butler 'Log Cabin', circa 1900-20. **$20**

'Sweet Leaf' smoking mixture, circa 1900. **$40**

Gallaher's 'Rich Dark Honeydew', circa 1900-20. **$40**

Carroll's 'Mick McQuaid' cut plug, circa 1900-10. **$40**

TOOLS

Medical, nautical and draftsman's instruments have always been recognized as precision made tools worthy of the attention of collectors.

Now the old tools of all professions, vocations and crafts are appreciated for their beautiful workmanship and charm.

Those particularly sought after are, the carpenter's mortise gauges and brace and bits made of ebony and brass, also butcher's cleavers and bone saws. Woodworking chisels will form a splendid collection on their own as will the infinite variety of different sized woodworking planes.

Certain items, of course, have been moving upwards in price for some time and this applies in particular to the wood plane. There are over fifty different types of plane, ranging from the 3in. plane used by violin makers to the 17in. jack plane, and nowadays, some of the early 'named' examples can fetch hundreds rather than tens of dollars.

A cooper's (barrel makers) hatchet with short handle. $80

Mid 19th century miter plane with brass box-shaped body, stamped G. Snelling and C. Keate, 7.1/8in. long. $350

An early 18th century lignum vitae and steel upholsterer's hammer, inscribed J. Sarney and 1716, 9½in. long. $1,210

A screwstem plow with boxwood stems and nuts, by J. Miller, Clayton St. (David Stanley Auctions) $140

An 18th century beechwood router or 'Old Woman's Tooth', 9½in. long. $1,500

A Jaguar tool kit in a fitted case. $100

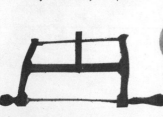

Late 19th century wooden framed fret saw. $30

A 19th century two-handled French floor plane. (David Stanley Auctions) $200

Pair of mahogany steel tipped trammels with knurled brass tightening screws, 9in. overall. (David Stanley Auctions) $230

A hand-operated diamond cutting machine with copper cutting wafers. (David Stanley Auctions) $95

A mid 18th century Dutch beechwood plane dated 1766, blade stamped Robt. Moor, 8in. long. $1,650

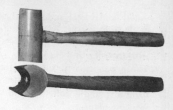

A Naval serving mallet of boxwood for serving shipped ropes. $30

Victorian scaffolder's hammer for tightening lashings in pinewood pole scaffolding. $40

A Stanley-Marsh No.100 miter machine, lacks saw. (David Stanley Auctions) $30

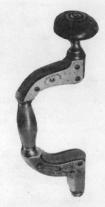

An ultimatum brace by Wm. Marples with boxwood infill, handle and head with ebony ring. (David Stanley Auctions) $3,100

An early R/H side axe, 11½in. edge, with star decoration, sharply cranked handle. (David Stanley Auctions) $85

A rosewood box plane with cast brass sole plate and steel blade by Hearnshaw Bros., 7½in. long. (Dacre, Son & Hartley) $130

A beech plow by Gabriel, with brass thumb screw at the end of the stems. (David Stanley Auctions. $1,400

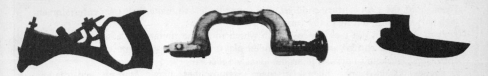

A Stanley No. 196 circular rebate plane. (David Stanley Auctions) $775

A beech button chuck brace with rosewood head and neck, by Deanes, London Bridge. (David Stanley Auctions) $70

An early goosewing axe with 18½in. blade, two smiths marks and simple decoration. (David Stanley Auctions) $140

A vetinary horse pill tool with boxwood handle that pushes the nickel grips through the brass tube, thus pushing the pill down the animal's throat. $175

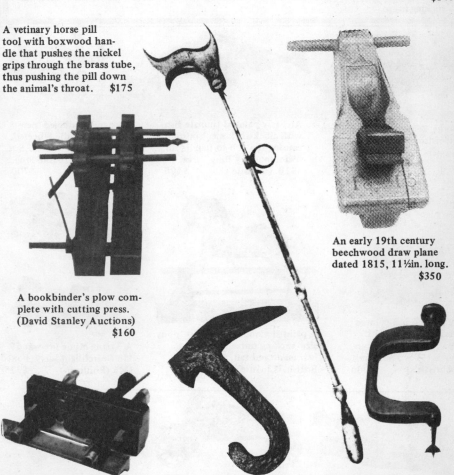

An early 19th century beechwood draw plane dated 1815, 11½in. long. $350

A bookbinder's plow complete with cutting press. (David Stanley Auctions) $160

A mahogany sash fillester with boxwood fence and stem wedges. $230

Iron wood jack for rope attachment after hammering into wood. $12

A shipwright's large ash brace with 18in. sweep and 2in. fixed center bit. (David Stanley Auctions) $215

TOYS

Throughout the 19th century children were generally left to make their own entertainment with only rarely an outing to the seaside or zoo.

They certainly did not lack for toys with which to amuse themselves however, for, apart from the familiar stuffed animals or wooden playthings, there was a multitude of the new optical and mechanical devices to arouse great wonder.

Zeotropes, kaleidoscopes, phenakistiscopes, stereoscopes, magic lanterns and thaumatropes, all products of the new age of inventions. There were board games, jigsaw puzzles and model theatres for rainy days, and tops, kites, hoops and skipping ropes for sunny weather.

From Germany, there were mechanical toys galore, simply waiting to be wound up; model trains, lead soldiers, doll's houses and, standing proudly aloof, the elegant Victorian rocking horse.

Dinky 28M green delivery van advertising "Atco Motor Mowers'. (Christie's) $500

An early painted tinplate fish, with clockwork mechanism causing the fish to flap its fin, 8¼in. long, by Bing, circa 1910. (Christie's) $400

A hand enameled 'new Orleans Paddle Wheeler', probably by Dent, U.S.A., circa 1903, 10½in. long. (Christie's) $700

A printed and painted tinplate beetle, EPL No. 431, by Lehmann, circa 1906, 3¾in. long. (Christie's) $200

A painted wood dapple gray 'pony size' rocking horse, with horse hair mane and tail, 56in. long, British. (Christie's) $600

A Triang Minic pre-war 59 ME Searchlight lorry, boxed (M). (Phillips) $325

An early painted metal gunboat with clockwork mechanism, by Bing, circa 1904, 10½in. long. (Christie's) $400

Gunthermann, Gordon Bennett clockwork racing car, finished in yellow with gold detail, 28cm. long. (Phillips) $7,000

Dinky 917, Guy van advertising 'Spratts'. (Christie's) $200

TOYS

German plush pull toy of a baby elephant by Steiff, 14in. overall. (Theriault's) $410

American wooden character doll of Felix, by Schoenhut, 9in. high. (Theriault's) $560

Unique Art tin wind-up L'il Abner and his Dogpatch Band, American, 1946, 8½in. high. (Robt. W. Skinner Inc.) $300

A clockwork automaton toy of a bisque headed doll pulling a wooden two-wheeled cart with driver, 13in. long. (Christie's) $2,000

A painted tinplate toy of a monkey on a four-wheel musical carriage, German, circa 1903, 7½in. long. (Christie's) $450

A gauge 1 signals gantry, with four signals, oil fired lamps and ladders on both sides, by Bing, circa 1910, 21in. high. (Christie's) $750

A Lehmann tinplate 'Oh My' dancer No. 690, German, circa 1912, in original cardboard box. $600

Meccano, No. 2 Constructor Car constructed as a tourer, boxed. (Phillips) $2,000

A Triang Minic pre-war Learner's car, boxed, with key (M). (Phillips) $525

A Bing hand-enameled early two-seater Benz racing car, with steerable front wheels, German, circa 1904, 11¼in. long. (Christie's) $13,000

A printed and painted tinplate model of a four-door limousine with clockwork mechanism, by Tipp & Co., circa 1928, 8¼in. long. (Christie's) $750

A Dinky model Guy van with upright radiator grill, unboxed. (Hobbs & Chambers) $85

German clockwork racing car with original tyres. $180

An early Lines Bros. pedal car, the wooden body painted suede gray with sprung chassis, 39in. long. (Lawrence Fine Art) $1,000

A tinplate toy gramophone, printed 'Made in Germany', 1930's, 8¼in. long. (Lawrence Fine Art) $120

'Popeye the Sailor', No. 268, a printed and painted tinplate toy of the cartoon sailor in a rowing boat, 14in. long, by the Hoge Mfg. Co., Inc., U.S.A., circa 1935. (Christie's) $2,250

A Lehmann tinplate Anxious Bride, No. 470, German, circa 1910. $1,000

A painted metal model of an Austin J40 Roadster pedal car, 64in. long, British, circa 1950. (Christie's) $1,250

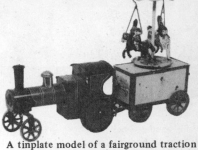

A tinplate model of a fairground traction engine, with a four-wheeled car containing a carousel, by Bing, circa 1906. (Christie's) $750

A Distler tinplate and clockwork fire engine, 37.5cm. long overall. $420

A Britains' farmer's gig, No. F28 with horse, unboxed. (Hobbs & Chambers) $30

'Bulky Mule, The Stubborn Donkey', EPL No. 425, by Lehmann, circa 1910, 7½in. long.(Christie's) $250

A Carette lithograph limousine, with clockwork mechanism, German, circa 1911, 8½in. long. (Christie's) $1,200

A painted tinplate model of a P2 Alfa Romeo racing car, with clockwork mechanism, by C.I. G., France, circa 1926, 21½in. long. (Christie's) $1,200

A Hess printed and painted tinplate toy of Dreadnought, with clockwork mechanism, circa 1911, 8½in. long. (Christie's) $120

'Mac 700', a printed tinplate motorbike with rider, by Arnold, W. Germany, circa 1955, 7½in. long. (Christie's) $400

A Magic Disk phenakisticope optical toy with 8 disks, each 7in. diam., a viewing disk, 9in. diam., and a Fantascope disk, 5in. diam. (Christie's) $750

A painted tinplate cat, 'Nina', EPL No. 790, by Lehmann, circa 1907, 11in. long. (Christie's) $1,750

'Mickey Mouse Organ Grinder', tinplate toy with clockwork and musical mechanisms, by Distler, circa 1930, 6in. long. (Christie's) $1,300

A Crown illuminated Panorama optical toy theater, illuminated by a candle mounted behind, 9½in. wide. (Christie's) $360

An early printed and painted tinplate automobile, 'Tut Tut', EPL No. 490, by Lehmann, circa 1910, 6¾in. long. (Christie's) $1,500

A Triang Minic pre-war taxi (M), boxed, with key. (Phillips) $600

A carved and painted rocking horse with hair mane and tail, America, circa 1880, 52in. long. (Robt. W. Skinner Inc.) $1,350

A boxed set of diecast Build-Yourself vehicles, by Solido. (Phillips) $90

TREEN

Treen is one of those collective terms which embrace a disjointed array of articles with the common factor being that they are all made of wood, and all have been produced on a lathe either in part or whole.

The majority are functional household articles, many originating in the kitchen, made from finely grained hardwoods such as yew, lignum vitae, sycamore and olivewood, which acquire a fine warm patina over the years.

Largely ignored little more than a decade ago, prices for good quality treen can now be measured in hundreds of dollars rather than tens.

Early 18th century American treen is particularly desirable and it is not unknown for a single bowl to fetch over $2,000.

The variety of objects embraced by the term is endless and includes bowls, spoons, goblets, coasters, molds, napkin rings, egg-cups, mortars, boxes and boot trees.

A miniature chamber candlestick with mahogany base inlaid with an end grain mosaic panel, 1¾in. high. $90

A mid 18th century boxwood cheese scoop, 7in. $225

An 18th century Scottish cog in walnut and beechwood, 11in. wide. $350

A George III mahogany coaster in the form of a wagon, 19 x 8in. $1,400

A 16th/17th century elm double-sided platter of square form with a salt sinking to each side, 9¾in. long. $690

An early 19th century rosewood letter rack with six fan-shaped divisions, 5 x 9in. $260

An 18th/19th century boxwood table salt, with a boxwood spoon and pestle, 4in. high. $310

A late 17th century lignum vitae Monteith, 10in. high, 12in. diam. $7,000

An 18th century oak tobacco jar with scrolled handles and turned lid, 11in. high. $300

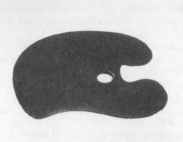

A Scandinavian beechwood washing bat, dated 1842, 15in. long. **$500**

A late 18th/early 19th century mahogany artist's palette, 18in. long. **$75**

A lignum vitae mortar and boxwood pestle, mortar 6½in., pestle 9½in. **$185**

A 19th century mahogany egg cup stand, 7½in. high. **$835**

A George III mahogany cistern, the vase shaped body with lead lining, 17in. diam. (Christie's) **$3,500**

An early 19th century mahogany cheese board, 10in. diam. **$530**

A treen bucket on ebonized turned stem with brass swing handle, 14½in. high. (Lawrence Fine Art) **$975**

A Biedermeier walnut cradle, the oval body with detachable tin liner, 52in. long. (Christie's) **$7,000**

A 19th century lignum vitae paperweight in the form of a pear, 5¼in. **$530**

TRENCH ART

Trench Art is a term embracing all those curious oddities made by our fighting troops from spent bullet and shell cases when they were not winging off mortars towards the enemy lines.

Most take the form of ashtrays or cigarette lighters, often sporting cryptic messages with names and dates which give an added interest, while other pieces are quite ambitious and take the form of aeroplanes, tanks and field guns.

Polished brass shell cases can make a useful addition to the hearth for housing spills and fireirons as can souvenir shells complete with the business end, when buffed and polished. Beware though, for it has been known for a First World War trophy to sit quite contentedly for decades by a roaring fire in a live condition — never assume they are harmless.

Brass trench art aeroplane made from bullet cases. $45

Combined lighter and ashtray dated 1944. $15

Second World War metal matchbox holder decorated with 'peace' symbols. $15

Leather riding crop with two 303 brass bullet cases forming the handle. $8

Brass bullet case button hook. $8

First World War lighter made from a bullet case. $6

Polished brass shell case, 12in. high. $16

Handmade World War I brass petrol lighter. $12

Cigarette lighter made from a brass bullet case. $10

A large brass and aluminum table lighter. $25

TSUBAS

Tsubas (hand protectors from a Japanese sword) are usually about 2in. across, are made of iron, brass or copper — occasionally with gold or silver decoration — and have a wedge-shaped hole in the center for the blade (tang). There are usually other openings for the sword knife (kogatawa) and skewer (kogai).

Some are simply patterned while others bear decoration, either inlaid or applied, depicting a variety of subjects including landscapes, animals, historical events and folklore. Later examples were sometimes decorated with cloisonne or Champleve enamel.

At first they were made by the swordsmith but, as they became more important, armorers took over their production until finally specialist craftsmen emerged who made nothing but tsubas.

A 19th century copper and sentoku hari-ishime hariawase tsuba, Mito Kinko School, 8.4cm. with fitted box. (Christie's) $2,625

Tsuba formed of red copper and sentoku plate, signed Tshiguro Masatsune. $4,500

A circular iron Soten tsuba, 7.3cm., signed Goshu ju Soheishi sei, details in gold nunome. (Wallis & Wallis) $150

A 19th century oval iron tsuba, signed Choshu ju Toyonobu saku (Okamoto School), 7.9cm.(Christie's) $330

Shakudo Nanako tsuba by Yanagawa Naomasa. $4,000

A 17th century Mokkogata iron tsuba, signed Izumi no Kami Koike Naomasa, 7.5cm. (Christie's) $260

Large armorer's tsuba by
Hamano Noriyuki. $2,500

Iron tsuba of the Hiragiya
School. $1,500

An 18th century circular
iron tsuba with black patina,
signed Echizen ju Kinai
saku, 8.6cm. (Christie's)
                               $830

An unsigned 19th century
oval Shibuichi tsuba,
6.4cm. (Christie's) $140

Rare copper tsuba decorated
in katakiri with a pair of
Sumo wrestlers. $3,000

An iron jakushu tsuba of
mokko form, 7.6cm.
(Wallis & Wallis) $100

Shibuichi tsuba by Seiryoken
Katsuhira featuring the three
Sake tasters. $10,000

An 18th century oval
shakudo-nanakoji tsuba,
unsigned, 7.1cm. (Christie's)
                               $260

A Sado School tsuba, 7.3cm.,
signed Sashu no ju Toshioki,
chiseled with a flower.
(Wallis & Wallis) $80

TUNBRIDGEWARE

In the 17th century, visitors flocked to take the waters at the spa town of Tunbridge Wells in Kent. Local craftsmen, eager to meet the demands of a growing souvenir trade, developed a method of producing thin sheets of patterned veneer known as Tunbridgeware or 'English mosaic'. Thin strips of different woods in a variety of colors, were set in an arranged pattern then stuck together to form a block from which thin sheets could be cut. This way the pattern could be repeated over and over again. The decorative veneer was applied to a great variety of objects and in particular to boxes.

The earliest pattern was made up of cube shapes and later veneers show a great number of intricate designs including flowers, birds and landscapes.

The popularity of Tunbridgeware continued throughout the 18th and 19th centuries and it is from this period that most examples originate; the last firm in production was Boyce, Brown and Kemp 1837-1927.

A rosewood jewelry box with mosaic borders, with velvet lined interior, 7in. wide. $200

A rosewood visiting card tray of rectangular shape, 10¾in. wide. $400

An English burr-walnut nautical writing box, 13½in. wide. $595

A mahogany and rosewood watch stand on inverted bun feet, 6½in. high. $200

A rosewood and Tunbridgeware tea caddy of waisted form, the domed top depicting Battle Abbey, 9in. wide. (Parsons, Welch & Cowell) $700

A thermometer stand by H. Hollanby, 4½in. high. $200

A rosewood book tray, the whole outlined with mosaic borders, 1ft.3in. wide. $600

A rosewood single division tea caddy, 5½in. wide. $300

A rosewood games box, the top and cavetto sides banded with 'Berlin woolwork' borders, 10½in. wide. $400

TYPEWRITERS

Many 19th century typewriters had a double keyboard with one key for each capital together with one for each of the small letters and the major disadvantage of most was that it was impossible to read the typed sheet until after the work had been completed.

The breakthrough came with a machine, based on a design by Sholes, incorporating the shift key mechanism – very much on the same principal as modern manual machines.

In the first ten years of manufacture 50,000 were sold by Remington, Oliver, Smith, Underwood and Yost; names still well to the fore in typewriter manufacture today.

Interest in these early machines has increased considerably and the trends of the last few years, points to a worthwhile investment.

An Edlemann typewriter on shaped cast iron base, German, circa 1897, 10½in. wide. $480

A Hall typewriter with rubber type sheet (defective), in walnut case with instructions in lid. (Christie's) $380

A Mignon Model 2 typewriter. $2,600

Rare Corona special folding typewriter in red lacquer body, circa 1910, 12¼in. wide. $440

A Lambert typewriter No. 2908, by The Lambert Typewriter Co., New York. (Christie's) $360

Williams No. 2 typewriter with grasshopper action type bars, length of platen, 8¼in., circa 1893. $700

American Colombia typewriter No. 2, with circular letter index, 9¾in. wide, circa 1890. $880

A Hammond No. 1 typewriter, American, with piano type ebony keys, circa 1884. $1,200

A Hall typewriter, No. 2498, in a mahogany case, American circa 1885, 15¼in. wide. $400

VALENTINE CARDS

On St. Valentine's Eve, it was a custom for young people to meet and draw by lot, one of a number of names of persons of the opposite sex. Once two names were paired, the gentleman was then bound to the service of his Valentine for the period of one year. This practice was adapted to form the custom we observe today; that of sending an anonymous greeting to a sweetheart. Valentine cards from about the 1850's were romantic with lashings of frills, lace, ribbons and flowers. Many survive, but not so many survive in perfect condition.

The Valentine postcard came into use around 1900 and, for twenty years or so, enjoyed a period of great popularity. The better examples in this category are good artist drawn, chromolitho cards by publishers such as Ettinger, Tuck, Hildesheimer, Wildt & Kray, Schwerdtfeger etc. Unfortunately, although many well known artists illustrated these cards, very few were ever signed.

True Love's Greeting, Royal Series by Max Ettinger, Series No. V90, chromo litho, embossed umbrella. $8

Long Have Loved Thee Truly. $7

Max Ettinger Series No. V125, 'Asylum for Lunatics'. $10

'My Love to You', Royal Series by Max Ettinger Series No. V86, printed in Germany. $6

'Faith, Hope and Charity', four in set, sometimes three in set. G. B. & Co. Series, embossed chromo litho with gold leaf applique. $4 each

Dove, heart and flowers, 'To My Valentine', Max Ettinger Series No. V75. $6

VALENTINE CARDS

A Valentine For Someone Often In My Thoughts. $4

Early Victorian Valentine in the form of a banknote. $25

To My Valentine, Raphael Tuck & Sons, 1930's. $5

Valentine Greetings, 'Though Walls Should Part Us', 1921. $6

I Love But Thee. $10

Forget Me Not For I'll Remember Thee. $10

My Heart Will Ever Be Thine, Forget Me Not. $10

'Maiden thy little heart to let'. $18

To Arms, to Arms, ye British Brave. $25

VANITY FAIR CARICATURES

An assemblage of Vanity Fair lithographs provides both a fascinating pictorial history of the latter half of the nineteenth century and an authentic collection of great charm.

A collection of original prints also offers an opportunity for great investment potential for many are irreplaceable with plates no longer in existence.

What kind of magazine was Vanity Fair? It would best be described as a combination of three magazines; 'Town & Country', 'New Yorker' and 'Harpers Bazaar'.

Published weekly from 1869 until 1914 Vanity Fair brought to the reader the eagerly awaited details of important society functions, the comings and goings of the Royal family, great satire, news of the week and up to date information on the fashions of the day. The undisputed highlight of each issue was the caricature, in color, of a well known personage.

These lithographs of extremely fine quality came in plate size for a single page of approximately 7.3/4in. x 12.7/8in. and double page size of approximately 19¼ x 13¼in. and were published complete with a biography. A lithograph complete with this historical background material will have greater value as a collectors' item.

Lithographs were published in a series from one upwards and, as a very general rule of thumb, the earlier the series the better, tho' this may be influenced in some cases by the rarity of the subject and condition of the print.

Quite apart from any possible market value the vast majority of people who collect these prints do so for the pleasure they give — and I can think of no better reason.

Isabella II, Queen of Spain, No. 2, 1st series, September 18, 1869. $170

Mr. Horace Greeley, candidate for the Presidency of the United States, No. 118, 4th series, July 20, 1872. $170

The Honorable Hamilton Fish, American
Secretary of State for Foreign Affairs, No.
112, 4th series, May 18, 1872. $160

Napoleon III, Emperor of the French, No. 1,
1st series, September 4, 1869. $400

Mr. Charles Francis Adams, No. 126, 4th
series, October 5, 1872. $70

Mr. Charles R. Darwin, No. 33, 3rd series,
September 30, 1871. $130

The King of Prussia, No. 8, 3rd series,
January 7, 1871. $95

The Nawab Nazim of Bengal, Behar and
Orissa, No. 8, 2nd series, April 16, 1870.
                                   $170

HRH The Duke of Edinburgh, No. 2, 6th
series, January 10, 1874. $150

Abdul Aziz, Sultan of Turkey, No. 5, 1st
Series, October 30, 1869. $200

The Honorable Charles Sumner, Member of the United States Senate, No. 113, 4th series, May 25, 1872. $70

Mr. William Powell Frith, RA, No. 63, 5th series, May 10, 1873. $75

Mr. Henry Irving, 6th series, December 19, 1874. $80

Victor Emanuel I, No. 7, 2nd series, January 29, 1870. $60

VINAIGRETTES

There were many thousands of small useful boxes and among the most precious — and the smallest — are those known by the unlikely name of 'vinaigrettes'.

Descendants of the pomander and, before that, the pomme d'ambre, vinaigrettes began to appear towards the end of the 18th century. Their function was to contain, under a pierced grille, a small piece of sponge or wadding soaked in aromatic oils and 'vinegars' whose vapors were thought to ward off disease and could be sniffed to counteract the less pleasant effluvia not uncommonly encountered in the days before efficient garbage collection.

These little boxes were carried either in a pocket, muff or purse or, were worn suspended from a chain on a chatelaine or pocket watch and some have little fixing rings attached. The inside was almost invariably gilded to avoid corrosion.

Occasionally made of gold but more commonly of silver, pinchbeck, glass or porcelain and sometimes inset with precious stones, vinaigrettes have the advantage over many collectible items in that they are usually particularly beautifully made and, being so often constructed of precious metals, they are fairly certain to resist those fluctuations of fashion which can so easily undermine the investment potential of less stable items.

Prices and values naturally vary according to the maker, quality, material, age and condition of the pieces. Vinaigrettes by Nathaniel Mills are particularly desirable, especially those with embossed scenic views on the lid.

A 19th century Chinese Export oblong vinaigrette with engine-turned base, by Khecheong of Canton, circa 1850. (Phillips) $240

An oblong silver 'Castletop' vinaigrette chased on the cover with a view of Westminster Abbey, by N. Mills, Birmingham, 1842, 1¾in. long. (Christie's) $1,300

A Victorian gilt lined, bright cut, shaped oblong vinaigrette with vacant scroll cartouche, by F. Clarke, Birmingham, 1846. (Christie's) $150

A George IV vinaigrette in the form of a purse, by Lawrence & Co., Birmingham, 1821, 3cm. long. (Lawrence Fine Art) $400

WALKING STICKS

Walking sticks have been collected for a very long time and a survey of the current market shows no decline in their popularity as collector's items.

Relevant factors to consider when starting any collection must be availability, variety and of course, space available to display the chosen objects. The walking stick seems to fulfil all of these requirements with ease.

A good collection will include examples on an international scale which in turn leads to a healthy exchange of information and objects in a field where everyone involved can indulge their own individual taste while selecting from the great variety of items available.

Some collectors will prefer walking sticks with handles of carved ivory, silver, hardstone or gold while others favor the simpler animal handles or the more humble and very individual 'country stick' which is usually made from a piece of wood selected from a hedgerow or special tree and carved according to the skill of the craftsman.

Walking sticks are often designed to serve a dual purpose, the shaft cleverly concealing the mechanism for a variety of functions. Since sticks were 'worn' as part of the 17th/18th century gentleman's dress the inclusion of such accessories as a watch, telescope or drinking flask seemed a very sensible idea. A typical example is the sword stick with a slender steel blade attached to the cane handle and concealed within the shaft of the stick.

This category has always had great appeal for collectors but anyone can join in and the chance of finding a unique interior fitting is always a possibility.

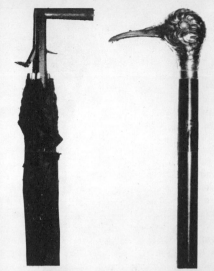

Rare percussion muzzle loading umbrella gun with Birmingham proof stamps, the brolly being ornamental, 35in. long, circa 1840. $1,200

Victorian lady's cane with silver snipe handle and ebonized shaft, 34in. long, circa 1880. $240

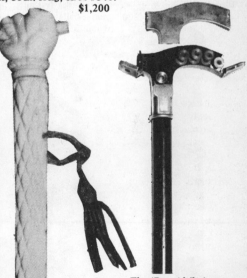

Mid 19th century carved whalebone stick, the handle carved in the form of hand grasping a scroll, 32in. long. $800

The 'Ben Akiba' camera cane invented by E. Kronke, Berlin 1903, and manufactured by A. Leh, with 24 exposures and ten spare rolls of film carried in the shaft, 35in. long. $8,000

A rare silver and enamel walking stick with tau-shaped handle and ebonized shaft, 33in. long, circa 1880. $1,300

Rosewood cane with carved wood walrus head handle with ivory tusks and gilt metal collar, circa 1880, 35in. long. $260

A Malacca shaft walking stick with carved wood dog handle the jaw hinged for holding silk gloves, 34in. long, circa 1870. $180

English stick with rosewood shaft and horn handle carved in the form of a dog, 34in. long, circa 1860. $320

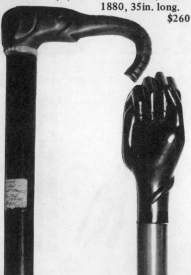
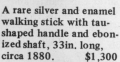

Mid 19th century cane with carved horn handle in the form of an elephant with a collar of turquoise, 35in. long. $180

Mid 19th century cane, the carved wood handle in the form of a hand entwined with a snake, 35in. long. $170

Victorian corkscrew cane with black horn handle and silver collar, bayonet fitting, 34in. long, circa 1880. $500

A heavy natural growth country walking stick with copper cap on top, 33in. long, circa 1840. $140

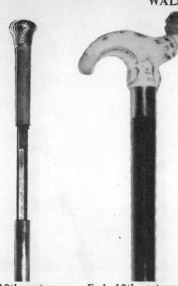

Late 19th century silver mounted swordstick with etched blade by Swaine, London, 34in. long, circa 1900. $360

Early 19th century Malacca shaft stick with German porcelain handle, 35in. long, circa 1825. $700

English cane with a Malacca shaft and carved wood handle in the form of a dog, 34in. long, circa 1850. $180

Japanese cane with Malacca shaft and good ivory handle carved with heads of rats, circa 1860. $600

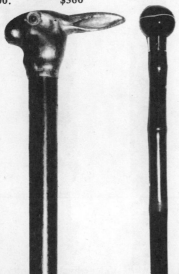

Ebonized shaft cane with a silver gilt handle in the form of a hare's head, 34in. long, dated 1912. $340

Mid 19th century bamboo shaft walking stick with 'tiger's eye' agate ball handle, 34in. long. $200

German stick with Malacca shaft and finely carved ivory handle featuring a seated lion, circa 1840. $800

A Georgian walking stick the exterior wrapped in colored baleen with space for candlestick, candleholder and spills, 35in. long, circa 1830. $1,100

An early Victorian telescope walking stick the horn screw-off handle fitted with a compass and presentation silver band, 34in. long, circa 1850. $1,200

Malacca shaft cane with carved wood handle in the form of a horse's head with gilt collar, circa 1880. $180

Simple country made stick with silver collar, 33in. long, mid 19th century. $50

Bamboo shafted walking stick incorporating a horse measure and spirit level armpiece, 35in. long, circa 1885. $260

Edwardian cane with duck's head handle formed of small jet beads, with silver collar dated 1910, 33in. long. $280

English country made dagger cane, the blade activated by centrifugal force through a brass trap door on top, circa 1850. $320

Walking stick with rosewood shaft and carved ivory handle in the form of a horse's head, 34in. long, circa 1865. $700

Unique English country walking stick carved overall with a foxhunt in full flight, the fox disappearing into the handle to escape the hounds, 35in. long, circa 1870. $360

WATCHSTANDS

Watchstands have been in use for some 400 years but, as with most other antique objects, the largest numbers of surviving (and, for the average collector, the only realistically priced) specimens date from the 19th century.

Early 19th century examples are typically of the one-pillar type, usually of wood but not uncommonly of brass, agate or marble. Some were of rigid construction, but better examples often contained a pivot which allowed the watch to be tilted to a convenient viewing angle. Because of the materials used in their construction, and because of their rudimentary design, watchstands of this type are placed at the lower end of the scale.

The "wellhead" design consists of two pillars joined at the top by an arch from which the watch is suspended. Another two-pillar design encloses a pivoted holder for the watch, and sometimes has a short, central pillar on which might be a small mirror or pin cushion. Others, without the central pillar, are usually dished to take rings, studs and other trinkets.

A third variety, known as the "triangular prismatic watchstand" from its shape, is usually of hard wood, often beautifully inlaid, and quite commonly has a small door at the back giving access to the velvet-lined interior. A variant on the same theme has opening front and back panels, the watch being safely contained inside for traveling.

Purpose-built traveling watchstands were made to several designs, usually with some souvenir-type decoration. Some have hinged lids which, in the in-use position, are propped open by a flap pivoted from the front of the piece and fitted with a stud or hook from which the watch hangs against its dished backing. These pieces are usually beautifully made, often with locks embellished with ivory, bone or brass escutcheons.

20th century American ebony and ivory watchstand, 6¼in. high. **$300**

A French Napoleonic prisoner-of-war carved bone watchstand, in the form of a classical arch supported by two Roman soldiers, height 8¾in., width 6in. **$360**

German porcelain watch holder entitled 'Gravelotte'. **$300**

WATCHES

Although watches with single hands were made in the 17th century it wasn't until the 18th century that the need for an accurate timepiece was required specifically as an aid to navigation aboard ship.

This prompted a number of significant developments such as the lever and cylinder escapement and established a wealth of watchmakers whose work is most sought after today. Among them are Mudge, Tompion, Graham, Quare, Frodsham, Breguet, Leroux, Barraud and Ellicott.

Watches were originally carried in the 'fob pocket' in the waistband of the trousers only moving up to the waistcoat pocket in the 19th century. Wrist watches are basically a product of the 20th century.

Recent manufacturers to look for are Rolex, Movado, Piguet, Cartier and Patek Philippe.

A gold World Time wristwatch, signed Patek Philippe & Co., Geneva, no. 929572, the leather strap with 18kt. gold buckle. (Christie's)
$20,000

A gold wristwatch, signed P. Philippe & Co., Geneve, nickel eighteen-jewel cal. 23-300PM movement. (Christie's) $1,500

A gold wristwatch within an 18kt. gold case, signed Audemars Piguet, with 14kt. mesh bracelet. (Christie's)
$1,100

A verge watch, the movement signed Daniel Delander, London, 334, 55mm. diam. (Christie's) $1,000

A chased and enameled platinum openface watch, signed P. Philippe & Co., no. 200063, 43mm. diam. (Christie's) $1,350

A gold duplex watch, the movement signed Radford, Leeds, No. 2588, 53mm. diam. (Christie's) $1,400

A multi-color gold filled hunter cased pocket watch, signed Illinois Watch Co., fifteen jewel movement, 53mm. diam. (Christie's) $275

A French gold and enamel cylinder watch, the movement signed Breguet A Paris, 51mm. diam. (Christie's) $2,300

A small gold openface five-minute repeating watch, signed Fayette S. Giles, 36mm. diam. (Christie's) $1,650

An 18kt. gold wristwatch, signed P. Philippe & Co., Geneve, nickel eighteen-jewel cal. 9'''-90 movement. (Christie's) $3,000

A lady's platinum wristwatch, signed P. Philippe & Co., Geneve. (Christie's) $725

A gold wristwatch, signed Patek Philippe & Co., Geneva, no. 794766, with 18-jewel cal. 23-300 movement. (Christie's) $2,000

A Swiss gold openface skeletonized quarter repeating verge watch with erotic automaton, circa 1820, 56mm. diam. (Christie's) $6,600

A silver pair cased verge watch with automaton, signed Sylvester, London, no. 6788, 55mm. diam. (Christie's) $900

A Dutch enamel and silver pair cased verge watch with false pendulum, signed Martineau, London, 52mm. diam. (Christie's) $1,500

A 19th century French gold quarter repeating Jaquemart automaton watch, 56mm. diam. (Phillips) $5,585

A gold hunter cased lever watch, signed J. Jurgensen, Copenhagen, 18kt. gold case, 50mm. diam. (Christie's) $1,430

Mid 19th century Swiss three-color gold, pearl, turquoise and pink stone watch. (Robt. W. Skinner Inc.) $815

An 18kt. gold wristwatch with fifteen jewel movement, signed Le Coultre Co., dated 1934. (Christie's) $1,600

A 9kt. gold combined cigarette lighter and watch by Dunhill, the base stamped Made in Switzerland, 5.3cm. high. (Lawrence Fine Art) $880

An 18kt. gold wristwatch, signed Patek Philippe & Co., Geneva, no. 743586, with an 18kt. gold mesh bracelet. (Christie's) $1,210

A slim gold and enamel open faced keywind watch with Lepine caliber movement. (Lawrence Fine Art) $1,060

A gold pocket chronometer, the movement signed John Arnold & Son, 53mm. diam. (Christie's) $7,620

A Swiss gold and enamel musical automaton verge watch, circa 1820, 60mm. diam. (Christie's) $19,000

A lady's platinum and diamond wristwatch, signed P. Philippe & Co., Geneve, no. 199809. (Christie's) $1,100

A gold hunter cased quarter repeating duplex watch, signed Courvoisier Freres, 18kt. gold case, 50mm. diam. (Christie's) $1,100

A gold center second wristwatch with perpetual calendar, signed Patek Philippe & Co., Geneva, no. 888001. (Christie's) $26,000

A 14kt. gold snake bracelet watch, 'Blancpain', 91gr. without movement. (Robt. W. Skinner Inc.) $1,700

A Concorde Watch Co. lady's watch, yellow metal set with peridots, topaz, diamonds and pearls. (Christie's) $3,250

An 18kt. gold wristwatch with 21-jewel movement, signed Corum. (Christie's) $380

An 18th century verge pocket watch with silver dial and case, by J. Hocker, Reading. (Capes, Dunn & Co.) $275

A gold openface quarter repeating watch with automaton, 18kt. gold case, 56mm. diam. (Christie's) $2,650

A gold duplex watch, the full plate movement signed John Newton, London, No. 604, 54mm. diam. (Christie's) $770

WEATHERVANES

If there was any doubt that collecting weathervanes is a subject for serious investment, it was dispelled recently in America when an entire auction was devoted to the sale of just one weathervane with historical connections to the patriot Paul Revere.

It is rumoured that weathervanes have been disappearing mysteriously from atop some of the highest churches in New York State as the result of daring helicopter raids at dawn, no less. A sure indication of their worth.

American weathervanes tend to be more adventurous in their design than their British counterpart and feature running horses, Red Indians, stagecoaches, sailing ships and butterflies as well as the universal cockerel.

A sulkie and rider with horse weathervane figure, attributed to T. W. Fiske, America, circa 1880, 36in. long. (Robt. W. Skinner Inc.) $2,500

Late 19th century running horse with jockey weathervane figure, possibly J. L. Mott & Co., circa 1880, America, 16in. long. (Robt. W. Skinner Inc.) $2,000

A 19th century running horse and hoop weathervane, America, 30in. long. (Robt. W. Skinner Inc.) $3,900

Ethan Allen running horse weathervane figure, America, circa 1880, 26½in. long. (Robt. W. Skinner Inc.) $600

A cast metal and copper rooster weathervane figure, American, circa 1890, 27in. high. (Robt. W. Skinner Inc.) $1,900

A molded copper stag weathervane, attributed to J. Harris & Co., Boston, circa 1879, 30½in. high. (Robt. W. Skinner Inc.) $28,000

An prospector's iron weathervane, Penn., circa 1900, 27½in. high. (Robt. W. Skinner Inc.) $750

Late 19th/early 20th century American gilt copper weathervane depicting a peacock, 29in. long overall. (Christie's) $3,520

A late 19th century American carved wooden weathervane in the form of Gabriel blowing his horn, 47in. long. (Christie's) $1,650

A 20th century grasshopper weathervane figure, the molded copper figure with verdigris, mounted on vertical shaft, 19in. high, America. (Robt. W. Skinner Inc.) $925

A cast metal and molded copper horse weathervane figure, attributed to J. Howard, circa 1880, 21in. high, 29in. long. (Robt. W. Skinner Inc.) $3,300

Mid 19th century American copper horse and groom weathervane, 20½in. high. (Robt. W. Skinner Inc.) $650

Late 19th century American copper weathervane depicting a cow, 14½in. high, 24in. long. (Christie's) $440

Late 19th century American copper weathervane in the form of a pig, 35in. long. (Christie's) $11,000

A locomotive and tender copper weathervane, America, circa 1882, 61in. long. (Robt. W. Skinner Inc.) $185,000

A molded copper 'North Wind' weathervane, in the form of a cherub's head blowing stylized air, 23in. high, 56½in. long. (Christie's) $18,700

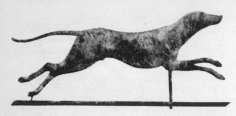

'Foxhound' weathervane, L. W. Cushing & Sons, Waltham, Mass., circa 1883, with traces of gold leaf and weathered verdigris surface, 27in. long. (Robt. W. Skinner Inc.) $12,500

A gilded centaur weathervane, probably A. L. Jewell & Co., Waltham, Mass., circa 1860, 30¼in. high, 40in. long. (Robt. W. Skinner Inc.) $130,000

'Flying Horse' weathervane, A. L. Jewell & Co., Waltham, Mass., circa 1870, 35½in. long. (Robt. W. Skinner Inc.) $7,000

Early 19th century gold leaf dove figure, America, 13in. high, 23in. wide. (Robt. W. Skinner Inc.) $1,300

Mid 19th century American copper cow weathervane, possibly from the Howard Co., 15½in. high. (Robt. W. Skinner Inc.) $800

A 19th century sheet iron silhouette weathervane, a prancing horse with military rider, 27in. long. (Robt. W. Skinner Inc.) $2,000

WEDGWOOD

Josiah Wedgwood established his first pottery at Burslem in 1759. In 1769 his Etruria factory was opened but the original Burslem factory closed in 1774. In 1940 the factory moved to Barlaston.

The Wedgwood pottery was renowned for its green glazed wares, its cream colored wares, black basalt, jasper and cane ware. Parian busts, marketed as Carrara busts, appeared in 1848 and bone porcelain was produced on a sizeable scale from 1878 onwards.

The company experimented in lithography which gave an imitation of oil painting on pottery and they also produced high quality relief decoration. At the end of the 19th century Wedgwood transfer printed tiles were very popular as were their basalt vases, majolica ware and pottery decorated with printed landscapes which was exported to America in large numbers.

Among the best known Wedgwood artists were A. and L. Powell who experimented in freehand designs, and K. Murray whose work was decorated with grooves and fluting.

A Wedgwood blue and white jasper bulb pot and cover, impressed mark and V, circa 1785, 24cm. high.(Christie's) $1,850

A pair of Wedgwood bronzed black basalt triton candlesticks of conventional type, impressed marks, circa 1880, 27cm. high. (Christie's) $1,000

A Wedgwood blue and white jasper portrait medallion of William Pitt The Younger, circa 1790, 9.5cm. high. (Christie's) $575

A Wedgwood charger, the cobalt blue ground with raised polychrome decoration, 38.5cm. diam. (Christie's) $1,200

A 19th century Wedgwood blue and white jasper vase, 12in. high. (Christie's) $735

A Wedgwood vase designed by Keith Murray, 16.5cm. high. (Christie's) $125

A Wedgwood blue jasper dip cylindrical coffee cup and deep saucer, impressed mark. (Christie's) $450

A pair of Wedgwood black basalt griffin candlesticks, circa 1795, 34cm. high. (Christie's) $1,840

A Wedgwood Fairyland luster octagonal bowl, printed Portland Vase mark in gold and pattern no. Z4968T, circa 1925, 16cm. wide. (Christie's) $1,150

A Wedgwood Fairyland luster circular bowl, the exterior painted with birds in flight on a green ground, 11in. diam. (Christie's) $520

A Wedgwood & Bentley black basalt hare's head stirrup cup, circa 1775, 16cm. high. (Christie's) $13,000

A Wedgwood pot pourri vase and pierced cover, the central area painted by H. Beardmore, signed, 34.5cm. high. (Phillips) $460

A Wedgwood comport, oval base surmounted by a stem modeled as dolphins supporting a conch shell, date code for 1884, 42.5cm. high. (Christie's) $1,160

A Wedgwood blue and white jasper oval plaque, portrait of J. Philip Elers, the potter, modeled by Wm. Hackwood, 10.7 x 7.4cm. (Lawrence Fine Art) $160

A Wedgwood terracotta bust of Locke, impressed mark and inscribed on the reverse, circa 1785, 21.5cm. high. (Christie's) $290

WHISTLES

New collectors tend to gather these little whistles without much system or discrimination then, realizing that there are so many different types and styles, they quickly start to specialize.

Others collect just military or police whistles including the bosun's call which is often made of silver and has a special fascination all of its own.

There are whistles for train guards and whistles for referees but most interesting of all are those disguised within the form of another object, such as, a penknife, spoon, peeper, Dog whistles and those in the form of a dog are particularly attractive, especially those made of porcelain by the Derby factory.

pencil, or tape measure.

Materials will include silver, gold, jet, agate, brass, porcelain, wood and ivory.

Silver dog whistle, dated 1898, Birmingham. $100

Victorian silver whistle with niello decoration. $200

Victorian silver whistle of bulbous form. $70

An 18th/19th century choir master's mahogany pitch pipe, 12½in. long. $290

The Acme Thunderer with plated chain, circa 1950. $5

A goldwashed silver and coral rattle whistle, hallmarked Birmingham, 1862, 6in. long. (Robt. W. Skinner Inc.) $470

A plated Metropolitan Police whistle. $6

A 19th century sheep's horn sheepdog whistle, 5in. long. $40

Scottish silver thistle whistle, dated 1906. $130

Rare George II bosun's whistle, London, 1740, 4¼in. long. $3,740

WINE GLASSES

Wine glasses began to replace metal goblets on rich men's tables from the 17th century onwards and since then glass workers have vied to produce more elegant and unusual designs.

Venetian glasses were always marked by the elaboration of the design; the Bohemians first discovered how to cut glass so that it looked like a jewel and their heavy, ruby colored goblets are now very valuable. Wine glasses were also used to pass opinions for the supporters of the Jacobite cause after the 1715 and 1745 rebellions drank their toasts out of glasses engraved with roses which symbolized their Stuart sympathies. These glasses now change hands at prices around $600 each. Some of the most elegant old glasses have air twist stems and others are decorated with gilt or are intricately engraved by skilled artists. Jacob Sang of Amsterdam was an 18th century engraver whose work is among the most beautiful in the world.

A color twist wine glass with waisted bucket bowl, circa 1760, 17cm. high. (Christie's) $2,800

A wine glass by David Wolff, the stem cut with diamond facets, 1790-95, 15cm. high. (Christie's) $5,000

The 'Beves' 'Amen' glass engraved with the Jacobite version of God Save the King, circa 1750, 18cm. high. $21,000

A composite stemmed wine glass of drawn trumpet shape, circa 1750, 18cm. high. (Christie's) $185

An 18th century serpent-stemmed glass, the funnel bowl supported on a merese, 18cm. high. (Christie's) $275

A baluster wine glass, the bell bowl with a small tear to the solid lower part, circa 1715, 14cm. high. (Christie's) $400

A 'Lynn' opaque twist wine glass with horizontally ribbed ogee bowl, circa 1775, 14cm. high. (Christie's) $500

The 'Breadalbane' Amen glass, the bowl engraved in diamond point, 1745-50, 20cm. high. (Christie's) $41,185

An opaque twist wine glass with octagonally molded ogee bowl, circa 1770, 14.5cm. high. (Christie's) $390

A composite stemmed engraved goblet with round funnel bowl with fruiting vinestock, 19cm. high. (Christie's) $400

An unrecorded signed Royal armorial goblet by Wm. Beilby, circa 1762, 25cm. high. (Christie's) $75,000

A facet cut shipping goblet attributed to Simon J. Sang, 1770-80, 23.5cm. high. (Christie's) $3,475

An incised twist wine glass with generous funnel bowl, on a conical foot, circa 1760, 14cm. high. (Christie's) $230

A composite stemmed goblet by Jacob Sang, supported on a beaded dumb-bell section above an inverted baluster stem, 1759, 18.3cm. high. (Christie's) $6,945

A Jacobite airtwist wine glass, the stem with a twisted air core entwined by spiral threads, circa 1750, 14.5cm. high. (Christie's) $435

A Beilby opaque twist wine glass, the funnel bowl decorated in white with a border of fruiting vine, circa 1770, 15cm. high. (Christie's) $1,300

A plain stemmed Jacobite wine glass, the funnel bowl with a seven-petaled rose and a bud, circa 1750, 15cm. high. (Christie's) $435

A facet stemmed friendship wine glass by Jacob Sang, 1761, 17.8cm. high. (Christie's) $10,855

A Beilby enameled opaque twist wine glass, circa 1770, 15.5cm. high. (Christie's) $900

A wine glass with ovoid bowl, by David Wolff, The Hague, 1780-90, 15.3cm. high. (Christie's) $3,475

A Jacobite airtwist wine glass, the stem with swelling waist knop filled with airtwist spirals, 16.5cm. high. (Christie's) $745

A faceted stemmed portrait wine glass, by David Wolff, The Hague, 1780-85, 15.8cm. high. (Christie's) $6,945

A Jacobite airtwist wine glass, the funnel bowl engraved with a rose and bud, circa 1750, 15cm. high. (Christie's) $780

A plain stemmed landscape wine glass by David Wolff, with conical foot, The Hague, 1790, 15cm. high. (Christie's) $7,960

WOOD POTTERY

Prior to the 18th century, the average piece of English pottery was a pretty crude affair but, with the discovery of a hard white stoneware suitable for more delicate modelling, a new era dawned.

Part of the glazing process involved throwing common salt on the pottery while it was still in the kiln, the heat causing it to combine with the surface of the object to form a vitreous coating – hence the term "saltglaze". Figures glazed in this way were extensively made in Staffordshire, notably by Wedgwood and Astbury, and later by the Wood family throughout the 18th and early 19th century.

Ralph Wood, Senior (1715–72) and his brother Aaron (1717–85), sons of a Chedleton miller, developed a unique style for their productions, perpetuated by their respective sons, Ralph Jr. (1748–95) and Enoch (1759–1840). Their products were particularly noted for their delicate coloring and fine design but Aaron's son, Enoch, was later tempted by the prospect of increased production, as a result of the industrial revolution, and a good deal of the quality associated with the family was lost in the process.

All of their wares are clearly marked. The rarest of these takes the form of an impressed 'R. Wood', which although taken to be the work of Ralph Wood Senior has been recorded as late as 1794; 22 years after his death.

Enoch Wood started his own factory in 1784 and later, in 1790, went into a partnership with James Caldwell which continued trading successfully until 1818. During this time they shipped vast quantities of their tableware to America marked 'Wood & Caldwell' impressed around an American eagle.

An Enoch Wood model of a stag, circa 1800, 29cm. high. (Christie's) $3,670

A Ralph Wood bust of Milton, on a shaped rectangular socle, circa 1790, 22cm. high. (Christie's) $865

Ralph Wood jug, modeled by Jean Voysey, circa 1788, 25cm. high. $850

A Ralph Wood group of the Vicar and Moses of conventional type, circa 1770, 21.5cm. high. (Christie's) $900

A Ralph Wood oval plaque portrait of a woman, perhaps Charlotte Corday, circa 1780, 20cm. high. (Christie's) $1,190

A Ralph Wood triple spill vase modeled as two entwined dolphins, circa 1775, 20cm. high. (Christie's) $2,375

WORCESTER

Robert Chamberlain and Co. began in 1783 at Worcester and continued in operation till 1850. In 1852, the company took the name of Kerr and Binns. By 1862, this company was renamed the Worcester Royal Porcelain Company.

Dessert ware and comports in glazed porcelain supported by parian figures are among the best known Worcester pieces and their Limoges ware was exhibited in the Paris International Exhibition of 1855. The firm is best known, however, for the heavily jeweled decoration of its table services. The effect was achieved by building up the decoration by many firings. In the 20th century the company was noted for high quality painting and lavish gilding. They also produced figures in ivory paste or white porcelain with bright glazes and enameled decorations. The birds modeled by D. Doughty are especially famous.

One of a pair of First Period Worcester blue scale oviform vases and covers, 16cm. high, square seal marks in underglaze blue. (Lawrence Fine Art) $2,630

A Worcester blue scale plate painted in the atelier of James Giles, circa 1770, 21cm. diam. (Christie's) $460

A Royal Worcester three-light candelabrum, by J. Hadley, 19in. high. (Reeds Rains) $1,300

A Worcester, Flight & Barr, canary-yellow ground flared flower pot with fixed gilt ring handles, circa 1805, 16cm. high. (Christie's) $2,000

Pair of Royal Worcester vases and covers in Sevres style, signed J. Rushton, date letter for 1870, 39cm. high. (Lawrence Fine Art) $3,030

A Royal Worcester figure of Karan Singh, the trinket maker, 13cm. high, from the Indian Craftsman Series, shape 1204, 1884. (Lawrence Fine Art) $550

A Hadley's Worcester lobed pear shaped jug with lion mask terminal and leaf molded handle, 9in. high. (Christie's)　$445

A Worcester blue and white faceted oval creamboat painted with the Root Pattern, circa 1758, 10cm. wide. (Christie's)　$1,455

A Royal Worcester pot pourri vase and pierced cover, with angular scroll handles, 24cm. high, printed mark in puce. (Lawrence Fine Art) $700

A Worcester Imari pattern armorial mug, blue square seal mark, circa 1770, 9cm. high. (Christie's)　$1,150

A Worcester blue and white baluster coffee pot and cover painted with an early version of the Plantation Pattern, circa 1754, 17cm. high. (Christie's)　$1,455

A Worcester yellow scale saucer dish painted with exotic birds and insects, circa 1765, 18.5cm. diam. (Christie's)　$5,520

A Worcester baluster mug with the monogram GG, circa 1770, 9cm. high. (Christie's)　$1,380

A Worcester plate painted in the atelier of James Giles in puce camaieu, circa 1770, 22.5cm. diam. (Christie's)　$2,600

A Worcester blue scale small jug with exotic birds among shrubs and trees, blue square seal mark, circa 1770, 9cm. high. (Christie's)　$1,530

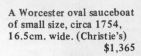

A Worcester blue and white chamber candlestick with scroll handle, blue W mark, circa 1770, 14.5cm. wide. (Christie's) $2,870

An oval Royal Worcester plaque, painted by John Stinton, signed, 16 x 24.5cm., printed mark in puce, 1906. (Lawrence Fine Art) $1,515

A Worcester oval sauceboat of small size, circa 1754, 16.5cm. wide. (Christie's) $1,365

A Royal Worcester reticulated globular vase in the manner of George Owen, inscribed January 4th 1895, 11cm. high. (Christie's) $650

A pair of Royal Worcester figures modeled as a lady and gentleman, 14in. high, circa 1887. (Christie's) $1,500

One of a pair of Royal Worcester vases painted by Stinton, signed, 6in. high. (Reeds Rains) $500

A Worcester plate painted in the atelier of James Giles, circa 1770, 22.5cm. diam. (Christie's) $850

A Worcester flared wine funnel painted in a famille verte palette with an Oriental holding a fan, circa 1755, 13.5cm. high. (Christie's) $17,250

A First Period Worcester apple-green teacup and saucer, crossed swords mark and 9 in underglaze blue. (Lawrence Fine Art) $575

INDEX

INDEX

INDEX

INDEX